AF718750

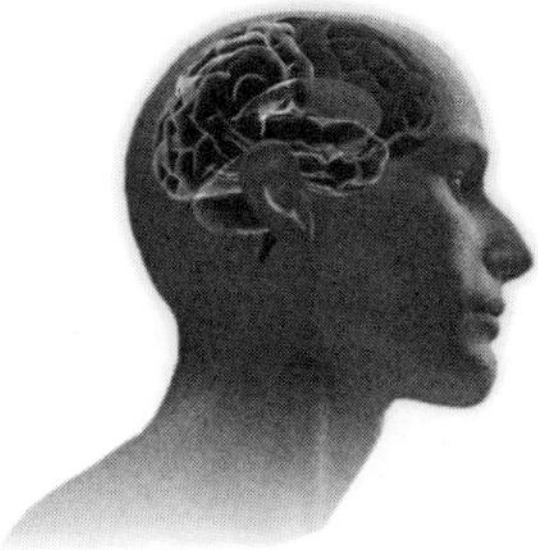

COMPUTATIONAL INTELLIGENCE AND ITS APPLICATIONS

Evolutionary Computation, Fuzzy Logic, Neural Network and Support Vector Machine Techniques

COMPUTATIONAL INTELLIGENCE AND ITS APPLICATIONS

Evolutionary Computation, Fuzzy Logic, Neural Network and Support Vector Machine Techniques

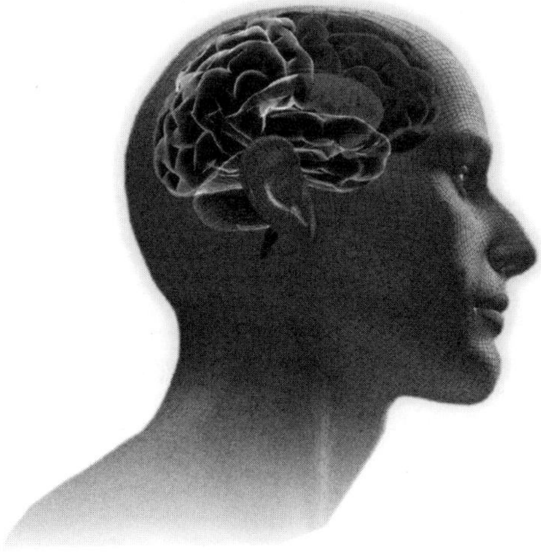

Editors

H. K. Lam

King's College London, UK

S. H. Ling • H. T. Nguyen

University of Technology, Australia

ICP

Imperial College Press

Published by

Imperial College Press
57 Shelton Street
Covent Garden
London WC2H 9HE

Distributed by

World Scientific Publishing Co. Pte. Ltd.
5 Toh Tuck Link, Singapore 596224
USA office: 27 Warren Street, Suite 401-402, Hackensack, NJ 07601
UK office: 57 Shelton Street, Covent Garden, London WC2H 9HE

British Library Cataloguing-in-Publication Data
A catalogue record for this book is available from the British Library.

COMPUTATIONAL INTELLIGENCE AND ITS APPLICATIONS
Evolutionary Computation, Fuzzy Logic, Neural Network and Support Vector Machine Techniques

Copyright © 2012 by Imperial College Press

All rights reserved. This book, or parts thereof, may not be reproduced in any form or by any means, electronic or mechanical, including photocopying, recording or any information storage and retrieval system now known or to be invented, without written permission from the Publisher.

For photocopying of material in this volume, please pay a copying fee through the Copyright Clearance Center, Inc., 222 Rosewood Drive, Danvers, MA 01923, USA. In this case permission to photocopy is not required from the publisher.

ISBN-13 978-1-84816-691-2
ISBN-10 1-84816-691-5

Printed in Singapore by World Scientific Printers.

Preface

Computational intelligence techniques are fast-growing and promising research topics that have drawn a great deal of attention from researchers for many years. This volume brings together many different aspects of the current research on intelligence technologies such as neural networks, support vector machines, fuzzy logics, evolutionary computing and swarm intelligence. The combination of these techniques provides an effective treatment toward some industrial and biomedical applications. Most real-world problems are complex and even ill-defined. Lack of knowledge on the problems or too much information makes the classical analytical methodologies difficult to apply and obtain reasonable results. Computational intelligence techniques demonstrate superior learning and generalization abilities on handling these complex and ill-defined problems. By using appropriate computational intelligence techniques, some essential characteristics and important information can be extracted to deal with the problems. It has been shown that various computational intelligence techniques have been successfully applied to a wide range of applications from pattern recognition and system modeling to intelligent control problems and biomedical applications.

This edited volume provides the state-of-the-art research on significant topics in the field of computational intelligence. It presents fundamental concepts and essential analysis of various computational techniques to offer a systematic and effective tool for better treatment of different applications. Simulation and experimental results are included to illustrate the design procedure and the effectiveness of the approaches. With collective experiences and the knowledge of leading researchers, the important problems and difficulties are fully addressed, concepts are fully explained and methodologies are provided to handle various problems.

This edited volume comprises 13 chapters which falls into 4 main categories: (1) Evolutionary computation and its applications, (2) Fuzzy logics and their applications, (3) Neural networks and their applications and (4) Support vector machines and their applications.

Chapter 1 compares three machine learning methods, support vector machines, AdaBoost and soft margin AdaBoost algorithms, to solve the pose estimation problem. Experiment results show that both the support vector machines-based method and soft margin AdaBoost-based method are able to reliably classify frontal and pose images better than the original AdaBoost-based method.

Chapter 2 proposes a particle swarm optimization for polynomial modeling in a dynamic environment. The performance of the proposed particle swarm optimization is evaluated by polynomial modeling based on a set of dynamic benchmark functions. Results show that the proposed particle swarm optimization can find significantly better polynomial models than genetic programming.

Chapter 3 deals with the problem of restoration of color-quantized images. A restoration algorithm based on particle swarm optimization with multi-wavelet mutation is proposed to handle the problem. Simulation results show that it can improve the quality of a half-toned color-quantized image remarkably in terms of both signal-to-noise ratio improvement and convergence rate and the subjective quality of the restored images can also be improved.

Chapter 4 deals with a non-invasive hypoglycemia detection for Type 1 diabetes mellitus (T1DM) patients based on the physiological parameters of the electrocardiogram signals. An evolved fuzzy inference model is developed for classification of hypoglycemia with rule optimization and membership functions using a hybrid particle swarm optimization method with wavelet mutation.

Chapter 5 studies the limit cycle behavior of weights of perceptron. It is proposed that the perceptron exhibiting the limit cycle behavior can be employed for solving a recognition problem when downsampled sets of bounded training feature vectors are linearly separable. Numerical computer simulation results show that the perceptron exhibiting the limit cycle behavior can achieve a better recognition performance compared to a multi-layer perceptron.

Chapter 6 presents an alternative information theoretic criterion (minimum description length) to determine the optimal architecture of neural networks according to the equilibrium between the model parameters and model errors. The proposed method is applied for modeling of various data using neural networks for verification.

Chapter 7 solves eigen-problems of matrices using neural networks. Several recurrent neural network models are proposed and each model is expressed as an individual differential equation, with its analytic solution being obtained. The convergence properties of the neural network models are fully discussed based on the solutions to these differential equations and the computing steps are designed toward solving the eigen-problems, with numerical simulations being provided to evaluate each model's effectiveness.

Chapter 8 considers the study of methods of automation for the insertion of self-tapping screws. A new methodology for monitoring the insertion of self-tapping screws is developed based on radial basis function neural networks, which are able to generalize and to correctly classify unseen insertion signals. The ability of the artificial neural networks to classify signals belongs to a single insertion case. Both the computer simulation and experimental results show that after a modest training period, the neural network is able to correctly classify torque signature signals.

Chapter 9 applies the theory behind both support vector classification and regression to deal with real-world problems. A classifier is developed which can accurately estimate the risk of developing heart disease simply from the signal derived from a finger-based pulse oximeter. The regression example shows how support vector machines can be used to rapidly and effectively recognize hand-written characters particularly designed for the so-called graffiti character set.

Chapter 10 proposes a control oriented modeling approach to depict nonlinear behavior of heart rate response at both the onset and offset of treadmill exercise to accurately regulate cardiovascular response to exercise for the individual exerciser.

Chapter 11 explores control methodologies to handle time variant behavior for heart rate dynamics at onset and offset of exercises. The effectiveness of the proposed modeling and control approach is shown from the regulation of dynamical heart rate response to exercise through simulation using Matlab.

Chapter 12 investigates real-time fault detection and isolation for heating, ventilation and air conditioning systems by using an online support vector machine. Simulation studies are given to show the effectiveness of the proposed online fault detection and isolation approach.

This edited volume covers state-of-the-art computational intelligence techniques and the materials are suitable for post-graduate students and researchers as a reference in engineering and science. Particularly, it is more suitable for researchers working on computational intelligence including evolutionary computation, fuzzy logics, neural networks and support vector machines. Moreover, a wide range of applications using computational intelligence techniques, such as biomedical problems, control systems, forecasting, optimization problems, pattern recognition and system modeling, are covered. These problems can be commonly found in industrial engineering applications. So, this edited volume can be a good reference, providing concept, techniques, methodologies and analysis, for industrial engineers applying computational intelligence to deal with engineering problems.

We would like to thank all the authors for their contributions to this edited volume. Thanks also to the staff members of the Division of Engineering, King's College London and the Faculty of Engineering and Information Technology, University of Technology, Sydney for their comments and support. The editor, H.K. Lam, would like to thank his wife, Esther Wing See Chan, for her patience, understanding, support and encouragement that make this work possible. Last but not least, we would like to thank the publisher Imperial College Press for the publication of this edited volume and the staff who have offered support during the preparation of the manuscript.

The work described in this book was substantially supported by grants from King's College London and University of Technology, Sydney.

H.K. Lam
S.H. Ling
H.T. Nguyen

Contents

PART 1

Evolutionary Computation and its Applications

Chapter 1

Maximal Margin Algorithms for Pose Estimation

Ying Guo and Jiaming Li
ICT Centre, CSIRO
PO Box 76, Epping, NSW 1710, Australia
ying.guo, jiaming.li@csiro.au

This chapter compares three machine learning methods to solve the pose estimation problem. The methods were based on support vector machines (SVMs), AdaBoost and soft margin AdaBoost (SMA) algorithms. Experiment results show that both the SVM-based method and SMA-based method are able to reliably classify frontal and pose images better than the original AdaBoost-based method. This observation leads us to compare the generalization performance of these algorithms based on their margin distribution graphs.

For a classification problem, features selection is the first step, and selecting better features results in better classification performance. The feature selection method described in this chapter is easy and efficient. Instead of resizing the whole facial image to a subwindow (as in the common pose estimation process), the prior knowledge in this method is only the eye location, hence simplifying its application. In addition, the method performs extremely well even when some facial features such as the nose or the mouth become partially or wholly occluded.

Experiment results show that the algorithm performs very well, with a correct recognition rate around 98%, regardless of the scale, lighting or illumination conditions associated with the face.

Contents

1.1. Introduction

Research in face detection, face recognition and facial expression usually focuses on using frontal view images. However, approximately 75% of faces in normal photographs are non-frontal [1]. Significant improvements in many computer vision algorithms dealing with human faces can be obtained if we can achieve an accurate estimation of the pose of the face, hence pose estimation is an important problem.

CSIRO has developed a real-time face capture and recognition system (SQIS - System for Quick Image Search) [2], which can automatically capture a face in a video stream and verify this against face images stored in a database to inform the operator if a match occurs. It is observed that the system performs better for the frontal images, so a method is required to separate the frontal images from pose images for the SQIS system.

Pose detection is hard because large changes in orientation significantly change the overall appearance of a face. Attempts have been made to use view-based appearance models with a set of view-labeled appearances (e.g. [3]). **Support vector machines** (SVMs) have been successfully applied to model the appearance of human faces which undergo nonlinear change across multiple views, and these have achieved good performance [4–7]. SVMs are linear classifiers that use the *maximal margin hyperplane* in a feature space defined by a kernel function. Here, *margin* is a measure of the generalization performance of a classifier. An example is classified correctly if and only if it has a positive margin. A large value of the margin indicates that there is little uncertainty in the classification of the point. They will be precisely explained in Section 1.3.

Recently, there has been great interest in ensemble methods for learning classifiers, and in particular in boosting algorithms [8], which is a general method for improving the accuracy of a basic learning algorithm. The best known boosting algorithm is the **AdaBoost** algorithm. These algorithms have proved surprisingly effective at improving generalization performance in a wide variety of domains, and for diverse base learners. For instance, Viola and Jones demonstrated that AdaBoost can achieve both good speed and performance in face detection [9]. However, research also showed that AdaBoost often places too much emphasis on misclassified examples which may just be noise. Hence, it can suffer from overfitting, particularly with a highly noisy data set. The **soft margin AdaBoost** algorithm [10] was introduced by using a regularization term to achieve a *soft margin algorithm*, which allows mislabeled samples to exist in the training data set, and improves the generalization performance of original AdaBoost.

Researchers have pointed out the equivalence between the mathematical programs underlying both SVMs and boosting, and formalized a correspondence. For instance, in [11], a given hypothesis set in boosting can correspond to the choice of a particular kernel in SVMs and vice versa. Both SVMs and boosting are *maximal margin algorithms*, whose generalization performance of a hypothesis f can be bounded in terms of the *margin* with respect to the training set. In this chapter, we will compare these *maximal margin algorithms*, SVM, AdaBoost and SMA, in one practical pattern recognition problem – pose estimation. We will especially analyze their generalization performance in terms of the margin distribution.

This chapter is directed toward a pose detection system that can classify the frontal images (within $\pm 25^o$) from pose images (greater angles), under different scale, lighting or illumination conditions. The method uses Principal Component Analysis (PCA) to generate a representation of the facial image's appearance, which is parameterized by geometrical variables such as the angle of the facial image. The *maximal margin algorithms* are then used to generate a statistical model, which captures variation in the appearance of the facial angle.

All the experiments were evaluated on the CMU PIE database [12], Weizmann database [13], CSIRO front database and CMU profile face testing set [14]. It is demonstrated that both the SVM-based model and SMA-based model are able to reliably classify frontal and pose images better than the original AdaBoost-based model. This observation leads us to discuss the generalization performance of these algorithms based on their margin distribution graphs.

The remainder of this chapter is organized as follows. We proceed in Section 1.2 to explain our approach and the feature extraction. In Section 1.3, we analyze the maximal margin algorithms, including the theoretic introduction of SVMs, AdaBoost and SMA. In Section 1.4, we will present some experiment results, and analyze different algorithms' margin distribution. The conclusions are discussed in Section 1.5.

1.2. Pose Detection Algorithm

1.2.1. *Procedure of pose detection*

Murase and Nayar [15] proposed a continuous compact representation of object appearance that is parameterized by geometrical variables such as object pose. In this pose estimation approach, the principal component analysis (PCA) is applied to make pose detection more efficient. PCA is a well-known method for computing the directions of greatest variance for a set of vectors. Here the training facial images are transformed into vectors first. That is, each $l \times w$ pixel window is vectorised to a $(l \times w)$-element vector $\mathbf{v} \in \mathbb{R}^N$, where $N = l \times w$. By computing the eigenvectors of the covariance matrix of a set of $\mathbf{v}$, PCA determines an orthogonal basis, called the eigen pose space (EPS), in which to describe the original vector $\mathbf{v}$, i.e. vector $\mathbf{v}$ is projected into a vector $\mathbf{x}$ in the subspace of eigenspace, where $\mathbf{x} \in \mathbb{R}^d$ and normally $d \ll N$.

According to the pose angle θ_i of the training image $\mathbf{v}_i$, the corresponding label y_i of each vector $\mathbf{x}_i$ is defined as

$$y_i = \begin{cases} +1 & |\theta_i| \leq 25^o \\ -1 & \text{otherwise.} \end{cases}$$

The next task is to generate a decision function $f(\mathbf{x})$ based on a set of training samples $(\mathbf{x}_1, y_1), \ldots, (\mathbf{x}_m, y_m) \in \mathbb{R}^d \times \mathbb{R}$. We call $\mathbf{x}$ *inputs* from the input space $\mathcal{X}$ and y *outputs* from the output space $\mathcal{Y}$. We will use the shorthand $\mathbf{s}_i = (\mathbf{x}_i, y_i)$, $\mathbf{X}^m = (\mathbf{x}_1, \ldots, \mathbf{x}_m)$, $Y^m = (y_1, \ldots, y_m)$ and $S^m = (\mathbf{X}^m, Y^m)$. The sequence S^m (sometimes also S) is generally called a *training set*, which is assumed to be distributed according to the product probability distribution $\mathrm{P}^m(\mathbf{x}, y)$. The maximal margin machine learning algorithms, such as the SVMs, AdaBoost and SMA, are applied to solve this binary classification problem. Figure 1.1 shows the procedure of the whole pose detection approach.

1.2.2. *Eigen Pose Space*

We chose 3003 facial images from the CMU PIE database under 13 different poses to generate the EPS. The details of PIE data set can be seen in [12], where the facial images are from 68 persons, and each person was photographed using 13 different poses, 43 different illumination conditions and 4 different expressions. Figure 1.2 shows the pose variations.

A mean pose image and set of orthonormal eigen poses are produced. The first eight eigen poses are shown in Fig. 1.3. Figure 1.4 shows the

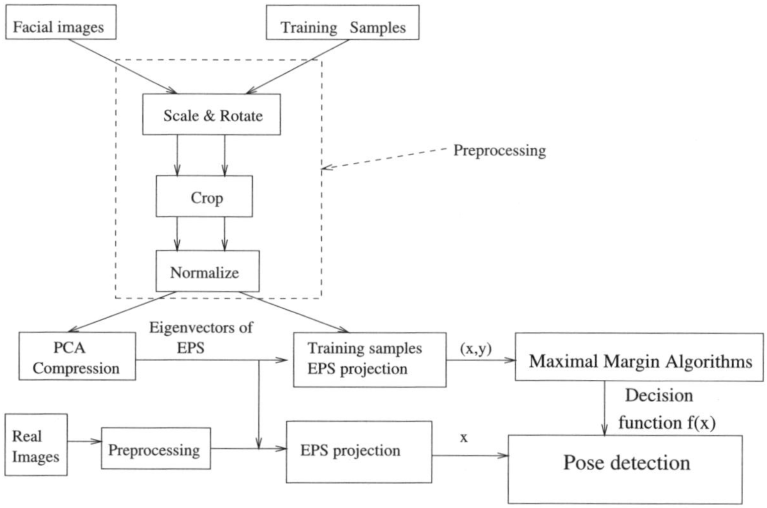

Fig. 1.1. Flow diagram of pose detection algorithm.

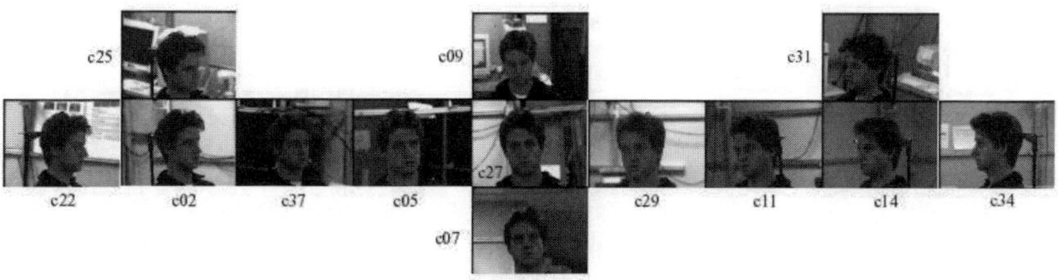

Fig. 1.2. The pose variation in the PIE database. The pose varies from full left profile to full frontal and on to full right profile. The nine cameras in the horizontal sweep are each separated by about 22.5^o. The four other cameras include one above and one below the central camera, and two in the corners of the room, which are typical locations for surveillance cameras.

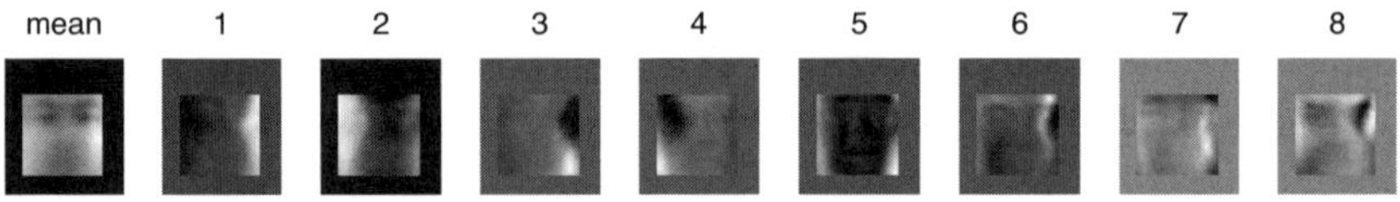

Fig. 1.3. Mean face and first eight eigen poses.

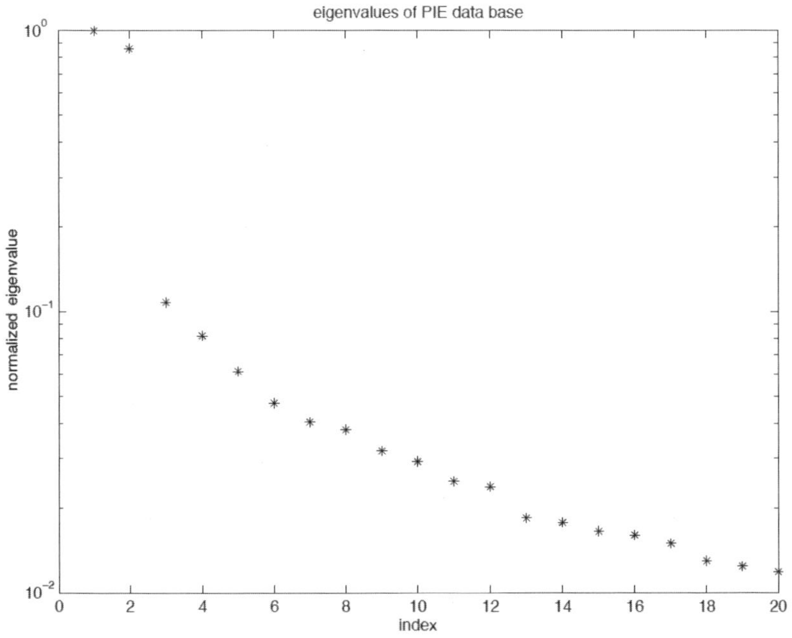

Fig. 1.4. Pose Eigenvalue Spectrum, normalized by the largest eigenvalue.

eigenvalue spectrum, which decreases rapidly. Good reconstruction is achieved using at most 100 eigenvectors, as shown in Fig. 1.5, where the sample face from the Weizmann database is compared with reconstructions using increasing numbers of eigenvectors. The number of eigenvectors is shown on the top of each reconstructed images. The first 100 eigenvectors were saved to construct the EPS.

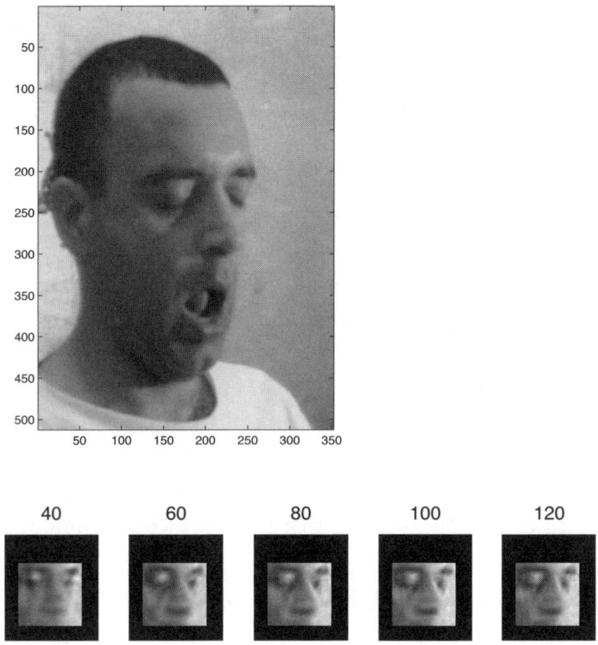

Fig. 1.5. Reconstructed image (Weizmann) using the eigen poses of the PIE data set. Top: original image. Bottom: sample (masked and relocated) and its reconstruction using the given numbers of eigenvectors. The number of eigenvectors is above each reconstructed image.

1.3. Maximal Margin Algorithms for Classification

As shown in the procedure (Fig. 1.1), the projection of a facial image to the EPS is classified as a function of the pose angle. A classifier is required to learn the relationship. We will apply three maximal margin algorithms, SVMs, AdaBoost and SMA.

Many binary classifier algorithms produce their output by thresholding a real valued function, such as neural network, support vector machine and combined classifiers produced by voting methods. It is obvious that it is often useful to deal with the continuous function directly, since the thresholded output contains less information. So it is easy to imagine that the real-valued output can be interpreted as a measure of generalization performance in pattern recognition. Such generalization performance is expressed in terms of *margin*. Next we define the *margin* of an example:

Definition 1.1 (Margin). *Given an example* $(\mathbf{x}, y) \in \mathbb{R}^d \times \{-1, 1\}$ *and a real-valued hypothesis* $f : \mathbb{R}^d \to \mathbb{R}$*, the margin of* $\mathbf{s}$ *with respect to* f *is defined as* $\gamma(\mathbf{s}) := yf(\mathbf{x})$.

From this definition, we can see that an example is classified correctly if and only if it has a positive margin. A large value of the margin indicates that there is little uncertainty in the classification of the point. Thus, we would expect that a hypothesis with large margins would have good generalization performance. In fact, it can be shown that achieving a large margin on the training set results in an improved bound on the generalization performance [16, 17]. Geometrically, for "well behaved" functions f, the distance between a point and the decision boundary will roughly correspond to the magnitude of the margin at that point. The learning algorithm which separates the samples with the maximal margin hyperplane is called the *maximal margin algorithm.* There are two main maximal margin algorithms: support vector machines and boosting.

1.3.1. *Support vector machines*

As a powerful classification algorithm, SVMs [18] generate the maximal margin hyperplane in a feature space defined by a kernel function. For the binary classification problem, the goal of an SVM is to find an optimal hyperplane $f(\mathbf{x})$ to separate the positive examples from the negative ones with maximum margin. The points which lie on the hyperplane satisfy $\langle \mathbf{w}, \mathbf{x} \rangle + b = 0$. The decision function which gives the maximum margin is

$$f(\mathbf{x}) = \operatorname{sign}\left(\sum_{i=1}^{m} y_i \alpha_i \langle \mathbf{x}, \mathbf{x}_i \rangle + b \right). \tag{1.1}$$

The parameter α_i is non-zero only for inputs $\mathbf{x}_i$ closest to the hyperplane $f(\mathbf{x})$ (within the functional margin). All the other parameters α_i are zero. The inputs with non-zero α_i are called *support vectors.* Notice $f(\mathbf{x})$ depends only on the inner products between inputs. Suppose the data are mapped to some other inner product space $\mathcal{S}$ via a nonlinear map $\Phi \colon \mathbb{R}^d \to \mathcal{S}$. Now the above linear algorithm will operate in $\mathcal{S}$, which would only depend on the data through inner products in $\mathcal{S}$: $\langle \Phi(\mathbf{x}_i), \Phi(\mathbf{x}_j) \rangle$. Boser, Guyon and Vapnik [19] showed that there is a simple function k such that $k(\mathbf{x}, \mathbf{x}_i) = \langle \Phi(\mathbf{x}), \Phi(\mathbf{x}_i) \rangle$, which can be evaluated efficiently. The function k is called a *kernel.* So we only need to use the kernel k in the optimization algorithm and never need to explicitly know what Φ is.

For linear SVM, the kernel k is just the inner product in the input space, i.e. $k(\mathbf{x}, \mathbf{x}_i) = \langle \mathbf{x}, \mathbf{x}_i \rangle$, and the corresponding decision function is (1.1). For nonlinear SVMs, there are a number of kernel functions which have been found to provide good performance, such as polynomials and radial basis function (RBF). The corresponding decision function for a nonlinear SVM is

$$f(\mathbf{x}) = \text{sign}\left(\sum_{i=1}^{m} y_i \alpha_i k(\mathbf{x}, \mathbf{x}_i) + b\right). \tag{1.2}$$

1.3.2. *Boosting*

Boosting is a general method for improving the accuracy of a learning algorithm. In recent years, many researchers have reported significant improvements in the generalization performance using boosting methods with learning algorithms such as C4.5 [20] or CART [21] as well as with neural networks [22].

A number of popular and successful boosting methods can be seen as gradient descent algorithms, which implicitly minimize some cost function of the margin [23–25]. In particular, the popular AdaBoost algorithm [8] can be viewed as a procedure for producing voted classifiers which minimize the sample average of an exponential cost function of the training margins.

The aim of boosting algorithms is to provide a hypothesis which is a voted combination of classifiers of the form sign $(f(\mathbf{x}))$, with

$$f(\mathbf{x}) = \sum_{t=1}^{T} \alpha_t h_t(\mathbf{x}), \tag{1.3}$$

where $\alpha_t \in \mathbb{R}$ are the classifier weights, h_t are base classifiers from some class $\mathcal{F}$ and T is the number of base classifiers chosen from $\mathcal{F}$. Boosting algorithms take the approach of finding voted classifiers which minimize the sample average of some cost function of the margin.

Nearly all the boosting algorithms iteratively construct the combination one classifier at a time. So we will denote the combination of the first t classifiers by f_t, while the final combination of T classifiers will simply be denoted by f.

In [17], Schapire *et al.* show that boosting is good at finding classifiers with large margins in that it concentrates on those examples whose margins are small (or negative) and forces the base learning algorithm to generate good classifications for those examples. Thus, boosting can effectively find a large margin hyperplane.

1.3.3. *Soft margin AdaBoost*

Although AdaBoost is remarkably successful in practice, AdaBoost's cost function often places too much emphasis on examples with large negative margins. It was shown theoretically and experimentally that AdaBoost is especially effective at increasing the margins of the training examples [17], but the generalization performance of AdaBoost is not guaranteed. Hence it can suffer from overfitting, particularly in high noise situations [26].

For the problem of approximating a smooth function from sparse data, regularization techniques [27, 28] impose constraints on the approximating set of functions. Rätsch *et al.* [10] show that versions of AdaBoost modified to use regularization are more robust for noisy data. Mason *et al.* [25] discuss the problem of approximating a smoother function based on boosting algorithms and a *regularization term* was also suggested to be added to the original cost function. This term represents the "mistrust" to a noisy training sample, and allows it to be misclassified (negative margin) in the training process. The final hypothesis $f(\mathbf{x})$ obtained this way has worse training error but better generalization performance compared to $f(\mathbf{x})$ of the original AdaBoost algorithm.

There is a broad range of choices for the *regularization term*, including many of the popular generalized additive models used in some regularization networks [29]. In the so-called *soft margin AdaBoost*, the regularization term $\eta_t(\mathbf{s}_i)$ is defined as

$$\eta_t(\mathbf{s}_i) = \left(\sum_{r=1}^{t} \alpha_r w_r(\mathbf{s}_i)\right)^2,$$

where w is the sample weight and t the training iteration index (cf. [10] for a detailed description). The soft margin of a sample $\mathbf{s}_i$ is then defined as

$$\tilde{\gamma}(\mathbf{s}_i) := \gamma(\mathbf{s}_i) + \lambda\eta_t(\mathbf{s}_i), \text{ for } i = 1, \cdots, m,$$

where λ is the *regularization constant* and $\eta_t(\mathbf{s}_i)$ the *regularization term.* A large value of $\eta(\mathbf{s}_i)$ for some patterns allow for some larger soft margin $\tilde{\gamma}(\mathbf{s}_i)$. Here λ balances the trade-off between goodness-of-fit and simplicity of the hypothesis. In the noisy case, SMA prefers hypotheses which do not rely on only a few samples with smaller values of $\eta(\mathbf{s}_i)$. So by using the regularization method, AdaBoost is not changed for easily classifiable samples, but only for the most difficult ones.

1.3.4. *Margin distribution*

In this chapter, we will compare these *maximal margin algorithms* in one practical pattern recognition problem, pose estimation. Our comparison will be based on the margin distribution of different algorithms over the training data. The key idea of this analysis is the following: In order to analyze the generalization error, one should consider more than just the training error, which is the number of incorrect classifications in the training set. One should also take into account the *confidence* of the classifications [30]. We will use margin as a measure of the classification confidence, for which it is possible to prove that an improvement in margin on the training set guarantees an improvement in the upper bound on the generalization error. For *maximal margin algorithms*, it is easy to see that slightly perturbing one training example with a large margin is unlikely to cause a change in the hypothesis f, and thus have little effect on the generalization performance of f. Hence, the distribution of the margin over the whole set of training examples is useful to analyze the confidence of the classification. To visualize this distribution, the fraction of examples whose margin is at most γ as a function of γ and normalized in $[-1, 1]$ is plotted and analyzed in the experiment part. These graphs are referred to as *margin distribution graphs* [17].

1.4. Experiments and Discussions

1.4.1. *Data preparation*

The databases used for experiments were collected from four databases: the CMU PIE database, the Weizmann database, the CSIRO front database and the CMU profile face database. These contain a total of 41567 faces, of which 22221 are frontal images, and 19346 are pose images. The training samples were randomly selected from the whole data set, and the rest to test the generalization performance of the technique. The training and testing were carried out based on the procedure for pose detection shown in Fig. 1.1.

In experiment *Group A*, we compared the performance of SVM, AdaBoost and soft margin AdaBoost on a small training sample set ($m = 500$), in order to save the computation time. Their margin distribution graphs were generated based on the training performance, which explains why SVM and SMA perform better than AdaBoost. In experiment *Group B*, we did experiments on a much larger training set ($m = 20783$) for the

SVM- and SMA-based techniques, in order to show the best performance these two techniques can achieve.

For the SVM, we chose the polynomial kernel with degree $d = 3$ and bias $b = 0$. For AdaBoost and SMA, we used radial basis function (RBF) networks with adaptive centers as the base classifier, and the number of base classifiers is $T = 800$. The effect of using different numbers of significant Principal Components (PCs), i.e. the signal components along the principal directions in the EPS, is also observed in the experiments. We will define the number of PCs as the PC-dimension. We tested the PC-dimensions between 10 and 80 in steps of 10. All the experiments were repeated five times, and the results were averaged over the five repeats.

1.4.2. *Data preprocessing*

As the prior knowledge of the system is the face's eye location, the x-y positions of both eyes were hand-labeled. The face images were normalized for rotation, translation and scale according to eye location. The subwindow of the face is then cropped using the normalized eyes distance. Because the new eye location is fixed without knowledge of the face's pose, the subwindow range is quite different based on different poses. For a large-angle pose face, the cropped subwindow cannot include the whole face. Figure 1.6 shows such face region extraction for nine poses of the PIE database with the corresponding angle on top.

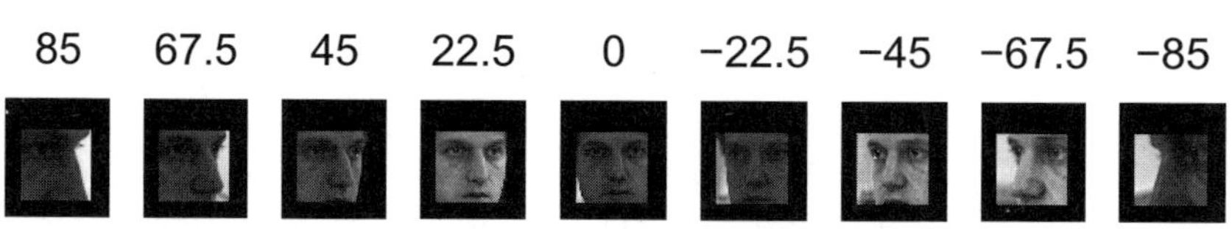

Fig. 1.6. Normalized and cropped face region for nine different pose angles. The degree of the pose is above the image. The subwindows only include eyes and part of nose for the $\pm 85^o$ pose images.

1.4.3. *Experiment results of Group A*

We compared SVM, original AdaBoost and SMA-based techniques in this group of experiments. In Table 1.1, the average generalization performance (with standard deviation) over the range of PC-dimensions is given. Our experiments show that the AdaBoost results are in all cases at least $2 \sim 4\%$ worse than both the SVM and SMA results. Figure 1.7 shows

Table 1.1. Performance of pose classifiers on different PC-dimensions.

PC-dim	testErr of SVM	testErr of Ada	testErr of SMA	Diff between Ada and SMA
10	$12.02 \pm 1.34\%$	$13.72 \pm 1.34\%$	$11.63 \pm 0.71\%$	2.09%
20	$9.07 \pm 0.56\%$	$10.71 \pm 0.81\%$	$7.26 \pm 0.38\%$	3.45%
30	$6.49 \pm 0.21\%$	$8.19 \pm 0.63\%$	$6.06 \pm 0.47\%$	2.13%
40	$5.72 \pm 0.64\%$	$7.87 \pm 0.92\%$	$5.05 \pm 0.19\%$	2.82%
50	$5.03 \pm 0.43\%$	$8.20 \pm 0.69\%$	$5.14 \pm 0.21\%$	3.06%
60	$4.79 \pm 0.39\%$	$7.32 \pm 1.04\%$	$4.63 \pm 0.61\%$	2.69%
70	$4.83 \pm 0.12\%$	$7.98 \pm 0.85\%$	$4.49 \pm 0.33\%$	3.52%
80	$4.60 \pm 0.26\%$	$8.03 \pm 0.74\%$	$4.87 \pm 0.27\%$	3.16%

one comparison of AdaBoost and SMA with PC-dimension $n = 30$. The training error of the AdaBoost-based technique converges to zero after only five iterations, but the testing error clearly shows the overfitting. For the SMA-based technique, because of the regularization term, the training error is not zero in most of the iterations, but the testing error keeps decreasing.

1.4.4. *Margin distribution graphs*

We will use the margin distribution graphs to explain why both SVM and SMA perform better than AdaBoost. Figure 1.8 shows the margin distribution for SVM, AdaBoost and SMA, indicated by solid, dashed and dotted lines, respectively. The margin of all AdaBoost are positive, which means all of the training data are classified correctly. For SVM and SMA, about 5% of the training data are classified incorrectly, while the margins of more than 90% of the points are bigger than those of AdaBoost.

We know that a large positive margin can be interpreted as a "confident" correct classification. Hence the generalization performance of SVM and SMA should be better than AdaBoost, which is observed in the experiment results (Table 1.1). AdaBoost tends to increase the margins associated with examples and converge to a margin distribution in which all examples try to have positive margins. Hence, AdaBoost can improve the generalization error of a classifier when there is no noise. But when there is noise in the training set, AdaBoost generates an overfitting classifier by trying to classify the noisy points with positive margins. In fact, in most cases, AdaBoost will modify the training sample distribution to force the learner to concentrate on its errors, and will thereby force the learner to concentrate on learning noisy examples. AdaBoost is hence called "hard margin" algorithm. For noisy data, there is always the trade-off between believing in the data or mistrusting it, because the data point could be mislabeled.

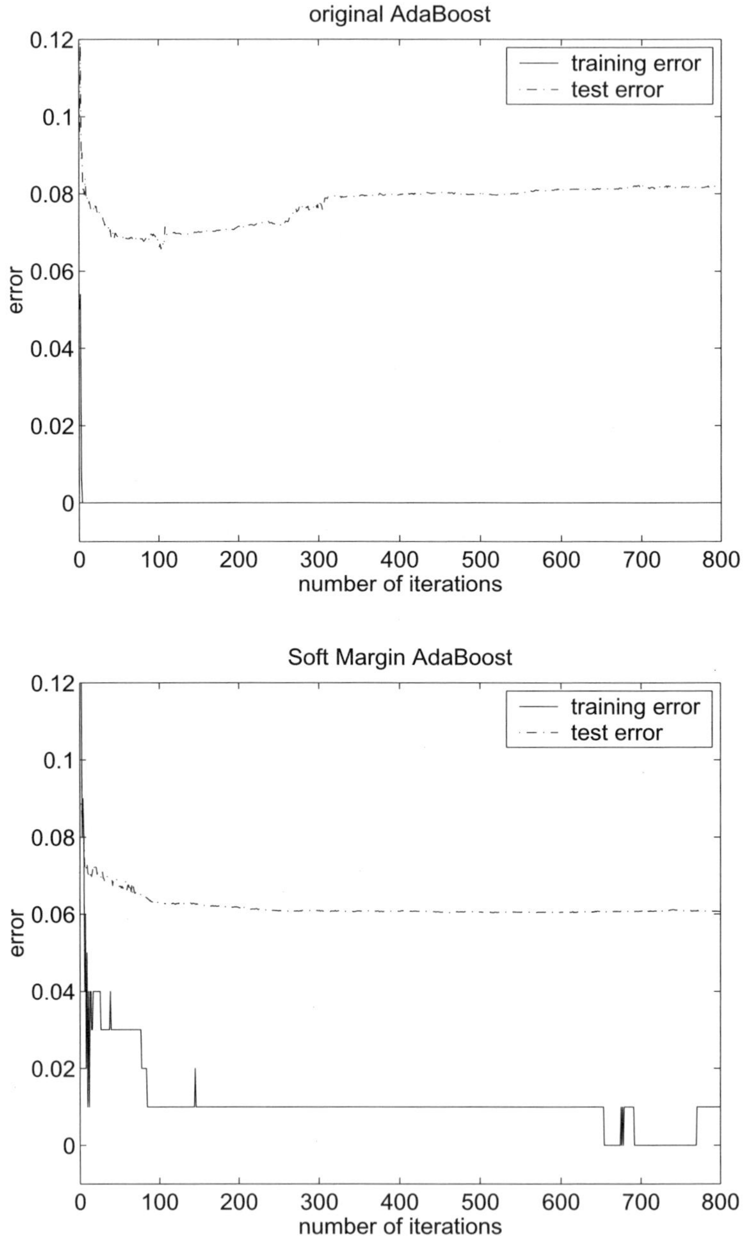

Fig. 1.7. Training and testing error graphs of original AdaBoost and SMA when training set size $m = 500$, and PC-dimension of the feature vector $n = 30$. The testing error of AdaBoost overfits to 8.19% while the testing error of SMA converges to 6.06%.

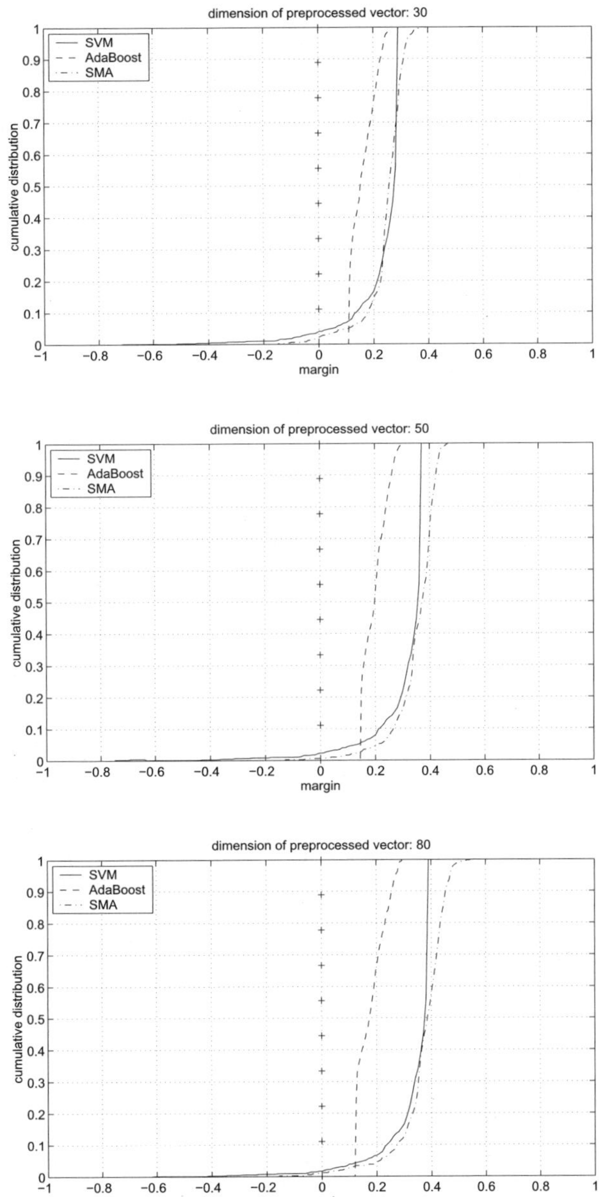

Fig. 1.8. Margin distribution graphs of SVM, AdaBoost and SMA on training set when training sample size $m = 500$, PC-dimension is $30, 50, 80$ respectively. For SVM and SMA, although about $1 \sim 2\%$ of the training data are classified incorrectly, the margins of more than 90% of the points are bigger than those of AdaBoost.

So the "hard margin" condition needs to be relaxed. For SVM, the original SVM algorithm [19] had poor generalization performance on noisy data as well. After the "soft margin" was introduced [31], SVMs tended to find a smoother classifier and converge to a margin distribution in which some examples may have negative margins, and have achieved much better generalization results. The SMA algorithm is similar, which tends to find a smoother classifier because of the balancing influence of the regularization term. So, SVM and SMA are called "soft margin" algorithms.

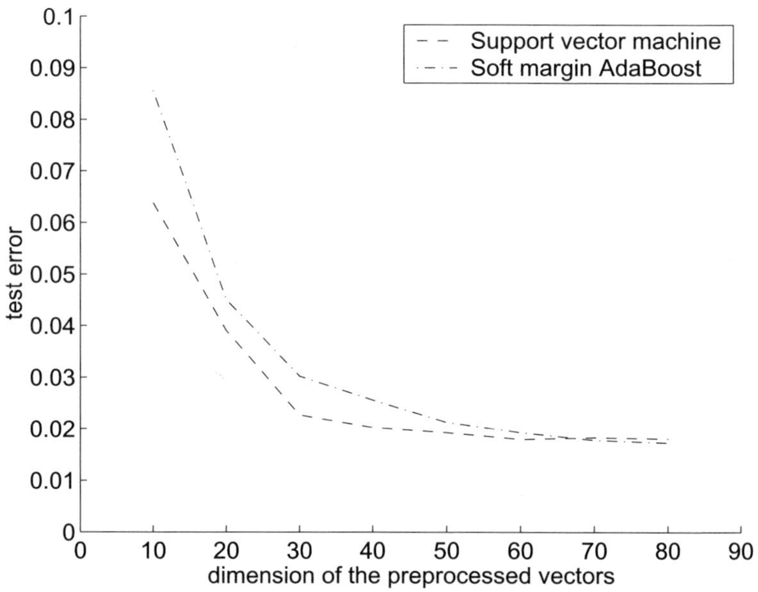

Fig. 1.9. The testing error of SVM and SMA versus the PC-dimension of the feature vector. As the PC-dimension increases, the testing errors decrease. The testing error is as low as 1.80% (SVM) and 1.72% (SMA) when the PC-dimension is 80.

1.4.5. *Experiment results of Group B*

From the experiment results in Section 1.4.3, we observed that both SVM- and SMA-based approaches perform better than AdaBoost, and we analyzed the reason in Section 1.4.4. In order to show the best performance of SVM and SMA techniques, we trained the SMA on more training samples ($m = 20783$), and achieved competitive results on pose estimation problem. Figure 1.9 shows the testing errors of the SVM- and SMA-based techniques versus the PC-dimension of the feature vector. The testing error is related to the PC-dimension of the feature vector. The performance in pose detection is better for a higher dimensional PCA representation. Especially, the testing error is as low as 1.80% and 1.72% when PC-dimension is 80. On the other hand, a low dimensional PCA representation can already provide satisfactory performance, for instance, the testing errors are 2.27% and 3.02% when PC-dimension is only 30.

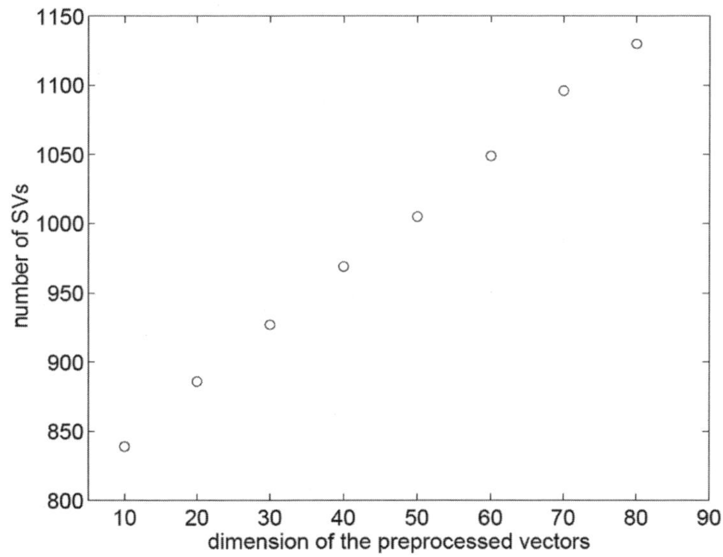

Fig. 1.10. The number of support vectors versus the dimension of the feature vectors. As the dimension increases, the number of support vectors increases as well.

Fig. 1.11. Test images correctly classified as profile. Notice these images include different facial appearance, expression, significant shadows or sun-glasses.

It is observed that the number of support vectors increases as the PC-dimension of the feature vectors for SVM-based technique (Fig. 1.10).

The proportion of support vectors to the size of the whole training set is less than 5.5%. Figure 1.11 shows some examples of the correctly classified pose images, which include different scale, lighting or illumination conditions.

1.5. Conclusion

The main strength of the present method is the ability to estimate the pose of the face efficiently by using the maximal margin algorithms. The experimental results and the margin distribution graphs show that the "soft margin" algorithms allow higher training errors to avoid the overfitting problem of "hard margin" algorithms, and achieve better generalization performance. The experimental results show that SVM- and SMA-based techniques are very effective for the pose estimation problem. The testing error on more than 20000 testing images was as low as 1.73%, where the images cover different facial features such as beards, glasses and a great deal of variability including shape, color, lighting and illumination.

In addition, because the only prior knowledge of the system is the eye locations, the performance is extremely good, even when some facial features such as the nose or the mouth become partially or wholly occluded. For our current interest in improving the performance of our face recognition system (SQIS), as the eye location is already automatically determined, this new pose detection method can be directly incorporated into the SQIS system to improve its performance.

References

[1] A. Kuchinsky, C. Pering, M. Creech, D. Freeze, B. Serra, and J. Gwizdka, Fotofile: A consumer multimedia organization and retrieval system, *M CHI 99 Conference Proceedings.* pp. 496–503, (1999).

[2] R. Qiao, J. Lobb, J. Li, and G. Poulton, Trials of the CSIRO face recognition system in a video surveillance environment, *Proceedings of the Sixth Digital Image Computing Techniques and Application.* pp. 246–251, (2002).

[3] S. Baker, S. Nayar, and H. Murase, Parametric feature detection, *International Journal of Computer Vision.* **27**(1), 27–50, (1998).

[4] S. Gong, S. McKenna, and J. Collins, An investigation into face pose distributions, *IEEE International Conference on Face and Gesture Recognition.* pp. 265–270, (1996).

[5] J. Ng and S. Gong, Performing multi-view face detection and pose estimation using a composite support vector machine across the view sphere, *Proceedings of the IEEE International Workshop on Recognition, Analysis, and Tracking of Faces and Gestures in Real-Time Systems.* pp. 14–21, (1999).

[6] Y. Li, S. Gong, and H. Liddell, Support vector regression and classification based multi-view face detection and recognition, *Proceedings of IEEE International Conference On Automatic Face and Gesture Recognition.* pp. 300–305, (2000).

[7] Y. Guo, R.-Y. Qiao, J. Li, and M. Hedley, A new algorithm for face pose classification, *Image & Vision Computing New Zealand IVCNZ.* (2002).

[8] Y. Freund and R. E. Schapire, A decision-theoretic generalization of on-line learning and an application to boosting, *Journal of Computer and System Sciences.* **55**(1), 119–139, (1997).

[9] P. Viola and M. Jones, Rapid object detection using a boosted cascade of simple features, *IEEE Conference on Computer Vision and Pattern Recognition.* (2001).

[10] G. Rätsch, T. Onoda, and K.-R. Müller, Soft margins for AdaBoost, *Machine Learning.* **42**(3), 287–320, (2001).

[11] G. Rätsch, B. Schölkopf, S. Mika, and K.-R. Müller. SVM and boosting: One class. Technical report, NeuroCOLT, (2000).

[12] T. Sim, S. Baker, and M. Bsat, The CMU Pose, Illumination, and Expression (PIE) database, *Proceedings of the IEEE International Conference on Automatic Face and Gesture Recognition.* (2002).

[13] Y. Moses, S. Ullman, and S. Edelman, Generalization to novel images in upright and inverted faces, *Perception.* **25**, 443–462, (1996).

[14] H. Schneiderman and T. Kanade, A statistical method for 3D object detection applied to faces and cars, *Proceedings of the IEEE Conference on Computer Vision and Pattern Recognition.* **1**, 746–751, (2000).

[15] H. Murase and S. K. Nayar, Visual learning and recognition of 3D objects from appearance, *International Journal of Computer Vision.* **14**(1), 5–24, (1995).

[16] M. Anthony and P. Bartlett, *A Theory of Learning in Artificial Neural Networks.* (Cambridge University Press, 1999).

[17] R. Schapire, Y. Freund, P. L. Bartlett, and W. S. Lee, Boosting the margin: A new explanation for the effectiveness of voting methods, *Annals of Statistics.* **26**(5), 1651–1686, (1998).

[18] V. Vapnik, *The Nature of Statistical Learning Theory.* (Springer, NY, 1995).

[19] B. E. Boser, I. M. Guyon, and V. N. Vapnik, A training algorithm for optimal margin classifiers, *Proceedings of the 5th Annual ACM Workshop on Computational Learning Theory.* pp. 144–152, (1992).

[20] J. R. Quinlan, *C4.5: Programs for Machine Learning.* (Morgan Kaufmann, San Marteo, CA, 1993).

[21] L. Breiman, J. H. Friedman, R. A. Olshen, and C. J. Stone, *Classification and Regression Trees.* (Wadsworth International Group, Belmont, CA, 1984).

[22] Y. Bengio, Y. LeCun, and D. Henderson. Globally trained handwritten word recognizer using spatial representation, convolutional neural networks and hidden markov models. In eds. J. Cowan, G. Tesauro, and J. Alspector, *Advances in Neural Information Processing Systems*, vol. 5, pp. 937–944. (Morgan Kaufmann, San Marteo, CA, 1994).

[23] L. Breiman, Prediction games and arcing algorithms, *Neural Computation.* **11**(7), 1493–1518, (1999).
[24] J. Friedman, T. Hastie, and R. Tibshirani, Additive logistic regression: a statistical view of boosting, *Annals of Statistics.* **28**(2), 400–407, (2000).
[25] L. Mason, J. Baxter, P. Bartlett, and M. Frean, *Functional Gradient Techniques for Combining Hypotheses.* (MIT Press, Cambridge, MA, 2000).
[26] A. Grove and D. Schuurmans, Boosting in the limit: Maximizing the margin of learned ensembles, *Proceedings of the Fifteenth National Conference on Artificial Intelligence.* pp. 692–699, (1998).
[27] A. N. Tikhonov, Solution of incorrectly formulated problems and the regularization method, *Soviet Mathematics. Doklady.* **4**, 1035–1038, (1963).
[28] A. N. Tikhonov and V. Y. Arsenin, *Solution of Ill-Posed Problems.* (Winston, Washington, DC, 1977).
[29] F. Girosi, M. Jones, and T. Poggio, Regularization theory and neural networks architectures, *Neural Computation.* **7**(2), 219–269, (1995).
[30] Y. Guo, P. L. Bartlett, J. Shawe-Taylor, and R. C. Williamson, Covering numbers for support vector machines, *IEEE Transactions on Information Theory.* **48**, 239–250, (2002).
[31] C. Cortes and V. Vapnik, Support vector networks, *Machine Learning.* **20**, 273–297, (1995).

Chapter 2

Polynomial Modeling in a Dynamic Environment based on a Particle Swarm Optimization

Kit Yan Chan and Tharam S. Dillon

Digital Ecosystems and Business Intelligence Institute, Curtin University of Technology, Perth, Australia
kit.chan@curtin.edu.au

In this chapter, a particle swarm optimization (PSO) is proposed for polynomial modeling in a dynamic environment. The basic operations of the proposed PSO are identical to the ones of the original PSO except that elements of particles represent arithmetic operations and polynomial variables of polynomial models. The performance of the proposed PSO is evaluated by polynomial modeling based on a set of dynamic benchmark functions in which their optima are dynamically moved. Results show that the proposed PSO can find significantly better polynomial models than genetic programming (GP) which is a commonly used method for polynomial modeling.

Contents

2.1. Introduction

Particle swarm optimization is inspired by the social behaviors of animals like fish schooling and bird flocking [1]. The swarm consists of a population of particles which aim to look for the optimal solutions, and the movement of each particle is based on both its best previous position recorded so far from the previous generations and the position of the best particle among all the particles. Diversity of the particles can be kept along the search by selecting suitable PSO parameters which provide a balance between the global exploration based on the position of best particle among all the particles in the swarm, and local exploration based on each individual element's best previous position recorded. Each particle can converge gradually toward the position of best particle among all the particles in the swarm and its best previous position recorded so far. Kennedy and Eberhart [2] demonstrated that PSO can solve hard optimization problems with satisfactory results.

However, there is no research involving PSO on polynomial modeling in a dynamic environment according to the authors' knowledge. This can be blamed on the fact that the polynomials consist of arithmetic operations and polynomial variables, which are difficult to represent by the commonly used continuous version of PSO (i.e. the original PSO [1]). In fact, recent literature shows that PSO has been applied to solve various combinatorial problems with satisfactory results [3–7] and the particles of the PSO-based algorithm can represent arithmetic operations and polynomial variables in polynomial models. These reasons motivated the author to apply a PSO-based algorithm on generating polynomial models.

In this chapter, a PSO has been proposed for polynomial modeling in a dynamic environment. The basic operations of the proposed PSO are identical to those of the original PSO [1] except that elements of particles of the PSO are represented by arithmetic operations and polynomial variables in polynomial models. To evaluate the performance of the PSO polynomial modeling in a dynamic environment, we compared the PSO with the GP, which is a commonly used method on polynomial modeling [8–11]. Based on the benchmark functions in which their optima are dynamically moved, polynomial modeling in dynamic environments can be evaluated. This evaluation indicates that the proposed PSO significantly outperforms the GP in polynomial modeling in a dynamic environment.

2.2. PSO for Polynomial Modeling

The polynomial model of an output response relating to polynomial variables can be described as follows:

$$y = f(x_1, x_2, ..., x_m) \tag{2.1}$$

where y is the output response, x_j, $j = 1, 2, ..., m$ is the j-th polynomial variable and f is a functional relationship, which represents the polynomial model. The polynomial model f can be found by a set of experimental data $\mathbf{D} = (\mathbf{x}^D(i), y^D(i))_{i=1}^{N_D}$ with the corresponding values of the

i-th experimental data $\mathbf{x}^D(i) = (x_1^D(i), x_2^D(i), ..., x_m^D(i)) \in R^m$ and corresponding value of the i-th response output $y^D(i) \in R$. With $\mathbf{D}$, f can be generated as a high-order high-dimensional Kolmogorov–Gabor polynomial:

$$y = a_0 + \sum_{i_1=1}^{m} a_{i_1} x_{i_1} + \sum_{i_1=1}^{m}\sum_{i_2=1}^{m} a_{i_1 i_2} x_{i_1} x_{i_2} + \\ \sum_{i_1=1}^{m}\sum_{i_2=1}^{m}\sum_{i_3=1}^{m} a_{i_1 i_2 i_3} x_{i_1} x_{i_2} x_{i_3} + ... + a_{123...m} \prod_{i_m=1}^{m} x_{i_m} \tag{2.2}$$

which is a universal format for polynomial modeling if the number of terms in (2.2) is large enough [12]. The polynomial model varies, if the polynomial coefficiencies vary dynamically. In this chapter, a PSO is proposed to generate polynomial models, while experimental data is available. The PSO uses a number of particles, which constitute a swarm, and each particle represents a polynomial model. Each particle traverses the search space looking for the optimal polynomial model.

Each particle in the PSO represents the polynomial variables ($x_1, x_2, ...,$ and x_m) and the arithmetic operations ($'+','-'$ and$'*'$) in the polynomial model as defined in (2.2). The i-th particle at generation t is defined as $P_i^t = (p_{i,1}^t, p_{i,2}^t, ..., p_{i,N_p}^t)$, where $N_p > m$; $i = 1, 2, ..., N_{pop}$; N_{pop} is the number of particles of the swarm; $P_{i,k}^t$ is the k-th element of the i-th particle at the t-th generation, and is in the range between zero to one, i.e. $P_{i,k}^t \in 0...1$. The elements in odd numbers (i.e. $P_{i,1}^t$, $P_{i,3}^t$, $P_{i,5}^t$, ...) are used to illustrate the polynomial variables, and the elements in even numbers (i.e. $P_{i,2}^t$, $P_{i,4}^t$, $P_{i,6}^t$, ...) are used to illustrate the arithmetic operations. For odd k, if $0 < P_{i,k}^t \le 1/(m+1)$, no polynomial variable is presented by the element $P_{i,k}^t$. If $1/(m+1) < P_{i,k}^t \le (l+1)/(m+1)$ with $l > 0$, $P_{i,k}^t$ represents the l-th polynomial variable, x_l.

In the polynomial model, $'+','-'$ and $'*'$ are the only three arithmetic operations. For even k, if $0 < P_{i,k}^t \le 1/3$, $1/3 < P_{i,k}^t \le 2/3$ and $2/3 < P_{i,k}^t \le 1$, the element $P_{i,k}^t$ represents the arithmetic operations $'+','-'$ and $'*'$ respectively. For example, the following particle with seven elements is used to represent a polynomial model with four polynomial variables (i.e. x_1, x_2, x_3 and x_4):

$P_{i,1}^t$	$P_{i,2}^t$	$P_{i,3}^t$	$P_{i,4}^t$	$P_{i,5}^t$	$P_{i,6}^t$	$P_{i,7}^t$
0.2	0.4	0.9	0.9	0.4	0.1	0.1

The elements in the particle are within the following ranges:

$P^t_{i,1}$	$P^t_{i,2}$	$P^t_{i,3}$	$P^t_{i,4}$	$P^t_{i,5}$	$P^t_{i,6}$	$P^t_{i,7}$
$0 < 0.2 \leq \frac{1}{5}$	$\frac{1}{3} < 0.4 \leq \frac{2}{3}$	$\frac{4}{5} < 0.9 \leq \frac{5}{5}$	$\frac{2}{3} < 0.9 \leq \frac{3}{3}$	$\frac{2}{5} < 0.4 \leq \frac{3}{5}$	$0 < 0.1 \leq \frac{1}{3}$	$0 < 0.1 \leq \frac{1}{5}$

Therefore this particle represents the following polynomial model:

$P^t_{i,1}$	$P^t_{i,2}$	$P^t_{i,3}$	$P^t_{i,4}$	$P^t_{i,5}$	$P^t_{i,6}$	$P^t_{i,7}$
0	$-$	x_4	$*$	x_2	$+$	0

which is equivalent to: $f_i(\mathbf{x}) = 0 - x_4 * x_2 + 0$ or $f_i(\mathbf{x}) = -x_4 * x_2$ The polynomial coefficients a_0 and a_1 are determined after the structure of the polynomial is generated, where the number of coefficients of the polynomial is two. The completed function can be represented as follows: $f_i(\mathbf{x}) = a_0 - a_1 * x_4 * x_2$. In this research, the polynomial coefficients are determined by an orthogonal least square algorithm [13, 14], which has been demonstrated to be effective in determining polynomial coefficients in models generated by the GP [15]. Details of the orthogonal least square algorithm can be found in [13, 14]. Each particle is evaluated based on the mean absolute error (MAE), which can reflect the differences between the predicted values of the polynomial model and the actual values of the data sets. The mean absolute error of the i-th particle at the t-th generation MAE^t_i can be calculated based on (2.3).

$$MAE^t_i = 100\% \times \sqrt{\frac{1}{N_D} \sum j = 1^{N_D} \left| \frac{y^D(j) - f^t_i(\mathbf{x}^D(j))}{y^D(j)} \right|} \tag{2.3}$$

where f^t_i is the polynomial model represented by the i-th particle P^t_i at the t-th generation, $(\mathbf{x}^D(j), y^D(j))$ is the j-th training data set, and N_D is the number of training data sets used for developing the polynomial model. The velocity $v^t_{i,j}$ (corresponding to the flight velocity in a search space) and the k-th element of the i-th particle at the t-th generation $p^t_{i,j}$ are calculated by the following formula:

$$v^t_{i,k} = K(v^{t-1}_{i,k} + \phi_1 \times rand() \times (pbest_{i,k} - p^{t-1}_{i,k} + \phi_2 \times rand() \times (gbest_k - p^{t-1}_{i,k})) \tag{2.4}$$

$$p^t_{i,k} = p^{t-1}_{i,k} + v^t_{i,k} \tag{2.5}$$

where

$pbest_i = [pbest_{i,1}, pbest_{i,2}, ..., pbest_{i,N_p}]$,
$gbest = [pbest_1, pbest_2, ..., pbest_{N_p}]$,
$k = 1, 2, ..., N_p$,

where the best previous position of a particle is recorded so far from the previous generation and is represented as $pbest_i$; the position of best particle among all the particles is represented as $gbest$; $rand()$ returns a uniform random number in the range of [0,1]; w is an inertia weight factor; φ_1 and φ_2 are acceleration constants; ϕ is a constriction factor derived from the stability analysis of (2.6) to ensure the system to be converged but not prematurely [16]. Mathematically, K is a function of φ_1 and φ_2 as reflected in the following equation:

$$p_{i,j}^{t} = p_{i,j}^{t-1} + v_{i,j}^{t} \tag{2.6}$$

where $\phi = \phi_1 + \phi_2$ and $\phi > 4$.

The PSO utilizes $pbest_i$ and $gbest$ to modify the current search point to avoid the particles moving in the same direction, but to converge gradually toward $pbest_i$ and $gbest$. In (2.4), the particle velocity is limited by a maximum value $v_{\max}$. The parameter $v_{\max}$ determines the resolution with which regions are to be searched between the present position and the target position. This limit enhances the local exploration of the problem space and it realistically simulates the incremental changes of human learning. If $v_{\max}$ is too high, particles might fly past good solutions. If $v_{\max}$ is too small, particles may not explore sufficiently beyond local solutions. $v_{\max}$ was often set at 10% to 20% of the dynamic range of the element on each dimension.

2.3. PSO vs. GP

A set of benchmark functions was employed to evaluate the effectiveness of the PSO on polynomial modeling in a dynamic environment. Comparison between the PSO and the genetic programming (GP), which is a commonly used method on polynomial modeling, was carried out. The GP parameters, which have been shown to be able to find good solutions for both static and dynamic system modeling [17], were also used: population size = 50; crossover rate = 0.5; mutation rate = 0.5; pre-defined number of generations = 1000; maximum depth of tree = 50; roulette wheel selection, point-mutation and one-point (two parents) were used. The PSO parameters, which can be referred to [18] and are shown in Table 2.1, were used in this research.

Table 2.1. The PSO parameters implemented.

Number of particles in the swarm	500
Number of elements in the particle	30
Acceleration constants ϕ_1 and ϕ_2	Both 2.05
Maximum velocity $v_{\max}$	0.2
Pre-defined number of generations	1000

The genetic programming GP based on a public GP toolbox developed in Matlab [17], which aims at modeling both dynamic and static systems, was used in this research. The benchmark functions shown in Table 2.2 have been employed to evaluate the performance of the GP and the PSO in polynomial modeling. The dynamic environment in polynomial modeling was simulated by moving the optimum of the benchmark function in a period of generations. All benchmark functions are in the ranges of the initialization areas $[X_{\min}, X_{\max}]^n$ as shown in Table 2.2. The dimension of each test function is $n = 4$. The Sphere and Rosenbrock functions are unimodal (a single local and global optimum), and the Rastrigin and Griewank functions are multimodal (several local optima). To simulate the dynamic environment, the optimum position $\mathbf{x}^+$ of each dynamic benchmark function in Table 2.2 is moved by adding or subtracting the random values in all dimensions by a severity parameter s, at every change of the environment. The choice of whether to add or subtract the severity parameter s on the optimum $\mathbf{x}^+$ was done randomly with an equal probability. The severity parameter s is defined by:

$$s = \begin{cases} +\Delta d(X_{\max} - X_{\min}), & \text{if } rand() \geq 0; \\ -\Delta d(X_{\max} - X_{\min}), & \text{if } rand() < 0; \end{cases} \tag{2.7}$$

where $\Delta d = 1\%$ or 10%.

Hence the optimal value $V_{\min}$ of each dynamic function can be represented by:

$$V_{\min} = F(\mathbf{x}^+ + x) = \min F(\mathbf{x} + s). \tag{2.8}$$

For each test run a different random seed was used. The severity was chosen relative to the extension (in one dimension) of the initialization area of each dynamic benchmark function. The different severities were chosen as 1% and 10% of the range of each dynamic benchmark function. The benchmark functions were periodically changed in every 5000

Table 2.2. Benchmark functions and initialization areas.

Benchmark functions	Initialization areas $[X_{\min}, X_{\max}]^n$
Sphere: $F_{Sph}(\mathbf{x}) = \sum_{i=1}^{n}(x_i+s)^2$	$[-50,50]^n$
Rosenbrock: $F_{Ros}(\mathbf{x}) = \sum_{i=1}^{n-1}\left(100\left((x_{i+1}+s)-(x_i+s)^2\right)^2+\left((x_i+s)-1\right)^2\right)$	$[-30,30]^n$
Rastrigin: $F_{Ras}(\mathbf{x}) = \sum_{i=1}^{n}\left((x_i+s)^2 - 10\cos(2\pi(x_i+s))+10\right)$	$[-5.12,5.12]^n$
Griewank: $F_{Gri}(\mathbf{x}) = \frac{1}{4000}\sum_{i=1}^{n}(x_i+s)^2 - \prod_{i=1}^{n}\cos\left(\frac{x_i+s}{\sqrt{i}}\right)+1$	$[-600,600]^n$

[1]The severity parameter s is defined by (8)

computational evaluations. Based on the benchmark function, 100 data sets were generated randomly in every generation. Each date set is in the form of $x_1^D(i), x_2^D(i), x_3^D(i), x_4^D(i), y_i^D(i))$, where $x_1^D(i), x_2^D(i), x_3^D(i) and x_4^D(i)$ were generated randomly in the range of $[X_{\min}, X_{\max}]^4$, and y_i^D was calculated based on the benchmark function with $i = 1, 2, ..., 100$. Based on the 100 data sets generated in each generation, the polynomial models in (2.2) can be obtained by the GP and the PSO. Since the optima of the benchmark functions moved in a period of generations, the dynamic environment can be simulated and the performance of both the GP and the PSO in modeling dynamic systems can be evaluated.

Thirty runs have been performed on both the GP and the PSO on polynomial modeling based on the benchmark functions with various severity parameters $\Delta d = 1\%$ or 10%. In each run, the smallest MAEs obtained by the best chromosome of the GP and the best particle of the PSO were recorded.

For the Sphere function that the optimum of the Sphere function varies by $\Delta d = 10\%$ in every 5000 computational evaluations, it can be observed from Fig. 2.1a that the PSO kept progressing in every 5000 computational evaluations while the optimum moved. However, the GP may not achieve smaller MAEs in every 5000 computational evaluations. Finally, the PSO obtained smaller MAEs than the ones obtained by the GP. For the Rosenbrock function with $\Delta d = 10\%$, it can be observed in Fig. 2.1b that the solution qualities of the PSO can be maintained in every 5000 computational evaluations while the optimum moved. However, the solution qualities of the GP are more unstable than the one obtained by the PSO in every 5000 computational evaluations. Finally, the PSO can reach smaller MAEs than the ones obtained by the GP. For the Rastrigin function with $\Delta d = 10\%$, Fig. 2.2a shows that the PSO kept progressing in every 5000 computational evaluations even when the optimum moved, while the GP may obtain larger MEAs after the optimum moves at every 5000 computational evaluations. Finally, the PSO can obtain a smaller MAE than the one obtained by the GP. For the Griewank function, similar characteristics can be found in Fig. 2.2b. Similar results can be found on solving the benchmark functions with $\Delta d = 10\%$. Therefore, it can be concluded that the PSO is more effective to adapt to smaller MAEs than the GP while the optimum of the benchmark functions move periodically in every 5000 computational evaluations. Also, the PSO can converge to smaller MAEs than the ones obtained by the GP in the benchmark functions. For the benchmark functions with $\Delta d = 1\%$, similar characteristics can be found.

Solely from the figures, it is difficult to compare the qualities and stabilities of solutions found by both methods. Tables 2.3 and 2.4 summarize the results for the benchmark functions. They show that the minimums, the maximums and the means of MAEs found by the PSO are smaller than those found by the GP in all the benchmark functions with $\Delta d = 1\%$ and 10% respectively. Furthermore, the variances of MAE found by the PSO are much smaller than those found by GP. These results indicate that the PSO can not only produce smaller MEAs but also produce more stable MEAs for polynomial modeling based on the benchmark functions with the dynamic environments. The t-test is then used to evaluate significance of performance difference between the PSO and the GP. Table 2.4 shows that all t-values between the PSO and the GP for all benchmark functions with $\Delta d = 1\%$ and 10% are higher than 2.15. Based on the normal distribution table, if the t-value is higher than 2.15, the significance is 98% confident level. Therefore, the performance of the PSO is significantly better than that of the GP with 98% confident level in polynomial modeling based on the benchmark functions with $\Delta d = 1\%$ and 10%.

Since maintaining population diversity in population-based algorithms like GP or PSO is a key in preventing premature convergence and stagnation in local optima [19, 20], it is essential to study population diversities of the two algorithms along the search. Various diversity measures, which involve calculation of distance between two individuals in both genetic

Table 2.3. Experimental results obtained by the GP and the PSO for the benchmark functions with $\Delta d = 1\%$.

Functions		PSO	GP
Sphere	Max value	2.3494	14.8534
	Min value	1.9575	2.6376
	Mean value	7.5622	11.9369
	Std value	0.3596	8.5927
	t-value	15.9874	
Griewank	Max value	5.9312	29.5903
	Min value	2.4252	7.6544
	Mean value	2.3309	13.6590
	Std value	0.3570	0.5724
	t-value	7.7275	
Rastrigrin	Max value	6.4475	42.4166
	Min value	2.2948	11.6546
	Mean value	1.8496	16.5391
	Std value	0.3384	0.5000
	t-value	6.7735	
Rosenbrock	Max value	97.0673	394.6
	Min value	25.2113	372.67
	Mean value	59.1312	1381.2
	Std value	18.2627	86.536
	t-value	4.9192	

programming [21, 22] and genetic algorithm [23] have been widely studied. However, those distance measures can only apply either on tree-based representation or string-based representation, which cannot be applied on measuring population diversities for all the two algorithms, since the representations of the two algorithms are not identical. Tree-based representation of individuals is used in the GP. String-based representation of individuals is used in the PSO. Either of the two types of distance measures can be applied on the three algorithms in which the types of representation are different.

To investigate population diversities of the algorithms, we measure the distance between two individuals by counting the number of different terms of the polynomials represented by the two individuals. If the terms in both polynomials are all identical, the distance between two polynomials is zero. The distance between two polynomials is larger with a greater number of different terms in the two polynomials. However, for each method we use the same for the polynomial and hence results can be compared. For example, f_1 and f_2 are two polynomials represented by:

$$f_1 = x_1 + x_2 + x_1x_3 + x_4^2 + x_1x_3x_5 \text{ and } f_2 = x_1 + x_2 + x_1x_5 + x_4 + x_1x_3x_5.$$

Table 2.4. Experimental results obtained by the GP and the PSO for the benchmark functions with $\Delta d = 10\%$.

Functions		PSO	GP
Sphere	Max value	6.0332	49.52
	Min value	2.1068	10.397
	Mean value	10.996	21.392
	Std value	3.8289	12.403
	t-value	7.9299	
Griewank	Max value	9.5221	32.942
	Min value	1.827	7.7071
	Mean value	6.229	17.227
	Std value	4.009	10.39
	t-value	7.6056	
Rastrigin	Max value	10.852	41.255
	Min value	2.2544	9.789
	Mean value	6.3097	18.089
	Std value	3.8387	8.8241
	t-value	6.4225	
Rosenbrock	Max value	100	1736.4
	Min value	27.298	504.3
	Mean value	71.449	760.42
	Std value	22.274	105.56
	t-value	7.472	

Both f_1 and f_2 contain the three terms x_1, x_2 and $x_1x_3x_5$, and the terms x_1x_3 and x_4^2 in f_1 and the terms x_1x_5 and x_4 in f_2 are different. Therefore the number of terms which are different in f_1 and f_2 is four, and the distance between f_1 and f_2 is defined to be four.

The diversity measure of the population at the g-th generation is defined by the mean of the distances of individuals which is denoted as:

$$\sigma_g = \frac{2}{N_p^2} \sum_{i=1}^{N_p} \sum_{j=i+1}^{N_p} d(s_g(i), s_g(j)) \tag{2.9}$$

where $s_g(i)$ and $s_g(j)$ are the i-th and the j-th individuals in the population at the g-th generation, and d is the distance measure between the two individuals.

The diversities of the populations along the generations were recorded for the two algorithms. Figure 2.3a shows the diversities of the Sphere functions with $\Delta d = 10\%$. It can be found from the figure that the diversities of the GP are the highest in the early generations. The diversities of the PSO are smaller than the ones of the GP in the early generations. However, diversities of the PSO can be kept until the late generations,

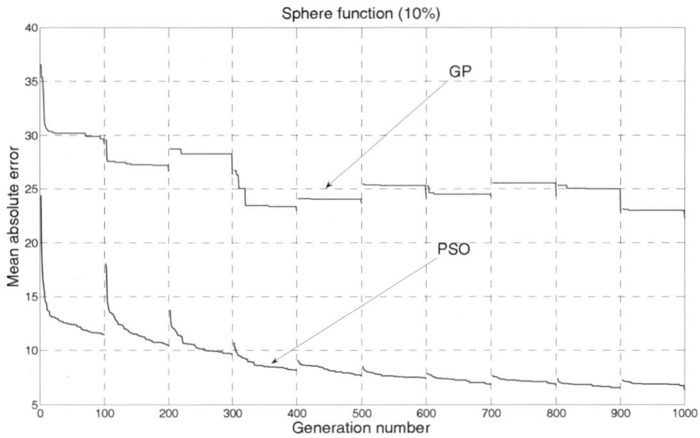

(a) Convergence plot for Sphere function with $\Delta d = 10\%$

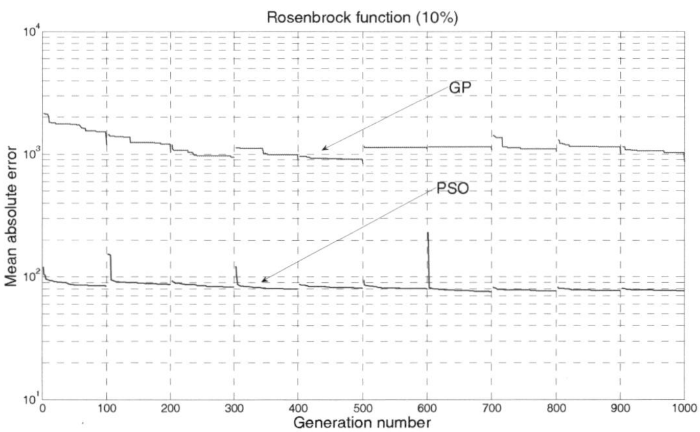

(b) Convergence plot for Rosenbrock function with $\Delta d = 10\%$

Fig. 2.1. Convergence plot for Sphere and Rosenbrock functions.

while the ones of the GP saturated to low levels in the mid generations. Figures 2.3b, 2.4a and 2.4b show the diversities of the two algorithms for Rosenbrock function, Rastrigin function and Griewank function with $\Delta d = 10\%$ respectively. The figures show similar characteristics to the one of the Sphere function in that the diversities of populations of the PSO can be kept along the generations, while the GP saturated to a low value after the early generations. For the benchmark functions with $\Delta d = 1\%$, similar characteristics can be found.

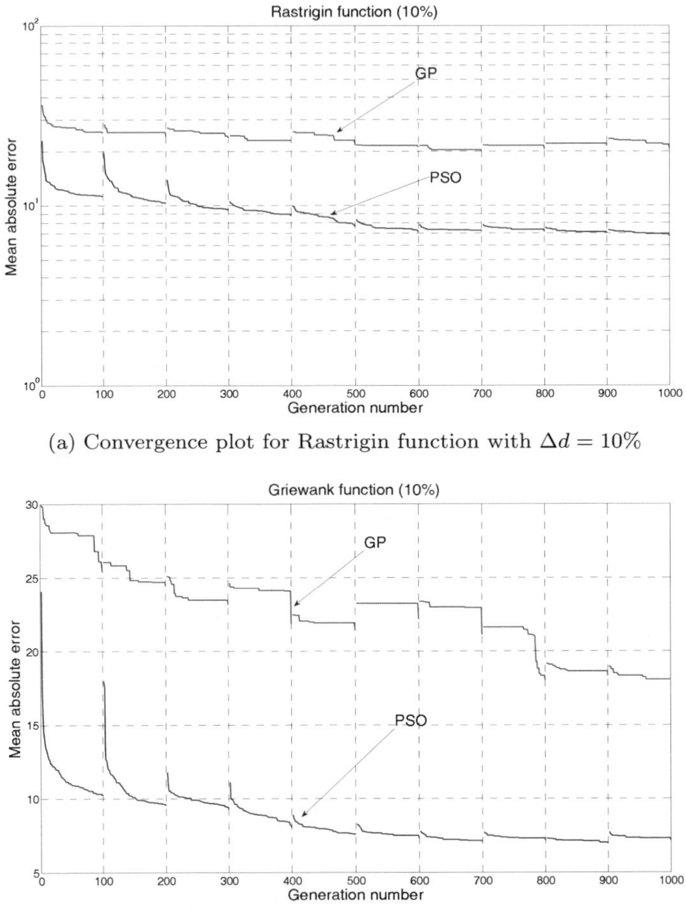

(a) Convergence plot for Rastrigin function with $\Delta d = 10\%$

(b) Convergence plot for Griewank function with $\Delta d = 10\%$

Fig. 2.2. Convergence plot for Rastrigin and Griewank functions.

Diversities of the population in the two algorithms are necessary to be maintained along the generations, so as to explore potential individuals with better scores throughout the search. If individuals of the population of the algorithm converge too early, the algorithm may trap into a sub-optimum. The algorithm is more likely to explore the solution space, while the diversity of the individuals of the algorithm can be maintained. The results indicate that diversities of the individuals in the PSO can be maintained along the search in both early and late generations, while the individuals

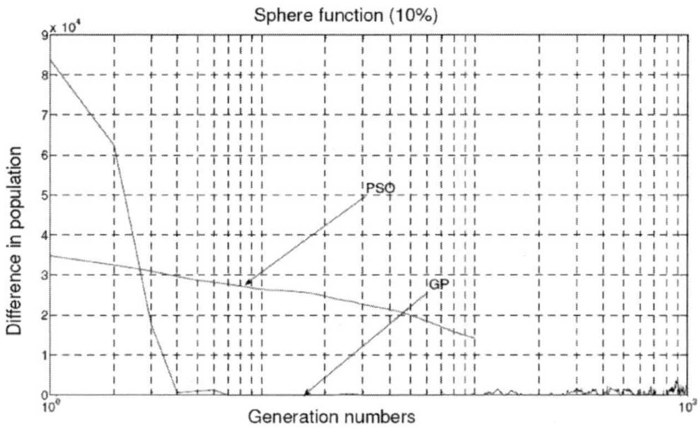

(a) Population diversities for Sphere function ($\Delta d = 10\%$)

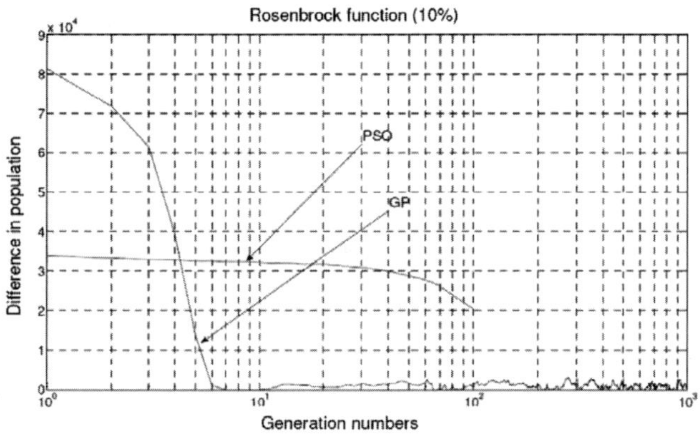

(b) Population diversities for Rosenbrock function ($\Delta d = 10\%$)

Fig. 2.3. Population diversities for for Sphere and Rosenbrock functions.

of the GP converged in the early generation. Therefore the results explain why the PSO can find better solutions than the ones obtained by the GP, while the PSO can maintain higher diversity than the other two algorithms.

2.4. Conclusion

In this chapter, a PSO has been proposed for polynomial modeling which aims at generating explicit models in the form of Kolmogorov–Gabor

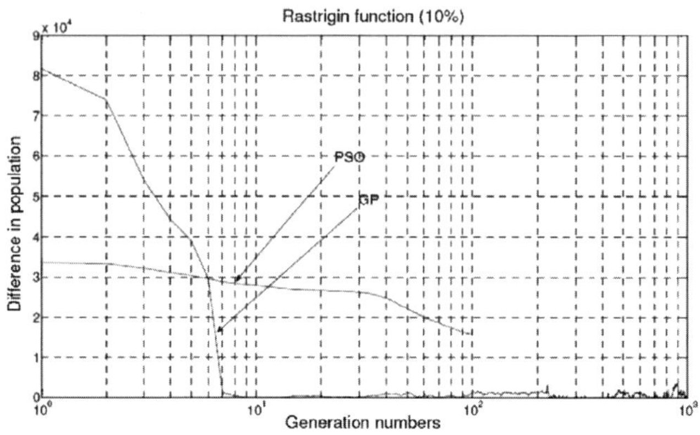

(a) Population diversities for Rastrigin function ($\Delta d = 10\%$)

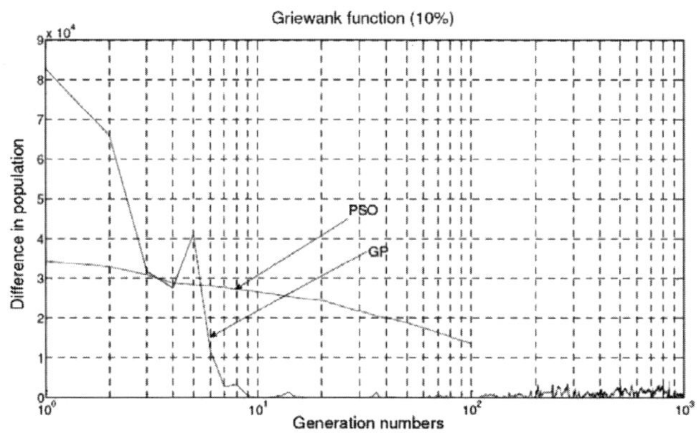

(b) Population diversities for Griewank function ($\Delta d = 10\%$)

Fig. 2.4. Population diversities for for Rastrigin and Griewank functions.

polynomials in dynamic environment. The operations of the PSO are identical to the ones of the original PSO except that elements of particles of the PSO are represented by arithmetic operations and polynomial variables, which are the components of the polynomial models. A set of dynamic benchmark functions in which their optima are dynamically moved was employed to evaluate the performance of the PSO. Comparison of the PSO and the GP, which is commonly used on polynomial modeling, was carried out by using the data generated based on the dynamic benchmark functions.

It was shown that the PSO perform significantly better than the GP in polynomial modeling. Enhancing the effectiveness of the proposed PSO in polynomial modeling in dynamic environments will be considered in the further work. It will be incorporated with the techniques implemented in the PSO which have been shown to be able to obtain satisfactory results on solving dynamic optimization problems [24, 25].

References

[1] R. Eberhart and J. Kennedy, A new optimizer using particle swarm theory, *Proceedings of the Sixth IEEE International Symposium on Micro Machine and Human Science.* pp. 39–43, (1995).

[2] J. Kennedy and R. Eberhart, *Swarm Intelligence.* (Morgan Kaufmann, 2001).

[3] Z. Lian, Z. Gu, and B. Jiao, A similar particle swarm optimization algorithm for permutation flowshop scheduling to minimize makespan, *Applied Mathematics and Computation.* **175**, 773–785, (2006).

[4] C. J. Liao, C. T. Tseng, and P. Luran, A discrete version of particle swarm optimization for flowshop scheduling problems, *Computer and Operations Research.* **34**, 3099–3111, (2007).

[5] Y. Liu and X. Gu, Skeleton network reconfiguration based on topological characteristics of scale free networks and discrete particle swarm optimization, *IEEE Transactions on Power Systems.* **22**(3), 1267–1274, (2007).

[6] Q. K. Pan, M. F. Tasgetiren, and Y. C. Liang, A discrete particle swarm optimization algorithm for the no-wait flowshop scheduling problem, *Computer and Operations Research.* **35**, 2807–2839, (2008).

[7] C. T. Tseng and C. J. Liao, A discrete particle swarm optimization for lot-streaming flowship scheduling problem, *European Journal of Operations Research.* **191**, 360–373, (2008).

[8] H. Iba, Inference of differential equation models by genetic programming, *Information Sciences.* **178**, 4453–4468, (2008).

[9] J. Koza, *Genetic Programming: On the Programming of Computers by Means of Natural Evolution.* (MIT Press, Cambridge. MA, 1992).

[10] K. Rodriguez-Vazquez, C. M. Fonseca, and P. J. Fleming, Identifying the structure of nonlinear dynamic systems using multiobjective genetic programming, *IEEE Transactions on Systems, Man and Cybernetics – Part A.* **34**(4), 531–545, (2004).

[11] N. Wagner, Z. Michalewicz, M. Khouja, and R. R. McGregor, Time series forecasting for dynamic environments: the dyfor genetic program model, *IEEE Transactions on Evolutionary Computation.* **4**(11), 433–452, (2007).

[12] D. Gabor, W. Wides, and R. Woodcock, A universal nonlinear filter predictor and simulator which optimizes itself by a learning process, *Proceedings of IEEE.* **108-B**, 422–438, (1961).

[13] S. Billings, M. Korenberg, and S. Chen, Identification of nonlinear outputaffine systems using an orthogonal least-squares algorithm, *International Journal of Systems Science.* **19**, 1559–1568, (1988).

[14] S. Chen, S. Billings, and W. Luo, Orthogonal least squares methods and their application to non-linear system identification, *International Journal of Control.* **50**, 1873–1896, (1989).

[15] B. McKay, M. J. Willis, and G. W. Barton, Steady-state modeling of chemical processes using genetic programming, computers and chemical engineering, *Computers and Chemical Engineering.* **21**(9), 981–996, (1997).

[16] R. C. Eberhart and Y. Shi, Comparison between genetic algorithms and particle swarm optimization, *Lecture Notes in Computer Science.* **1447**, 611–616, (1998).

[17] J. Madar, J. Abonyi, and F. Szeifert, Genetic programming for the identification of nonlinear input – output models, *Industrial and Engineering Chemistry Research.* **44**, 3178–3186, (2005).

[18] M. O. Neill and A. Brabazon, Grammatical swarm: The generation of programs by social programming, *Natural Computing.* **5**, 443–462, (2006).

[19] A. Ekart and S. Nemeth, A metric for genetic programs and fitness sharing, *Proceedings of the European Conference of Genetic Programming.* pp. 259–270, (2000).

[20] R. I. McKay, Fitness sharing genetic programming, *Proceedings of the Genetic and Evolutionary Computation Conference.* pp. 435–442, (2000).

[21] E. K. Burke, S. Gustafson, and G. Kendall, Diversity in genetic programming: an analysis of measures and correlation with fitness, *IEEE Transactions on Evolutionary Computation.* **8**(1), 47–62, (2004).

[22] X. H. Nguyen, R. I. McKay, D. Essam, and H. A. Abbass, Toward an alternative comparison between different genetic programming systems, *Proceedings of the European Conference on Genetic Programming.* pp. 67–77, (2004).

[23] B. Naudts and L. Kallel, A comparison of predictive measures of problem difficulty in evolutionary algorithms, *IEEE Transactions on Evolutionary Computation.* **4**(1), 1–15, (2000).

[24] T. Blackwell and J. Branke, Multiswarms, exclusion, and anti-convergence in dynamic environments, *IEEE Transactions on Evolutionary Computation.* **10**(4), 459–472, (2006).

[25] S. Janson and M. Middendorf, A hierarchical particle swarm optimizer for noisy and dynamic environments, *Genetic Programming and Evolvable Machines.* **7**, 329–354, (2006).

Chapter 3

Restoration of Half-toned Color-quantized Images Using Particle Swarm Optimization with Multi-wavelet Mutation

Frank H.F. Leung, Benny C.W. Yeung and Y.H. Chan

Centre for Signal Processing,
Department of Electronic and Information Engineering,
The Hong Kong Polytechnic University,
Hung Hom, Kowloon, Hong Kong
enfrank@inet.polyu.edu.hk *

Restoration of color-quantized images is rarely addressed in the literature, especially when the images are color-quantized with half-toning. Many existing restoration algorithms are inadequate to deal with this problem because they were proposed for restoring noisy blurred images only. In this chapter, a restoration algorithm based on Particle Swarm Optimization with multi-wavelet mutation (MWPSO) is proposed to solve the problem. This algorithm makes good use of the available color palette and the mechanism of a half-toning process to derive useful *a priori* information for the restoration. Simulation results show that it can improve the quality of a half-toned color-quantized image remarkably in terms of both signal-to-noise ratio improvement and convergence rate. The subjective quality of the restored images can also be improved.

Contents

*The work described in this chapter was substantially supported by a grant from the Research Grants Council of the Hong Kong Special Administrative Region, China (Project No. PolyU 5224/08E).

3.1. Introduction

Color quantization is a process of reducing the number of colors in a digital image by replacing them with some representative colors selected from a palette [1]. It is widely used because it can save transmission bandwidth and data storage requirements in many multimedia applications. When color quantization is performed, certain degradation of quality will be introduced owing to the limited number of colors used to produce the output image. The most common artifact is the false contour. False contours occur when the available palette colors are not enough to represent a gradually changing region. Another common artifact is the color shift. In general, the smaller the color palette size is used, the more severe the defects will be.

Half-toning is a reprographic technique that converts a continuous-tone image to a lower resolution, and it is mainly for printing [2–6]. Error diffusion is one of the most popular half-toning methods. It makes use of the fact that the human visual system is less sensitive to higher frequencies, and during diffusion, the quantization error of a pixel is diffused to the neighboring pixels so as to hide the defects and to achieve a more faithful reproduction of colors.

Restoring a color-quantized image back to the original image is often necessary. However, most of the recent restoration algorithms mainly concern the restoration of noisy and blurred color images [7–14]; literature for restoring half-toned color-quantized images is seldom found. The restoration can be formulated as an optimization problem. Since error diffusion is a nonlinear process, conventional gradient-oriented optimization algorithms might not be suitable to solve the addressed problem.

In this chapter, we make use of a proposed particle swarm optimization with multi-wavelet mutation (MWPSO) algorithm to restore half-toned color-quantized images. It is an evolutionary computation algorithm that works very well on various optimization problems. By taking advantage of the wavelet theory, which increases the searching space for the PSO at the early stage of evolution, the chance of converging to local minima is lowered. The process of color quantization with error diffusion will first be detailed. Then the application of the proposed MWPSO to the restoration of the degraded images will be discussed. The results demonstrate that the MWPSO can achieve a remarkable improvement in terms of convergence rate and signal-to-noise ratio.

3.2. Color Quantization With Half-toning

A color image generally consists of three color planes, namely, O_r, O_g and O_b, which represent the red, green and blue color planes of the image respectively. Accordingly, the $(i,\, j)$-th color pixel of a 24-bit full-color image of size $N \times N$ pixels consists of three color components. The intensity values of these three components form a 3D vector $\vec{O}_{(i,\, j)} = (O_{(i,\, j)r},\, O_{(i,\, j)g},\, O_{(i,\, j)b})$, where $O_{(i,\, j)c} \in [0 \quad 1]$ is the intensity value of the c color component of the $(i,\, j)$-th pixel. Here, we assume that the maximum and the minimum intensity values of a pixel are one and zero respectively.

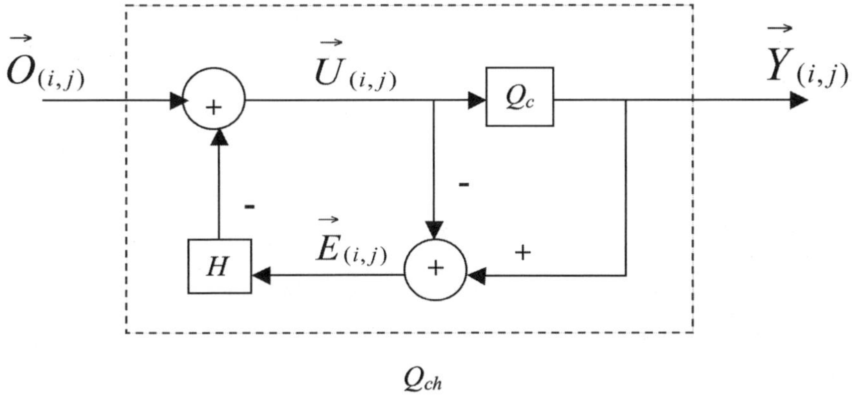

Fig. 3.1. Color quantization with half-toning.

Figure 3.1 shows the system that performs color quantization with error diffusion. The input image is scanned in a row-by-row fashion from top to bottom and from left to right. The relationship between the original image $\vec{O}_{(i,\, j)}$ and the encoded image $\vec{Y}_{(i,\, j)}$ is described by

$$U_{(i,\, j)c} = O_{(i,\, j)c} - \sum_{(k,\, l) \in \Omega} H_{(i,\, j)c} E_{(i-k,\, j-l)c} \tag{3.1}$$

$$\vec{E}_{(i,\, j)} = \vec{Y}_{(i,\, j)} - \vec{U}_{(i,\, j)} \tag{3.2}$$

$$\vec{Y}_{(i,\, j)} = Q_c[\vec{U}_{(i,\, j)}] \tag{3.3}$$

where $\vec{U}_{(i,\, j)} = (U_{(i,\, j)r},\, U_{(i,\, j)g},\, U_{(i,\, j)b})$ is a state vector of the system, $\vec{E}_{(i,\, j)}$ is the quantization error of the pixel at position $(i,\, j)$ and $H_{(i,\, j)c}$ is a coefficient of the error diffusion filter for the c color component. Ω is the corresponding causal support region of $H_{(i,j)c}$.

The operator $Q_c[\cdot]$ performs a 3D vector quantization. Specifically, the 3D vector $\vec{U}_{(i,j)}$ is compared with a set of representative color vectors stored in a previously generated color palette $V = \{\widehat{v_i} : i = 1, 2, \ldots, N_c\}$. The best-matched vector in the palette is selected based on the minimum Euclidean distance criterion. In other words, a state vector $\vec{U}_{(i,j)}$ is represented by the color $\widehat{v_k}$ if and only if $\|\vec{U}_{(i,j)} - \widehat{v_k}\| \leq \|\vec{U}_{(i,j)} - \widehat{v_l}\|$ for all $l = 1, 2, \ldots, N_c$; $l \neq k$. Once the best-matched vector is selected from the color palette, its index is recorded and the quantization error $\vec{E}_{(i,j)} = \widehat{v_k} - \vec{U}_{(i,j)}$ is diffused to pixel (i, j)'s neighborhood as described in (3.1). Note that in order to handle the boundary pixels, $\vec{E}_{(i,j)}$ is defined to be zero when (i, j) falls outside the image. Without loss of generality, in this chapter, we use a typical Floyd–Steinberg error diffusion kernel as $H_{(i,j)c}$ to perform the half-toning. The recorded indices of the color palette will be used again in future to reconstruct the color-quantized image of the restored image.

3.3. Formulation of Restoration Algorithm

3.3.1. *PSO with multi-wavelet mutation (MWPSO)*

Consider a swarm $X(t)$ at the t-th iteration. Each particle $\mathbf{x}^p(t) \in X(t)$ contains κ elements $x_j^p(t) \in \mathbf{x}^p(t)$ at the t-th iteration, where $p = 1, 2, \ldots, \gamma$ and $j = 1, 2, \ldots, \kappa$; γ denotes the number of particles in the swarm. First, the particles of the swarm are initialized and then evaluated based on a defined fitness value. The objective of PSO is to minimize the fitness value (cost value) of a particle through iterative steps. The swarm evolves from iteration t to $t + 1$ by repeating the procedures as shown in Fig. 3.2.

The velocity $v_j^p(t)$(corresponding to the flight speed in a search space) and the coordinate $x_j^p(t)$ of the j-th element of the p-th particle at the t-th generation can be calculated using the following formula:

$$\begin{aligned} v_j^p(t) =& \Big(w \cdot v_j^p(t-1) + \varphi_1 \cdot rand_j^p()\Big) \cdot \Big(pbest_j^p - x_j^p(t-1)\Big) \\ &+ \varphi_2 \cdot rand_j^p() \cdot \Big(gbest_j - x_j^p(t-1)\Big) \end{aligned} \tag{3.4}$$

$$x_j^p(t) = x_j^p(t-1) + k \cdot v_j^p(t) \tag{3.5}$$

```
Begin
        t→0                 //Iteration number
        initialize X(t)     //The Swarm for iteration t
        evaluate f(X(t))    //The fitness function
while (not termination condition) do
        begin
                t→t+1
                // Process of standard PSO//
                record the best current position among all particles as gbest
                record the best current position for each particle as pbest
                update velocity v(t) and position of each particle based on gbest and pbest
                if v(t) > v_max
                        v(t) = v_max
                end
                if v(t) < -v_max
                        v(t) = -v_max
                end
                // End of the process of standard PSO//
                Perform multi-wavelet mutation operation with μ_m and N_m
                reproduce a new X(t)
                evaluate f(X(t))
        end
end
```

Fig. 3.2. Pseudo code for MWPSO.

where

$$pbest^p = [pbest_1^p \quad pbest_2^p \quad \dots \quad pbest_\kappa^p]$$

and

$$gbest = [gbest_1 \quad gbest_2 \quad \dots \quad gbest_\kappa].$$

The best previous position of a particle is recorded and represented as $pbest^p$; the position of the best particle among all the particles is represented as $gbest$; w is an inertia weight factor; φ_1 and φ_2 are acceleration constants; $rand_j^p()$ returns a random number in the range of [0 1]; k is a constriction factor derived from the stability analysis of (3.5) to ensure the system can converge but not prematurely.

PSO utilizes $pbest^p$ and $gbest$ to modify the current search point in order to prevent the particles from moving in the same direction, but to converge gradually toward $pbest^p$ and $gbest$. A suitable selection of the inertia weight w provides a balance between the global and local explorations. Generally, w can be dynamically set with the following equation:

$$w = w_{max} - \frac{w_{max} - w_{min}}{T} \times t \tag{3.6}$$

where t is the current iteration number, T is the total number of iteration, w_{max} and w_{min} are the upper and lower limits of the inertia weight, and are set to 1.2 and 0.1 respectively in this chapter.

In (3.4), the particle velocity is limited by a maximum value v_{max}. The parameter v_{max} determines the resolution of region between the present position and the target position to be searched. This limit enhances the local exploration of the problem space, affecting the incremental changes of learning.

Before generating a new $X(t)$, the mutation operation is performed: every particle of the swarm will have a chance to mutate governed by a probability of mutation $\mu_m \in [0\ 1]$, which is defined by the user. For each particle, a random number between zero and one will be generated; if μ_m is larger than the random number, this particle will be selected for the mutation operation. Another parameter called the element probability $N_m \in [0\ 1]$ is then defined by the user to control the number of elements in the particle that will mutate in each iteration step. For instance, if $\mathbf{x}^p(t) = [x_1^p(t), x_2^p(t), \ldots, x_\kappa^p(t)]$ is the selected p-th particle, the expected number of elements that undergo mutation is given by

$$\text{Expected number of mutated elements} = N_m \times \kappa \tag{3.7}$$

We propose a multi-wavelet mutation operation for realizing the mutation. The exact elements for doing mutation in a particle are randomly selected. The resulting particle is given by $\bar{\mathbf{x}}^p(t) = [\bar{x}_1^p(t), \bar{x}_2^p(t), \ldots, \bar{x}_\kappa^p(t)]$. If the j-th element is selected for mutation, the operation is given by

$$\bar{x}_j^p(t) = \begin{cases} x_j^p(t) + \sigma \times \left(para_{max}^j - x_j^p(t)\right) & \text{if } \sigma > 0 \\ x_j^p(t) + \sigma \times \left(x_j^p(t) - para_{min}^j\right) & \text{if } \sigma \le 0 \end{cases} \tag{3.8}$$

Using the Morlet wavelet as the mother wavelet, we have

$$\sigma = \frac{1}{\sqrt{a}} e^{-\left(\frac{\varphi}{a}\right)^2/2} \cos\left(5\left(\frac{\varphi}{a}\right)\right) \tag{3.9}$$

The value of the dilation parameter a is set to vary with the value of t/T in order to realize a fine-tuning effect, where T is the total number of iteration and t is the current iteration number. In order to perform a local search when t is large, the value of a should increase as t/T increases so as to reduce the significance of the mutation. Hence, a monotonic increasing function governing a and t/T is proposed as follows:

$$a = e^{-\ln(g)\times(1-\frac{t}{T})^{\zeta_{wm}}+\ln(g)} \tag{3.10}$$

where ζ_{wm} is the shape parameter of the monotonic increasing function, g is the upper limit of the parameter a.

3.3.2. *The fitness function*

The proposed MWPSO is applied to restore half-toned color-quantized images. Let X be the output image of the restoration. Obviously, when the restored image X is color-quantized with error diffusion, the output should be close to the original half-toned image Y. Suppose $Q_{ch}[\cdot]$ (as shown in Fig. 3.1) denotes the operator that performs the color quantization with half-toning, then we should have

$$Y \approx Q_{ch}[X] \tag{3.11}$$

Based on the above criterion, the cost function for the restoration problem can be defined as

$$fitness = \sum |Y - Q_{ch}[X]| \tag{3.12}$$

If $fitness = 0$, it implies the restored image X and the original image O provide the same color quantization results. In other words, the cost function of (3.12) provides a good measure to judge if X is a good estimate of O.

3.3.3. *Restoration with MWPSO*

Let $X_{cur}(t-1)$ be the group of the current estimates of the restored image (the swarm) at a particular iteration, $t-1$, $X^p_{cur}(t)$ be the p-th particle of the swarm, and E^p_{cur} be its corresponding fitness value. According to (3.4) and (3.5), the new estimate of the restored image is given by

$$X^p_{new}(t) = X^p_{cur}(t-1) + k \cdot v^p(t) \tag{3.13}$$

where k is a constriction factor. Before evaluating the fitness of each particle, the multi-wavelet mutation is performed. The mutation operation realizes a fine tuning upon many times of iteration. After each time of iteration, E^p_{new}, which is the fitness for $X^p_{new}(t)$, is then evaluated. If $E^p_{new} < E^p_{cur}$, $X^p_{cur}(t)$ is updated to $X^p_{new}(t)$. Furthermore, if $E^p_{new} < E_{best}$, where E_{best} is the fitness value of the best estimate *gbest* so far, then *gbest* will be updated by $X_{new}^{p}(t)$. In summary, we have

$$X_{cur}^{p}(t) = \begin{cases} X_{new}^{p}(t) & \text{if } E_{new}^{p} < E_{cur}^{p} \\ X_{cur}^{p}(t-1) & \text{otherwise} \end{cases} \tag{3.14}$$

and

$$gbest = \begin{cases} X_{new}^{p}(t) & \text{if } E_{new}^{p} < E_{best} \\ gbest & \text{otherwise} \end{cases} \tag{3.15}$$

3.3.4. *Experimental setup*

On realizing the MWPSO restoration, the following simulation conditions are used:

- Shape parameter of the wavelet mutation (ζ_{wm}): 0.2
- Probability of mutation (μ_m): 0.2
- Element probability (N_m): 0.3
- Acceleration constant φ_1: 2.05
- Acceleration constant φ_2: 2.05
- Constriction factor k: 0.005
- Parameter g: 10000
- Swarm size: 8
- Number of iteration: 500
- Initial population $X(0)$: All the particles are initialized to be the Gaussian filtered output of the original half-toned image Y
- Initial global best *gbest*: The original half-toned image Y
- Initial previous best $pbest^{p}$: The zero matrix

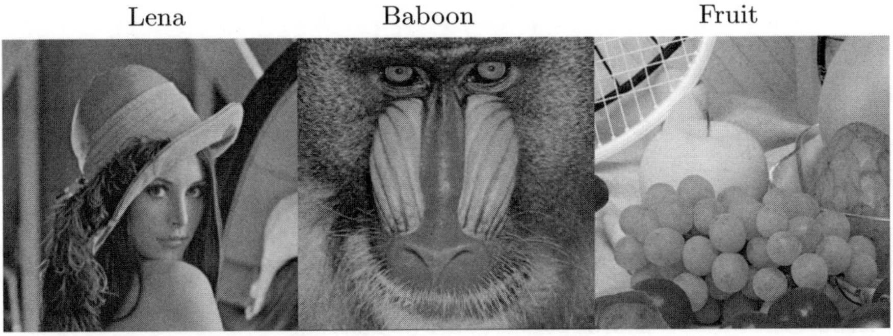

Fig. 3.3. Original images used for testing the proposed restoration algorithm.

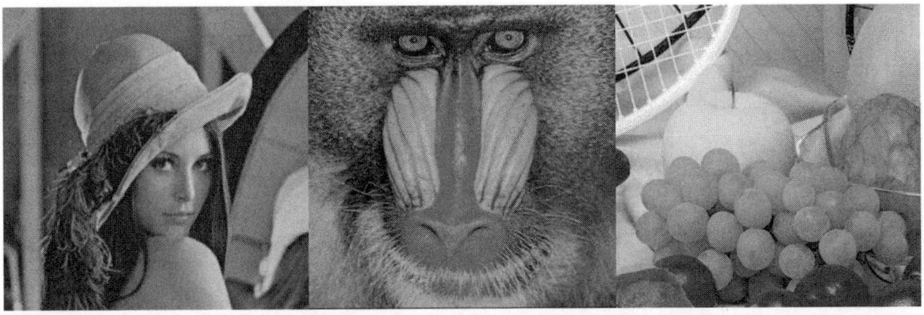

Fig. 3.4. Half-toned images with 256-color palette size.

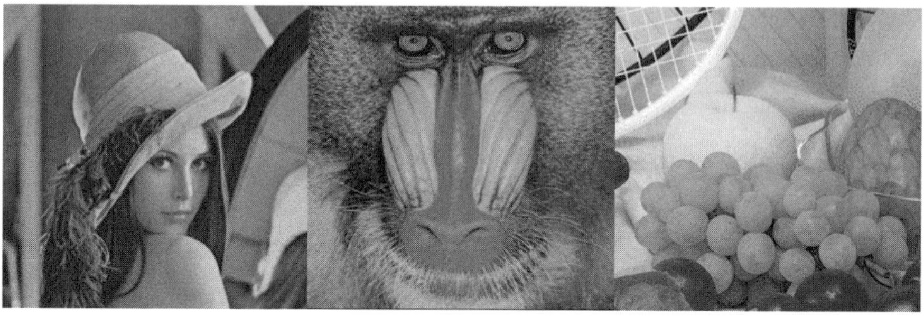

Fig. 3.5. Half-toned images with 128-color palette size.

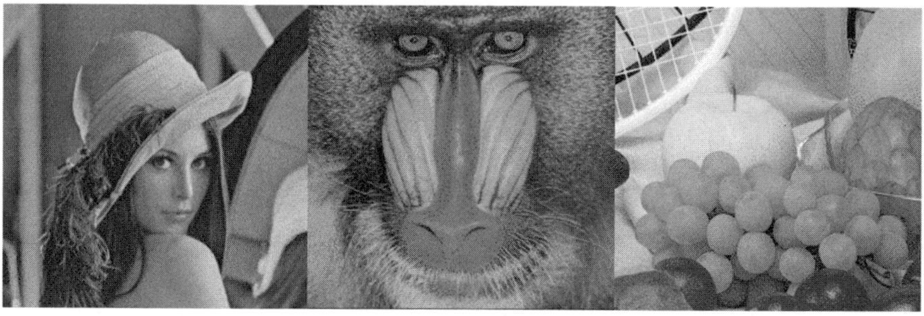

Fig. 3.6. Half-toned images with 64-color palette size.

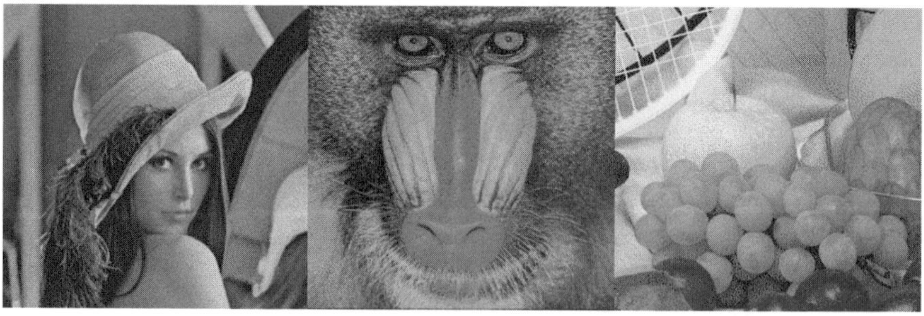

Fig. 3.7. Half-toned images with 32-color palette size.

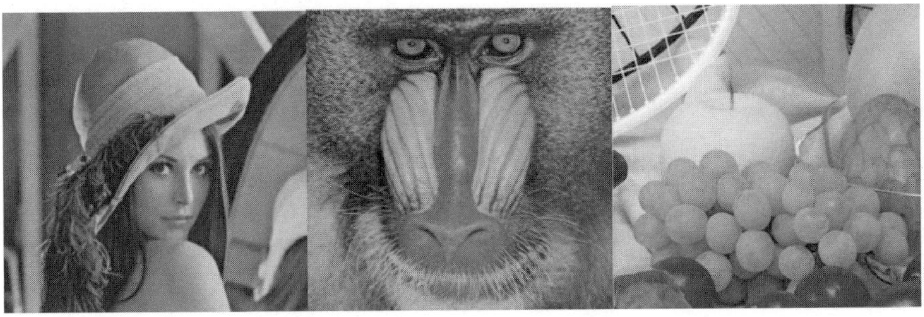

Fig. 3.8. MWPSO restored images with 256-color palette size.

Fig. 3.9. MWPSO restored images with 128-color palette size.

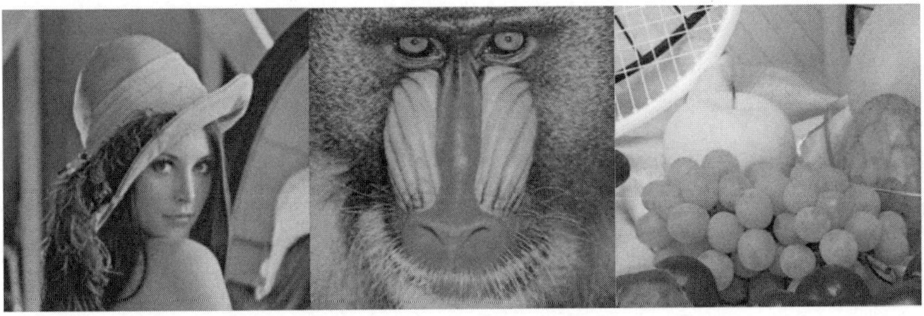

Fig. 3.10. MWPSO restored images with 64-color palette size.

Fig. 3.11. MWPSO restored images with 32-color palette size.

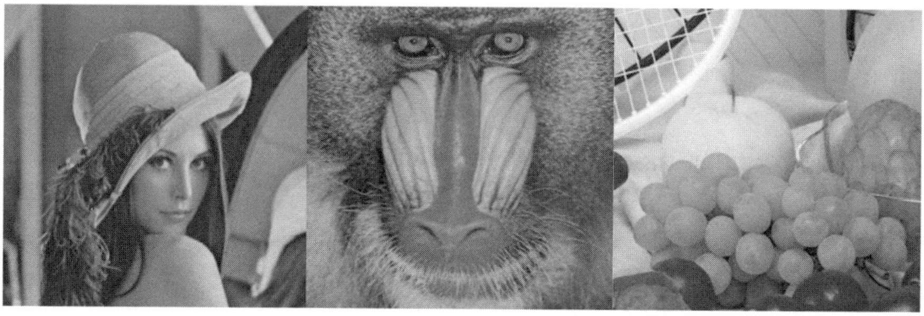

Fig. 3.12. SA restored images with 256-color palette size.

Fig. 3.13. SA restored images with 128-color palette size.

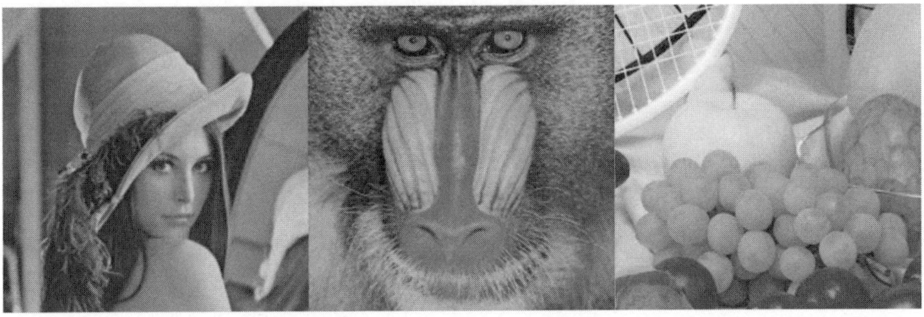

Fig. 3.14. SA restored images with 64-color palette size.

Fig. 3.15. SA restored images with 32-color palette size.

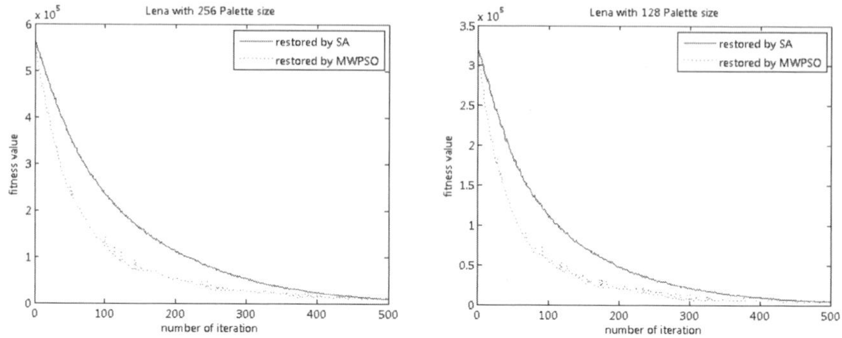

Fig. 3.16. Comparisons between SA and MWPSO for Lena with 256- and 128-color palette size.

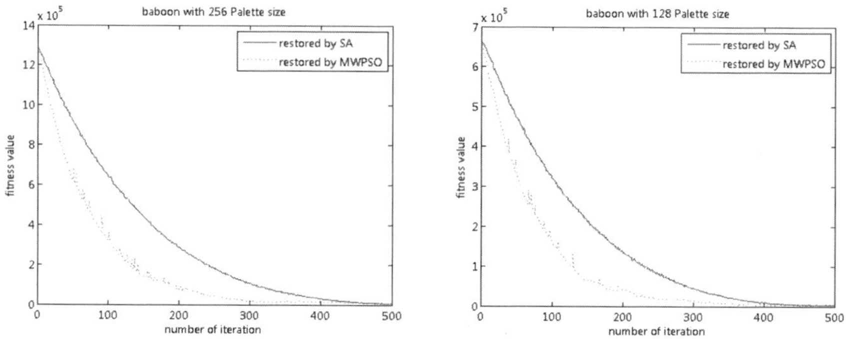

Fig. 3.17. Comparisons between SA and MWPSO for Baboon with 256- and 128-color palette size.

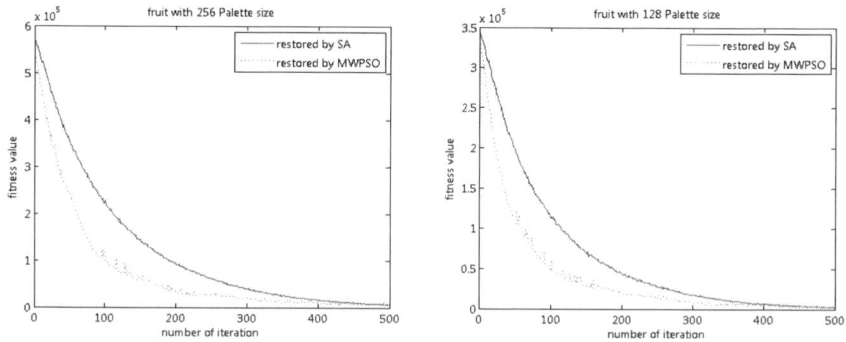

Fig. 3.18. Comparisons between SA and MWPSO for Fruit with 256- and 128-color palette size.

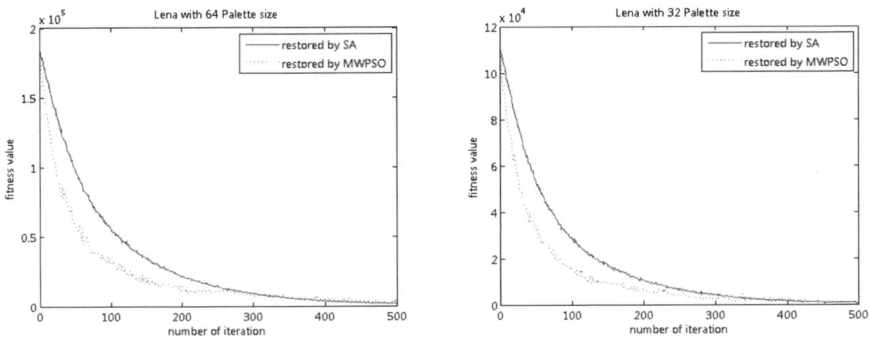

Fig. 3.19. Comparisons between SA and MWPSO for Lena with 64- and 32-color palette size.

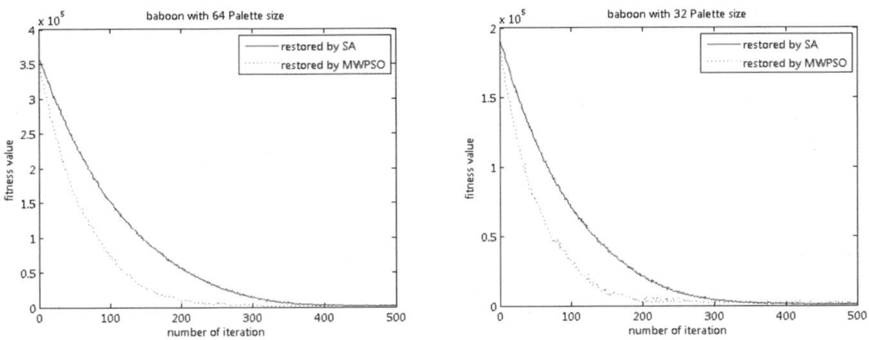

Fig. 3.20. Comparisons between SA and MWPSO for Baboon with 64- and 32-color palette size.

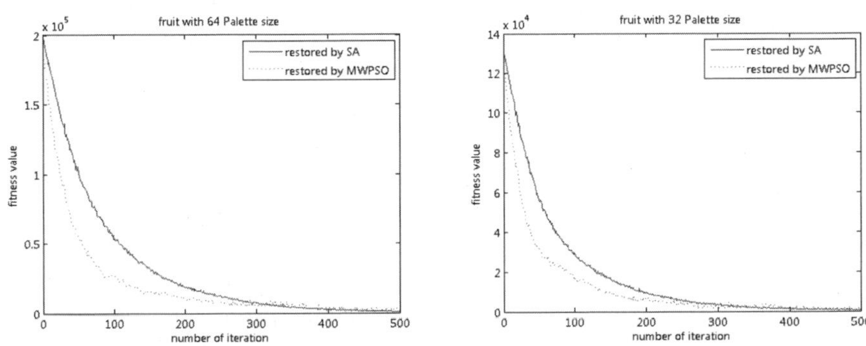

Fig. 3.21. Comparisons between SA and MWPSO for Fruit with 64- and 32-color palette size.

Table 3.1. Fitness and SNRI of two algorithms for restoring the half-toned image Lena.

Lena with 256-color Palette size		
	MWPSO	SA
SNRI	**6.7736**	6.7123
Best fitness	**8945**	8957

Lena with 128-color Palette size		
	MWPSO	SA
SNRI	**8.1969**	8.1944
Best fitness	**3849**	3851

Lena with 64-color Palette size		
	MWPSO	SA
SNRI	9.4404	**9.566**
Best fitness	**1604**	1652

Lena with 32-color Palette size		
	MWPSO	SA
SNRI	**11.522**	11.4903
Best fitness	**649**	677

3.4. Result and Analysis

Simulations have been carried out to evaluate the performance of the proposed algorithm. Three *de facto* standard 24-bit full-color images of size 256×256 pixels are used, and all the test images are shown in Fig. 3.3. These test images are color-quantized to produce the corresponding images (Y). The color-quantized images with 256-color palette size, 128-color palette size, 64-color palette size and 32-color palette size are shown in Fig 3.4 to 3.7 respectively.

Color palettes of different sizes are generated using the median-cut algorithm [2]. On doing color quantization, half-toning is performed with error diffusion, and the Floyd–Steinberg diffusion filter [3] is used. The proposed restoration algorithm is used to restore the half-toned color-quantized images.

For comparison, simulated annealing (SA) is also applied to do the restoration. The performance of SA and the proposed MWPSO are reflected in terms of the signal-to-noise ratio improvement (SNRI) achieved when the algorithms are used to restore the color-quantized images "Lena", "Baboon" and "Fruit". The simulation condition for SA is basically the

Table 3.2. Fitness and SNRI of two algorithms for restoring the half-toned image Baboon.

Baboon with 256-color Palette size		
	MWPSO	SA
SNRI	**2.6854**	2.6706
Best fitness	**5410**	5445

Baboon with 128-color Palette size		
	MWPSO	SA
SNRI	**4.3301**	4.3293
Best fitness	**2189**	2277

Baboon with 64-color Palette size		
	MWPSO	SA
SNRI	5.5836	**5.616**
Best fitness	**1045**	1166

Baboon with 32-color Palette size		
	MWPSO	SA
SNRI	**5.8208**	5.8186
Best fitness	**750**	760

same as that of the proposed MWPSO. The control parameter of SA, *gamma*, is set to be equal to the parameter k of the MWPSO. The number of iteration is set at 500. The experimental results in terms of SNRI and the convergence rate are summarized in Tables 3.1 to 3.3 and Figs 3.16 to 3.21 respectively. The SNRI is defined as:

$$SNRI = 10 \log \frac{\sum_{(i,j)} \left\| \vec{O}_{(i,j)} - \vec{Y}_{(i,j)} \right\|^2}{\sum_{(i,j)} \left\| \vec{O}_{(i,j)} - \vec{X}_{best(i,j)} \right\|^2} \tag{3.16}$$

where $\vec{O}_{(i,j)}$, $\vec{Y}_{(i,j)}$ and $\vec{X}_{best(i,j)}$ are the (i, j)-th pixels of the original, the half-toned color-quantized and the optimally restored images respectively.

From Figs 3.16 to 3.21, we can see that the final results achieved by SA and MWPSO are similar: both of them converge to some similar values. It means that both algorithms can reach the same optimal point. However, we can see that the proposed MWPSO exhibits a higher convergence rate. Also, from Tables 3.1 to 3.3, MWPSO converges to smaller fitness values in all experiments and offers higher SNRI in most of the experiments.

Table 3.3. Fitness and SNRI of two algorithms for restoring the half-toned image Fruit.

Fruit with 256-color Palette size		
	MWPSO	SA
SNRI	**7.5598**	7.5155
Best fitness	**6372**	6394

Fruit with 128-color Palette size		
	MWPSO	SA
SNRI	**9.9556**	9.9186
Best fitness	**2400**	2417

Fruit with 64-color Palette size		
	MWPSO	SA
SNRI	**10.8616**	10.8607
Best fitness	**982**	1012

Fruit with 32-color Palette size		
	MWPSO	SA
SNRI	**11.7873**	11.7815
Best fitness	**478**	574

3.5. Conclusion

In this chapter, we used the MWPSO as the restoration algorithm for half-toned color-quantized images. The half-toned color quantization and the application of the proposed MWPSO have been described. Simulation results demonstrate that the proposed algorithm performs better in terms of convergence rate and SNRI than the conventional SA algorithm. By using MWPSO, the number of particles used for searching is increased, and more freedom is given to search the optimal result thanks to the multi-wavelet mutation. This explains the improved searching ability and the convergence rate. The chance for the particles being trapped in some local optimal point is also reduced.

References

[1] M. T. Orchard and C. A. Bouman, Color quantization of images, *IEEE Transactions on Signal Processing.* **39**(12), 2677–2690, (1991).

[2] P. Heckbert, Color image quantization for frame buffer displays, *Computer Graphics.* **16**(4), 297–307, (1982).

[3] R. Ulichney, *Digital Halftoning.* (MIT Press, Cambridge, MA, 1987).

[4] R. S. Gentile, E. Walowit, and J. P. Allebach, Quantization and multi-level halftoning of color images for near original image quality, *Proceedings of the SPIE 1990*. pp. 249–259, (1990).
[5] S. S. Dixit, Quantization of color images for display/printing on limited color output devices, *Computer Graphics*. **15**(4), 561–567, (1991).
[6] X. Wu, Color quantization by dynamic programming and principal analysis, *ACM Transactions on Graphics*. **11**(4), 372–384, (1992).
[7] M. Barni, V. Cappellini, and L. Mirri, Multichannel m-filtering for color image restoration. pp. 529–532, (2000).
[8] G. Angelopoulosnd and I. Pitas, Multichannel wiener filters in color image restoration, *IEEE Transactions on CASVT*. **4**(1), 83–87, (1994).
[9] N. P. Galatsanos, A. K. Katsaggelos, R. T. Chin, and A. D. Hillery, Least squares restoration of multichannel images, *IEEE Transactions on Signal Processing*. **39**(10), 2222–2236, (1991).
[10] N. P. Galatsanos and R. T. Chin, Restoration of color images by multichannel kalman filtering, *IEEE Transactions on Signal Processing*. **39** (10), 2237–2252, (1991).
[11] B. R. Hunt and O. Kubler, Karhunen-loeve multispectral image restoration, part 1: theory, *IEEE Transactions on Acoustic Speech Signal Processing*. **32** (3), 592–600, (1984).
[12] H. Altunbasak and H. J. Trussell, Colorimetric restoration of digital images, *IEEE Transactions on Image Processing*. **10**(3), 393–402, (2001).
[13] K. J. Boo and N. K. Bose, Multispectral image restoration with multisensor, *IEEE Transactions on Geosci. Remote Sensing*. **35**(5), 1160–1170, (1997).
[14] N. P. Galatsanos and R. T. Chin, Digital restoration of multichannel images, *IEEE Transactions on Acoustic Speech Signal Processing*. **37**, 415–421, (1989).

PART 2
Fuzzy Logics and their Applications

Chapter 4

Hypoglycemia Detection for Insulin-dependent Diabetes Mellitus: Evolved Fuzzy Inference System Approach

S.H. Ling, P.P. San and H.T. Nguyen

Centre for Health Technologies,
Faculty of Engineering and Information Technology,
University of Technology, Sydney, NSW, Australia,
steve.ling@uts.edu.au

Insulin-dependent diabetes mellitus is classified as Type 1 diabetes and it can be further classified as immune-mediated or idiopathic. Hypoglycemia is a common and serious side effect of insulin therapy in patients with Type 1 diabetes. In this chapter, we measure physiological parameters continuously to provide a non-invasive hypoglycemia detection for Type 1 diabetes mellitus (T1DM) patients. Based on the physiological parameters of the electrocardiogram (ECG) signal, such as heart rate, corrected QT interval, change of heart rate and change of corrected QT interval, an evolved fuzzy inference model is developed for classification of hypoglycemia. To optimize the rules and membership functions of the fuzzy system, a hybrid particle swarm optimization with wavelet mutation (HPSOWM) is introduced. For the clinical study, 15 children with Type 1 diabetes are volunteered overnight. All the real data sets are collected from the Department of Health, Government of Western Australia and are randomly organized into a training set (10 patients) and testing set (5 patients). The results show that the evolved fuzzy inference system approach performs well in terms of sensitivity and specificity.

Contents

4.1. Introduction

Hypoglycemia is the medical term for a state produced by a lower level of blood glucose. It is characterized by a mismatch between the action of insulin, the ingestion of food and energy expenditure. The most common forms of hypoglycemia occur as a complication of treatment with insulin or oral medications. Hypoglycemia is less common in non-diabetic people, but can occur at any age because of many causes. Among these causes are excessive insulin produced in the body, inborn errors, medications and poisons, alcohol, hormone deficiencies, prolonged starvation, alterations of metabolism associated with infection and organ failure. In [1, 2] it was discussed that diabetic patients, especially those who have been treated with insulin, are at risk of developing hypoglycemia while it is less likely to occur in non-insulin-dependent patients who are taking sugar-lowering medicine for diabetes. Most surveys in [3] have demonstrated that the tighter the glycemic control, and the younger the patient, the greater frequency of both mild and severe hypoglycemia.

The level of blood glucose low enough to define hypoglycemia may be different for different people in different circumstances, and for different purposes and occasionally has been a matter of controversy. Most healthy adults maintain fasting glucose levels above 70 mg/dL, (3.9 $mmol/L$) and develop symptoms of hypoglycemia when the glucose level falls below 55 mg/dL, (3.0 $mmol/L$). In [4], it has been reported that the severe hypoglycemic episodes are defined in those whose documented blood glucose level is 50 mg/dL, (2.8 $mmol/L$) and the patients are advised to take the necessary treatment. Hypoglycemia is treated by restoring the blood glucose level to normal by the investigation or administration of carbohydrate foods. In some cases, it is treated by injection or infusion of glucagon.

The symptoms of hypoglycemia occur when not enough glucose is supplied to the brain, in fact the brain and nervous system need a certain level of glucose to function. The two typical symptoms of hypoglycemia arise from the activation of the autonomous central nervous systems (autonomic symptoms) and reduced cerebral glucose consumption (neuroglycopenic symptoms). Autonomic symptoms such as headache, extreme hunger, blurry or double vision, fatigue, weakness and sweating are activated before neuroglycopenic symptoms follow. As discussed in [5, 6] the initial condition of the presence of hypoglycemia can only be identified when autonomic symptoms occur and allow the patient to recognize correct ensuing episodes. The neuroglycopenic symptoms such as confusion, seizures and loss of consciousness (coma) arise due to insufficient glucose flow to the brain [7].

In cases of hypoglycemia presented in [8, 9], the symptoms occured without the patients being aware of them, at any time while driving, or during sleeping. Nocturnal hypoglycemia is particularly dangerous because it reduces sleep and may obscure autonomic counter-regulatory responses, so that an initially mild episode may become severe. The risk of hypoglycemia is high during night time, since 50% of all severe episodes occur at that time [10]. Deficient glucose counter-regulation may also lead to severe hypoglycemia even with modest insulin elevations. Regulation of nocturnal hypoglycemia is further complicated by the dawn phenomenon. This is a consequence of nocturnal changes in insulin sensitivity secondary to growth hormone secretion: a decrease in insulin requirements approximately between midnight and 5 am followed by an increase in requirements between 5 am and 8 am. Thus, hypoglycemia is one of the complications of diabetes most feared by patients.

Current technologies used in the diabetes diagnostic testing and self-monitoring market have already been improved to the extent that any additional improvements would be minimal. For example, glucose meter manufacturers have modified their instruments to use as little as 2 μl of blood and produce results within a minute. Technology advancement in this market is expected to occur using novel design concepts. An example of such technology is the non-invasive glucose meter. There is a limited number of non-invasive blood glucose monitoring systems currently available in the market but each has specific drawbacks in terms of functioning, cost, reliability and obtrusiveness. Intensive research has been devoted to the development of hypoglycemia alarms, exploiting principles that range from detecting changes in the electroencephalogram (EEG) or skin conductance (due to sweating) to measurements of subcutaneous tissue glucose concentrations by glucose sensors. However, none of these have been proved sufficiently.

A significant contribution is made by the use of fuzzy reasoning systems to the modeling and design of a non-invasive hypoglycemia monitor with physiological responses. During hypoglycemia, the most profound physiological changes are caused by activation of the sympathetic nervous system. Among them, the strongest responses are sweating and increased cardiac output. As discussed in [8, 11, 12] sweating is mediated through sympathetic cholinergic fibres, while the change in cardiac output is due to an increase in heart rate and stroke volume. In [13, 14] the possibility of hypoglycemia-induced arrhythmias and experimental hypoglycemia have been shown to prolong QT intervals and dispersion in both non-diabetic subjects and those with Type 1 and Type 2 diabetes.

The classification models for numerous medical diagnosis such as diabetic nephropathy [15], acute gastrointestinal bleeding [16] and pancreatic cancer [17] have been developed by the use of the statical regression methods in [18]. However, statical regression models are accurate over the range of patients' data. In addition, it can only be applied if the patients' data is distributed due to the developed regression model, and the correlation between dependent and independent variables does not exist. If the patients' data is irregular, the developed regression models have an unnaturally wide possibility range.

Another commonly used method to generate classification models for heart disease [19] and Parkinson's disease [20] is genetic programming as discussed in [21]. To generate classification models with nonlinear terms in polynomial forms, the genetic operation is used, while the least square algorithm is used to determine the contribution of each nonlinear term of the model classification. According to fuzziness of measures, it is unavoidable that the patients' data involves uncertainty. Since the genetic programming with least square algorithm does not consider the fuzziness of uncertainty during measurement, it cannot give the best classification model for diagnosis purposes.

To carry out modeling and classification for medical diagnosis purposes of ECG and EEG in [22–24] much attention has been devoted to computational technologies such as fuzzy systems [25], support vector machine [26] and neural networks [27]. Not only in EEG and ECG classifications, the advanced computational intelligent techniques have been applied to cardiovascular response [28, 29], breast cancer and blood cell [30], skull and brain [31, 32], dermatologic disease [17], heart disease [33], radiation therapy [34] and lung sound [35] etc. Each technology has its own advantages, for example, fuzzy system is famous because of its decision making ability. Due to its human experts' representation, the system's output can be determined by a set of linguistic rules which can be understood easily. As discussed in [36] neural networks (NNs) have been used as a universal function approximator due to their good approximation capability. To develop classification models for medical diagnosis purposes as presented in [37] NNs are used due to their generalization ability in addressing both the nonlinear and fuzzy nature of patients' data. In [38] support vector machines (SVMs) have proven good performance for classification and have also been used in various applications. Because they tackle binary classification problems, SVMs have been used in the classification of cardiac signal [39].

Since the traditional optimization methods of least square algorithms and gradient descent methods have a problem of trapping in local optima, evolutionary algorithms such as PSO [40], genetic algorithm (GA) [41] differential evolution (DE) [42] and ant colony optimization [43] have been introduced. These algorithms are efficient global optimization algorithms and make it easy to handle multimodel problems. As discussed in [9, 23, 44–47] the combination of optimization methods and evolutionary algorithms eventually gives a good performance in clinical applications.

A hybrid particle swarm optimization-based fuzzy reasoning model has been developed for early detection of hypoglycemic episodes using physiological parameters, such as heart rate (HR) and corrected QT interval (QT_c) of ECG signal. The fuzzy reasoning model (FRM) [25, 48] is good in representing expert knowledge and linguistic rules that can be easily understood by human beings. In this chapter, it has been proved that the overall performance of a hypoglycemia detection system is distinctly improved in terms of sensitivity and specificity by introducing FRM. To optimize fuzzy rules and fuzzy membership functions of FRM, a global learning algorithm called hybrid particle swarm optimization with wavelet mutation (HPSOWM) is presented [49]. Since PSO is a powerful random global search technique for optimization problems, by using it, the global optimum solution over a domain can be obtained instantly. By introducing wavelet mutation in PSO, the drawback of possible trapping in local optima in PSO can be overcome easily. Also, a fitness function is introduced to reduce the risk of the overtraining phenomenon [50]. A real hypoglycemia study is given in Section 4.3 to show that the proposed detector can successfully detect the hypoglycemic episodes in T1DM.

The organization of this chapter is as follows. In Section 4.2, the details of the development of hybrid particle swarm optimization based on the fuzzy reasoning model is presented. To show the effectiveness of our proposed methods, the results of early detection of nocturnal hypoglycemic episodes in T1DM are discussed in Section 4.3 before a conclusion is drawn in Section 4.4.

4.2. Hypoglycemia Detection System: Evolved Fuzzy Inference System Approach

Even though current technologies used in diabetes diagnosis testing and self-monitoring have already been improved to some extent, technological advancement in the market is expected to come from the use of novel design concepts, i.e the development of the non-invasive glucose meter. There is a limited number of non-invasive blood glucose monitoring systems currently available on the market. However, each has its own drawbacks in terms of functioning, cost, reliability and obtrusiveness. To measure glucose levels up to 3 times per hour for 12 hours, the Gluco Watch G2 Biographer was designed and developed by Cygnus Inc, in which the autosensor is attached to the skin and provides 12 hours of measurement. The product uses reverse iontophoresis to extract and measure the levels of glucose non-invasively using interstitial fluid. Before each measurement, the device needs calibrating and takes two hours. The gel pads, costly disposable components, are required whenever using these devices and may cause skipped readings during measurement because of sweating. The worst case is that the device has a time delay of about 10 to 15 minutes. Due to its limited ability, the device is no longer available on the market.

Although real-time glucose monitoring systems (CGMS) are now available to give real-time estimations of glucose levels, they still lack the sensitivity to be used as an alarm. In [51, 52] the median error for MiniMed Medtronic CGMS was reported as 10 to 15% at a plasma glucose of 4 to 10 mmol/l and the inaccuracy of CGMS in detecting of hypoglycemia is reported in [53]. In addition, for the Abbott Freestyle Navigator CGMS, the sensor accuracy was the lowest during hypoglycemia (3.9 mmol/l), with the median absolute relative difference (ARD) being 26.4% [54]. As these are median values, the error may be significantly greater and, as a result, those sensors are not to be used as an alarm. Intensive research has been devoted to the development of hypoglycemia alarms, exploiting principles that range from detecting changes in the EEG or skin conductance [11]. However, none of these have proved sufficiently reliable or unobtrusive.

During hypoglycemia, the most profound psychological changes are caused by activation of the sympathetic nervous systems [55]. Among them, the strongest responses are sweating and increased cardiac output. [12–14] Sweating is mediated through sympathetic cholinergic fibres, while the change in cardiac output is due to an increase in heart rate and stroke volume [14]. The possibility of hypoglycemia induced arrhythmias and experimental hypoglycemia has been shown to prolong QT intervals and dispersion in both non-diabetic subjects and in those with Type 1 and Type 2 diabetes. In this chapter, the physiological parameters for detection of hypoglycemic episodes in T1DM were collected by the use of a continuous non-invasive hypoglycemia monitor in [56] in which an alarm system is available for warning at various stages of hypoglycemia.

To realize the early detection of hypoglycemic episodes in T1DM, a hybrid PSO-based fuzzy reasoning model is developed with four physiological inputs and one decision output, as shown in Fig. 4.1. The four physiological inputs of the system are HR, QT_c of the electrocardiogram signal, ΔHR, and ΔQT_c and the output is the binary status of hypoglycemia(h) which gives +1 when hypoglycemia is presented (positive hypoglycemia) while −1 represents non-hypoglycemia (negative hypoglycemia).

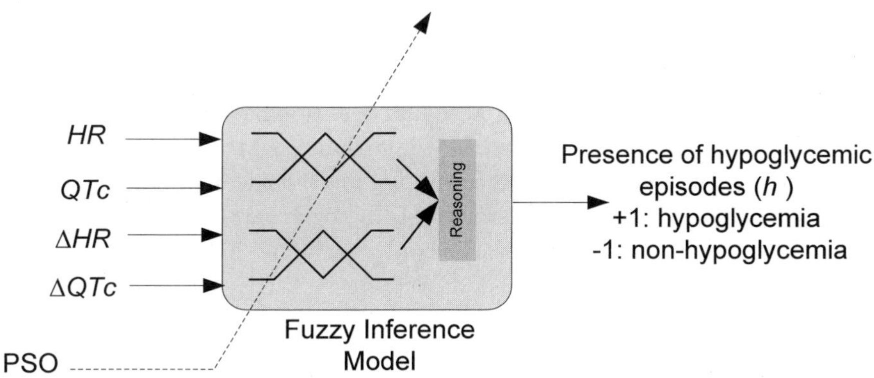

Fig. 4.1. PSO-based fuzzy inference system for hypoglycemia detection.

The ECG parameters which will be investigated in this research involve the parameters in depolarization and repolarization stages of electrocardiography. The concern points are Q point, R peak, T wave peak and T wave end, as shown in Fig. 4.2. The peak of T wave is searched in the section of 300 ms after R peak. In this section, the maximum peak is defined as the peak of T wave. Q point is searched in the section of 120 ms in the left side of R peak. The Q point is found by investigating the sequential gradients of negative-negative-positive/zero-positive/zero from the right side. These concerned points are used to obtain the ECG parameters which are used for inputs in the hypoglycemia detection. QT is the interval

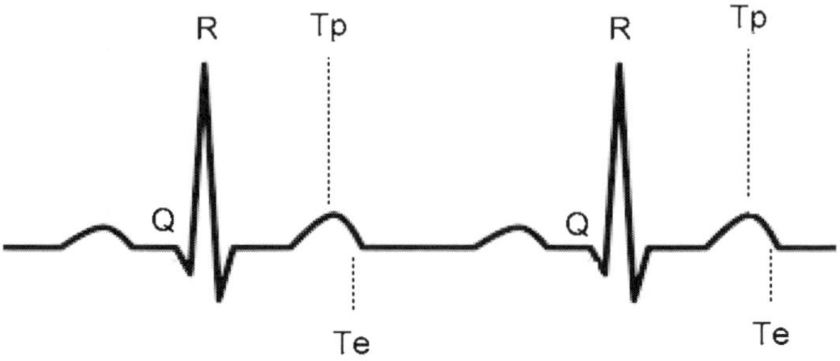

Fig. 4.2. The concerned points: Q, R, Tp and Te, which are used to find the ECG parameters.

between Q and T_p points. QT_c is $\sqrt{\frac{QT}{RR}}$ in which RR is the interval between R peaks. Heart rate is $\frac{60}{RR}$.

4.2.1. *Fuzzy inference system*

The detailed methodologies of the fuzzy reasoning model (FRM) are discussed in Section 4.2.1.1 by showing that FRM plays a vital role in modeling the correlation between the physiological parameters HR, QT_c, ΔHR and ΔQT_c and status of hypoglycemia (h). The three FRM components such as fuzzification, reasoning by if-then rule and defuzzification are also discussed in Sections 4.2.1.1, 4.2.1.2 and 4.2.1.3 respectively.

4.2.1.1. *Fuzzification*

The first step is to take the inputs and determine the degree of membership to which they belong to each of the appropriate fuzzy sets via membership functions. In this study, there are four inputs, HR, QT_c, ΔHR, and ΔQT_c. The degree of the membership function is shown in Fig. 4.3. For input HR, a bell-shaped function, $\mu_{N_{HR}^k}(HR(t))$ is given when $m_{HR}^k \neq \max\{\mathbf{m}_{HR}\}$ or $\min\{\mathbf{m}_{HR}\}$.

$$\mu_{N_{HR}^k}(HR(t)) = e^{\frac{-(HR(t)-m_{HR}^k)^2}{2\varsigma_{HR}^k}}, \qquad (4.1)$$

where

$$\mathbf{m}_{HR} = \left[m_{HR}^1 \; m_{HR}^2 \; \cdots \; m_{HR}^k \; \cdots \; m_{HR}^{m_f}\right],$$

k=1, 2, ..., m_f, m_f denotes the number of membership function, t=1, 2, ..., n_d, n_d denotes the number of input-output data pairs, parameter m_{HR}^k and ς_{HR}^k are the mean value and the standard deviation of the member function, respectively.

When $m_{HR}^k = \min\{\mathbf{m}_{HR}\}$

$$\mu_{N_{HR}^k}(HR(t)) = \begin{cases} 1 & \text{if } HR(t) \le \min\{\mathbf{m}_{HR}\} \\ e^{\frac{-(HR(t)-m_{HR}^k)^2}{2\varsigma_{HR}^k}} & \text{if } HR(t) > \min\{\mathbf{m}_{HR}\} \end{cases}, \tag{4.2}$$

when $m_{HR}^k = \max\{\mathbf{m}_{HR}\}$

$$\mu_{N_{HR}^k}(HR(t)) = \begin{cases} 1 & \text{if } HR(t) \ge \max\{\mathbf{m}_{HR}\} \\ e^{\frac{-(HR(t)-m_{HR}^k)^2}{2\varsigma_{HR}^k}} & \text{if } HR(t) < \max\{\mathbf{m}_{HR}\} \end{cases}. \tag{4.3}$$

Similarly, the degree of the membership function for input QT_c $(\mu_{N_{QT_c}^k}(QT_c(t)))$, ΔHR $(\mu_{N_{\Delta HR}^k}(\Delta HR(t)))$, ΔQT_c $(\mu_{N_{\Delta QT_c}^k}(\Delta QT_c(t)))$ is same as input heart rate.

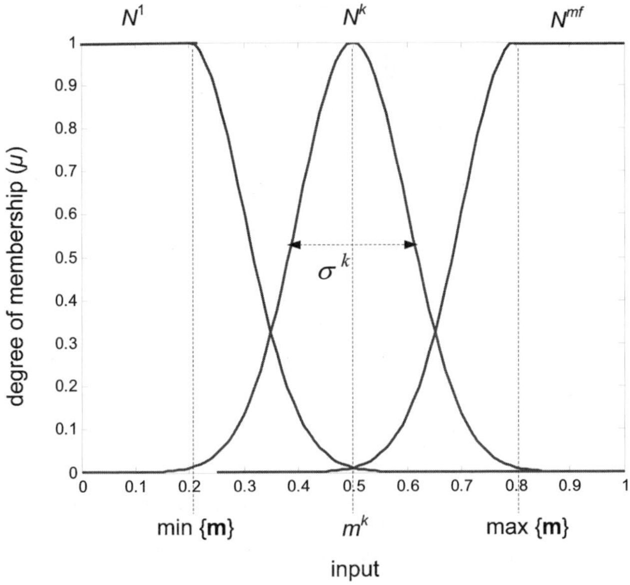

Fig. 4.3. Fuzzy inputs.

4.2.1.2. *Fuzzy reasoning*

With these fuzzy inputs (HR, QT_c, ΔHR, ΔQT_c) and fuzzy output (presence of hypoglycemia, y), the behavior of the FRM is governed by a set of fuzzy if-then rules in the following format:

$$\begin{gathered} \textit{Rule } \gamma: \textbf{ IF } HR(t) \text{ is } N_{HR}^{k}(HR(t)) \textbf{ AND } QT_c(t) \text{ is } N_{QT_c}^{k}(QT_c(t)) \textbf{ AND} \\ \Delta HR(t) \text{ is } N_{\Delta HR(t)}^{k}(\Delta HR(t)) \textbf{ AND } \Delta QT_c(t) \text{ is } N_{\Delta QT_c(t)}^{k}(\Delta QT_c(t)) \\ \textbf{THEN } y(t) \text{ is } w_\gamma. \end{gathered} \tag{4.4}$$

where $N_{HR}^{k}(HR(t))$, $N_{QT_c}^{k}(QT_c(t))$, $N_{\Delta HR}^{k}(\Delta HR(t))$ and $N_{\Delta QT_c(t)}^{k}$ are fuzzy terms of rule γ, γ=1, 2, ..., n_r; n_r denotes number of rules and n_r is equal to $(m_f)^{n_{in}}$ where n_{in} represents the number of input to FRM; $w_\gamma \in [0, 1]$ is the fuzzy singleton to be determined.

4.2.1.3. *Defuzzification*

Defuzzification is the process of translating the output of the fuzzy rules into a scale. The presence of hypoglycemia $h(t)$ is given by:

$$h(t) = \begin{cases} -1 & \text{if } y(t) < 0 \\ +1 & \text{if } y(t) \geq 0 \end{cases}, \tag{4.5}$$

where,

$$y(t) = \sum_{\gamma=1}^{n_r} m_\gamma(t) w_\gamma, \tag{4.6}$$

and

$$m_\gamma(t) = \frac{\mu_{N_z^k(z(t))}}{\sum_{\gamma=1}^{n_r} \mu_{N_z^k(z(t))}} \tag{4.7}$$

where

$$\begin{aligned} \mu_{N_z^k(z(t))} = (\mu_{N_{HR}^k}(HR(t))) \times (\mu_{N_{QT_c}^k}(QT_c(t))) \\ \times (\mu_{N_{\Delta HR}^k}(\Delta HR(t))) \times (\mu_{N_{\Delta QT_c}^k}(\Delta QT_c(t))) \end{aligned} \tag{4.8}$$

All the parameters of FRM, $\mathbf{m}_{HR}$, ς_{HR}, $\mathbf{m}_{QT_c}$, ς_{QT_c}, $\mathbf{m}_{\Delta HR}$, $\varsigma_{\Delta HR}$, $\mathbf{m}_{\Delta QT_c}$, $\varsigma_{\Delta QT_c}$ and $\mathbf{w}$ are tuned by the hybrid particle swarm optimization with wavelet mutation [49].

4.2.2. *Particle swarm optimization with wavelet mutation*

To optimize the parameters of the fuzzy reasoning model, a global learning algorithm called hybrid particle swarm optimization with wavelet mutation [49] is investigated in the system. PSO is a novel optimization method which is firstly developed in [40]. It models the processes of the sociological behavior associated with bird flocking, and is one of the evolutionary computation techniques. It uses a number of particles that constitute a swarm. Each particle traverses the search space looking for the global optimum. In this section, HPSOWM is introduced and the detailed algorithm of HPSOWM is presented in Algorithm 4.2.1.

Algorithm 4.2.1: PSEUDO CODE FOR HPSOWM($X(t)$)

$t \leftarrow 0$
Initialize $X(t)$
output $(f(X(t)))$
while <not termination condition>
do
    $t \leftarrow t + 1$
    Update $v(t)$ and $x(t)$ based on (4.9) to (4.12)
    if $v(t) > v_{\max}$
      then $v(t) = v_{\max}$
    if $v(t) < v_{\min}$
      then $v(t) = v_{\min}$
    Perform wavelet mutation operation with μ_m
    Update $\bar{x}_j^p(t)$ based on (4.13) to (4.15)
    output $(X(t))$
    output $(f(X(t)))$
return $(\hat{\mathbf{x}})$
comment: return the best solution

From Algorithm 4.2.1, $X(t)$ is denoted as a swarm at the t-th iteration. Each particle $\mathbf{x}^p(t) \in X(t)$ contains κ elements $x_j^p(t)$ at the t-th iteration, where $p = 1, 2, ..., \theta$ and $j = 1, 2, ..., \kappa$; θ denotes the number of particles in the swarm and κ is the dimension of a particle. First, the particles of the swarm are initialized and then evaluated by a defined fitness function. The objective of HPSOWM is to minimize the fitness function (cost function) $f(X(t))$ of particles iteratively. The swarm evolves from iteration t to $t+1$

by repeating the procedures as shown in Algorithm 4.2.1. The operations are discussed as follows.

The velocity $v_j^p(t)$(corresponding to the flight speed in a search space) and the position $x_j^p(t)$ of the j-th element of the p-th particle at the t-th generation can be calculated using the following formulae:

$$v_j^p(t) = k\cdot\{\{w\cdot v_j^p(t-1)\}+\{\varphi_1\cdot r_1(\tilde{x}_j^p - x_j^p(t-1))\}+\{\varphi_2\cdot r_2(\hat{x}_j - x_j^p(t-1))\}\} \tag{4.9}$$

and

$$x_j^p(t) = x_j^p(t-1) + v_j^p(t). \tag{4.10}$$

where $\tilde{x}^p = [\tilde{x}_1^p, \tilde{x}_2^p, \ldots, \tilde{x}_k^p]$ and $\hat{\mathbf{x}} = [\ \hat{x_1}\ \hat{x_2}\ , ...\hat{x_\kappa}\ ]$, $j = 1, 2, ..., \kappa$. The best previous position of a particle is recorded and represented as $\tilde{x}$; the position of best particle among all the particles is represented as $\hat{x}$; w is an inertia weight factor; r_1 and r_2 are acceleration constants which return a uniform random number in the range of [0,1]; k is a constriction factor derived from the stability analysis of 4.10 to ensure the system is converged but not prematurely [57]. Mathematically, k is a function of φ_1 and φ_2 as reflected in the following equation:

$$k = \left(\frac{2}{|2 - \varphi - \sqrt{\varphi^2 - 4\varphi}|}\right) \tag{4.11}$$

where $\varphi = \varphi_1 + \varphi_2$ and $\varphi > 4$. PSO utilizes $\tilde{x}$ and $\hat{x}$ to modify the current search point to avoid the particles moving in the same direction, but to converge gradually toward $\tilde{x}$ and $\hat{x}$. A suitable selection of the inertia weight w provides a balance between the global and local explorations. Generally, w can be dynamically set with the following equation [57]:

$$w = w_{\max} - \left(\frac{w_{\max} - w_{\min}}{T}\right) \times T \tag{4.12}$$

where t is the current iteration number, T is the total number of iterations, $w_{\max}$ and $w_{\min}$ are the upper and lower limits of the inertia weight, $w_{\max}$ and $w_{\min}$ are set to 1.2 and 0.1 respectively.

In 4.9, the particle velocity is limited by a maximum value $v_{\max}$. The parameter $v_{\max}$ determines the resolution with which regions are to be searched between the present position and the target position. This limit enhances the local exploration of the problem space and it realistically simulates the incremental changes of human learning. If $v_{\max}$ is too high, particles might fly past good solutions. If $v_{\max}$ is too small, particles may not explore sufficiently beyond local solutions. From experience, $v_{\max}$ is often set at 10% to 20% of the dynamic range of the element on each dimension. Next, the mutation operation is used to mutate the element of particles.

4.2.2.1. *Wavelet mutation*

The wavelet mutation (WM) operation exhibits a solution stability and a fine-tuning ability. Every particle element of the swarm will have a chance to mutate governed by a probability of mutation, $\mu_m \in [0\ 1]$, which is defined by the user. For each particle element, a random number between zero and one will be generated such that if it is less than or equal to p_m, the mutation will take place on that element. For instance, if $\mathbf{x}^p(t) = [x_1^p(t), x_2^p(t), ..., x_\kappa^p(t)]$ is the selected p-th particle and the element of particle $x_j^p(t)$ is randomly selected for mutation (the value of $x_j^p(t)$ is inside the particle element's boundaries $[\rho^j_{\min}, \rho^j_{\max}]$), the resulting particle is given by $\bar{\mathbf{x}}^p(t) = [\bar{x}_1^p(t), \bar{x}_2^p(t), ..., \bar{x}_\kappa^p(t)]$

$$\bar{x}_j^p(t) = \begin{cases} x_j^p(t) + \sigma \times (\rho^j_{\max} - x_j^p(t)) & \text{if } \sigma > 0 \\ x_j^p(t) + \sigma \times (x_j^p(t) - \rho^j_{\min}) & \text{if } \sigma < 0 \end{cases} \tag{4.13}$$

where $j \in 1, 2, ...\kappa$, κ denotes the dimension of particle and the value of σ is governed by Morlet wavelet function [58]:

$$\sigma = \psi_{a,0}(\varphi) = \frac{1}{\sqrt{a}}\psi\left(\frac{\varphi}{a}\right) = \frac{1}{\sqrt{a}}e^{\frac{-\left(\frac{\varphi}{a}\right)^2}{2}}\cos\left(5\left(\frac{\varphi}{a}\right)\right) \tag{4.14}$$

The amplitude of $\psi_{a,0}(\varphi)$ will be scaled down as the dilation parameter a increases. This property is used to do the mutation operation in order to enhance the searching performance. According to 4.14, if σ is positive and approaching one, the mutated element of the particle will tend to have the maximum value of $x_j^p(t)$. Conversely, when σ is negative ($\sigma \le 0$) approaching -1, the mutated element of the particle will tend to the minimum value of $x_j^p(t)$. A larger value of $|\sigma|$ gives a larger searching space for $x_j^p(t)$. When $|\sigma|$ is small, it gives a smaller searching space for fine-tuning. As over 99% of the total energy of the mother wavelet function is contained in the interval $[-2.5, 2.5]$, it can be generated from $[-2.5, 2.5] \times a$ randomly. The value of the dilation parameter a is set to vary with the value of $\frac{t}{T}$ in order to meet the fine-tuning purpose, where T is the total number of iterations and t is the current number of iterations. In order to perform a local search when t is large, the value of a should increase as $\frac{t}{T}$ increases so as to reduce the significance of the mutation. Hence, a monotonic increasing function governing a and $\frac{t}{T}$ is proposed in the following form:

$$a = e^{-ln(g)\times\left(1-\frac{t}{T}\right)^{\zeta_{wm}}+ln(g)} \tag{4.15}$$

where ζ_{wm} is the shape parameter of the monotonic increasing function and g is the upper limit of the parameter a. The effects of the various values of the shape parameter ζ_{wm} and parameters g to a with respect to ζ_{wm} are shown in Figs 4.4 and 4.5, respectively. In this figure, g is set as 10000. Thus, the value of a is between 1 and 10000. Referring to 4.14, the maximum value of σ is 1 when the random number of $\varphi = 0$ and $a = 1$ ($\frac{t}{T} = 0$). Then referring to 4.13, the resulting particle $\bar{x}_j^p(t) = x_j^p(t) + 1 \times (\rho_{\max}^j - x_j^p(t)) = \rho_{max}^j$. It ensures that a large search space for the mutated element is given. When the value $\frac{t}{T}$ is near to 1, the value of a is so large that the maximum value of σ will become very small. For example, at $\frac{t}{T}$=0.9 and $\zeta_{wm} = 1$, the dilation parameter $a = 4000$; if the random value of φ is zero, the value of σ will be equal to 0.0158. With $\bar{x}_j^p(t) = x_j^p(t) + 0.0158 \times (\rho_{\max}^j - x_j^p(t))$, a smaller searching space for the mutated element is given for fine-tuning. Changing the parameter ζ_{wm} will change the characteristics of the monotonic increasing function of the wavelet mutation. The dilation parameter a will take a value so as to perform fine-tuning faster as ζ_{wm} is increasing. It is chosen by trial and error, which depends on the kind of optimization problem. When ζ_{wm} becomes larger, the decreasing speed of the step size (σ) of the mutation becomes faster. In general, if the optimization problem is smooth and symmetric, the searching algorithm is easier to find the solution and the fine-tuning can be done in the early stage. Thus, a larger value of ζ_{wm} can be used to increase the step size of the early mutation. After the operation of wavelet mutation, a new swarm is generated. This new swarm will repeat the same process. Such an iterative process will be terminated if the pre-defined number of iterations is met.

4.2.3. *Choosing the HPSOWM parameters*

HPSOWM is seeking a balance between the exploration of new regions and the exploitation of the already sampled regions in the search spaces.

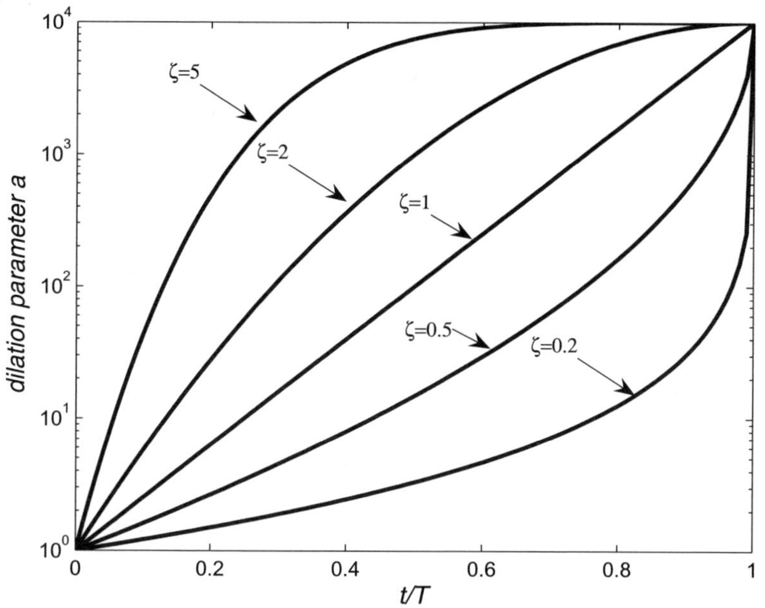

Fig. 4.4. Effect of the shape parameter ζ_{wm} to a with respect to $\frac{t}{T} = 0$.

This balance, which critically affects the performance of HPSOWM, is governed by the right choices of the control parameters: Swarm size (θ), the probability of mutation (μ_m), the shape parameter (ζ_{wm}) and parameter g of wavelet mutation. Some views about these parameters are given as follows:

(i) Increasing swarm size (θ) will increase the diversity of the search space, and reduce the probability that HPSOWM prematurely converges to a local optimum. However, it also increases the time required for the population to converge to the optimal region in the search space.

(ii) Increasing the probability of mutation (μ_m) tends to transform the search into a random search such that when $\mu_m = 1$, all elements of particles will mutate. This probability gives us an expected number ($\mu_m \times \theta \times \kappa$) of elements of particles that undergo the mutation operation. In other words, the value of μ_m depends on the desired number of elements of particles that undergo the mutation operation. Normally, when the dimension is very low (number of elements of particles is less than 5, μ_m is set at 0.5 to 0.8). When the dimension is around 5 to 10, μ_m is set

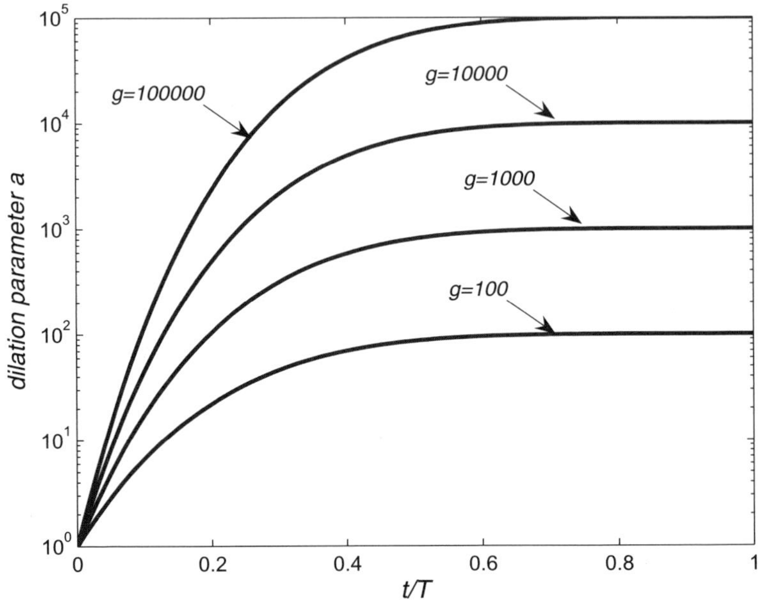

Fig. 4.5. Effect of the parameter g to a with respect to $\frac{t}{T} = 0$.

at 0.3 to 0.4. When the dimension is in the range of 11 to 100, μ_m is set at 0.1 to 0.2. When the dimension is in the range of 101 to 1000, normally μ_m is set at 0.05 to 0.1. Lastly, when the dimension is very high (number of elements of particles is larger than 1000), μ_m is set at < 0.05. The rationale to set this selection criterion is: when the dimension is high, μ_m should be set to be a smaller value; when the dimension is low, μ_m should be set to be a larger value. This is because if the dimension is high and μ_m is set to be a larger number, then the number of elements of particles undergoing mutation operation will be large. It will increase the searching time and more importantly it destroys the current information about the application in each iteration as all elements of particles are randomly assigned. Generally speaking, by choosing the value of μ_m, the ratio of the number of elements of particles undergoing mutation operation to the population size can be maintained to prevent the searching process turning to a random searching one. Thus, the value of μ_m is based on this selection criterion and chosen by trial and error through experiments for good performance for all functions.

(iii) The dilation parameter a is governed by the monotonic increasing function 4.15, and this monotonic increasing function is controlled by two parameters. They are called shape parameter ζ_{wm} and parameter g. Changing the parameter ζ_{wm} will change the characteristics of the monotonic increasing function of the wavelet mutation. The dilation parameter a will take a value so as to perform fine-tuning faster as ζ_{wm} is increasing. It is chosen by trial and error, which depends on the kind of optimization problem. When ζ_{wm} becomes larger, the decreasing speed of the step size (σ) of the mutation becomes faster. In general, if the optimisation problem is smooth and symmetric, it is easier to find the solution and the fine-tuning can be done in early iteration. Thus, a larger value of ζ_{wm} can be used to increase the step size of the early mutation. Parameter g is the value of the upper limit of dilation parameter a. A larger value of g implies that the maximum value of a is larger. In other words, the maximum value of ζ_{wm} will be smaller (smaller searching limit is given). Conversely, a smaller value of g implies that the maximum value of a is smaller. On the other hand, the maximum value of $|\Sigma|$ will be larger (larger searching limit is given). In our point of view, fixing one parameter and adjusting another parameter to control the monotonic increasing function is more convenient to find a good setting.

4.2.4. *Fitness function and training*

In this system, HPSOWM is employed to optimize the fuzzy rules and membership functions by finding out the best parameters of the FSM. The function of the fuzzy reasoning model is to detect the hypoglycemic episodes accurately. To measure the performance of the biomedical classification test, sensitivity and specificity are introduced [59]. The sensitivity measures the proportion of actual positives which are correctly identified and the specificity measures the proportion of negatives which are correctly identified. The definitions of the sensitivity (ξ) and the specificity (η) are given as follows:

$$\xi = \frac{N_{TP}}{N_{TP} + N_{FN}} \tag{4.16}$$

$$\eta = \frac{N_{TN}}{N_{TN} + N_{FP}} \tag{4.17}$$

where N_{TP} is the number of true positives which implies the sick people correctly the diagnosed as sick; N_{FN} is the number of the false negatives which implies sick people wrongly diagnosed as healthy; N_{FP} is the number of false positives which implies healthy people wrongly diagnosed as sick; and N_{TN} is the number of true negatives which implies healthy people correctly diagnosed as healthy. The values of these are within zero to one. The objective of the system is to maximize the sensitivity and the specificity, thus, the fitness function, $f(\xi, \eta)$ is defined as follows:

$$f(\xi, \eta) = \xi + \frac{\eta_{\max} - \eta}{\eta_{\max}} \tag{4.18}$$

where $\eta_{\max}$ is the upper limit of the specificity. The objective is to maximize the fitness function of 4.18 which is equivalent to maximize the sensitivity and the specificity. In 4.18, the specificity is limited by a maximum value $\eta_{\max}$. The parameter $\eta_{\max}$ is used to fix the region of specificity and find the optimal sensitivity in this region. In particular, the $\eta_{\max}$ can be set from zero to one and different sensitivity with different specificity values can be determined. With this proposed fitness function, the ROC curve for this hypoglycemia detection can be found satisfactory. The ROC curve is commonly used in medical decision making and is a useful technique for visualizing the classification performance. The classification results with ROC curve of the proposal method will be illustrated in Section 4.3.

4.3. Results and Discussion

Fifteen children with T1DM (14.6 ± 1.5 years) volunteered for the 10-hour overnight hypoglycemia study at the Princess Margaret Hospital for Children in Perth, Western Australia, Australia. Each patient is monitored overnight for the natural occurrence of nocturnal hypoglycemia. Data are collected with approval from Women's and Children's Health Service, Department of Health, Government of Western Australia and with informed consent. A comprehensive patient information and consent form is formulated and approved by the Ethics Committee. The consent form includes the actual consent and a revocation of consent page. Each patient receives this information consent form at least two weeks prior to the start of the studies. He/she has the opportunity to raise questions and concerns with any medical advisors, researchers and the investigators. For the children participating in this study, the parent or guardian signed the relevant forms.

The required physiological parameters are measured by the use of the non-invasive monitoring system in [56], while the actual blood glucose levels (BGL) are collected for reference using Yellow Spring Instruments. The main parameters used for the detection of hypoglycemia are the heart rate and corrected QT interval. The actual blood glucose profiles for 15 T1DM children [56] are shown in Fig. 4.6. The responses from 15 T1DM children exhibit significant changes during the hypoglycemia phase against the non-hypoglycemia phase. Normalization is used to reduce patient-to-patient variability and to enable group comparison by dividing the patient's heart rate and corrected QT interval by his/her corresponding values at time zero.

The study shows that the detection of hypoglycemic episodes (BGL $\leq 2.8\ mmol/l$ and BGL $\leq 3.3\ mmol/l$) using these variables is based on a hybrid PSO with wavelet mutation-based fuzzy reasoning model developed from the obtained clinical data. In effect, it estimates the presence of hypoglycemia at sample period k_s based on the basis of the data at sampling period k_s and the previous data at sampling period $k_s - 1$. In general, the sampling period is 5 minutes and approximately 35 to 40 data points are used for each patient. The overall data set consisted of a training set and a testing set, 10 patients for training and 5 patients for testing are randomly selected. For these, the whole data set included both hypoglycemia data part and non-hypoglycemia data part. By using HPSOWM which is used to find the optimized fuzzy rules and membership functions of FRM, the basic settings of the parameters of the HPSOWM are shown as follows:

- Swarm size θ : 50;
- Constant c_1 and c_2 : 2.05;
- Maximum velocity $v_{\max}$: 0.2 or 20%;
- Probability of mutation μ_m: 0.5;
- The shape parameter of wavelet mutation ζ_{wm} [49] : 2;
- The constant value g of wavelet mutation [49] : 10000;
- Number of iteration T : 1000.

Table 4.1. Simulation Results.

	Training		Testing		
Method	Sensitivity	Specificity	Sensitivity	Specificity	Area of ROC curve
EFIS	89.23%	39.87%	81.40%	41.82%	71.46%
EMR	78.46%	39.23%	72.09%	41.82%	64.19%

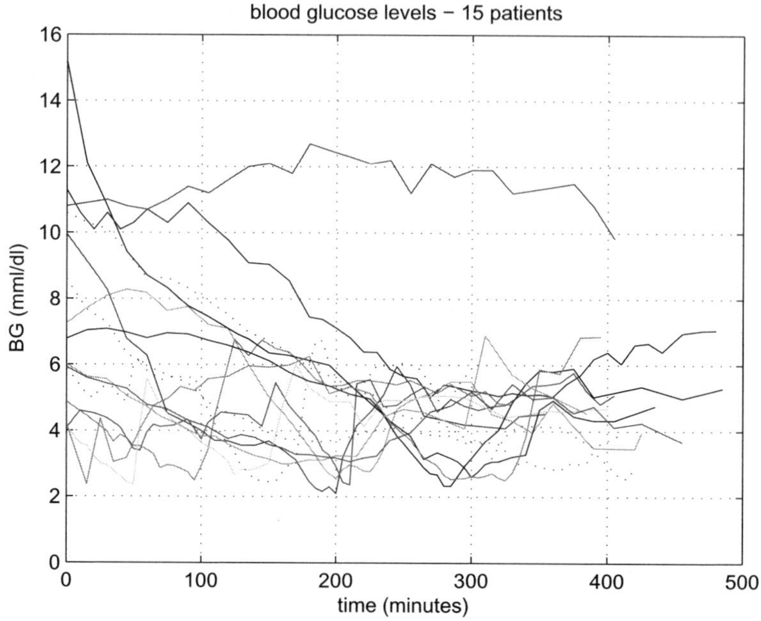

Fig. 4.6. Actual blood glucose level profiles in 15 T1DM children.

The clinical results of hypoglycemia detection with different approaches, fuzzy interference system (FIS) and evolved multiple-regression (EMR) are tabulated in Table 4.1. By the use of proposed FIS, the test sensitivity and specificity are about 81.4% and 41.82%, while the detection of EMR gives 72.09% and 41.82%. From Table 4.1, we can say that the training and testing results of FIS performs better than EMR in terms of the sensitivity and specificity. In comparison studies of area of ROC curves for FIS (71.46%) and EMR (64.19%) in Fig. 4.7, it can be distinctly seen that the proposed FIS detection system has higher accuracy than that of detection with EMR. Thus, the proposed detection system gives satisfactory results with higher accuracy.

4.4. Conclusion

A hybrid particle swarm optimization-based fuzzy inference system is developed, in this chapter, to detect the hypoglycemic episodes for diabetes patients. The results in Section 4.3 indicate that the hypoglycemic episodes

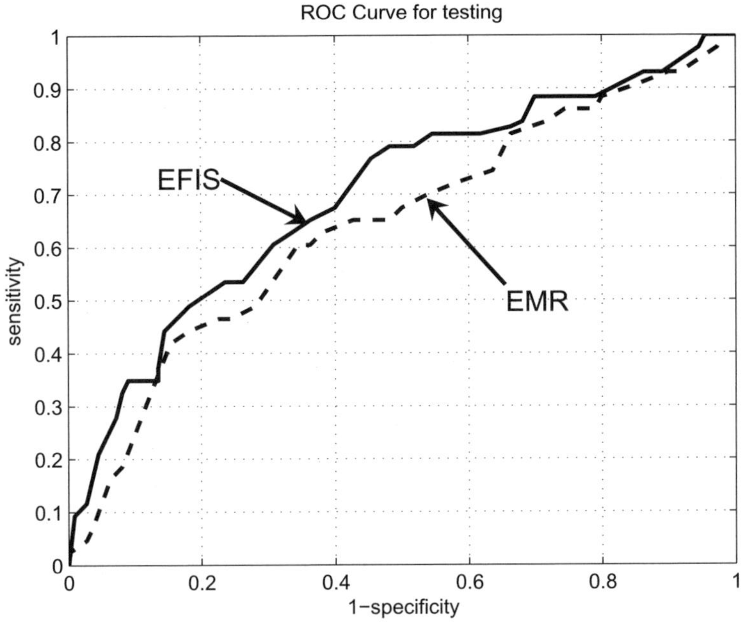

Fig. 4.7. ROC curve for testing.

in T1DM children can be detected non-invasively and continuously from the real-time physiological responses (heart rate, corrected QT interval, change of heart rate and change of corrected QT interval). To optimize the fuzzy rules and membership functions, a hybrid particle swarm optimization is presented where wavelet mutation operation is introduced to enhance the optimization performance. A real T1DM study is given to illustrate that the proposed algorithm produces better results compared with a multiple regression algorithm in terms of the sensitivity and specificity. To conclude, the performance of the proposed algorithm for detection of hypoglycemic episodes for T1DM is satisfactory, as the sensitivity is 81.40% and specificity is 41.82% for hypoglycemia defined less than 3.3 $mmol/l$.

References

[1] T. Duning and B. Ellger, Is hypoglycaemia dangerous?, *Best Practice and Research Clinical Anaesthesiology.* **23**(4), 473–485, (1996).

[2] M. Egger and G. D. Smith, Hypoglycaemia awareness and human insulin, *The Lancet.* **338**(8772), 950–951, (1991).

[3] D. J. Becker and C. M. Ryan, Hypoglycemia: A complication of diabetes therapy in children, *Trends in Endocrinology and Metabolism.* **11**(5), 198–202, (2000).

[4] D. R. Group, Adverse events and their association with treatment regimens in the Diabetes Control and Complications Trial, *Diabetes Care.* **18**, 1415–1427, (1995).

[5] D. R. Group, Epidemiology of severe hypoglycemia in the diabetes control and complication trial, *The American Journal of Medicine.* **90**(4), 450–459, (1991).

[6] M. A. E. Merbis, F. J. Snoek, K. Kanc, and R. J. Heine, Hypoglycaemia induces emotional disruption, *Patient Education and Counseling.* **29**(1), 117–122, (1996).

[7] P. E. Cryer, Symptoms of hypoglycemia, thresholds for their occurrence and hypoglycemia unawareness, *Endocrinology and Metabolism Clinics of North America.* **28**(3), 495–500, (1999).

[8] G. Heger, K. Howorka, H. Thoma, G. Tribl, and J. Zeitlhofer, Monitoring set-up for selection of parameters for detection of hypoglycaemia in diabetic patients, *Medical and Biological Engineering and Computing.* **34**(1), 69–75, (1996).

[9] S. Pramming, B. Thorsteinsson, I. Bendtson, and C. Binder, Symptomatic hypoglycaemia in 411 type 1 diabetic patients, *Diabetic medicine : A Journal of the British Diabetic Association.* **8**(3), 217–222, (1991).

[10] J. C. Pickup, Sensitivity glucose sensing in diabetes, *Lancet.* **355**, 426–427, (2000).

[11] E. A. Gale, T. Bennett, I. A. Macdonald, J. J. Holst, and J. A. Matthews, The physiological effects of insulin-induced hypoglycaemia in man: responses at differing levels of blood glucose, *Clinical Science.* **65**(3), 263–271, (1983).

[12] N. D. Harris, S. B. Baykouchev, and J. L. B. Marques, A portable system for monitoring physiological responses to hypoglycaemia, *Journal of Medical Engineering and Technology.* **20**(6), 196–202, (1996).

[13] R. B. Tattersall and G. V. Gill, Unexplained death of type 1 diabetic patients, *Diabetic Medicine.* **8**(1), 49–58, (1991).

[14] J. L. B. Marques1, E. George, S. R. Peacey, N. D. Harris, and T. C. I. A. Macdonald, Altered ventricular repolarization during hypoglycaemia in patients with diabetes, *Diabetic Medicine.* **14**(8), 648–654, (1997).

[15] B. H. Cho, H. Yu, K. Kim, T. H. Kim, I. Y. Kim, and S. I. Kim, Application of irregular and unbalanced data to predict diabetic nephropathy using visualization and feature selection methods, *Artificial Intelligence in Medicine archive.* **42**(1), 37–53, (2008).

[16] A. Chu, H. Ahn, B. Halwan, B. Kalmin, E. L. V. Artifon, A. Barkun, M. G. Lagoudakis, and A. Kumar, A decision support system to facilitate management of patients with acute gastrointestinal bleeding, *Artificial Intelligence in Medicine Archive.* **42**(3), 247–259, (2008).

[17] C. L. Chang and C. H. Chen, Applying decision tree and neural network to increase quality of dermatologic diagnosis, *Expert Systems with Applications.* **36**(2), 4035–4041, (2009).

[18] G. A. F. Seber and A. J. Lee, *Linear regression analysis.* (John Wiley & Sons, New York, 2003).

[19] S. M. Winkler, M. Affenzeller, and S. Wagner, Using enhanced genetic programming techniques for evolving classifiers in the context of medical diagnosis, *Genetic Programming and Evolvable Machines.* **10**(2), 111–140, (2009).

[20] T. S. Subashini, V. Ramalingam, and S. Palanivel, Breast mass classification based on cytological patterns using RBFNN and SVM, *Source Expert Systems with Applications: An International Journal Archive.* **36**(3), 5284–5290, (2009).

[21] H. F. Gray and R. J. Maxwell, Genetic programming for classification and feature selection: analysis of 1H nuclear magnetic resonance spectra from human brain tumour biopsies, *NMR in Biomedicine.* **11**(4), 217–224, (1998).

[22] C. M. Fira and L. Goras, An ECG signals compression method and its validation using NNs, *IEEE Transactions on Biomedical Engineering.* **55** (4), 1319–1326, (2008).

[23] W. Jiang, S. G. Kong, and G. D. Peterson, ECG signal classification using block-based neural networks, *IEEE Transactions on Neural Networks.* **18** (6), 1750–1761, (2007).

[24] A. H. Khandoker, M. Palaniswami, and C. K. Karmakar, Support vector machines for automated recognition of obstructive sleep apnea syndrome from ECG recordings, *IEEE Transactions on Information Technology in Biomedicine.* **13**(1), 37–48, (2009).

[25] J. S. Jang and C. T. Sun, *Neuro-Fuzzy and Soft Computing: A Computational Approach to Learning and Machine Intelligence.* (Prentice Hall, Upper Saddle River, NJ, 1997).

[26] C. Cortes and V. Vapnik, Support-vector networks, *Machine Learning.* **20** (3), 273–297, (1995).

[27] A. K. Jain, J. Mao, and K. M. Mohiuddin, Artificial neural networks: a tutorial, *IEEE Computer Society.* **29**(3), 31–44, (1996).

[28] K. H. Chon and R. J. Cohen, Linear and nonlinear ARMA model parameter estimation using an artificial neural network, *IEEE Transactions on Biomedical Engineering.* **44**(3), 168–174, (1997).

[29] W. W. Melek, Z. Lu, A. Kapps, and B. Cheung, Modeling of dynamic cardiovascular responses during G-transition-induced orthostatic stress in pitch and roll rotations, *IEEE Transactions on Biomedical Engineering.* **49** (12), 1481–1490, (2002).

[30] S. Wang and W. Min, A new detection algorithm (NDA) based on fuzzy cellular neural networks for white blood cell detection, *IEEE Transactions on Information Technology in Biomedicine.* **10**(1), 5–10, (2006).

[31] Y. Hata, S. Kobashi, K. Kondo, Y. Kitamura, and T. Yanagida, Transcranial ultrasonography system for visualizing skull and brain surface aided by fuzzy expert system, *IEEE Transactions on Systems, Man, and Cybernetics - Part B.* **35**(6), 1360–1373, (2005).

[32] S. Kobashi, Y. Fujiki, M. Matsui, and N. Inoue, Genetic programming for classification and feature selection: analysis of 1H nuclear magnetic

resonance spectra from human brain tumour biopsies, *IEEE Transactions on Systems, Man, and Cybernetics, Part B.* **36**(1), 74–86, (2006).

[33] R. Das, I. Turkoglu, and A. Sengur, Effective diagnosis of heart disease through neural networks ensembles, *An International Journal Source Expert Systems with Applications.* **36**(4), 7675–7680, (2009).

[34] E. I. Papageorgiou, C. D. Stylios, and P. P. Groumpos, An integrated two-level hierarchical system for decision making in radiation therapy based on fuzzy cognitive maps, *IEEE Transactions on Biomedical Engineering.* **50** (12), 1326–1339, (2003).

[35] P. A. Mastorocostas and J. B. Theocharis, A stable learning algorithm for block-diagonal recurrent neural networks: application to the analysis of lung sounds, *IEEE Transactions on Systems, Man, and Cybernetics.* **36**(2), 242–254, (2006).

[36] M. Brown and C. Harris, *Neural Fuzzy Adaptive Modeling and Control.* (Prentice Hall, Upper Saddle River, NJ, 1994).

[37] J. Reggia and S. Sutton, Self-processing networks and their biomedical implications, *Proceedings of the IEEE.* **76**(6), 580–592, (1988).

[38] D. Meyer, F. Leisch, and K. Hornik, The support vector machine under test, *Neurocomputing.* **55**(6), 169–186, (2003).

[39] N. Acir, A support vector machine classifier algorithm based on a perturbation method and its application to ECG beat recognition systems, *Expert Systems with Applications.* **31**(1), 150–158, (2006).

[40] J. Kennedy and R. Eberhart. Particle swarm optimization. In *Proceedings of IEEE International Conference on Neural Networks*, pp. 1942–1948, (1995).

[41] Z. Michalewicz, *Genetic algorithms + data structures = evolution programs (2nd, extended ed.).* (Springer–Verlag, Berlin, 1994).

[42] R. Storn and K. Price, Differential evolutiona simple and efficient heuristic for global optimization over continuous spaces, *Journal of Global Optimization.* **11**, 341–359, (1997).

[43] M. Dorigo and T. Stuzle, *Ant Colony Optimization.* (MIT Press, Cambridge, MA, 2004).

[44] Nuryani, S. Ling, and H. Nguyen. Hypoglycaemia detection for type 1 diabetic patients based on ECG parameters using fuzzy support vector machine. In *Proceedings of International Joint Conference on Neural Networks*, pp. 2253–2259, (2010).

[45] A. Keles, S. Hasiloglu, K. Ali, and Y. Aksoy, Neuro-fuzzy classification of prostate cancer using NEFCLASS-J, *Computers in Biology and Medicine.* **37**(11), 1617–1628, (2007).

[46] R. J. Oentaryo, M. Pasquier, and C. Quek, GenSoFNN-Yager: A novel brain-inspired generic self-organizing neuro-fuzzy system realizing Yager inference, *Expert Systems with Application.* **35**(4), 1825–1840, (2008).

[47] S. Osowski and H. Tran, ECG beat recognition using fuzzy hybrid neural network, *IEEE Transactions on Biomedical Engineering.* **48**(11), 875–884, (2001).

[48] H. Mamdani and S. Assilian, An experiment in linguistic synthesis with a fuzzy logic controller, *International Journal of Man–Machine Studies.* **7**(1), 1–13, (1975).

[49] S. H. Ling and H. C. C. Iu, Hybrid particle swarm optimization with wavelet mutation and its industrial applications, *IEEE Transactions on Systems, Man, and Cybernetics–Part B: Cybernetics.* **38**(3), 743–763, (2008).

[50] M. L. Astion, M. H. Wener, R. G. Thomas, and G. G. Hunder, Overtraining in neural networks that interpret clinical data, *Clinical Chemistry.* **39**(9), 1998–2004, (1993).

[51] Diabetes in Research Children Network (DirecNet) Study Group, Evaluation of factors affecting CGMS calibration, *Diabetes technology and therapeutics.* **8**(3), 318–325, (2006).

[52] M. J. Tansey and R. W. Beck, Accuracy of the modified continuous glucose monitoring system (CGMS) sensor in an outpatient setting: results from a diabetes research in children network (DirecNet) study, *Diabetes Technology and Therapeutics.* **7**(1), 109–114, (2005).

[53] F. F. Maia and L. R. Arajo, Efficacy of continuous glucose monitoring system to detect unrecognized hypoglycemia in children and adolescents with type 1 diabetes, *Arquivos Brasileiros De Endocrinologia E Metabologia.* **49**(4), 569–574, (2005).

[54] R. L. Weinstein, Accuracy of the freestyle navigator CGMS: comparison with frequent laboratory measurements, *Diabetes Care.* **30**, 1125–1130, (2007).

[55] S. R. Heller and I. A. MacDonald, Physiological disturbances in hypoglycaemia: effect on subjective awareness, *Clinical Science.* **81**(1), 1–9, (1991).

[56] H. T. Nguyen, N. Ghevondian, and T. W. Jones, Neural-network detection of hypoglycemic episodes in children with Type 1 diabetes using physiological parameters, *Proceedings of the 28th Annual International Conference of the IEEE Engineering in Medicine and Biology Society.* pp. 6053–6056, (2006).

[57] R. C. Eberhart and Y. Shi, Comparing inertia weights and constriction factors in particle swarm optimization, *Proceedings of the IEEE Congress on Evolutionary Computing.* pp. 84–88, (2000).

[58] I. Daubechies, *Ten Lectures on Wavelets.* (Society for Industrial and Applied Mathematics, Philadelphia, 1992).

[59] D. G. Altman and J. M. Bland, Statistics notes: Diagnostic tests 1: sensitivity and specificity, *Clinical Chemistry.* (308), 1552–1552, (1994).

PART 3

Neural Networks and their Applications

Chapter 5

Study of Limit Cycle Behavior of Weights of Perceptron

C.Y.F. Ho and B.W.K. Ling

School of Engineering, University of Lincoln
Lincoln, Lincolnshire, LN6 7TS, United Kingdom
wling@lincoln.ac.uk

In this chapter, limit cycle behavior of weights of perceptron is discussed. First, the weights of a perceptron are bounded for all initial weights if there exists a nonempty set of initial weights that the weights of the perceptron are bounded. Hence, the boundedness condition of the weights of the perceptron is independent of the initial weights. Second, a necessary and sufficient condition for the weights of the perceptron exhibiting a limit cycle behavior is discussed. The range of the number of updates for the weights of the perceptron required to reach the limit cycle is estimated. Finally, it is suggested that the perceptron exhibiting the limit cycle behavior can be employed for solving a recognition problem when downsampled sets of bounded training feature vectors are linearly separable. Numerical computer simulation results show that the perceptron exhibiting the limit cycle behavior can achieve a better recognition performance compared to a multi-layer perceptron.

Contents

5.1. Introduction

Since the implementation cost of a perceptron is low and a perceptron can classify linearly separable bounded training feature vectors [1–3], perceptrons [4–8] are widely applied in many pattern recognition systems.

However, as the values of the output of the perceptron are binary, they can be represented by symbols and the dynamics of the perceptron are governed by symbolic dynamics. Symbolic dynamics is very complex because limit cycle and chaotic behaviors may occur. One of the properties of symbolic dynamical systems is that the system state vectors may be bounded for some initial system state vectors while they may not be bounded for other initial system state vectors. Hence, it is expected that the boundedness condition of the weights of the perceptron would also depend on the initial weights. In fact, the boundedness condition of the weights of the perceptron is not completely known yet. As the boundedness property is very important because of safety reasons, this chapter studies the boundedness condition of the weights of the perceptron.

It is well known from the perceptron convergence theorem [1–3] that the weights of the perceptron will converge to a fixed point within a finite number of updates if the set of bounded training feature vectors is linearly separable, and the weights may exhibit a limit cycle behavior if the set of bounded training feature vectors is nonlinearly separable. However, the exact condition for the weights of the perceptron exhibiting the limit cycle behavior is unknown. A perceptron exhibiting the limit cycle behavior is actually a neural network with time periodically varying coefficients. In fact, this is a generalization of the perceptron with constant coefficients. Hence, better performances will result if the downsampled sets of bounded training feature vectors are linearly separable. By knowing the exact condition for the weights of the perceptron exhibiting limit cycle behaviors, one can operate the perceptron accordingly so that better performances are achieved. Besides, the range of the number of updates for the weights of the perceptron to reach the limit cycle is also unknown when the weights of the perceptron exhibit the limit cycle behavior. The range of the number of updates for the weights of the perceptron to reach the limit cycle relates to the rate of the convergence of the training algorithm. Hence, by knowing the range of the number of updates for the weights of the perceptron to reach the limit cycle, one can estimate the computational effort of the training algorithm. The details of these issues will be discussed in Section 5.4.

The outline of this chapter is as follows. Notations used throughout this chapter will be introduced in Section 5.2. It will be discussed in Section 5.3 that the weights of the perceptron are bounded for all initial weights if there exists a nonempty set of initial weights that the weights of the perceptron is bounded. A necessary and sufficient condition for the weights of the perceptron exhibiting the limit cycle behavior will be discussed in Section 5.4. Also, the range of the number of updates for the weights of the perceptron to reach the limit cycle will be estimated in the same section. Numerical computer simulation results will be shown in Section 5.5 to illustrate that the perceptron exhibiting the limit cycle behavior can achieve a better recognition performance compared to a multi-layer perceptron. Finally, a conclusion will be drawn in Section 5.6.

5.2. Notations

Denote N as the number of the bounded training feature vectors and d as the dimension of these bounded training feature vectors. Denote the elements in the bounded training feature vectors as $x_i(k)$ for $i = 1, 2, \ldots, d$ and for $k = 0, 1, \ldots, N-1$. Define $\mathbf{x}(k) \equiv [1, x_1(k), \ldots, x_d(k)]^T$ for $k = 0, 1, \ldots, N-1$ and $\mathbf{x}(Nn+k) = \mathbf{x}(k)\ \forall n \geq 0$ and for $k = 0, 1, \ldots, N-1$, where the superscript ^{T} denotes the transposition operator. Denote the weights of the perceptron as $w_i(n)$ for $i = 1, 2, \ldots, d$ and $\forall n \geq 0$. Denote the threshold of the perceptron as $w_0(n)\ \forall n \geq 0$ and the activation function of the perceptron as

$$Q(z) = \begin{cases} 1 & z \geq 0 \\ -1 & z < 0 \end{cases} .$$

Define $\mathbf{w}(n) \equiv [w_0(n), w_1(n), \ldots, w_d(n)]^T\ \forall n \geq 0$ and denote the output of the perceptron as $y(n)\ \forall n \geq 0$, then $y(n) = Q(\mathbf{w}^T(n)\mathbf{x}(n))\ \forall n \geq 0$. Denote the desired output of the perceptron corresponding to $\mathbf{x}(n)$ as $t(n)$ $\forall n \geq 0$. Assume that the perceptron training algorithm [9] is employed for the training, so the updated rule for the weights of the perceptron is as follows:

$$\mathbf{w}(n+1) = \mathbf{w}(n) + \frac{t(n) - y(n)}{2}\mathbf{x}(n)\ \forall\ n \geq 0. \tag{5.1}$$

Denote the absolute value of a real number as $|.|$ and the 2-norm of a vector as $\|\mathbf{v}\| \equiv \sqrt{\sum_{i=1}^{d} v_i^2}$, where $\mathbf{v} \equiv [v_1, \ldots, v_d]^T$. Denote K as the maximum 2-norm of the vectors in the set of bounded training feature vectors, that is $K \equiv \max_{0 \leq k \leq N-1} \|\mathbf{x}(k)\|$. Denote $\emptyset$ as the empty set.

5.3. Global Boundness Property

Since $y(n) \in \{1, -1\}$ $\forall n \geq 0$, the values of $y(n)$ can be represented as symbols and the dynamics of the perceptron is governed by symbolic dynamics. As discussed in Section 5.1 the boundedness condition of the system state vectors of general symbolic dynamical systems depends on the initial system state vectors, so one may expect that different initial weights would lead to different boundedness conclusions. However, it is found that if there exists a nonempty set of initial weights that leads to the bounded behavior, then all initial weights will lead to the bounded behavior. That means, the boundedness condition of the weights of the perceptron is independent of the initial weights. This result is stated in Theorem 5.1 and is useful because engineers can employ arbitrary initial weights for the training and the boundedness condition of the weights is independent of the choice of the initial weights. Before we discuss this result, we need the following lemmas:

Lemma 5.1. *Assume that there are two perceptrons with the initial weights* $\mathbf{w}(0)$ *and* $\mathbf{w}^*(0)$. *Suppose that the set of the bounded training feature vectors and the corresponding set of desired outputs of these two perceptrons are the same, then* $(\mathbf{w}(k) - \mathbf{w}^*(k))^T \frac{Q((\mathbf{w}^*(k))^T\mathbf{x}(k)) - Q((\mathbf{w}(k))^T\mathbf{x}(k))}{2}\mathbf{x}(k) \leq 0 \forall k \geq 0$.

The importance of Lemma 5.1 is for deriving the result in Lemma 5.2 stated below, which is essential for deriving the main result on the boundedness condition of the weights of the perceptron stated in Theorem 5.1.

Lemma 5.2. *If* $\frac{\|\mathbf{x}(k)\|^2}{2} < |(\mathbf{w}(k) - \mathbf{w}^*(k))^T\mathbf{x}(k)|$, *then* $\|\mathbf{w}(k) - \mathbf{w}^*(k)\|^2 \geq \|\mathbf{w}(k+1) - \mathbf{w}^*(k+1)\|^2$.

The importance of Lemma 5.2 is for deriving the result in Theorem 5.1 stated below, which describes the main result on the boundedness condition of the weights of the perceptron.

Theorem 5.1. *If* $\exists \mathbf{w}^*(0) \in \mathbb{R}^{d+1}$ *and* $\exists \tilde{B} \geq 0$ *such that* $\|\mathbf{w}^*(k)\| \leq \tilde{B}$ $\forall k \geq 0$, *then* $\exists B'' \geq 0$ *such that* $\|\mathbf{w}(k)\| \leq B''$ $\forall k \geq 0$ *and* $\forall \mathbf{w}(0) \in \mathbb{R}^{d+1}$.

For practical applications, the weights of the perceptron are required to be bounded because of safety reasons. Suppose that there exists a nonempty set of initial weights such that the weights of the perceptron are bounded. Otherwise, the perceptron is useless. Without Theorem 5.1, we do not know what exact initial weights will lead to the bounded behavior. However, by Theorem 5.1, we can conclude that it is not necessary to know the exact initial weights which lead to the bounded behavior. This is because once there exists a nonempty set of initial weights that leads to the bounded behavior, then all initial weights will lead to the bounded behavior. The result implies that engineers can employ arbitrary initial weights for the training and the boundedness condition is independent of the choice of the initial weights. This phenomenon is counter-intuitive to the general understanding of symbolic dynamical systems because the system state vectors of general symbolic dynamical systems may be bounded for some initial system state vectors, but exhibit an unbounded behavior for other initial system state vectors. It is worth noting that the weights of the perceptron may exhibit complex behaviors, such as limit cycle or chaotic behaviors.

Corollary 5.1. *Define a nonlinear map* $\tilde{Q}\colon \mathbb{R}^{d+1} \to \mathbb{R}^{d+1}$ *such that* $\tilde{Q}(\mathbf{w}(n)) \equiv [q_0(n), \ldots, q_{N-1}(n)]^T$, *where*

$$q_j(n) \equiv \begin{cases} t(j) & j \neq mod(n, N) \\ Q(\mathbf{w}^T(n)\mathbf{x}(n)) & otherwise \end{cases}$$

$\forall n \geq 0$ *and for* $j = 0, 1, \ldots, N-1$. *If* $\exists \mathbf{w}^*(0) \in \mathbb{R}^{d+1}$ *and* $\exists B \geq 0$ *such that* $\|\mathbf{w}^*(k)\| \leq B\ \forall k \geq 0$, *then* $\sum_{\forall n \geq 0} t(j) - q_j(n) = 0$ *for* $j = 0, 1, \ldots, N-1$.

This corollary states a sufficient condition for the boundedness of the weights of the perceptron. Hence, this corollary can be used for testing whether the weights of the perceptron are bounded or not.

It is worth noting that the difference between the block diagram of the perceptron shown in Fig. 5.1 and that of conventional interpolative sigma delta modulators [10] is that $\tilde{Q}(\cdot)$ is a periodically time varying system with period N, while the nonlinear function in conventional interpolative sigma delta modulators is a memoryless system. Moreover, $\tilde{Q}(\cdot)$ is not a quantization function, while that in conventional interpolative sigma delta modulators is a quantization function. Hence, the boundedness condition derived in Theorem 5.1 is not applicable to the conventional sigma delta modulators.

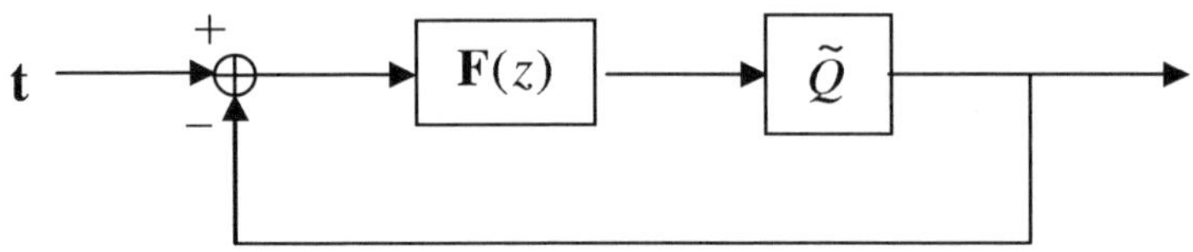

Fig. 5.1. A block diagram for modeling the dynamics of the weights of the perceptron.

5.4. Limit Cycle Behavior

In Section 5.3, the boundedness condition of the weights of the perceptron has been discussed. However, even when the weights of the perceptron are bounded, it is not guaranteed that the weights of the perceptron will converge to limit cycles. In this section, a necessary and sufficient condition for the occurrence of the limit cycle is discussed and the result is stated in Lemma 5.3. These results are important because perceptrons exhibiting limit cycle behaviors are actually time periodically varying neural networks, which are the generalization of neural networks with constant coefficients. Hence, it can achieve better performances, such as better recognition rate. By applying the result in Lemma 5.3, the perception can be operated under the limit cycle behaviors and better performances could be achieved. The range of the number of updates for the weights of the perceptron to reach the limit cycle is estimated. This result is discussed in Theorem 5.2 and Lemma 5.4. In addition, by applying the results in Theorem 5.2 and Lemma 5.4, one can estimate the computational effort of the training algorithm, which is also very important for practical applications.

Lemma 5.3. *Suppose that q_1 and q_2 are co-prime and M and N are positive integers. That is $q_1 M = q_2 N$. Then $\mathbf{w}^*(n)$ is periodic with period M if and only if* $\sum_{j=0}^{M-1} \frac{t(kM+j) - Q((\mathbf{w}^*(kM+j))^T \mathbf{x}(kM+j))}{2} \mathbf{x}(kM+j) = \mathbf{0}$ *for* $k = 0, 1, \ldots, q_1 - 1$.

Lemma 5.3 can be described as follows: By duplicating q_2 sets of bounded training feature vectors and dividing all of them to q_1 groups with M bounded training feature vectors in each group, then the sign or the null combinations, that is, 1 or 0 or -1, of these M bounded training feature vectors in each group will be zero, where the sign or the null coefficients are exactly equal to half of the difference between the desired outputs and the true outputs of the perceptron.

Lemma 5.3 is the generalization of the existing result on the necessary and sufficient condition for the weights of the perceptron exhibiting from the fixed point behavior to the limit cycle behavior with the period being any positive rational multiple of the number of bounded training feature vectors. Here, we have M hyperplanes and N bounded training feature vectors, so the weights of the perceptron exhibit the periodic behavior with period M. Note that neither the number of hyperplanes is necessarily equal to a positive integer multiple of the number of bounded training feature vectors nor vice versa, that is neither $M = k_1 N$ for $k_1 \in \mathbb{Z}^+$ nor $N = k_2 M$ for $k_2 \in \mathbb{Z}^+$ is necessarily required. When $M = 1$, $q_1 = N$ and $q_2 = 1$, Lemma 5.3 reduces to the existing perceptron convergence theorem. In this case, Lemma 5.3 implies that $\mathbf{w}^*(n)$ is periodic with period 1 if and only if $\frac{t(k)-Q((\mathbf{w}^*(k))^T\mathbf{x}(k))}{2}\mathbf{x}(k) = \mathbf{0}$ $k = 0, 1, \ldots, N-1$.

This is equivalent to $\mathbf{w}^*(n)$ exhibiting a fixed point behavior if and only if

$\frac{t(k)-Q((\mathbf{w}^*(k))^T\mathbf{x}(k))}{2} = \mathbf{0}$ for $k = 0, 1, \ldots, N-1$.

In other words, $\mathbf{w}^*(n)$ exhibits a fixed point behavior if and only if the set of bounded training feature vectors is linearly separable.

Since the limit cycle behavior is a bounded behavior, by combining Lemma 5.3 and Theorem 5.1 together, we can conclude that the weights of the perceptron will be bounded for all initial weights if there exists a nonempty set of initial weights $\mathbf{w}^*(0)$ such that $\sum_{j=0}^{M-1} \frac{t(kM+j) - Q((\mathbf{w}^*(kM+j))^T\mathbf{x}(kM+j))}{2}\mathbf{x}(kM+j) = \mathbf{0}$ for $k = 0, 1, \ldots, q_1 - 1$.

However, it does not imply that the weights of the perceptron will eventually exhibit a limit cycle behavior for all initial weights. The perceptron may still exhibit complex behaviors, such as chaotic behaviors, for some initial weights.

Suppose that the perceptron converges to a limit cycle with the equivalent instantaneous initial weights $\mathbf{w}^*(0)$, that is $\exists n_0 \geq 0$ such that $\mathbf{w}(k+nM) = \mathbf{w}^*(k)$ for $k = 0, 1, \ldots, M-1$ and for $n \geq n_0$, where $\mathbf{w}^*(k+nM) = \mathbf{w}^*(k)$ $\forall n \geq 0$ and for $k = 0, 1, \ldots, M-1$. Then it is important to estimate the range of the number of updates for $\mathbf{w}(0)$ to reach $\{\mathbf{w}^*(k)$ for $k = 0, 1, \ldots, M-1\}$. This is because the number of updates for $\mathbf{w}(0)$ to reach the limit cycle relates to the rate of the convergence of the perceptron and the computational effort of the training algorithm.

Theorem 5.2. *Define* $\mathbf{X} \equiv [\mathbf{x}(0), \ldots, \mathbf{x}(N-1)]$. *Suppose that* $rank(\mathbf{X}\mathbf{X}^T) = d+1$. *Define* $\tilde{\mathbf{X}} \equiv \mathbf{X}^T(\mathbf{X}\mathbf{X}^T)^{-1}$. *Denote* λ_{max} *and* λ_{min} *as the maximum and minimum eigenvalues of* $\tilde{\mathbf{X}}\tilde{\mathbf{X}}^T$, *respectively. Define* $\mathbf{C}_{nq_2N+kN+j} \equiv [\ddot{C}_{0,nq_2N+kN+j}, \ldots, \ddot{C}_{N-1,nq_2N+kN+j}]^T$ $\forall j \in \{0,1,\ldots,N-1\}$, $\forall k \in \{0,1,\ldots,q_2-1\}$ *and* $\forall n \geq 1$, *in which* $\ddot{C}_{i,nq_2N+kN+j} = \sum_{p=0}^{n-1}\sum_{l=0}^{q_2-1} \frac{t(i)-Q((\mathbf{w}(pq_2N+lN+i))^T\mathbf{x}(i))}{2} + \sum_{l=0}^{k-1} \frac{t(i)-Q((\mathbf{w}(nq_2N+lN+i))^T\mathbf{x}(i))}{2} + \frac{t(i)-Q((\mathbf{w}(nq_2N+kN+i))^T\mathbf{x}(i))}{2}$ *for* $i \leq j$, *where* $i = 0,1,\ldots,N-1$, $j = 0,1,\ldots,N-1$, $k = 0,1,\ldots,q_2-1$ *and* $\forall n \geq 1$, *and* $\ddot{C}_{i,nq_2N+kN+j} = \sum_{p=0}^{n-1}\sum_{l=0}^{q_2-1} \frac{t(i)-Q((\mathbf{w}(pq_2N+lN+i))^T\mathbf{x}(i))}{2} + \sum_{l=0}^{l-1} \frac{t(i)-Q((\mathbf{w}(nq_2N+lN+i))^T\mathbf{x}(i))}{2}$ *for* $i > j$, *where* $i = 0,1,\ldots,N-1$, $j = 0,1,\ldots,N-1$, $k = 0,1,\ldots,q_2-1$ *and* $\forall n \geq 1$. *Assume that* $\mathbf{w}(nq_2N+kN+j) = \mathbf{w}^*(j)$ *for some* $j \in \{0,1,\ldots,N-1\}$, *for some* $k \in \{0,1,\ldots,q_2-1\}$ *and for some* $n \geq 1$, *where* $\mathbf{w}^*(nM+k) = \mathbf{w}^*(k)$ $\forall n \geq 0$ *and for* $k = 0,1,\ldots,M-1$. *Define* $\tilde{\mathbf{C}}_j \equiv \tilde{\mathbf{X}}(\mathbf{w}^*(j)-\mathbf{w}(0))$ *for* $j = 0,1,\ldots,M-1$. *Then* $\frac{\|\tilde{\mathbf{C}}_j\|^2}{\lambda_{max}} \leq \|\mathbf{X}\mathbf{C}_{nq_2N+kN+j}\|^2 \leq \frac{\|\tilde{\mathbf{C}}_j\|^2}{\lambda_{min}}$ $\forall j \in \{0,1,\ldots,N-1\}$, $\forall k \in \{0,1,\ldots,q_2-1\}$ *and* $\forall n \geq 1$.

Although the range of the number of updates for the weights of the perceptron to reach the limit cycle is equal to $\|\mathbf{C}_{nq_2N+kN+j}\|_1$, it can be reflected through $\|\mathbf{X}\mathbf{C}_{nq_2N+kN+j}\|^2$. Hence, Theorem 5.2 provides an idea on the range of the number of updates for the weights of the perceptron to reach the limit cycle, which is useful for the estimation of the computational effort of the training algorithm. In order to estimate the bounds for $\|\mathbf{C}_{nq_2N+kN+j}\|_1$, denote m' as the number of the differences between the output of the perceptron based on $\mathbf{w}(0)$ and that based on $\mathbf{w}^*(0)$, that is $m' = \sum_{\forall n} \left|\frac{Q((\mathbf{w}^*(n))^T\mathbf{x}(n)) - Q((\mathbf{w}(n))^T\mathbf{x}(n))}{2}\right|$.

Then we have the following result:

Lemma 5.4. *If* $\mathbf{w}(nq_1M+kM+j) = \mathbf{w}^*(j)$ *for some* $j \in \{0,1,\ldots,M-1\}$, *for some* $k \in \{0,1,\ldots,q_1-1\}$ *and for some* $n \geq 1$, *by defining*

$$c \equiv \sum_{j=0}^{q_1 M-2} \sum_{k=j+1}^{q_1 M-1} (\mathbf{w}^*(k) - \mathbf{w}(k))^T \frac{Q((\mathbf{w}^*(j))^T \mathbf{x}(j)) - y(j)}{2} \mathbf{x}(j), \textit{ then } m' \geq$$

$$\frac{c + \sum_{k=0}^{q_1-1} \sum_{j=0}^{M-1} \|\mathbf{w}^*(kM+j) - \mathbf{w}(kM+j)\|^2}{\| \sum_{p=0}^{q_1-1} \sum_{i=0}^{M-1} \mathbf{w}^*(pM+i) - \mathbf{w}(pM+i) \| K}.$$

The importance of Lemma 5.1 is to estimate the minimum number of updates for the weights of the perceptron to reach the limit cycle and it is useful for the estimation of the computation effort of the training algorithm. It is worth noting that the minimum number of updates for the weights of the perceptron to reach the limit cycle depends on the initial weights. Similar result can be obtained by generalizing the conventional perceptron convergence theorem with zero initial weights to arbitrarily initial weights when the set of bounded training feature vectors is linearly separable.

5.5. Application of Perceptron Exhibiting Limit Cycle Behavior

Since time divisional multiplexing systems are widely used in many communications and signal processing systems, a time divisional multiplexing system is employed for an illustration. Consider an example that sixteen voices from four African boys, four Asian boys, four European girls and four American girls are multiplexed into a single channel. As two dimensional bounded training feature vectors are easy for an illustration, the dimension of the bounded feature vectors is chosen to be equal to two. Without loss of generality, denote the bounded training feature vectors of these voices as $\mathbf{x}(i)$ for $i = 0, 1, \ldots, 15$, and the corresponding desired outputs as $t(i)$ for $i = 0, 1, \ldots, 15$. Suppose that the voices generated by the boys are denoted as -1, so $t(4n+1) = t(4n+2) = -1$ for $n = 0, 1, 2, 3$, while the voices generated by the girls are denoted as 1, so $t(4n) = t(4n+3) = 1$ for $n = 0, 1, 2, 3$. Suppose that the means of the bounded training feature vectors corresponding to African boys are $[-1, 1]^T$, $[-0.9, 1]^T$, $[-1, 0.9]^T$ and $[-0.9, 0.9]^T$, that corresponding to Asian boys are $[1, -1]^T$, $[0.9, -1]^T$, $[1, -0.9]^T$ and $[0.9, -0.9]^T$ that corresponding to American girls are $[1, 1]^T$, $[0.9, 1]^T$, $[1, 0.9]^T$ and $[0.9, 0.9]^T$ and that corresponding to European girls are $[-1, -1]^T$, $[-0.9, -1]^T$, $[-1, -0.9]^T$ and $[-0.9, -0.9]^T$. Each speaker generates 100 bounded feature vectors for transmission and the channel is corrupted by an additive white Gaussian noise with zero mean and variance equal to 0.5. These bounded feature vectors are used for testing. Figure 5.2 shows the distribution of these bounded testing feature vectors. On the other hand, the 16 noise-free bounded training feature vectors are trained using the conventional perceptron training algorithm.

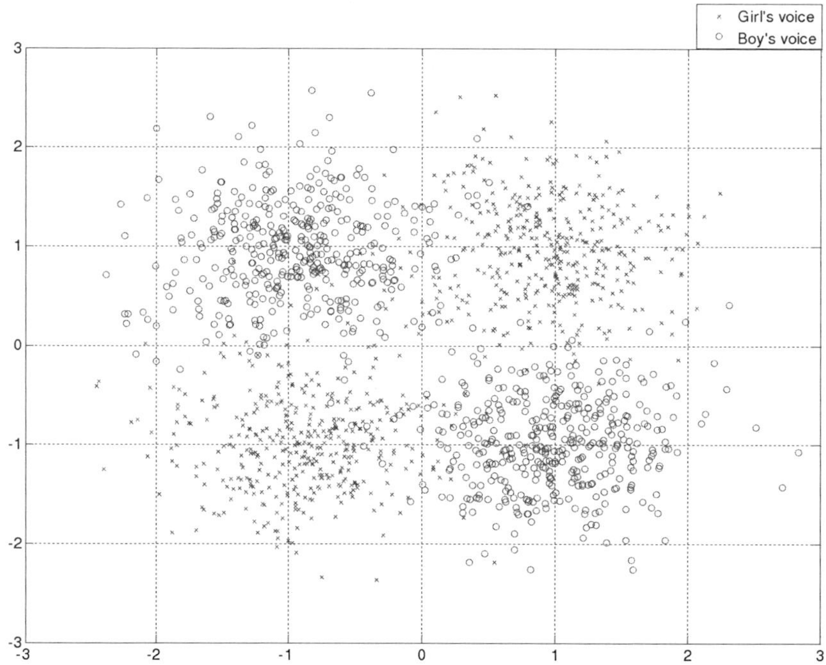

Fig. 5.2. Distribution of bounded testing feature vectors.

As the set of bounded training feature vectors is nonlinearly separable, the conventional perceptron training algorithm does not converge to a fixed point and the perceptron exhibits the limit cycle behavior with period four. A perceptron exhibiting the limit cycle behavior is actually a neural network with time periodically varying coefficients. In fact, this is a generalization of the perceptron with constant coefficients. Hence, better performances are resulted if the downsampled sets of bounded training feature vectors are linearly separable. The reason is as follows: Assume that $\mathbf{w}^*(nM+k) = \mathbf{w}^*(k)\ \forall n \geq 0$ and for $k = 0, 1, \ldots, M-1$. Suppose that N is an integer multiple of M, that is $\exists z \in \mathbb{Z}^+$ such that $N = zM$. By downsampling the set of the bounded training feature vectors by M, we have M downsampled sets of bounded training feature vectors, denoted as $\{\mathbf{x}(kM+i)\}$ for $i = 0, 1, \ldots, M-1$ and for $k = 0, 1, \ldots, z-1$. For each downsampled set of bounded training feature vectors, if these z samples are linearly separable, then $\mathbf{w}^*(i)$ for $i = 0, 1, \ldots, M-1$ can be employed for the classification and the recognition error will be exactly equal to zero. Hence, the perceptron exhibiting the limit cycle behavior significantly improves the recognition performance.

Refer to the example discussed above, by defining the classification rule as follows: Assign $\mathbf{x}(k)$ to class -1 if $Q((\mathbf{w}^*(k))^T\mathbf{x}(k)) = 1$, and assign $\mathbf{x}(k)$ to class 1 if $Q((\mathbf{w}^*(k))^T\mathbf{x}(k)) = -1$, as well as by running the conventional perceptron training algorithm with zero initial weights, then it is found that the weights of perceptron are bounded and converge to a limit cycle. This implies that the weights of the perceptron will also be bounded if other initial weights are employed. We generated other initial weights randomly and found that the weights of the perceptron are really bounded. This demonstrates the validity of Theorem 5.1. For the zero initial weight, it is found that the recognition error is 2.25%. For comparison, a two layer perceptron is employed for solving the corresponding nonlinearly separable problem. It is well known that if the weights of the perceptrons are selected as $\mathbf{w}_1^* \equiv [\frac{1}{2}, \frac{1}{2}, \frac{1}{2}]^T$, $\mathbf{w}_2^* \equiv [-\frac{1}{2}, \frac{1}{2}, \frac{1}{2}]^T$ and $\mathbf{w}_3^* \equiv [0, -\frac{1}{2}, \frac{1}{2}]^T$, then the output of the two layer perceptron, defined as $y'(k) = Q([1, Q((\mathbf{w}_1^*)^T\mathbf{x}(k)), Q((\mathbf{w}_2^*)^T\mathbf{x}(k))]^T\mathbf{w}_3^*)$, will solve the XOR nonlinear problem, and it can be checked easily that the recognition error for the set of the noise-free bounded training feature vectors is exactly equal to zero. Hence, these coefficients are employed for the comparison. It is found that the recognition error based on the two layer perceptron is 14.56%, while that based on the perceptron exhibiting a limit cycle behavior is only 2.25%. This demonstrates that the perceptron exhibiting the limit cycle behavior outperforms the two layer perceptron.

5.6. Conclusion

Unlike other symbolic dynamical systems, the boundedness condition of the perceptron is independent of the initial weights. That means, if there exists a nonempty set of initial weights that the weights of the perceptron are bounded, then the weights of a perceptron will be bounded for all initial weights. Also, it is suggested that the perceptron exhibiting the limit cycle behavior can be employed for solving a recognition problem when the downsampled sets of bounded training feature vectors are linearly separable.

References

[1] M. Gori and M. Maggini, Optimal convergence of on-line backpropagation, *IEEE Transactions on Neural Networks.* **7**(1), 251–254, (2002).

[2] S. J. Wan, Cone algorithm: An extension of the perceptron algorithm, *IEEE Transactions on Systems, Man and Cybernetics.* **24**(10), 1571–1576, (1994).

[3] M. Brady, R. Raghavan, and J. Slawny, Gradient descent fails to separate, *Proceedings of the IEEE International Conference on Neural Networks, 1988.* pp. 649–656, (2002).

[4] T. B. Ludermir, A. Yamazaki, and C. Zanchettin, An optimization methodology for neural network weights and architectures, *IEEE Transactions on Neural Networks.* **17**(6), 1452–1459, (2006).

[5] S. G. Pierce, Y. Ben-Haim, K. Worden, and G. Manson, Evaluation of neural network robust reliability using information-gap theory, *IEEE Transactions on Neural Networks.* **17**(6), 1349–1361, (2006).

[6] C. F. Juang, C. T. Chiou, and C. L. Lai, Hierarchical singleton-type recurrent neural fuzzy networks for noisy speech recognition, *IEEE Transactions on Neural Networks.* **18**(3), 833–843, (2007).

[7] R. W. Duren, R. J. Marks, P. D. Reynolds, and M. L. Trumbo, Real-time neural network inversion on the SRC-6e reconfigurable computer, *IEEE Transactions on Neural Networks.* **18**(3), 889–901, (2007).

[8] S. Wan and L. E. Banta, Parameter incremental learning algorithm for neural networks, *IEEE transactions on Neural Networks.* **17**(6), 1424–1438, (2006).

[9] M. Basu and Q. Liang, The fractional correction rule: a new perspective, *Neural Networks.* **11**(6), 1027–1039, (1998).

[10] C. Y. F. Ho, B. W. K. Ling, and J. D. Reiss, Estimation of an Initial Condition of Sigma–Delta Modulators via Projection Onto Convex Sets, *IEEE Transactions on Circuits and Systems I: Regular Papers.* **53**(12), 2729–2738, (2006).

Chapter 6

Artificial Neural Network Modeling with Application to Nonlinear Dynamics

Yi Zhao

Harbin Institute of Technology Shenzhen Graduate School
Shenzhen, China
zhao.yi@hitsz.edu.cn

Artificial neural network (ANN) is well known for its strong capability to handle nonlinear dynamical systems, and this modeling technique has been widely applied to the nonlinear time series prediction problem. However, this application needs more cautions as overfitting is the serious problem endemic to neural networks. The conventional method of avoiding overfitting is to avoid fitting the data too precisely while it cannot determine the exact model size directly. In this chapter, we employ an alternative information theoretic criterion (minimum description length) to determine the optimal architecture of neural networks according to the equilibrium between the model parameters and model errors. When applied to various time series, we find that the model with the optimal architecture both generalizes well and accurately captures the underlying dynamics. To further confirm the dynamical character of the model residual of the optimal neural network, the surrogate data method from the regime of nonlinear dynamics is then described to analyze such model residual so as to determine whether there is significant deterministic structure not captured by the optimal neural network. Finally, a diploid model is proposed to improve the prediction precision under the condition that the prediction error is considered to be deterministic. The systematic framework composed of the preceding modules is validated in sequence, and illustrated with several computational and experimental examples.

Contents

6.1. Introduction

Nonlinear dynamics has a significant impact on a variety of applied fields, ranging from mathematics to mechanics, from meteorology to economy, from population to biomedical signal analysis. That is, a great many phenomena are subject to nonlinear dynamics. For this reason, establishing effective models to capture or learn the nonlinear dynamic mechanism of the object system and to solve further prediction and control problems becomes a critical issue. Considering the length of this chapter, we will focus on one of the primary model applications: neural networks (NN) modeling for nonlinear time series prediction. Some other applications, such as pattern recognition, control and classification, can be found in [1–3].

In the previous research, there are many linear methods with mutation emerging, such as the famous autoregressive and moving average (ARMA) model. This model family proposed by Box *et al.* four decades ago has been widely used to solve the prediction problem with great success [4]. The ARMA model is composed of two parts: the autoregressive part, AR(p) predicting the current observation based on a linear function of the p previous ones, and the moving average part, MA(q) calculating the mean of the time series with the moving windows with the windows size q. Furthermore, the primary limitation of ARMA models is the assumption of the linear relation between independent and dependent variables. The ARMA models are applicable only to stationary time series modeling. Those constraints, therefore, limit the application range and prediction accuracy of related ARMA models. Meanwhile, artificial neural networks (ANN) have been suggested to handle the complicated time series. They are quite effective in modeling nonlinearity between the input and output variables and in particular, the multi-layer feedforward neural network with the given sigmoid activation function is able to approximate any nonlinear continuous function in arbitrary closed interval. Cybenko first proved the preceding assertion in 1989 [5]. Then Kurt Hornik showed that this universal approximation was closely related to the architecture of the network but not limited to the specific activation function of the neural network [6]. Afterwards, concerning model optimization, the architecture becomes the first factor to be considered. In addition, in 1987, Lapedes and Farber explained that ANN can be used for modeling and predicting nonlinear time series in a simulated case study [7].

Supported by these theoretical proofs, feedforward neural networks became much more popular for modeling nonlinear complicated system. Several prediction models based on ANN have been presented. Wilson and Sharda employed an ANN model to predict the bankruptcy and found it performed significantly better than the classical multivariate discrimination method [8]. Tseng *et al.* proposed a hybrid prediction model combining the seasonal autoregressive integrated moving average model and the backpropagation neural network to predict two kinds of sales data: the Taiwan machinery industry and soft drink production value. The result shows that this combination brings better prediction than the single model and other kind of models [9]. Chang *et al.* demonstrated that the traditional approach of sales forecasting integrated with the appropriate artificial intelligence was highly competitive in the practical business service [10]. D. Shanthi *et al.* employed the ANN model trained by backpropagation algorithm to forecast the thrombo-embolic stock disease and obtained high predictive accuracy [11]. In summary, ANN exhibits superiority for nonlinear time series prediction.

The significant advantage of ANN modeling can be mainly ascribed to its imitation of the biologically nervous system, a massive highly connected array of nonlinear excitatory "neuron". The high-degree freedom in the neural network architecture provides the potential to model complicated nonlinearity, but it also brings about uncertain conditions when dealing with those complicated systems. It is thus expected to build neural networks with a fairly large number of neurons to take the challenge. However, people usually found that large neural networks just made small prediction errors on the training data but failed to fit to novel data or even performed worse (i.e. overfitted). So the crucial issue in developing a neural network is generalization of the network: the network not only fits the training data well but also responds properly to novel inputs. To solve this problem satisfactorily requires a selection technique to ensure the neural network makes the reliable and accurate prediction.

Usual methods to improve overfitting are known as: early stopping and statistical regularization techniques, such as weights decaying and Bayesian learning [12–14]. As Zhao and Small discussed [15], the validation set required in the method of early stopping should be representative of all points in the training set, and the training algorithm cannot converge too fast. The weights decaying method modifies the performance function, the mean sum of squares of the model errors to the sum of the mean sum of squares of the model errors and the network parameters. The key problem of this method is that it is difficult to seek equilibrium between the modified two parts.

For Bayesian learning, the optimal regularization parameter, the previous balance is determined in an automatical way [14]. The promising feature of Bayesian learning is that it can measure how many network parameters are effectively used for the given application. Although it gives an indicator of wasteful parameters, this method cannot build a compact (or smaller) optimal neural network.

In this chapter, we describe an alternative approach, which estimates exactly the optimal structure of the neural network for time series prediction. We focus on feedforward multi-layer neural networks, which has been proved to be qualified for modeling nonlinear functions. The criterion is a modification and competitive to the initial minimum description length (MDL) [16].

This method is based on the well-known principle of minimum description length rooted in the theory of algorithmic complexity [17]. J. Rissanen proposed the issue of model selection as a problem in data compression with a series of papers starting with [18]. Judd and Mees developed this principle to selection for local linear models [19], and then Small and Tse extended the previous analysis to selection for radius basis function models [20]. Zhao and Small generalized the previous results to neural network architectures [15]. Several other modifications to the method of minimum description length can be found in the literature according to their own demands [21–24].

Another technique, surrogate data method, is also described in this chapter. Surrogate data tests are examples of Monte Carbo hypothesis tests [25]. The standard surrogate data method, suggested and implemented by Theiler *et al.* has been widely applied in the literature [26]. This method aims to determine whether the given time series has a statistically significant deterministic component, or is just consistent with identical independent distribution (i.i.d.) noise. We will introduce this idea at length in Section 6.4.

In summary, we employ the method of MDL to select the optimal model from a number of neural network candidates for the specific time series prediction, and afterward apply the standard surrogate data method to the residual of the optimal model (i.e. the prediction error) to determine whether there is significant deterministic structure not captured by the optimal neural network estimated by MDL. This combination of MDL for model selection and surrogate data method for model residual validation can enhance the model prediction ability effectively. In the case that the prediction error contains deterministic dynamics a diploid model is introduced to handle this scenario at the end of this chapter.

This chapter is organized as follows. Some basic ideas about ANN are briefly described in Section 6.2, and the MDL method developed for selecting optimal neural networks is presented in Section 6.3; in the next section, we discuss the application of the surrogate data method to analyze model residuals. A diploid model is proposed in Section 6.5 to further improve the prediction precision if necessary. Finally, we have the conclusion of this chapter.

6.2. Model Structure

The modeling process by ANN to build a model for dynamical systems is a process to extract the deterministic dynamics that govern the evolution of the system and then establish an ANN model to describe it effectively. As mentioned previously, the multi-layer feedforward neural network is applicable to approximate any nonlinear function under certain conditions. So, in this chapter, this type of neural network is our interest.

Common to all neural network architectures is the connection of input vector, neurons (or nodes) and then output layers to establish numerous interconnected pathways from input to output. Figure 6.1 shows the architecture of a multilayer neural network.

Given an input vector $x = (x_{t-1}, x_{t-2}, \cdots, x_{t-d})$, the transfer function of this neural network is mathematically described by

$$y(x) = b_0 + \sum_{i=1}^{k} v_i f\Big(\sum_{j=1}^{d}(\omega_{i,j} x_{t-j} + b_i)\Big). \tag{6.1}$$

The input vectors where b_0,b_i, v_i, $\omega_{i,j}$ are parameters, k represents the number of neurons in the hidden layer, and $f(\cdot)$is the activation function of neurons. As shown in the figure below, there is one hidden layer, but notice that the multiple hidden layers are also optional. The input

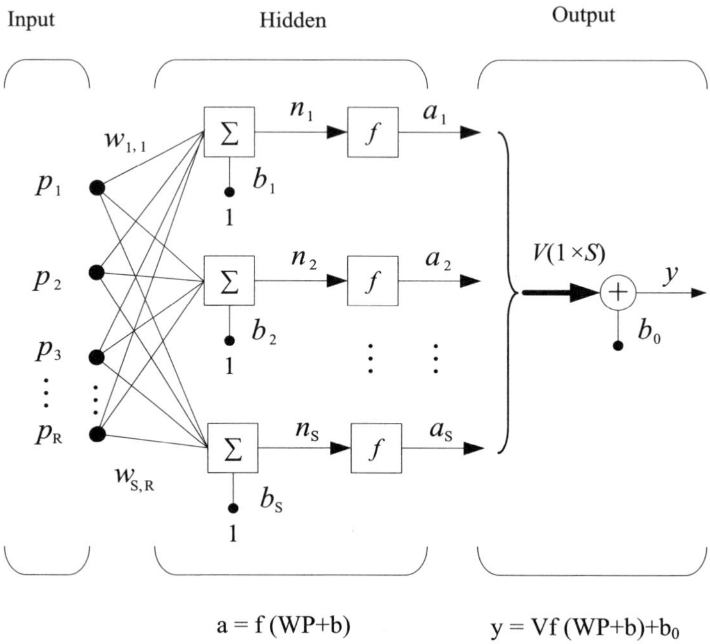

Fig. 6.1. The multilayer network is composed of the input, hidden and output layers [27].

vector is denoted by $P = \{p_1, p_2, \cdots, p_d\}$ and the output (or prediction value) is denoted by y. $W = \{w_{ij} | i = 1, \cdots, k, j = 1, \cdots, d\}$ and $V = \{v_i | i = 1, \cdots, k\}$ are weights associated with connections between layers; $b = \{b_i | i = 0, 1, \cdots, k\}$ are biases.

The process of training the neural network is to update these preceding parameters iteratively according to the mean square error between the original target and the prediction on it. The time series is divided into two sets: training and test sets. The first data set is used to train the neural network. Intuitively, it modifies the weights until the every output is close to the corresponding expectation. One of the classical training algorithms for feedforward neural networks is error back propagation. Hence, the neural network is sometimes called a backpropagation neural network. A number of training algorithms, including Levenberg–Marquardt (LM) algorithm were developed with the respective specifications [28]. For example, the LM training algorithm is known as fast convergence.

Obviously, the performance of the neural network heavily relies on the successful training of the model. But success training does not mean wonderful training on the training set. Trained neural networks, especially for back propagation networks, make small prediction errors on the training set, and yet, give poor prediction on another novel data set. This phenomenon has been recognized as overfitting. It is an old but hot issue endemic to neural network modeling. It widely occurs in any resultant neural networks, in particular those with a large number of neurons. This leads to the consequence that the performance of neural networks in some comparative experiments is not superior to or as good as other classical techniques. So, how many neurons should be put in the hidden layer is a crucial step to establish an optimal model. The next section will explain the details of MDL method to solve this problem and avoid overfitting.

6.3. Avoid Overfitting by Model Selection

There are several typical methods applicable to model selection. Akaike proposed his information criterion (AIC) based on a weighted function of fitting of a maximum log-likelihood model [29]. The motivation of AIC and its assumptions was the subject of some discussion in [18, 30, 31]. From a practical point, the AIC tends to overfit the data [32, 33]. To address this problem, Wallace *et al.*, therefore, developed the minimum message length (MML) [34]. Like MDL, MML chooses the hypothesis minimizing the code-length of the data but its codes are quite different from those in MDL. In addition, the Bayesian information criterion (BIC), also known as Schwarz's information criterion (SIC) is also an option [18, 31, 35].

It is clear that MDL criterion is related to other well-known model selection criterion. From our point of view, the AIC and BIC perform best for linear models; for nonlinear models description length style information criteria are better. We found that MDL in particular is robust and relatively easy to realize with reasonable assumption [15].

6.3.1. *How it works*

The basic principle of minimum description length is to estimate both the cost of describing the model parameters and model prediction errors. Let k be the number of neurons in the neural network. Λ represents all the parameters of the given neural network. As shown in Fig. 6.1, given the size of input vector, the number of parameters is completely determined by the number of neurons. We thus consider establishing the description length function of the neural network with respective to its neurons [15]. When we build a series of neural networks with varying neurons, we can also compute a series of description length of these models, which forms a DL curve along the x-axis of neurons.

Let E(k) be the cost of counting the model prediction errors and M(k) be the cost of counting the model parameters. The description length of the data with respect to this model is then given by the sum [20]:

$$D(k) = E(k) + M(k) \tag{6.2}$$

Intuitively, the typical tendency of E(k) and M(k) is that if the model size increases M(k) increases and E(k) decreases, which corresponds to the more model parameters and more potential modeling ability (i.e. less prediction error) respectively. The minimum description length principle states that the optimal model is the one that minimizes D(k).

Let $\{y_i\}_{i=1}^N$ be a time series of N measurements and

$$f(y_{i-1}, y_{i-2}, \cdots, y_{i-d}; \Lambda_k)$$

be the neural network output, given d previous inputs and parameters of the neural network described by $\Lambda_k = (\lambda_1, \lambda_2, \cdots, \lambda_k)$ associated with k neurons. The prediction error is thus given by $e_i = f(y_{i-1}, y_{i-2}, \cdots, y_{i-d}; \Lambda_k) - y_i$. For any Λ_k the description length of the model $f(\cdot; \Lambda_k)$ is given by [15]:

$$M(k) = L(\Lambda_k) = \sum_{i=1}^{k} \ln \frac{c}{\delta_i} \tag{6.3}$$

where c is a constant and represents the number of bits required in the representation of floating points, and δ_i is interpreted as the optimal precision of the parameter λ_i.

Rissanen [16] showed that E(k) is the negative logarithm of the likelihood of the errors $e = \{e_i\}_{i=1}^N$ under the assumed probability distribution of those errors:

$$E(k) = -\ln Prob(e) \tag{6.4}$$

For the general unknown probability distribution of errors, the estimation of E(k) would be rather complicated. However, it is reasonable to assume that the model residual is consistent with the normal Gaussian distribution according to central limit theorem, as N is adequately large.

We get the simplified equation

$$E(k) = \frac{N}{2} + \ln(\frac{2\pi}{N})^{\frac{N}{2}} + \ln(\sum_{i=1}^{N} e_i^2)^{\frac{N}{2}} \tag{6.5}$$

For the multilayer neural network described in the previous section, its parameters are completely denoted by $\Lambda_k = \{b_0, b_i, v_i, w_{i,j} | i = 1. \cdots, k, j = 1, \cdots, d\}$. Of these parameters, the weights v_i and the bias b_0 are all linear, the remaining parameters $w_{i,j}$ and $b_i (i = 1, \cdots, k, j = 1, \cdots, d)$ are nonlinear. Fortunately, the activation function $f(\cdot)$ is approximately linear in the region of interest so we suppose that the precision of the nonlinear parameters is similar to that of the linear one and employ the linear parameters to give the precision of the model, δ_i.

To account for the contribution of all linear and nonlinear parameters to M(k), instead of the contribution of only linear ones, we define $n_p(i)$ as the effective number of the parameters associated with the ith neuron contributed to the description length of the neural network [15]. So M(k) is updated by:

$$M(k) = \sum_{i=1}^{k} n_p(i) \ln \frac{\gamma}{\delta_i} \tag{6.6}$$

where δ_i is the relative precision of the weight $v_i \in \{v_1, v_2, \cdots, v_k\}$, and $n_p(i)$ will be a variable with respect to different neurons. But in order to make the problem tractable we make one further approximation that $n_p(i)$ is fixed for all i and then replace $n_p(i)$ with n_p.

However, the exact value of n_p is so difficult to calculate that we give $\hat{n}_p$ the embedding dimension by using False Nearest Neighbors (FNN) to approximate n_p [36]. In (6.3), $\hat{n}_p = 1$. That is, the previous work [20] just paid attention to the linear parameters and ignored contribution of those nonlinear ones. But for our neural networks $\hat{n}_p$ is in the range from one to $d + 2$. Embedding dimension represents the dimension of the phase space required to unfold a point in that phase space, i.e. it represents the effective number of inputs for a model.

With necessary but reasonable assumption and approximation, we establish a tractable description length function with respect to the number of neurons (i.e. all the associated parameters). The minimal value of this function takes the guidance of the optimal neural network, which makes the trade-off between the model parameters and corresponding model residual intuitively.

6.3.2. *Case study*

In this section, we present this analysis in two case studies: including a known dynamics system (Section A) and an experimental data set (Section B). The test system is the Rössler system with the addition of dynamic noise. We then describe the application of this model selection technique to experimental recordings of human pulse data during normal sinus rhythm.

When realizing description length, we notice that DL curves fluctuate somewhat or even dramatically for the practical data. It is very likely to give a wrong estimation of the minimum point. The independent construction of a series of neural networks correspondingly results in fluctuation of DL curves but the potential tendency estimated by DL curves still exists. The nonlinear curve fitting procedure is considered to smooth such perturbation and provide an accurate estimation of the actual minimum [15].

We first define a function, which takes a variable (the number of neurons) and coefficient vector to fit the original curve. The form of E(k) is consistent with that of a decreasing exponent function. So $ae^{-bk}(a > 0, b > 0)$ is used to reflect E(k). M(k) can be regarded appropriately as the linear function about the number of neurons. Thus a linear function, ck is defined to approximate M(k). d is required to compensate for an arbitrary constant missing from the computation of DL. So the defined function is $F(a, b, c, d; k) = ae^{-bk} + ck + d$, where a, b, c and d are the required coefficients. Note that the previous function is the empirical approximation of the true tendency of the DL curve.

Next, according to $\min\limits_{a,b,c,d} \sum\limits_{i=1}^{k} (F(a, b, c, d; i) - D(i))^2$, we obtain the coefficient vector (a, b, c, d). Finally, we substitute a, b, c, d, with estimated values and determine the solution of k that makes the fitted curve minimal. The fitted DL curve provides a smooth estimation of the original description length, and reflects the true tendency. The new estimation regarding the minimal description length appears to be robust, especially for complicated experimental data.

A. Computational experiments

Consider a reconstruction of the Rössler system with dynamic noise. The equations of the Rössler system are given by $\dot{x}(t) = -y(t) - z(t)$, $\dot{y}(t) = x(t) + a * y(t)$, $\dot{z}(t) = b + z(t) * [x(t) - c]$ with parameters $a = 0.1$, $b = 0.1$, $c = 18$ to generate the chaotic data [37]. Here we set the iteration step t_s to 0.25. By dynamic noise we mean that system noise is added to the

x-component data prior to prediction of the succeeding state. That is, we integrate this equation iteratively and then use the integrated results added with random noise as initial data for the next step. So the random noise is coupled into the generated data. The magnitude of the noise is set at 10% of the magnitude of the data. We generate 2000 points of this system of which 1600 points are selected to train the neural network and the rest are the testing data. We calculate a description length of 20 neural networks constructed with different neurons from 1 to 20, as shown in Fig. 6.2.

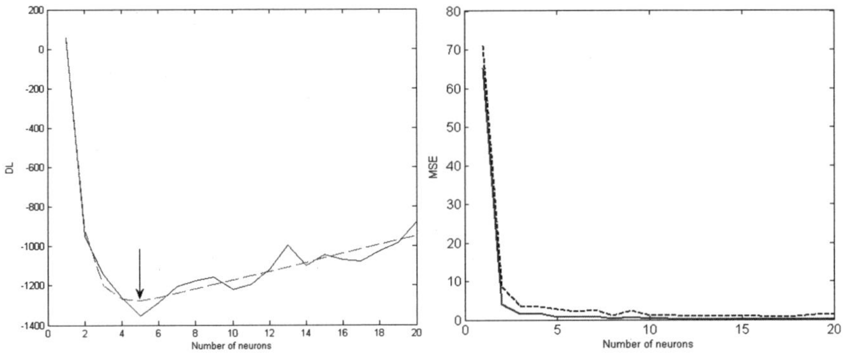

Fig. 6.2. Description Length (solid line) of neural networks for modeling the Rössler system (left panel) has the minimum point at five, and the fitted curve (dashed line) attains the minimum at the same point. In the right panel the solid line is the mean square error of training set and the dotted line is that of testing data.

We observe that both the DL and fitted curves denote that the optimal number of neurons is five. That is, the neural network with five neurons is the optimal model according to the principle of the minimum description length. Mean square error of the testing set gives little help in indicating the appearance of overfitting.

As a comparison, we chose other three networks with different numbers of neurons to perform a free-run prediction for the testing set. Concerning free-run prediction, the prediction value is based on the current and previous prediction values, in a comparison of the so-called one-step prediction. The predicted x-component data is converted into three vectors, $x(t)$, $x(t+3)$ and $x(t+5)$ ($t \in [1, 395]$) to construct the phase space shown in Fig. 6.3. The network with five neurons exactly captures the dynamics of the Rössler system but the neural network with more neurons is apt to overfit. As the test data is chaotic Rössler data, the corresponding attractor should be full of reconstructed trajectories, as shown in Fig. 6.3(b).

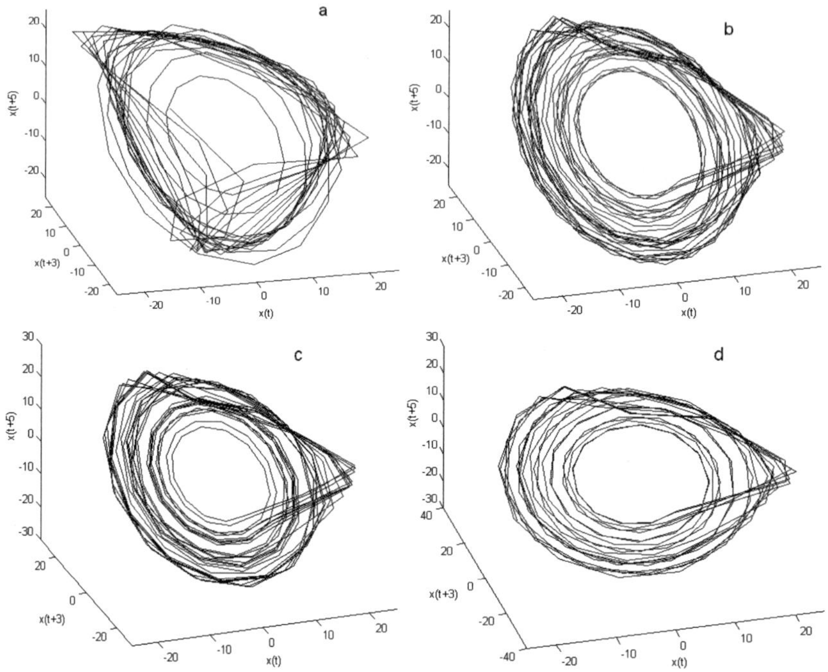

Fig. 6.3. Four reconstructions of free-run predictions of neural networks with 3, 5, 7 and 15 neurons.

B. Experimental data

Generally, experimental data are more complicated than computational data since the measurement of these data is usually contaminated with observational noise somewhat and also the deterministic dynamics governing the evolution of the real system is unknown. Hence, experimental data are much more difficult to predict accurately. We apply this information theoretic method to experimental recordings of human pulse data to validate its practicality.

We randomly utilize 2550 points to build neural networks and the consecutive 450 data points to test these well-trained models. Note that in the previous simulation example, the FNN that is used to estimate $\hat{n}_p$ curve drops to zero and remains at zero, but for practical ECG data the process is similar to that of noisy signal (i.e. it cannot reach zero). The inflection point of the FNN curve in this case points out the value of $\hat{n}_p$. Figure

6.4 describes description length and mean square error for this application respectively.

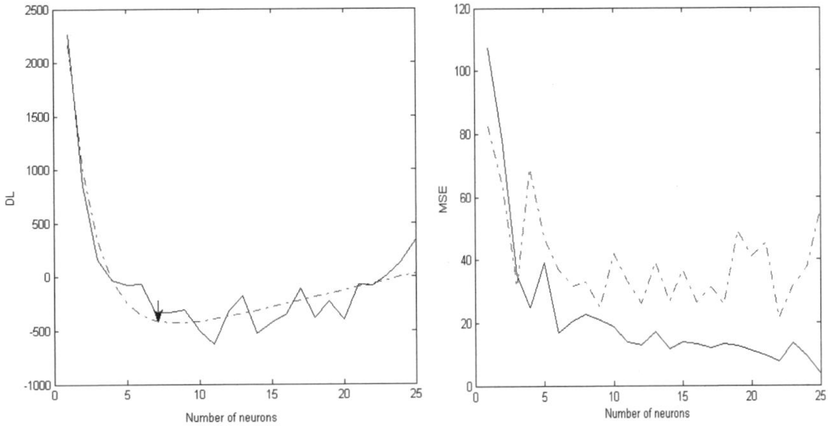

Fig. 6.4. Description length (solid line) and the fitted curve (dashed line) of ECG data (left panel) estimate the minimal points at the 11 and 7 point respectively. The right one is the mean square error of training set (solid line) and testing set (dotted line).

The DL curve suggests the optimal number of neurons is 11, but the fitted curve estimates that the optimal number of neurons is 7. In this experiment the mean square error (MSE) of testing data cannot give valuable information regarding the possibility of overfitting either. We thus deliberately select neural networks with both 7 and 11 neurons for verification. As in the previous case, another 2 neural networks with 5 neurons and 17 neurons are also used for comparison. All the free-run predictions obtained by these models are illustrated in Fig. 6.5

Networks with 7 neurons can predict the testing data accurately, but prediction of the network with 11 neurons is overfitted over the evolution of the time. So we confirm that the fitted curve shows robustness against fluctuation. The neural network with 7 neurons can provide adequate fitting to both training and novel data, and networks with more neurons, such as 11, overfit. Although referring to the DL line one may decide the wrong optimal number of neurons, the fitted curve reflects the true tendency hidden in the original DL estimation. For the computational data, both the original DL curve and the fitted one can provide the same or close estimation while taking the practical data into consideration, it is demonstrated the nonlinear curve fitting is necessary and effective.

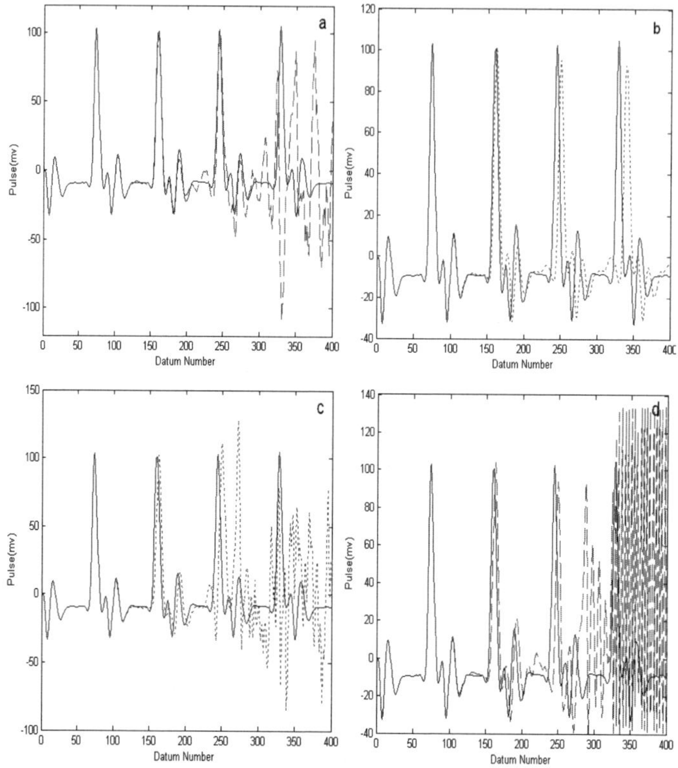

Fig. 6.5. Free-run prediction (dotted line) and actual ECG data (solid line) for 4 neural networks with 5, 7, 11 and 17 neurons.

By observation, readers are persuaded that the short-term prediction given by the selected optimal neural network is nearly perfect and these optimal models accurately capture the underlying deterministic dynamics of the given time series. However, how close is close enough? The model residual always exists as long as the target data and its prediction are not the same. So it could be hasty to make the previous conclusion without investigation of the model residual. Readers are referred to the next section, where we discuss how to examine the dynamical characters of this residual in a statistical way. If the model residual is merely random noise, it then gives a positive support to the performance of optimal neural networks as well as the proposed information theoretic criterion. If the model residual still contains significant determinism, it then indicates that these models are not omnipotent to deal with the original time series. We, therefore, present a solution to enhance the capability of the current neural network modeling in Section 6.5. One may find some interesting contents.

6.4. Surrogate Data Method for Model Residual

The surrogate data method has been widely applied in the literature. It was proposed to analyze whether the observed data is consistent with the given null hypothesis. Here, the observed data is the previous model residual. Hence, we employ the surrogate data method to answer the question in the last section. The given hypothesis is whether such data is consistent with random noise, known as NH0.

In fact, this technique can also be used prior to modeling to find whether the data comes from the deterministic dynamics or merely random noise. In the latter case, it is wasteful to make the prediction on it. Stochastic process tools may be more applicable to model such data. Consequently, the surrogate data method before modeling provides an indirect evidence of predictability of the data.

6.4.1. *Linear surrogate data*

The principle of surrogate data hypothesis testing is to generate an ensemble of artificial surrogate data (surrogates in short) by using a surrogate generation algorithm and ensure that the generated surrogates follow the certain null hypothesis. One then applies some test statistics to both surrogates and the original data to observe whether the original data is consistent with the given hypothesis. Commonly employed standard hypotheses include [38]:

- NH0: The data is independent and identically distributed (i.i.d.) noise.
- NH1: The data is linearly filtered noise.
- NH2: The data is a static monotonic nonlinear transformation of linearly filtered noise.

If the test statistic value for the data is distinct from the ensemble of values estimated for surrogates, then one can reject the given null hypothesis as being a likely origin of the data. If the test statistic value for the data is consistent with that for surrogates, then one may not reject the null hypothesis. Consequently, surrogate data provides a rigorous way to apply the statistical hypothesis testing to exclude experimental time series from the family of certain dynamics. One can apply it to determine whether an observed time series has a statistically significant deterministic component, or just is random noise.

There are three algorithms to generate surrogate data corresponding to the hypotheses above, known as Algorithm 0, Algorithm 1 and Algorithm 2. We only describe Algorithm 0 that we use. For Algorithm 0, the sequence of the data is randomly shuffled. Such shuffling will destroy any temporal autocorrelation of the original data. In essence such surrogates are random but consistent with the same probability distribution as that of the original.

To test the hypothesis of surrogate data one must select an appropriate statistic criterion. Among available optional criteria, correlation dimension is a popular choice [39]. By the value of correlation dimension, one can differentiate the time series with different dynamics. For example, the correlation dimension for a closed curve (a periodic orbit) is one and a strange (fractal) set can have a correlation dimension that is not an integer. Correlation dimension is now a standard tool in the area of nonlinear dynamics analysis. We adopt Gaussian Kernel Algorithm (GKA) [40] to estimate correlation dimension.

6.4.2. *Systematic flowchart*

Reviewing the workflow or basic ideas introduced previously, we summarize the contents in sequence by using a flowchart, as listed in Fig. 6.6. In summary, we incorporate neural network, MDL as well as the nonlinear curve fitting and the surrogate data method into one comprehensive modeling module for time series prediction [41, 42]. In other words, the modeling module constitutes three sub-modules with their respective purposes.

6.4.3. *Identification of model residual*

The surrogate data method is used to investigate the model residual of the optimal neural network selected by MDL for the previous two cases. We generate 50 surrogates of the prediction error for each case. The given hypothesis is NH0, i.e. such prediction error is consistent with the i.i.d noise. Suitable embedding dimension is required to estimate the correlation dimension as it is a scale invariant measured on the phase space reconstruction. There is no universal criterion to select the embedding dimension so we employ embedding dimension deviating from two to nine to calculate correlation dimension. The delayed time of phase space reconstruction is chosen to one the same as the time lag of the input vector.

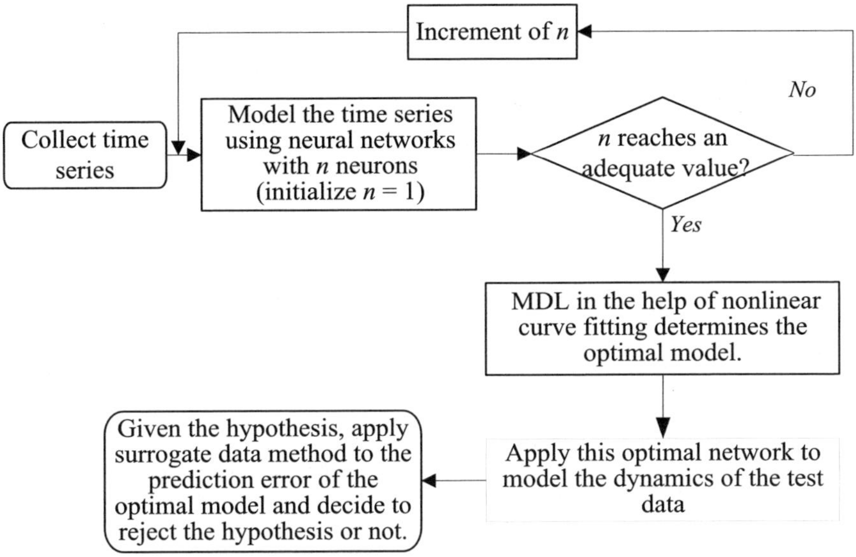

Fig. 6.6. Systematic integration of neural networks, MDL, and the surrogate data method to capture the dynamics of the observed time series.

Based on whether correlation dimension of the model error is out of or in the range of correlation dimension for the surrogates, we can determine whether to reject or fail to reject this given hypothesis. Typical results are depicted in Fig. 6.7.

One can find that the correlation dimension of the original error stays in the range of the mean plus or minus one standard deviation between $d_e = 2$ and $d_e = 6$. Moreover, most of them are close to the average, which means correlation dimension of the original data is close to the center of the distribution of correlation dimension for all the surrogates. Therefore, the original data is not distinguishable from the results of the surrogates. Consequently we cannot reject the given hypothesis. This result indicates that the previous prediction errors are consistent with random noise (i.e. there is no significant determinism in the prediction error). In other words, we conclude that the optimal neural networks estimated by MDL accurately capture the underlying dynamics in both cases.

Note that the behavior of correlation dimension calculated by GKA with embedding dimension higher than six becomes unstable. Large embedding dimension yields unexpected correlation dimension that is even lower than zero for some surrogates. This means that such embedding dimension is

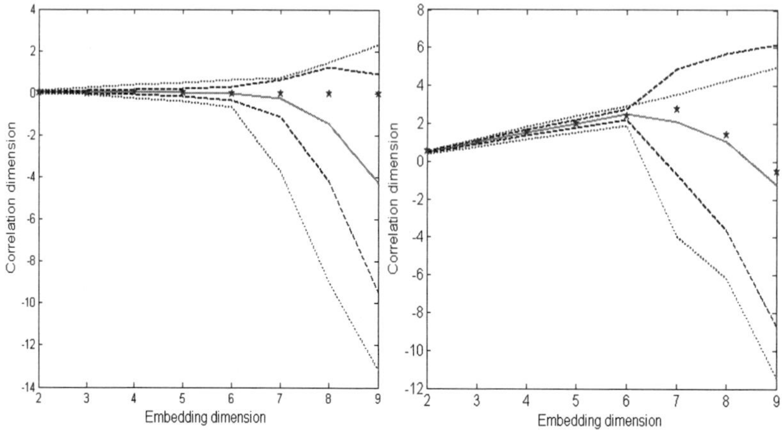

Fig. 6.7. Analysis of the prediction error for the Rössler system (left panel) and human pulse data (right panel). Stars are the correlation dimension of the original model residual of the optimal model; the solid line is the mean of correlation dimension of 50 surrogates at every embedding dimension; two dashed lines denote the mean plus one standard deviation (the upper line) and the mean minus one standard deviation (the lower line); two dotted lines are the maximum and minimum correlation dimension among these surrogates.

inappropriate to estimate correlation dimension. So the proper embedding dimension should be lower than six in both cases.

6.4.4. *Further investigation*

However, it may be possible that the surrogate data method failed to distinguish the deterministic components even though significant determinism exists. To address this problem, we further consider another experiment in which we add the prediction error with (deterministic but independent) observational "noise". The "noise" is from the Rössler system given in the third section. We take the prediction error of pulse modeling as an example.

The magnitude of x-component data is set at 2% of the magnitude of the original prediction error. So the added noise is considerably smaller in contrast to the original prediction error. Relevant results under this scenario are presented in Fig. 6.8, which reveals the deviation between the correlation dimension of the "new" model residual and its surrogates.

Since the deterministic Rössler dynamics is added to the original prediction error, new data should contain the deterministic dynamics. In

Fig. 6.8 we can observe that the correlation dimension of this new error is even further away from the maximal boundary of correlation dimension for surrogate between $d_e = 2$ and $d_e = 6$. So we can reject the given hypothesis that the original error is the i.i.d noise. It is consistent with our expectation. Again, numerical problems with GKA are evident for $d_e \geq 7$.

We notice that the surrogate data method can exhibit the existence of this deterministic structure in the model residual even if it is weak in comparison with the original signal. On the contrary, if there is no difference between the model prediction and data, the surrogate data method can also exhibit corresponding consistency.

We apply the surrogate data method to the residual of the optimal model (i.e. the prediction error). It estimates correlation dimension for this prediction error and its surrogates under the given hypothesis (NH0): the prediction error is consistent with i.i.d noise. According to results, we cannot reject that the prediction error is i.i.d noise. We conclude that with the test statistic at our disposal, the predictions achieved by the optimal neural network and original data are indistinguishable. Combination of neural networks, minimum description length and the surrogate data method provides a comprehensive framework to handle time series prediction. We feel that this technique is important and will be applicable to a wide variety of real-world data.

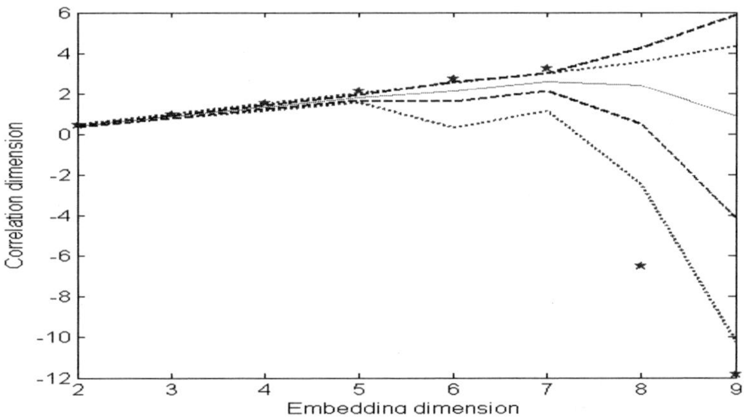

Fig. 6.8. Application of the surrogate data method to the prediction error contaminated with deterministic dynamics. All the donation of curves and symbol are the same as the previous graph.

6.5. The Diploid Model Based on Neural Networks

In the previous section, all the prediction is made based on a single model. However, the observed data may come from various different dynamics. So a single model is not qualified for handling this kind of complicated data. Section 6.4.4 gave an example to describe this case. The single model usually just captures one dominating dynamic but fails to respond to other relatively weak dynamics also hidden in the data. Thus, new integrated model structures are developed to model those data with more dynamics.

It has been well verified that the prediction can be improved significantly by the combination of different methods [43, 44]. Several combining schemes have been proposed to enhance the ability of the neural network. Horn described a combined system of the two feedforward neural networks to predict the future value [45]. Lee *et al.* proposed an integrated model with backpropagation neural networks and self organizing feature map (SOFM) model for bankruptcy prediction [46]. Besides that, the combination of autoregressive integrated moving average model (ARIMA) and neural networks are often mentioned as a common practice to improve prediction accuracy of the practical time series [47, 48]. They both show that the prediction error of the combined model is smaller than just the single model, which exhibits the advantages of the combined model. Inspired by the previous works, we develop an idea of the diploid model for predicting complicated data.

We construct the diploid neural network in a series way, which is defined as the series-wound model (Fig. 6.9). The principle of series-wound diploid model is that after the prediction of model I, its prediction error is used as the input data for model II to compensate the error of model I. The final results will be the sum of each output of both models.

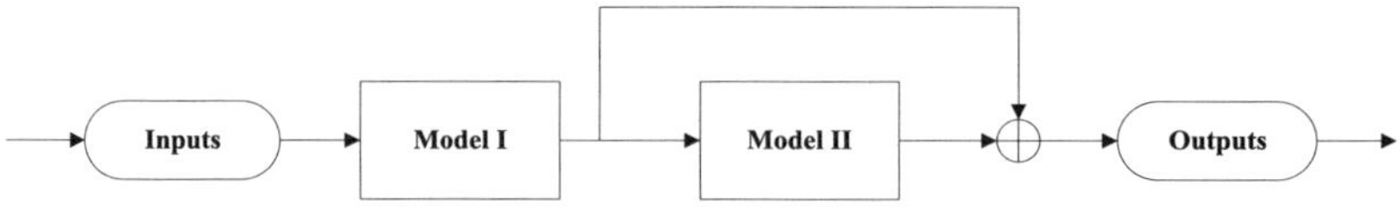

Fig. 6.9. The diploid neural networks constructed in a series-wound.

Suppose that model I is represented by the function $f(\cdot)$, and model II is represented by the function $S(\cdot)$. We briefly describe the principle of the diploid series-wound model as follow:

Model I gives its prediction on the long-term tendency, $\hat{x}_t = f(x)$, where $x = \{x_{t-1}, x_{t-2}, \cdots, x_{t-d}\}$, d is the number of input data and $\hat{x}_t$ denotes the prediction value of model I. Then model II is used for remedying the residual of model I. So we use the prediction error of the previous model as the training set to train it. That is, it aims to capture the short-term dynamics left in the previous model residual. So model II makes its predictions given by the equation $\hat{\hat{x}}_t = S(e)$, where $e = \{e_{t-1}, e_{t-2}, \cdots, e_{t-l}\}$ and l denotes the number of predictions that the previous model obtained. The sum of both equations gives the final prediction on the original time series with the equation $\bar{x}_{t+1} = S(e) + f(x)$. It compensates the missing components of the first prediction with the new prediction of the second model. The final prediction is expected to capture both underlying short-term and long-term tendencies of the data.

As we know, the complicated time series is usually generated by several different dynamics. For simplicity, it is reasonable to classify those dynamics into two categories: fast dynamics and slow dynamics, which determine the short-term and long-term varying tendencies of the time series respectively. We wish to develop an approach of double multi-layer feed-forward neural networks, denominated as the diploid model to capture both dynamics. The large time-scale inputs are fed to the first (global) network while the small time-scale inputs are selected for the second (local) network. At step one an optimal global neural network determined by the minimal description length makes its respective prediction on the original time series to follow the slow dynamics. Local dynamics exist in the model residual of the first one. At step two a local neural network is constructed to remedy global model prediction, i.e. capture the fast dynamics in the previous model residual.

In addition, the surrogate data method can provide an auxiliary measure to confirm the dynamic character of the model residual at each stage so as to validate the performance of the single model and the diploid model. Significantly, this new strategy introduces a new path for establishing the diploid ANN to deal with complex systems.

6.6. Conclusion

The modeling technique concerning artificial neural networks has been widely applied to capture nonlinear dynamics. Here, we address only one of these primary applications: prediction of nonlinear time series. Our interest is to seek the optimal (or appropriate) architecture of the multi-layer neural network to avoid overfitting and further provide adequate generalization for general time series prediction.

In the previous related works, researchers usually focused on optimization of the inherent parameters of the neural networks or training strategies. So these methods do not directly estimate how many neurons of the neural network are sufficient to a specific application. In this chapter, we describe an information theoretic criterion based on minimum description length to decide the optimal model. Moreover, the nonlinear fitted function is defined to reflect the tendency of the original DL curve so as to smooth its fluctuation. The experimental results demonstrate that the fitted curve is quite effective and robust in both computational and practical data sets.

To further confirm the performance of the optimal neural networks, we utilize the standard surrogate data method to analyze the prediction error obtained by these neural networks based on MDL. If the model residual is consistent with the given hypothesis of random noise, it then indicates that there is no deterministic structure in the residual. That is, the optimal model accurately follows dynamics of the data. A comprehensive procedure that integrates the neural network modeling with the surrogate data method is illustrated in this work. Application of the surrogate data method to the model residual paves the way for evaluating the performance of corresponding models. If the result is negative, more cautions are required to use the current model. Or another advanced model is suggested. The idea of a diploid model is then presented to deal with the complex system prediction. It aims to follow both short-term and long-term varying tendencies of the time series. The related work is in progress, and the preliminary results show its great advantage of modeling the simulated time series composed of components of the Lorenz system and Ikeda map.

Acknowledgments

This work was supported by the China National Natural Science Foundation Grant No. 60801014, the Natural Science Foundation Grant of Guangdong Province No. 9451805707002363 and the Scientific Plan of Nanshan District, Shenzhen, China.

References

[1] B. Lippmann, Pattern classification using neural networks, *Communications Magazine.* **27**, 47–50, (1989).

[2] P. J. Antsaklis, Neural networks for control systems, *Neural Networks.* **1**, 242–244, (1990).
[3] G. P. Zhang, Neural networks for classification: A survey, *IEEE Transactions on Systems, Man, and Cybernetics – Part C: Application and Review.* **30**, 451–462, (2000).
[4] G. E. P. Box, G. M. Jenkins, and G. C. Reinsel, *Time Series Analysis: Forecasting and Control.* (Prentice Hall, Upper Saddle River, 1994).
[5] P. J. Antsaklis, Approximations by superpositions of sigmoidal functions, *Mathematics of Control, Signals, and Systems.* **2**, 303–314, (1990).
[6] K. Hornik, Approximation capabilities of multilayer feedforward networks, *Neural Networks.* **4**, 251–257, (1991).
[7] A. Lapedes and R. Farber, Nonlinear signal processing using neural network prediction and system modeling, *Technical Report.* (1987).
[8] R. L. Wilson and R. Sharda, Bankruptcy prediction using neural networks, *Decision Support Systems.* **11**, 545–557, (1994).
[9] F.-M. Tseng, H.-C. Yu, and G.-H. Tzeng, Combining neural network model with seasonal time series ARIMA model, *Technological Forecasting and Social Change.* **69**, 71–87, (2002).
[10] P. C. Chang, C. Y. Lai, and K. R. Lai, A hybrid system by evolving case-based reasoning with genetic algorithm in wholesaler's returning book forecasting, *Decision Support Systems.* **42**, 1715–1729, (2006).
[11] D. Shanthi, G. Sahoo, and N. Saravanan, Designing an artificial neural network model for the prediction of Thrombo-embolic stroke, *International Journals of Biometric and Bioinformatics.* **3**, 10–18, (2009).
[12] A. Weigend, On overfitting and the effective number of hidden units, *Proceedings of the 1993 Connectionist Models Summer School.* pp. 335–342, (1994).
[13] J. E. Moody, S. J. Hanson, and R. P. Lippmann, The effective number of parameters: An analysis of generalization and regularization in nonlinear learning systems, *Advances in Neural Information Processing Systems.* **4**, 847–854, (1992).
[14] D. J. C. MacKay, Bayesian interpolation, *Neural Computation.* **4**, 415–447, (1992).
[15] Y. Zhao and M. Small, Minimum description length criterion for modeling of chaotic attractors with multilayer perceptron networks, *IEEE Transactions on Circuit and Systems-I: Regular Papers.* **53**, 722–732, (2006).
[16] J. Rissanen, *Stochastic Complexity in Statistical Inquiry.* (World Scientific, Singapore, 1989).
[17] M. Li and P. Vitnyi, *An Introduction of Kolmogorov and its Applications.* (Springer–Verlag, Berlin, 2009).
[18] J. Rissanen, Modeling by the shortest data description, *Automatica.* **14**, 465–471, (1978).
[19] K. Judd and A. Mees, On selecting models for nonlinear time series, *Physica D.* **82**, 426–444, (2009).
[20] M. Small and C. K. Tse, Minimum description length neural networks for time series prediction, *Physical Review E.* **66**, (2009).

[21] L. Xu, Advances on BYY harmony learning: Information theoretic perspective generalized projection geometry and independent factor autodetermination, *Neural Networks.* **15**, 885–902, (2004).
[22] C. Alippi, Selecting accurate, robust, and minimal feedforward neural networks, *IEEE. Transactions on Circurits and Systems I: Regular Papers.* **49**, 1799–1810, (2002).
[23] H. Bischof and A. Leonardis, Finding optimal neural networks for land use classification, *IEEE Transactions on Geoscience and Remote Sensing.* **36**, 337–341, (1998).
[24] X. M. Gao, Modeling of speech signals using an optimal neural network structure based on the PMDL principle, *IEEE Transactions on Speech and Audio Processing.* **6**, 177–180, (1998).
[25] A. Galka, *Topics in Nonlinear Time Series Analysis with Applications for ECG Analysis.* (World Scientific, Singapore, 2000).
[26] D. W. Baker and N. L. Carter, Testing for nonlinearity in time series: the method of surrogate data, *Physica D.* **58**, 77–94, (1972).
[27] H. Demuth and M. Beale, *Neural Network Toolbox User's Guide.* (The Math Works, USA, 1998).
[28] M. T. Hagan and M. Menhaj, Training feedforward networks with the Marquardt algorithm, *Neural Networks.* **5**, 989–993, (1994).
[29] H. Akaike, A new look at the statistical model identification, *IEEE Transactions on Automatic Control.* **19**, 716–723, (1974).
[30] G. Schwarz, Estimating the dimension of a model, *The Annals of Statistics.* **6**, 461–464, (2009).
[31] M. Stone, Comments on model selection criteria of Akaike and Schwarz, *The Royal Statistical Society.* **41**, 276–278, (1979).
[32] J. Rice, Bandwidth choice for nonparameteric regression, *The Annals of Statistics.* **12**, 1215–1230, (1984).
[33] Z. Liang, R. J. Jaszczak, and R. E. Coleman, Parameter estimation of finite mixtures using the EM algorithm and information criteria with application to medical image processing, *IEEE Transactions on Nuclear Science.* **39**, 1126–1133, (1992).
[34] C. Wallace and D. Boulton, An information measure for classification, *Computing Journal.* **11**, 185–195, (1972).
[35] B. A. Barron and J. Rissanen, The minimum description length principle in coding and modeling, *IEEE Transactions on Information Theory.* **4**, 2743–2760, (1972).
[36] M. B. Kennel, R. Brown, and H. D. I. Abarbanel, Determining embedding dimension for phase-space reconstruction using a geometrical construction, *Physical Review A.* **45**, 3403–3411, (1992).
[37] O. E. Rossler, An equation for continuous chaos, *Physics Letters A.* **57**, 397–398, (1976).
[38] J. Theiler, Testing for nonlinearity in time series: The method of surrogate data, *Physica. D.* **58**, 77–94, (1992).
[39] M. Small and C. K. Tse, Applying the method of surrogate data to cyclic time series, *Physica D.* **164**, 182–202, (2002).

[40] D. Yu, Efficient implementation of the Gaussian kernel algorithm in estimating invariants and noise level from noisy time series data, *Physical Review E.* **61**, 3750, (2000).
[41] Y. Zhao and M. Small, Equivalence between "feeling the pulse" on the human wrist and the pulse pressure wave at fingertip, *International Journal of Neural Systems.* **15**, 277–286, (2005).
[42] Y. Zhao, J. F. Sum, and M. Small, Evidence consistent with deterministic chaos in human cardiac data: Surrogate and nonlinear dynamical modeling, *International Journal of Bifurcations and Chaos.* **18**, 141–160, (2008).
[43] S. Makridakis, Why combining works, *International Journal of Forecasting.* **5**, 601–603, (1989).
[44] F. Palm and A. Zellner, To combine or not to combine? Issue of combining forecasts, *International Journal of Forecasting.* **11**, 687–701, (1992).
[45] G. D. Horn and I. Ginzburg, Combined neural networks for time series analysis, *Neural Information Processing Systems - NIPS.* **6**, 224–231, (1994).
[46] K. C. Lee, I. Han, and Y. Kwon, Hybrid neural network models for bankruptcy predictions, *Decision Support Systems.* **18**, 63–72, (1996).
[47] G. P. Zhang, Time series forecasting using a hybrid ARIMA and neural network model, *Neurocomputing.* **50**, 159–175, (2003).
[48] L. Aburto and R. Weber, Improved supply chain management based on hybrid demand forecasts, *Applied Soft Computing.* **7**, 136–144, (2007).

Chapter 7

Solving Eigen-problems of Matrices by Neural Networks

[1]Yiguang Liu, [1]Zhisheng You, [2]Bingbing Liu and [1]Jiliu Zhou

[1] *Video and Image Processing Lab, School of Computer Science & Engineering, Sichuan University, China 610065,*
liuyg@scu.edu.cn

[2] *Data Storage Institute, A* STAR, Singapore 138632*

How to efficiently solve eigen-problems of matrices is always a significant issue in engineering. Neural networks run in an asynchronous manner, and thus applying neural networks to address these problems can attain high performance. In this chapter, several recurrent neural network models are proposed to handle eigen-problems of matrices. Each model is expressed as an individual differential equation, with its analytic solution being derived. Subsequently, the convergence properties of the neural network models are fully discussed based on the solutions to these differential equations. Finally, the computation steps are designed toward solving the eigen-problems, with numerical simulations being provided to evaluate the effectiveness of each model.

This chapter consists of three major parts, with each approach in these three parts being in the form of neural networks. Section 7.1 presents how to solve the eigen-problems of real symmetric matrices; Sections 7.2 and 7.3 are devoted to addressing the eigen-problems of anti-symmetric matrices; Section 7.4 aims at solving eigen-problems of general matrices, which are neither symmetric nor anti-symmetric.

Finally, conclusions are made in Section 7.5 to summarize the whole chapter.

Contents

7.1. A Simple Recurrent Neural Network for Computing the Largest and Smallest Eigenvalues and Corresponding Eigenvectors of a Real Symmetric Matrix

Using neural networks to compute eigenvalues and eigenvectors of a matrix is both quick and parallel. Fast computation of eigenvalues and eigenvectors has many applications, e.g. primary component analysis (PCA) for image compression and adaptive signal processing etc. Thus, many research works in this field have been reported [1–11]. Zhang Yi *et al.* [8] proposed a recurrent neural network (RNN) to compute eigenvalues and eigenvectors of a real symmetric matrix, which is as follows

$$\frac{dx(t)}{dt} = -x(t) + \left[x^T(t)\,x(t)\,A + \left(1 - x^T(t)\,Ax(t)\right)I\right]x(t),$$

where $t \geq 0$, $x = (x_1, \cdots, x_n)^T \in R^n$ represents the states of neurons, I is an identity matrix, the matrix $A \in R^{n\times n}$ waiting for computing eigenvalues and eigenvectors is symmetric. Obviously, this neural network is wholly equivalent to the following neural networks

$$\frac{dx(t)}{dt} = x^T(t)\,x(t)\,Ax(t) - x^T(t)\,Ax(t)\,x(t). \tag{7.1}$$

We propose a new neural network that is applicable to computing eigenvalues and eigenvectors of real symmetric matrices, which is described as follows

$$\frac{dx(t)}{dt} = Ax(t) - x^T(t)\,x(t)\,x(t)\,, \tag{7.2}$$

where $t \geq 0$, definitions of A and $x(t)$ accord with A and $x(t)$ in Equation (7.1). When $A - x^T(t)\,x(t)$ is looked at as synaptic connection weights that vary with $x^T(t)\,x(t)$ and is regarded as a function of $x^T(t)\,x(t)$, and the neuron activation functions are supposed as pure linear functions, Equation (7.2) can be seen as a recurrent neural network (RNN (7.2)). Evidently, RNN (7.2) is simpler than RNN (7.1), which has important meanings for electronic designing; the connection is much less than RNN (7.1), and the electronic circuitry of RNN (7.2) is more concise than RNN (7.1). Therefore, the realization of RNN (7.2) is easier than RNN (7.1). Moreover, the performance is close to that of RNN (7.1), which can be seen in Section 7.1.3.

7.1.1. *Preliminaries*

All eigenvalues of A are denoted as $\lambda_1 \geq \lambda_2 \geq \cdots \geq \lambda_n$, and their corresponding eigenvectors and eigensubspaces are denoted as $\mu_1, \cdots, \mu_n$ and $V_1, \cdots, V_n$. $\lceil x \rceil$ denotes the most minimal integer which is not less than x. $\lfloor x \rfloor$ denotes the most maximal integer which is not larger than x.

Lemma 7.1. *$\lambda_1 + \alpha \geq \lambda_2 + \alpha \geq \cdots \geq \lambda_n + \alpha$ are eigenvalues of $A + \alpha I$ $(\alpha \in R)$ and $\mu_1, \cdots, \mu_n$ are the eigenvectors corresponding to $\lambda_1 + \alpha, \cdots, \lambda_n + \alpha$.*

Proof: From

$$A\mu_i = \lambda_i \mu_i, \quad i = 1, \cdots, n.$$

It follows that

$$A\mu_i + \alpha\mu_i = \lambda_i\mu_i + \alpha\mu_i, i = 1, \cdots, n$$

i.e.

$$(A + \alpha I)\,\mu_i = (\lambda_i + \alpha)\,\mu_i, i = 1, \cdots, n.$$

Therefore, this lemma is correct.

When RNN (7.2) approaches equilibrium state, we get the following relation from Equation (7.2)

$$A\xi = \xi^T\xi\xi,$$

where $\xi \in R^n$ is the equilibrium vector. If $\|\xi\| \neq 0$, ξ is an eigenvector, and the corresponding eigenvalue λ is

$$\lambda = \xi^T \xi. \tag{7.3}$$

7.1.2. *Analytic solution of RNN*

Theorem 7.1. *Denote $S_i = \frac{\mu_i}{\|\mu_i\|}$. $z_i(t)$ denotes the projection value of $x(t)$ onto S_i, then the analytic solution of RNN (7.2) is presented as*

$$x(t) = \frac{\sum\limits_{i=1}^{n} z_i(0) \exp(\lambda_i t) S_i}{\sqrt{1 + \sum\limits_{j=1}^{n} z_j^2(0) \int_0^t \exp(2\lambda_j \tau) d\tau}}. \tag{7.4}$$

Proof: Recurring to the properties of real symmetric matrices, we know $S_1, \cdots, S_n$ construct a normalized perpendicular basis of $R^{n\times n}$. So, $x(t) \in R^n$ can be presented as

$$x(t) = \sum_{i=1}^{n} z_i(t) S_i. \tag{7.5}$$

Taking Equation (7.5) into Equation (7.2), we get

$$\frac{d}{dt} z_i(t) = \lambda_i z_i(t) - \sum_{j=1}^{n} z_j^2(t) z_i(t),$$

when $z_i(t) \neq 0$

$$\lambda_i - \frac{1}{z_i(t)} \frac{d}{dt} z_i(t) = \sum_{j=1}^{n} z_j^2(t).$$

Therefore

$$\lambda_i - \frac{1}{z_i(t)} \frac{d}{dt} z_i(t) = \lambda_r - \frac{1}{z_r(t)} \frac{d}{dt} z_r(t) \quad (r = 1, \cdots, n),$$

so

$$\frac{z_i(t)}{z_r(t)} = \frac{z_i(0)}{z_r(0)} \exp[(\lambda_i - \lambda_r) t] \tag{7.6}$$

for $t \geq 0$. From Equation (7.2), we can also get

$$\frac{d}{dt}\left[\frac{1}{z_r^2(t)}\right] = -2\lambda_r \frac{1}{z_r^2(t)} + 2\sum_{j=1}^{n}\left[\frac{z_j(t)}{z_r(t)}\right]^2. \tag{7.7}$$

Taking Equation (7.6) into Equation (7.7), we have

$$\frac{d}{dt}\left[\frac{1}{z_r^2(t)}\right] = -2\lambda_r \frac{1}{z_r^2(t)} + 2\sum_{j=1}^{n}\left[\frac{z_j(0)}{z_r(0)}\right]^2 \exp\left[2(\lambda_j - \lambda_r)t\right],$$

i.e.

$$\frac{\exp(2\lambda_r t)}{z_r^2(t)} - \frac{1}{z_r^2(0)} = 2\sum_{j=1}^{n}\left[\frac{z_j(0)}{z_r(0)}\right]^2 \int_0^t \exp(2\lambda_j \tau)\, d\tau,$$

so

$$z_r(t) = \frac{z_r(0)\exp(\lambda_r t)}{\sqrt{1 + 2\sum\limits_{j=1}^{n} z_j^2(0)\int_0^t \exp(2\lambda_j \tau)\, d\tau}}. \tag{7.8}$$

So, from Equations (7.5), (7.6) and (7.8), it follows that

$$\begin{aligned} x(t) &= \sum_{i=1}^{n} z_i(t) S_i \\ &= \sum_{i=1}^{n} \frac{z_i(t)}{z_r(t)} z_r(t) S_i \\ &= \sum_{i=1}^{n} \frac{z_i(0)}{z_r(0)} \exp\left[(\lambda_i - \lambda_r)t\right] \frac{z_r(0)\exp(\lambda_r t) S_i}{\sqrt{1+2\sum\limits_{j=1}^{n} z_j^2(0)\int_0^t \exp(2\lambda_j \tau) d\tau}} \\ &= \frac{\sum\limits_{i=1}^{n} z_i(0)\exp(\lambda_i t) S_i}{\sqrt{1+2\sum\limits_{j=1}^{n} z_j^2(0)\int_0^t \exp(2\lambda_j \tau) d\tau}}. \end{aligned} \tag{7.9}$$

So, Theorem 7.2 shown in the following can be achieved.

7.1.3. *Convergence analysis of RNN*

Theorem 7.2. *For nonzero initial vector $x(0) \in V_i$, the equilibrium vector ξ may be trivial or $\xi \in V_i$. If $\xi \in V_i$, $\xi^T \xi$ is the eigenvalue λ_i.*

Proof: Since $x(0) \in V_i$, $V_i \perp V_j$ $(1 \le j \le n, j \ne i)$, the projections of $x(0)$ onto V_j $(1 \le j \le n, j \ne i)$ are zero. Therefore, from Equation (7.9), it follows that

$$
\begin{aligned}
x(t) &= \frac{\sum_{k=1}^{n} z_k(0)\exp(\lambda_k t)S_k}{\sqrt{1+2\sum_{j=1}^{n} z_j^2(0)\int_0^t \exp(2\lambda_j\tau)d\tau}} \\
&= \frac{z_i(0)\exp(\lambda_i t)S_i}{\sqrt{1+2\sum_{j=1}^{n} z_j^2(0)\int_0^t \exp(2\lambda_j\tau)d\tau}} \\
&\in V_i,
\end{aligned}
$$

so, $\xi \in V_i$. From Equation (7.3), we know $\xi^T\xi$ is the eigenvalue λ_i.

Theorem 7.3. *If nonzero initial vector $x(0) \notin V_i\,(i = 1, \cdots, n)$ and the equilibrium vector $\|\xi\| \neq 0$, then $\xi \in V_1$, $\xi^T\xi$ is the largest eigenvalue λ_1.*

Proof: Since $x(0) \notin V_i\,(i = 1, \cdots, n)$, the projection of $x(0)$ onto V_i $(1 \le i \le n)$ is nonzero, i.e.

$$z_i(0) \neq 0 \quad (1 \le i \le n).$$

From Theorem 7.1, it follows that

$$
\begin{aligned}
x(t) &= \frac{\sum_{i=1}^{n} z_i(0)\exp(\lambda_i t)S_i}{\sqrt{1+2\sum_{j=1}^{n} z_j^2(0)\int_0^t \exp(2\lambda_j\tau)d\tau}} \\
&= \frac{z_1(0)\exp(\lambda_1 t)S_1+\sum_{i=2}^{n} z_i(0)\exp(\lambda_i t)S_i}{\sqrt{1+2z_1^2(0)\int_0^t \exp(2\lambda_1\tau)d\tau+2\sum_{j=2}^{n} z_j^2(0)\int_0^t \exp(2\lambda_j\tau)d\tau}},
\end{aligned}
$$

and $\lambda_1 \le 0$ will make $\|\xi\| = 0$. So $\lambda_1 > 0$ and

$$x(t) = \frac{z_1(0)S_1+\sum_{i=2}^{n} z_i(0)\exp[(\lambda_i-\lambda_1)t]S_i}{\sqrt{\exp(-2\lambda_1 t)+\frac{z_1^2(0)}{\lambda_1}[\exp(2\lambda_1 t)-1]\exp(-2\lambda_1 t)+2\sum_{j=2}^{n} z_j^2(0)\int_0^t \exp[(2\lambda_j\tau)-(2\lambda_1 t)]d\tau}}.$$

Therefore, it holds that

$$
\begin{aligned}
\xi &= \lim_{t\to\infty} x(t) \\
&= \lim_{t\to\infty} \frac{z_1(0)S_1+\sum_{i=2}^{n} z_i(0)\exp[(\lambda_i-\lambda_1)t]S_i}{\sqrt{\exp(-2\lambda_1 t)+\frac{z_1^2(0)}{\lambda_1}[\exp(2\lambda_1 t)-1]\exp(-2\lambda_1 t)+2\sum_{j=2}^{n} z_j^2(0)\int_0^t \exp[(2\lambda_j\tau)-(2\lambda_1 t)]d\tau}}, \\
&= \sqrt{\frac{\lambda_1}{z_1^2(0)}}\, z_1(0)\, S_1 \\
&\in V_1
\end{aligned}
\tag{7.10}
$$

and

$$\begin{aligned}\xi^T\xi &= \sqrt{\tfrac{\lambda_1}{z_1^2(0)}}z_1\left(0\right)S_1^T S_1\sqrt{\tfrac{\lambda_1}{z_1^2(0)}}z_1\left(0\right) \\ &= \lambda_1.\end{aligned} \tag{7.11}$$

From Equations (7.10) and (7.11), we know this theorem is proved.

Theorem 7.4. *Replace A with $-A$, If nonzero initial vector $x\left(0\right) \notin V_i\left(i = 1, \cdots, n\right)$ and the equilibrium vector $\|\xi\| \neq 0$, then $\xi \in V_n$, $\lambda_n = -\xi^T\xi$.*

Proof: Replace A with $-A$, it follows that

$$\frac{dx\left(t\right)}{dt} = -Ax\left(t\right) - x^T\left(t\right)x\left(t\right)x\left(t\right). \tag{7.12}$$

For RNN (7.12), from Theorem 7.3, we know that if $|x\left(0\right)| \neq 0$, $x\left(0\right) \notin V_i\left(i = 1, \cdots, n\right)$ and the equilibrium vector $\|\xi\| \neq 0$, ξ belongs to the eigenspace corresponding to the largest eigenvalue of $-A$. Because the eigenvalues of $-A$ are $-\lambda_n \geq -\lambda_{n-1} \geq \cdots \geq -\lambda_1$. Therefore, $\xi \in V_n$ and $\xi^T\xi = -\lambda_n$, i.e. $\lambda_n = -\xi^T\xi$.

Theorem 7.5. *When A is positive definite, RNN (7.2) cannot compute λ_n by replacing A with $-A$. When A is negative definite, RNN (7.2) cannot compute λ_1*

Proof: When A is positive definite, the eigenvalues $\lambda_1 \geq \lambda_2 \geq \cdots \geq \lambda_n > 0$, there exists a vector $\varsigma \in R^n$ which matches $\varsigma^T\varsigma = \lambda_1$. Therefore, the RNN (7.2) will converge to a nonzero vector $\xi \in R^n$ that matches $\xi^T\xi = \lambda_1$. Replace A with $-A$, since $0 > -\lambda_n \geq -\lambda_{n-1} \geq \cdots \geq -\lambda_1$, there does not exist a vector $\varsigma \in R^n$, which matches $\varsigma^T\varsigma = -\lambda_n$. So, when A is positive definite, RNN (7.2) will converge to zero vector when A is replaced by $-A$. While if A is negative definite, there does not exist a vector that matches $\varsigma^T\varsigma = \lambda_1$, RNN (7.2) will converge to zero. However, there exists a vector $\zeta \in R^n$, which matches $\xi^T\xi = -\lambda_n$, so, RNN (7.2) can compute λ_n by replacing A with $-A$ when A is negative definite.

Theorem 7.6. *When A is positive definite, if A in RNN (7.2) is replaced with $-\left(A - \lceil\lambda_1\rceil I\right)$, then λ_n can be computed from the equilibrium vector ξ as*

$$\lambda_n = -\xi^T\xi + \lceil\lambda_1\rceil. \tag{7.13}$$

for the nonzero initial vector $x\left(0\right) \notin V_i\left(i = 1, \cdots, n\right)$.

Proof: Let $\lambda_n^{'}$ denote the smallest eigenvalue of $(A - \lceil\lambda_1\rceil I)$. Since A is positive definite, so, the smallest eigenvalue of $(A - \lceil\lambda_1\rceil I)$ is negative, therefore ξ is nonzero when A is replaced by $-(A - \lceil\lambda_1\rceil I)$, from Theorem 7.4, it follows that

$$\lambda_n^{'} = -\xi^T\xi. \tag{7.14}$$

From Lemma 7.1, we know that

$$\lambda_n^{'} = \lambda_n - \lceil\lambda_1\rceil. \tag{7.15}$$

From Equations (7.14) and (7.15), it follows Equation (7.13).

Theorem 7.7. *When A is negative definite, if A in RNN (7.2) is replaced with $(A - \lfloor\lambda_n\rfloor I)$, then λ_1 can be computed from the equilibrium vector ξ as*

$$\lambda_1 = \xi^T\xi + \lfloor\lambda_n\rfloor. \tag{7.16}$$

for nonzero initial vector $x(0) \notin V_i\ (i = 1, \cdots, n)$.

Proof: As similar to the proof of Theorem 7.6, the proof of this theorem is thus omitted.

Theorem 7.8. *The trajectory of RNN (7.2) will converge to zero or spherical surface whose radius is the square root of a positive eigenvalue of A.*

Proof: From Equation (7.9), we know

$$x(t) = \frac{\sum\limits_{i=1}^{n} z_i(0)\exp(\lambda_i t) S_i}{\sqrt{1 + 2\sum\limits_{j=1}^{n} z_j^2(0)\int_0^t \exp(2\lambda_j\tau)\,d\tau}},$$

for the equilibrium vector ξ, if $0 > \lambda_1 \geq \lambda_2 \geq \cdots \geq \lambda_n$, it follows that

$$\begin{aligned}
\xi &= \lim_{t\to\infty} x(t) \\
&= \lim_{t\to\infty} \frac{\sum\limits_{i=1}^{n} z_i(0)\exp(\lambda_i t)S_i}{\sqrt{1+2\sum\limits_{j=1}^{n} z_j^2(0)\int_0^t \exp(2\lambda_j\tau)d\tau}} \\
&= \frac{\sum\limits_{i=1}^{n} z_i(0)\lim\limits_{t\to\infty}\exp(\lambda_i t)S_i}{\sqrt{1+2\lim\limits_{t\to\infty}\sum\limits_{j=1}^{n} z_j^2(0)\int_0^t \exp(2\lambda_j\tau)d\tau}} \\
&= 0.
\end{aligned} \tag{7.17}$$

Suppose $\lambda_1 \geq \lambda_2 \geq \cdots \geq \lambda_k > 0 \geq \lambda_{k+1} \geq \cdots \geq \lambda_n$. The first nonzero projection is $z_p(0) \neq 0 \quad (1 \leq p \leq n)$. Then we get two cases:

1) If $1 \leq p \leq k$, it follows that

$$\begin{aligned}
\xi &= \lim_{t\to\infty} x(t) \\
&= \lim_{t\to\infty} \frac{\sum_{i=p}^{k} z_i(0)\exp(\lambda_i t)S_i + \sum_{i=k+1}^{n} z_i(0)\exp(\lambda_i t)S_i}{\sqrt{1+2\sum_{j=1}^{n} z_j^2(0)\int_0^t \exp(2\lambda_j\tau)d\tau}} \\
&= \frac{z_p(0)S_p + \lim_{t\to\infty}\sum_{i=p+1}^{k} z_i(0)\exp(\lambda_i t-\lambda_p t)S_i + \lim_{t\to\infty}\sum_{i=k+1}^{n} z_i(0)\exp(\lambda_i t-\lambda_p t)S_i}{\sqrt{1+\lim_{t\to\infty}\left\{z_p^2(0)[1-\exp(-2\lambda_p t)]/\lambda_p + 2\sum_{j=p+1}^{n} z_j^2(0)\int_0^t \exp(2\lambda_j\tau-2\lambda_p t)d\tau\right\}}} \\
&= z_p(0)\sqrt{\lambda_p/z_p^2(0)}S_p,
\end{aligned}$$

so

$$\begin{aligned}
\|\xi\| &= \sqrt{\xi^T\xi} \\
&= \sqrt{z_p^T(0)\,z_p(0)\sqrt{\lambda_p/z_p^2(0)}\sqrt{\lambda_p/z_p^2(0)}S_p^T S_p} \\
&= \sqrt{\lambda_p}.
\end{aligned} \tag{7.18}$$

2) If $k+1 \leq p \leq n$, it follows that

$$\begin{aligned}
\xi &= \lim_{t\to\infty} x(t) \\
&= \lim_{t\to\infty} \frac{\sum_{i=p}^{n} z_i(0)\exp(\lambda_i t)S_i}{\sqrt{1+2\sum_{p=1}^{n} z_j^2(0)\int_0^t \exp(2\lambda_j\tau)d\tau}}. \\
&= 0
\end{aligned} \tag{7.19}$$

From Equations (7.17), (7.18) and (7.19), we know that the theorem is correct.

7.1.4. *Steps to compute λ_1 and λ_n*

In this section, we provide the steps to compute the largest eigenvalue and the smallest eigenvalue of a real symmetric matrix $B \in R^{n\times n}$ with RNN (7.2), which are as follows:

7.1.5. *Simulation*

We provide three examples to evaluate the method integrated by RNN (7.2) and the five steps for computing the smallest eignevalue and the largest

Table 7.1. Steps computing λ_1 and λ_n.

Step 1	Replace A with B. If equilibrium vector $\|\xi\| \neq 0$, we get $\lambda_1 = \xi^T\xi$.
Step 2	Replace A with $-B$. If equilibrium vector $\|\xi\| \neq 0$, we get $\lambda_n = -\xi^T\xi$. If λ_1 has been received, go to step 5. Otherwise, go to step 3. If $\|\xi\| = 0$, go to step 4.
Step 3	Replace A with $(B - \lfloor\lambda_n\rfloor I)$, and we get $\lambda_1 = \xi^T\xi + \lfloor\lambda_n\rfloor$. Go to step 5.
Step 4	Replace A with $-(B - \lceil\lambda_1\rceil I)$, and we get $\lambda_n = -\xi^T\xi + \lceil\lambda_1\rceil$. Go to step 5.
Step 5	End.

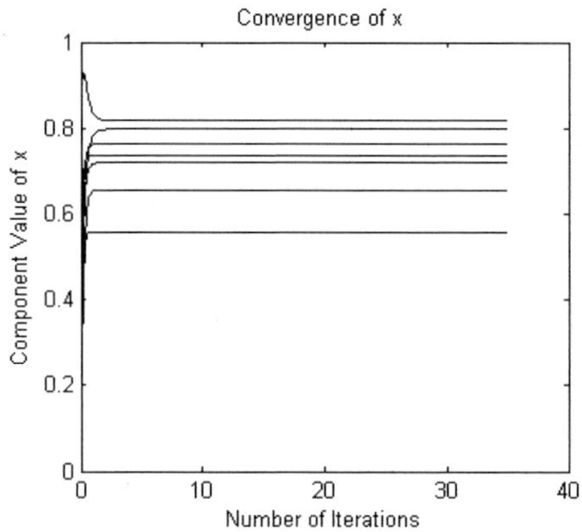

Fig. 7.1. The trajectories of the components of x when A is replaced with B.

eigenvalue of a real symmetric matrix. The simulating platform we used is Matlab.

Example 1: A real 7×7 symmetric matrix is randomly generated as

$$B = \begin{pmatrix} 0.4116 & 0.3646 & 0.5513 & 0.6659 & 0.5836 & 0.6280 & 0.4079 \\ 0.3646 & 0.4668 & 0.3993 & 0.4152 & 0.4059 & 0.4198 & 0.3919 \\ 0.5513 & 0.3993 & 0.9862 & 0.4336 & 0.6732 & 0.2326 & 0.8687 \\ 0.6659 & 0.4152 & 0.4336 & 0.5208 & 0.5422 & 0.5827 & 0.5871 \\ 0.5836 & 0.4059 & 0.6732 & 0.5422 & 0.3025 & 0.8340 & 0.4938 \\ 0.6280 & 0.4198 & 0.2326 & 0.5827 & 0.8340 & 0.9771 & 0.3358 \\ 0.4079 & 0.3919 & 0.8687 & 0.5871 & 0.4938 & 0.3358 & 0.1722 \end{pmatrix}.$$

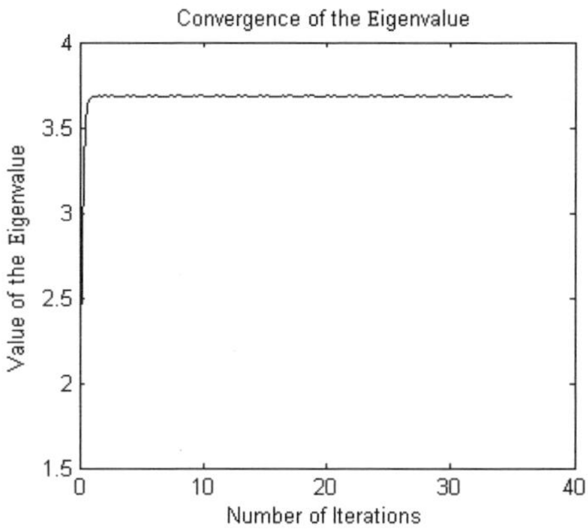

Fig. 7.2. The trajectories of $\lambda_1(t) = x^T(t)x(t)$ when A is replaced with B.

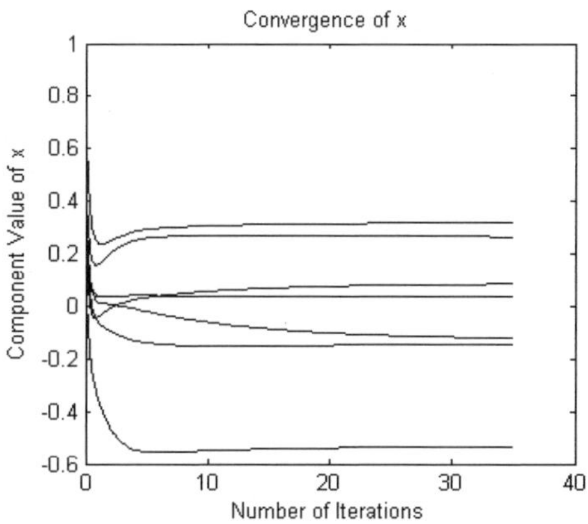

Fig. 7.3. The trajectories of the components of x when A is replaced with $-B$.

Through step 1, we get

$$\xi_1 = (0.7199\ 0.5577\ 0.8172\ 0.7356\ 0.7637\ 0.7979\ 0.6542)^T.$$

So, $\lambda_1 = \xi_1^T \xi_1 = 3.6860$. The trajectories of $x_i(t) \quad (i = 1, 2, \cdots, 7)$ and $\lambda_1(t) = x(t)^T x(t) = \sum_{i=1}^{7} x_i^2(t)$ are shown in Figs 7.1 and 7.2. From Figs 7.1 and 7.2, we can see that RNN (7.2) quickly reaches the equilibrium state and the largest eigenvalue is obtained. Through step 2, we get $\xi_n = (-0.1454\ 0.0388\ 0.3184\ 0.2658\ -0.1201\ 0.0846\ -0.5324)^T$ and $\lambda_n = -\xi_n^T \xi_n = -0.4997$. The trajectories of $x_i(t) \quad (i = 1, 2, \cdots, 7)$ and

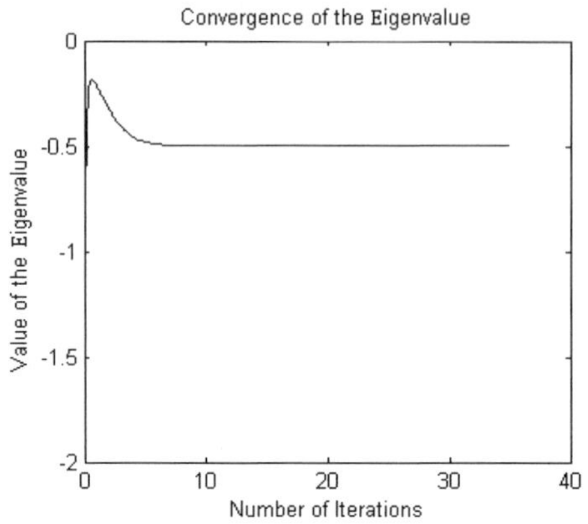

Fig. 7.4. The trajectories of $\lambda_n(t) = -x^T(t)x(t)$ when A is replaced with $-B$.

$\lambda_n(t) = -x(t)^T x(t) = -\sum_{i=1}^{7} x_i^2(t)$ are shown in Figs 7.3 and 7.4. By using Matlab to directly compute the eigenvalues of B, we get the "ground truth" largest eigenvalue $\lambda_1^{'} = 3.6862$ and the smallest eigenvalue $\lambda_n^{'} = -0.4997$.

Therefore, compare the results received by the RNN (7.2) approach with the ground truth, the absolute difference values are

$$\left|\lambda_1 - \lambda_1^{'}\right| = 0.0002,$$

and

$$\left|\lambda_n - \lambda_n^{'}\right| = 0.0000.$$

This verifies that the RNN (7.2) can compute the largest eigenvalue and the smallest eigenvalue of B successfully.

Example 2: Use Matlab to generate a positive matrix that is

$$C = \begin{pmatrix} 0.6495 & 0.5538 & 0.5519 & 0.5254 \\ 0.5538 & 0.8607 & 0.7991 & 0.5583 \\ 0.5519 & 0.7991 & 0.8863 & 0.4508 \\ 0.5254 & 0.5583 & 0.4508 & 0.6775 \end{pmatrix},$$

the ground truth eigenvalues of C directly computed by Matlab are $\lambda' = (0.0420\ 0.1496\ 0.3664\ 2.5160)$. From step 1, we can get $\lambda_1 = 2.5159$, the trajectories of $x(t)$ and $x^T(t)x(t)$ which will approach to λ_1 are shown in Figs 7.5 and 7.6. For step 2, the trajectories of $x(t)$ and $\lambda_n = -x^T(t)x(t)$ are shown in Figs 7.7 and 7.8. The equilibrium vector $\xi_n = (-0.0010\ -0.0028\ 0.0025\ 0.0015)^T$ and $\lambda_n = -\xi_n^T \xi_n = -1.7615 \times 10^{-5}$, obviously, λ_n is approaching to zero. So use step 4 to compute the smallest eigenvalue, and replace A with

$$C' = -\left(C - \lceil \lambda_1 \rceil I\right) = -\begin{pmatrix} -2.3505 & 0.5538 & 0.5519 & 0.5254 \\ 0.5538 & -2.1393 & 0.7991 & 0.5583 \\ 0.5519 & 0.7991 & -2.1137 & 0.4508 \\ 0.5254 & 0.5583 & 0.4508 & -2.3225 \end{pmatrix},$$

the trajectories of $x(t)$ and $-x^T(t)\,x(t)$ that will approach to the smallest eigenvalue of C' are shown in Figs 7.9 and 7.10. In the end, we get that the equilibrium vector is $\xi_n^* = (-0.4405\ -1.1408\ 1.0296\ 0.6342)^T$ and the small eigenvalue of C

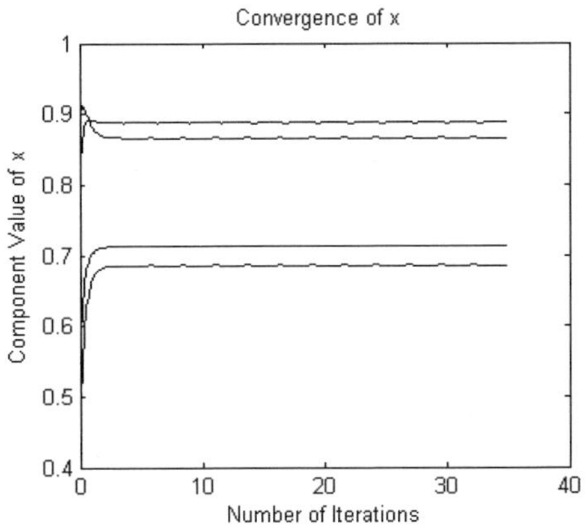

Fig. 7.5. The trajectories of components of x when A is replaced with C.

$$\begin{aligned} \lambda_n^* &= -\xi_n^{*T}\xi_n^* + \lceil \lambda_1 \rceil \\ &= -2.9578 + 3 \\ &= 0.0422 \end{aligned}$$

$\lambda_1 = 2.5159$ and $\lambda_n^* = 0.0422$ are the results computed by RNN (7.2). Compared with the ground true values $\lambda_1^{'} = 2.5160$ and $\lambda_n^{'} = 0.0420$, we can see that λ_1 is very close to $\lambda_1^{'}$, with the absolute difference being 0.0001, and λ_n^* is close to $\lambda_n^{'}$ as well the absolute difference being 0.0002.

This verifies that using step 4 to compute the smallest eigenvalue of a real positive symmetric matrix is effective.

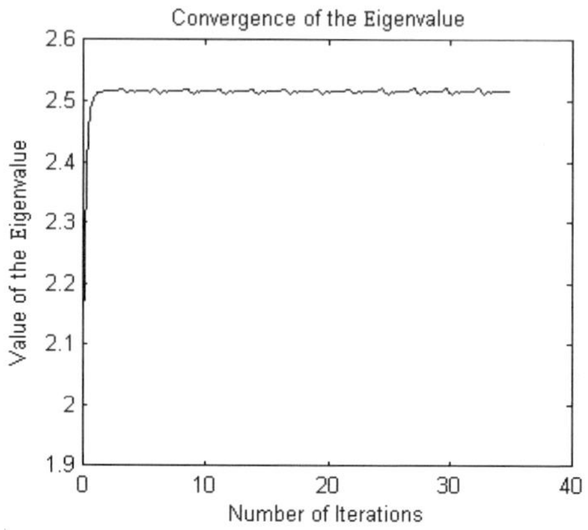

Fig. 7.6. The trajectories of $x^T(t)x(t)$ when A is replaced with C.

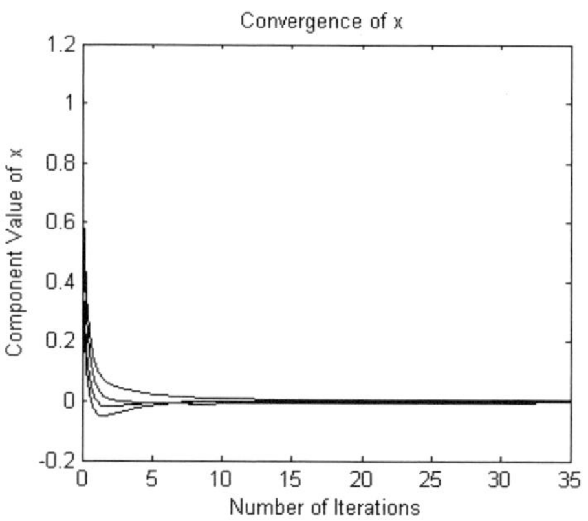

Fig. 7.7. The trajectories of components of x when A is replaced with $-C$.

Example 3: Use matrix $D = -C$ to evaluate RNN (7.2).

Obviously, D is negative definite and its true eigenvalues are $\lambda' =$ (- 2.5160 - 0.3664 - 0.1496 - 0.0420). Replace A with D, from step 1, we find the received eigenvalue is 2.1747×10^{-5}, we cannot decide whether this value is the true largest eigenvalue. Through step 2, the smallest eigenvalue is received $\lambda_4 = -2.5159$. Using step 3, we get $\lambda_1 = -0.0420$. Comparing λ_4 and λ_1 to $\lambda_4^{'}$ and $\lambda_1^{'}$, it can be found that using step 3 to compute the largest eigenvalue is successful.

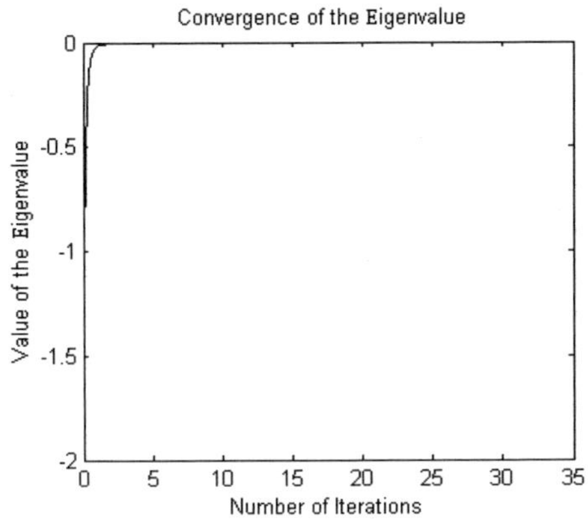

Fig. 7.8. The trajectories of $-x^T(t)x(t)$ when A is replaced with $-C$.

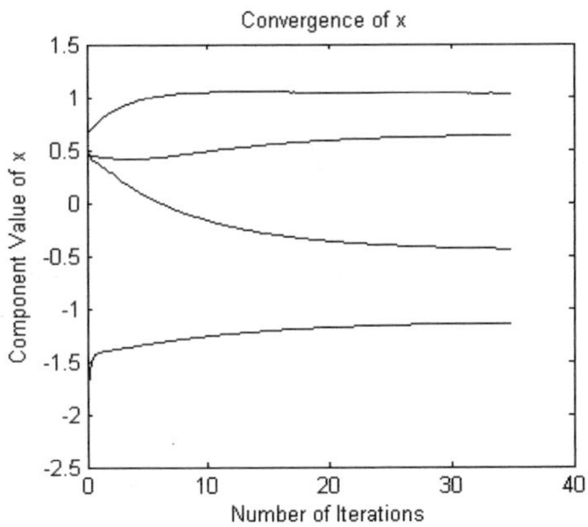

Fig. 7.9. The trajectories of components of x when A is replaced with C'.

7.1.6. *Section summary*

In this section, we presented a recurrent neural network, and designed steps to compute the largest eigenvalue and smallest eigenvalue of a real symmetric matrix using this neural network. This method depicted by the recurrent neural network and the five steps is not only adaptive to non-definite matrix but also to positive definite and negative definite matrix. Three examples were provided to evaluate the validity of this method, with B being a non-definite matrix, C being a positive definite matrix and D being a negative definite matrix. All of the results obtained

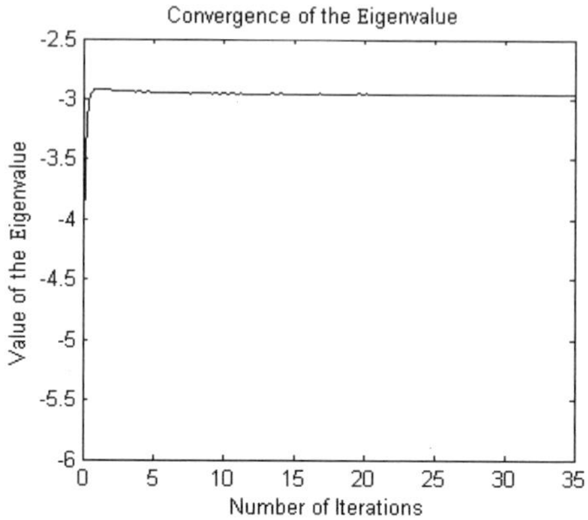

Fig. 7.10. The trajectories of $-x^T(t)x(t)$ when A is replaced with C'.

by applying this method were highly close to the corresponding ground truth values. Compared with other approaches based on neural networks, this recurrent neural network is simpler and can be realized more easily.

Actually there exists an improved form of the neural network presented in Equation (7.2), which is

$$\frac{dx\left(t\right)}{dt} = Ax\left(t\right) - sgn\left[x^T\left(t\right)\right]x\left(t\right)x\left(t\right), \tag{7.20}$$

where definitions of A, t and $x\left(t\right)$ are the same to those of Equation (7.2), and $sgn\left[x_i\left(t\right)\right]$ returns 1 if $x_i\left(t\right) > 0$, 0 if $x_i\left(t\right) = 0$ and -1 if $x_i\left(t\right) < 0$. Evidently, this new form is more concise than the neural network presented in Equation (7.2). Interested readers can refer to [12] for the analytic solution, convergence analysis and numerical valuations of this new form in detail.

7.2. A Recurrent Neural Network for Computing the Largest Modulus Eigenvalues and Their Corresponding Eigenvectors of an Anti-symmetric Matrix

As we argued in Section 7.1, the ability of quick computation of eigenvalues and eigenvectors has many important applications, and using neural networks to compute eigenvalues and eigenvectors of a matrix has outstanding features like high parallelism and quickness. That is the reason why many research works have been reported [1–11, 13, 14] in this field. However, the received results mainly focus on solving eigenvalues and eigenvectors for real symmetric matrices. According to the authors' knowledge, approaches based on neural networks to extract eigenvalues and eigenvectors of a real anti-symmetric matrix are rarely found in the literature.

In this section, we propose a recurrent neural network (RNN), in order to compute eigenvalues and eigenvectors for real anti-symmetric matrices. The proposed RNN is

$$\frac{dv(t)}{dt} = \left[A'g + A'g' - |v(t)|^2\right] v(t) \tag{7.21}$$

where $t \geq 0$, $v(t) \in R^{2n}$, $g = \begin{pmatrix} I_0 & I \\ I_0 & I_0 \end{pmatrix}$, $g' = \begin{pmatrix} I_0 & I_0 \\ -I & I_0 \end{pmatrix}$, $A' = \begin{pmatrix} A & I_0 \\ I_0 & A \end{pmatrix}$. I is an $n \times n$ unit matrix. I_0 is an $n \times n$ zero matrix. A is the real anti-symmetric matrix whose eigenvalues are to be computed. $|v(t)|$ denotes the modulus of $v(t)$. With $v(t)$ being taken as the states of neurons, $\left[A'g + A'g' - |v(t)|^2\right]$ being regarded as synaptic connection weights and the activation functions being assumed as pure linear functions, Equation (7.21) describes a continuous time recurrent neural network.

Denote $v(t) = \left(y^T(t)\; z^T(t)\right)^T$, $y(t) = (y_1(t), y_2(t), \cdots, y_n(t)) \in R^n$ and $z(t) = (z_1(t), z_2(t), \cdots, z_n(t)) \in R^n$, Equation (7.21) is equal to

$$\begin{cases} \frac{dy(t)}{dt} = Az(t) - \sum\limits_{j=1}^{n} \left[y_j^2(t) + z_j^2(t)\right] y(t) \\ \frac{dz(t)}{dt} = -Ay(t) - \sum\limits_{j=1}^{n} \left[y_j^2(t) + z_j^2(t)\right] z(t) \end{cases}. \tag{7.22}$$

Denote

$$x(t) = y(t) + \mathrm{i}z(t), \tag{7.23}$$

where i is the imaginary unit, Equation (7.22) is equal to

$$\frac{dy(t)}{dt} + \mathrm{i}\frac{dz(t)}{dt} = -A\mathrm{i}\left[y(t) + \mathrm{i}z(t)\right] - \sum_{j=1}^{n} \left[y_j^2(t) + z_j^2(t)\right] \left[y(t) + \mathrm{i}z(t)\right],$$

i.e.

$$\frac{dx(t)}{dt} = -Ax(t)\,\mathrm{i} - x^T(t)\,\bar{x}(t)\,x(t), \tag{7.24}$$

where $\bar{x}(t)$ denotes the complex conjugate values of $x(t)$. From Equations (7.21), (7.22) and (7.24), we know that analyzing the convergence properties of Equation (7.24) is equal to analyzing that of RNN (7.21).

7.2.1. *Preliminaries*

Lemma 7.2. *The eigenvalues of A are pure imaginary numbers or zero.*

Proof: let λ be an eigenvalue of A, and v is its corresponding eigenvector. Because $v^T\bar{\lambda}\bar{v} = v^T\overline{\lambda v} = v^T\overline{Av} = v^T A\bar{v} = \left(A^T v\right)^T \bar{v} = (-Av)^T \bar{v} = (-\lambda v)^T \bar{v} = -\lambda v^T \bar{v}$, so

$$\left(\bar{\lambda} + \lambda\right) v^T \bar{v} = \left(\bar{\lambda} + \lambda\right) |v|^2 = 0.$$

For $|v| \neq 0$, thus $\bar{\lambda} + \lambda = 0$, this indicates that the value of the real component of λ is zero. So, λ is a pure imaginary number or zero.

Lemma 7.3. *If $\eta\, i$ is an eigenvalue of A, and μ is the corresponding eigenvector, then $-\eta\, i$ is an eigenvalue of A too, and $\bar{\mu}$ is the eigenvector corresponding to $-\eta\, i$.*

Proof: from $A\mu = \eta\,\mathrm{i}\mu$, we get $\overline{A\mu} = \overline{\eta\,\mathrm{i}\mu}$, i.e. $A\bar{\mu} = (-\eta\,\mathrm{i})\,\bar{\mu}$. So, we can draw the conclusion.

Based on Lemmas 7.2 and 7.3, all eigenvalues of A are denoted as $\lambda_1\,\mathrm{i}, \lambda_2\,\mathrm{i}, \cdots, \lambda_n\,\mathrm{i}$ which match $|\lambda_1| \geq |\lambda_2| \geq \cdots \geq |\lambda_n|$, $\lambda_{2k} = -\lambda_{2k-1}$ and $\lambda_{2k-1} \geq 0$ ($k = 1, \cdots, \lfloor n/2 \rfloor$, $\lfloor n/2 \rfloor$ denotes the most maximal integer that is not larger than $n/2$). Corresponding complex eigenvectors and complex eigensubspaces are denoted as $\mu_1, \cdots, \mu_n$ and $V_1, \cdots, V_n$.

Lemma 7.4. *For matrix A, if two eigenvalues $\lambda_k\, i \neq \lambda_m\, i$, then $\mu_k \perp \mu_m$, namely the inner product $\langle \mu_k, \mu_m \rangle = 0$, $k, m \in [1, n]$.*

Proof: from $A\mu_k = \lambda_k\,\mathrm{i}\mu_k$ and $A\mu_m = \lambda_m\,\mathrm{i}\mu_m$, we get $\mu_k^T\overline{\lambda_m \mathrm{i}\mu_m} = \mu_k^T\overline{\lambda_m\,\mathrm{i}\mu_m} = \mu_k^T\overline{A\mu_m} = \mu_k^T A\bar{\mu}_m = \left(A^T\mu_k\right)^T \bar{\mu}_m = (-A\mu_k)^T \bar{\mu}_m$
$= -\lambda_k\,\mathrm{i}\mu_k^T \bar{\mu}_m$, thus,

$$\left(\overline{\lambda_m\,\mathrm{i}} + \lambda_k\,\mathrm{i}\right) \mu_k^T \bar{\mu}_m = 0. \tag{7.25}$$

From Lemma 7.2, we know $\lambda_k\,\mathrm{i}$ and $\lambda_m\,\mathrm{i}$ are imaginary numbers. From $\lambda_k\,\mathrm{i} \neq \lambda_m\,\mathrm{i}$, it follows that

$$\left(\overline{\lambda_m\,\mathrm{i}} + \lambda_k\,\mathrm{i}\right) \neq 0. \tag{7.26}$$

From Equations (7.25) and (7.26), it easily follows that

$$\mu_k^T \bar{\mu}_m = 0, \tag{7.27}$$

i.e.

$$\langle \mu_k, \mu_m \rangle = 0.$$

Therefore $\mu_k \perp \mu_m$.

When RNN (7.21) approaches equilibrium state, we get the following formula from Equation (7.24)

$$-A\xi\,\mathrm{i} = \xi^T \bar{\xi}\xi, \tag{7.28}$$

where $\xi \in C^n$ is the equilibrium vector. When ξ is an eigenvector of A, $\lambda\mathrm{i}\,(\lambda \in R)$ is supposed to be the corresponding eigenvalue, then

$$A\xi = \lambda\,\mathrm{i}\xi. \tag{7.29}$$

From Equations (7.28) and (7.29), it follows that

$$\lambda = \xi^T \bar{\xi}. \tag{7.30}$$

7.2.2. *Analytic solution of RNN*

Theorem 7.9. *Denote $S_k = \frac{\mu_k}{|\mu_k|}$, x_k denotes the projection value of $x(t)$ onto S_k, then the analytic solution of Equation (7.24) is*

$$x(t) = \frac{\sum\limits_{k=1}^{n} [y_k(0) + \ iz_k(0)] \exp(\lambda_k t) S_k}{\sqrt{1 + 2\sum\limits_{j=1}^{n} \left[z_j^2(0) + y_j^2(0)\right] \int_0^t \exp(2\lambda_j \tau)\, d\tau}} \tag{7.31}$$

for all $t \geq 0$.

Proof: from Lemma 7.4, we know that $S_1, S_2, \cdots, S_n$ construct an orthonormal basis of $C^{n\times n}$. Since $x_k = y_k(t) + \mathrm{i}\, z_k(t)$, thus

$$x(t) = \sum_{k=1}^{n} (z_k(t) + \mathrm{i}\, y_k(t)) S_k. \tag{7.32}$$

Take Equation (7.32) into Equation (7.24), as S_k is a normalized complex eigenvector of A, from the denotation of $\lambda_k i$, we know the corresponding eigenvalue is $\lambda_k i$, thus

$$\begin{aligned}
&\sum_{k=1}^{n} \left[\tfrac{d}{dt} z_k(t) + \mathrm{i}\, \tfrac{d}{dt} y_k(t)\right] S_k \\
&= -\sum_{k=1}^{n} A\left[z_k(t) + \mathrm{i}\, y_k(t)\right] S_k\, \mathrm{i} - \sum_{k=1}^{n} \left[z_k^2(t) + y_k^2(t)\right] \sum_{k=1}^{n} \left[z_k(t) + \mathrm{i}\, y_k(t)\right] S_k \\
&= -\sum_{k=1}^{n} \lambda_k \mathrm{i}\, S_k \left[z_k(t) + \mathrm{i}\, y_k(t)\right] \mathrm{i} - \sum_{k=1}^{n} \left[z_k^2(t) + y_k^2(t)\right] \sum_{k=1}^{n} \left[z_k(t) + \mathrm{i}\, y_k(t)\right] S_k \\
&= \sum_{k=1}^{n} \lambda_k S_k \left[z_k(t) + \mathrm{i}\, y_k(t)\right] - \sum_{k=1}^{n} \left[z_k^2(t) + y_k^2(t)\right] \sum_{k=1}^{n} \left[z_k(t) + \mathrm{i}\, y_k(t)\right] S_k,
\end{aligned}$$

therefore

$$\frac{d}{dt}z_k(t) = \lambda_k z_k(t) - \sum_{j=1}^{n} \left[z_j^2(t) + y_j^2(t)\right] z_k(t), \tag{7.33}$$

$$\frac{d}{dt}y_k(t) = \lambda_k y_k(t) - \sum_{j=1}^{n} \left[z_j^2(t) + y_j^2(t)\right] y_k(t). \tag{7.34}$$

From Equation (7.33), we get

$$\lambda_k - \frac{1}{z_k(t)}\frac{d}{dt}z_k(t) = \sum_{j=1}^{n} \left[z_j^2(t) + y_j^2(t)\right] = \lambda_r - \frac{1}{z_r(t)}\frac{d}{dt}z_r(t),$$

where $r \in [1, n]$, so

$$\frac{1}{z_r(t)}\frac{d}{dt}z_r(t) - \frac{1}{z_k(t)}\frac{d}{dt}z_k(t) = \lambda_r - \lambda_k,$$

i.e.

$$\frac{z_r(t)}{z_k(t)} = \frac{z_r(0)}{z_k(0)} \exp\left[(\lambda_r - \lambda_k)t\right]. \tag{7.35}$$

From Equation (7.34), we analogously get

$$\frac{y_r(t)}{y_k(t)} = \frac{y_r(0)}{y_k(0)} \exp\left[(\lambda_r - \lambda_k)t\right]. \tag{7.36}$$

From Equations (7.33) and (7.34), we get

$$\lambda_k - \frac{1}{z_k(t)}\frac{d}{dt}z_k(t) = \lambda_r - \frac{1}{y_r(t)}\frac{d}{dt}y_r(t),$$

i.e.

$$\frac{y_r(t)}{z_k(t)} = \frac{y_r(0)}{z_k(0)} \exp\left[(\lambda_r - \lambda_k)t\right]. \tag{7.37}$$

From Equation (7.21), we also get

$$\frac{1}{z_k^3(t)}\frac{d}{dt}z_k(t) = \frac{\lambda_k}{z_k^2(t)} - \sum_{j=1}^{n} \left[\frac{z_j^2(t)}{z_k^2(t)} + \frac{y_j^2(t)}{z_k^2(t)}\right],$$

i.e.

$$\frac{d}{dt}\frac{1}{z_k^2(t)} + 2\frac{\lambda_k}{z_k^2(t)} = 2\sum_{j=1}^{n} \left[\frac{z_j^2(t)}{z_k^2(t)} + \frac{y_j^2(t)}{z_k^2(t)}\right]. \tag{7.38}$$

Take Equations (7.35) and (7.37) into Equation (7.38), it follows that

$$\frac{d}{dt}\left[\frac{\exp\left(2\lambda_k t\right)}{z_k^2\left(t\right)}\right]=2\sum_{j=1}^{n}\left[\frac{z_j^2\left(0\right)+y_j^2\left(0\right)}{z_k^2\left(0\right)}\right]\exp\left(2\lambda_j t\right), \tag{7.39}$$

Integrating two sides of Equation (7.39) with respect to t from 0 to t', we get

$$\frac{\exp\left(2\lambda_k t'\right)z_k^2\left(0\right)}{z_k^2\left(t'\right)}=1+2\sum_{j=1}^{n}\left[z_j^2\left(0\right)+y_j^2\left(0\right)\right]\int_0^{t'}\exp\left(2\lambda_j t\right)dt,$$

so

$$z_k^2\left(t'\right)=\frac{\exp\left(2\lambda_k t'\right)z_k^2\left(0\right)}{1+2\sum\limits_{j=1}^{n}\left[z_j^2\left(0\right)+y_j^2\left(0\right)\right]\int_0^{t'}\exp\left(2\lambda_j t\right)dt},$$

therefore

$$z_k\left(t'\right)=\frac{\exp\left(\lambda_k t'\right)z_k\left(0\right)}{\sqrt{1+2\sum\limits_{j=1}^{n}\left[z_j^2\left(0\right)+y_j^2\left(0\right)\right]\int_0^{t'}\exp\left(2\lambda_j t\right)dt}}, \tag{7.40}$$

or,

$$z_k\left(t'\right)=\frac{-\exp\left(\lambda_k t'\right)z_k\left(0\right)}{\sqrt{1+2\sum\limits_{j=1}^{n}\left[z_j^2\left(0\right)+y_j^2\left(0\right)\right]\int_0^{t'}\exp\left(2\lambda_j t\right)dt}}.$$

For the above formula, when $t'=0$, we get

$$z_k\left(0\right)=-z_k\left(0\right),\quad k=1,2,\cdots,n.$$

When $z\left(0\right)$ is a nonzero vector, there exists

$$z_d\left(0\right)\neq -z_d\left(0\right)\quad\left(d\in\left[1,2,\cdots,n\right]\right),$$

so, we take only Equation (7.40) as correct.

Analogously, from Equations (7.34), (7.36) and (7.37), we get

$$y_k\left(t'\right)=\frac{\exp\left(\lambda_k t'\right)y_k\left(0\right)}{\sqrt{1+2\sum\limits_{j=1}^{n}\left[z_j^2\left(0\right)+y_j^2\left(0\right)\right]\int_0^{t'}\exp\left(2\lambda_j t\right)dt}}. \tag{7.41}$$

Therefore, from Equations (7.40) and (7.41), it follows that

$$\begin{aligned} x(t) &= \sum_{k=1}^{n} x_k(t) S_k \\ &= \sum_{k=1}^{n} [y_k(t) + \mathrm{i}\, y_k(t)] S_k \\ &= \frac{\sum_{k=1}^{n} \left[y_k(0) + \mathrm{i}\, z_k(0)\right] \exp(\lambda_k t) S_k}{\sqrt{1 + 2\sum_{j=1}^{n} \left[z_j^2(0) + y_j^2(0)\right] \int_0^t \exp(2\lambda_j \tau) d\tau}} \end{aligned} \quad . \tag{7.42}$$

for all $t \geq 0$. So the theorem is proved.

7.2.3. *Convergence analysis of RNN*

Theorem 7.10. *If nonzero initial vector $x(0) \in V_m$, then the equilibrium vector $\xi = 0$ or $\xi \in V_m$. If $\xi \in V_m$, $i\xi^T \bar{\xi}$ is the eigenvalue $\lambda_m i$.*

Proof: because $x(0) \in V_m$ and $V_m \perp V_j \quad (j \neq m)$, thus

$$x_j(0) = 0, \quad j \neq m. \tag{7.43}$$

From Theorem 7.9 and Equation (7.43), we get

$$x(t) = \frac{[y_m(0) + \mathrm{i} y_m(0)] \exp(\lambda_m t) S_m}{\sqrt{1 + 2\left[z_m^2(0) + y_m^2(0)\right] \int_0^t \exp(2\lambda_m \tau) d\tau}}. \tag{7.44}$$

when the equilibrium vector ξ exists, there exists the following relationship

$$\xi = \lim_{t \to \infty} x(t). \tag{7.45}$$

From Equations (7.44) and (7.45), it follows that: When $\lambda_m < 0$

$$\xi = 0. \tag{7.46}$$

When $\lambda_m = 0$

$$\begin{aligned} x(t) &= \lim_{t \to \infty} \frac{[y_m(0) + \mathrm{i} y_m(0)] S_m}{\sqrt{1 + 2\left[z_m^2(0) + y_m^2(0)\right] t}} \\ &= 0 \end{aligned} \tag{7.47}$$

When $\lambda_m > 0$

$$\begin{aligned} \xi &= \lim_{t \to \infty} \frac{\left[y_m(0) + \mathrm{i}\, y_m(0)\right] S_m}{\sqrt{\exp(-2\lambda_m t) + \frac{1}{\lambda_m}\left[z_m^2(0) + y_m^2(0)\right] \left[1 - \exp(-2\lambda_m t)\right]}} \\ &= \frac{\left[y_m(0) + \mathrm{i}\, y_m(0)\right] S_m}{\sqrt{\frac{1}{\lambda_m}\left[z_m^2(0) + y_m^2(0)\right]}} \\ &\in V_m \end{aligned} \quad . \tag{7.48}$$

From Equations (7.46), (7.47) and (7.48), it concludes that $\xi = 0$ or $\xi \in V_m$. When $\xi \in V_m$, from Equation (7.48), it follows that

$$\begin{aligned}\xi^T\bar{\xi}\mathrm{i} &= \frac{\left[y_m(0)+\mathrm{i}\,y_m(0)\right]S_m}{\sqrt{\frac{1}{\lambda_m}[z_m^2(0)+y_m^2(0)]}}\frac{\left[y_m(0)-\mathrm{i}\,y_m(0)\right]\bar{S}_m}{\sqrt{\frac{1}{\lambda_m}[z_m^2(0)+y_m^2(0)]}}\mathrm{i} \\ &= \lambda_m\mathrm{i}\end{aligned}. \tag{7.49}$$

From Equations (7.46)∼(7.49), the theorem can be concluded.

Theorem 7.11. *If nonzero initial vector $x(0) \notin V_m \quad (m = 1, \cdots, n)$, then the equilibrium vector $\xi \in V_1$ or $\xi = 0$, $\xi^T\bar{\xi}i$ is the eigenvalue $\lambda_1 i$. If $\lambda_2 i$ exists, $-\lambda_1\, i$ is the eigenvalue $\lambda_2 i$, and $\bar{\xi}$ is eigenvector corresponding to $\lambda_2 i$.*

Proof: because $x(0) \notin V_m \quad (m = 1, \cdots, n)$, so $x_k(t) \neq 0 \quad (1 \le k \le n)$. From the denotation of $\lambda_1\,\mathrm{i}, \lambda_2\,\mathrm{i}, \cdots, \lambda_n\,\mathrm{i}$, it follows that

$$\lambda_1 \ge 0.$$

From Theorem 7.9 and Equation (7.45), when $\lambda_1 = 0$, we get

$$\begin{aligned}\xi &= \lim_{t\to\infty}\frac{\sum_{k=1}^{n}\left[y_k(0)+\mathrm{i}\,y_k(0)\right]\exp(\lambda_k t)S_k}{\sqrt{1+2\sum_{j=1}^{n}\left[z_j^2(0)+y_j^2(0)\right]\int_0^t\exp(2\lambda_j\tau)d\tau}} \\ &= \lim_{t\to\infty}\frac{\sum_{k=1}^{n}\left[y_k(0)+\mathrm{i}\,y_k(0)\right]S_k}{\sqrt{1+2\sum_{j=1}^{n}\left[z_j^2(0)+y_j^2(0)\right]t}} \\ &= 0\end{aligned}, \tag{7.50}$$

and

$$\xi^T\bar{\xi}\mathrm{i} = 0 = \lambda_1\,\mathrm{i}, \tag{7.51}$$

when $\lambda_1 > 0$, we get

$$\xi = \lim_{t\to\infty}\frac{\left[y_1(0)+\mathrm{i}\,y_1(0)\right]S_1+\sum_{k=2}^{n}\left[y_k(0)+\mathrm{i}\,y_k(0)\right]\exp[(\lambda_k-\lambda_1)t]S_k}{\sqrt{\exp(-2\lambda_1 t)+2\left[z_1^2(0)+y_1^2(0)\right]\int_0^t\exp[2\lambda_1(\tau-t)]d\tau+2\sum_{j=2}^{n}\left[z_j^2(0)+y_j^2(0)\right]\int_0^t\exp(2\lambda_j\tau-2\lambda_1 t)d\tau}},$$

thus

$$\begin{aligned}\xi &= \sqrt{\frac{\lambda_1}{\left[z_1^2(0)+y_1^2(0)\right]}}\left[y_1(0)+\mathrm{i}y_1(0)\right]S_1 \\ &\in V_1\end{aligned}, \tag{7.52}$$

and

$$\begin{aligned}\xi^T\bar{\xi}\,\mathrm{i} &= \sqrt{\tfrac{\lambda_1}{\left[z_1^2(0)+y_1^2(0)\right]}}\left[y_1(0)+\mathrm{i}y_1(0)\right]S_1\sqrt{\tfrac{\lambda_1}{\left[z_1^2(0)+y_1^2(0)\right]}}\left[y_1(0)-\mathrm{i}y_1(0)\right]\bar{S}_1 \\ &= \lambda_1\mathrm{i}\end{aligned} \tag{7.53}$$

If $\lambda_2\mathrm{i}$ exists, from the denotation of $\lambda_1\,\mathrm{i}, \lambda_2\,\mathrm{i}, \cdots, \lambda_n\,\mathrm{i}$, we know

$$\lambda_2\,\mathrm{i} = \overline{\lambda_1\,\mathrm{i}} = -\lambda_1\,\mathrm{i}, \tag{7.54}$$

and from Equation (7.54) and Lemma 7.2, it easily follows

$$A\bar{\xi} = \lambda_2\,\mathrm{i}\,\bar{\xi}, \tag{7.55}$$

so $\bar{\xi}$ is the eigenvector corresponding to $\lambda_2\,\mathrm{i}$.

From Equations (7.50), (7.51), (7.52), (7.53), (7.54) and (7.55), it is concluded that the theorem is correct.

Theorem 7.12. *If $x(0) \neq 0$, the modulus of trajectory $|x(t)|$ will converge to zero or $\lambda_k > 0 \quad (1 \leq k \leq n)$.*

Proof: Rearrange $\lambda_1, \lambda_2, \cdots, \lambda_n$ into order $\lambda_1^r > \lambda_2^r > \cdots > \lambda_n^r$. From Theorem 1, we know

$$x(t) = \frac{\sum\limits_{k=1}^{n}\left[y_k(0) + iz_k(0)\right]\exp\left(\lambda_k^r t\right)S_k}{\sqrt{1 + 2\sum\limits_{j=1}^{n}\left[z_j^2(0) + y_j^2(0)\right]\int_0^t \exp\left(2\lambda_j^r\tau\right)d\tau}}.$$

Since $\lambda_1 \geq 0$,

$$\lambda_1^r \geq 0,$$

the supposition $\lambda_1^r > \cdots \lambda_q^r \geq 0 > \lambda_{q+1}^r \cdots \lambda_n^r$ is rational. Suppose the first nonzero component of $x(t)$ is $x_p(0) \neq 0$ $(1 \leq p \leq n)$. Then there are two cases:

1) If $1 \leq p \leq q$, it follows that

$$\begin{aligned}\xi &= \lim_{t\to\infty} x(t) \\ &= \lim_{t\to\infty}\frac{\sum\limits_{k=p}^{q}\left[y_k(0)+iz_k(0)\right]\exp\left(\lambda_k^r t\right)S_k + \sum\limits_{k=q+1}^{n}\left[y_k(0)+iz_k(0)\right]\exp\left(\lambda_k^r t\right)S_k}{\sqrt{1+2\sum\limits_{j=1}^{n}\left[z_j^2(0)+y_j^2(0)\right]\int_0^t\exp\left(2\lambda_j^r\tau\right)d\tau}} \\ &= \frac{\left[y_p(0)+iz_p(0)\right]S_p + \lim\limits_{t\to\infty}\sum\limits_{k=p+1}^{n}\left[y_k(0)+iz_k(0)\right]\exp\left(\lambda_k^r t-\lambda_p^r t\right)S_k}{\lim\limits_{t\to\infty}\sqrt{\exp\left(-2\lambda_p^r t\right)+\left[z_p^2(0)+y_p^2(0)\right]\left[1-\exp\left(-2\lambda_p^r t\right)\right]/\lambda_p^r+2\sum\limits_{j=p+1}^{n}\left[z_j^2(0)+y_j^2(0)\right]\int_0^t\exp\left(2\lambda_j^r\tau-2\lambda_p^r t\right)d\tau}} \\ &= \frac{\left[y_p(0)+iz_p(0)\right]\sqrt{\lambda_p^r}}{\sqrt{z_p^2(0)+y_p^2(0)}}S_p,\end{aligned}$$

so

$$
\begin{aligned}
|\xi| &= \sqrt{\xi^T \bar{\xi}} \\
&= \sqrt{\frac{[y_p(0)+iz_p(0)]\sqrt{\lambda_p^r}}{\sqrt{z_p^2(0)+y_p^2(0)}} S_p^T \frac{[y_p(0)+iz_p(0)]\sqrt{\lambda_p^r}}{\sqrt{z_p^2(0)+y_p^2(0)}} \bar{S}_p} \, . \\
&= \lambda_p^r
\end{aligned}
\tag{7.56}
$$

2) If $k+1 \le p \le n$, it follows that

$$
\begin{aligned}
\xi &= \lim_{t\to\infty} x(t) \\
&= \lim_{t\to\infty} \frac{\sum_{k=p}^{n} [y_k(0)+iz_k(0)] \exp(\lambda_k^r t) S_k}{\sqrt{1+2\sum_{j=1}^{n} \left[z_j^2(0)+y_j^2(0)\right] \int_0^t \exp\left(2\lambda_j^r \tau\right) d\tau}} \, . \\
&= 0
\end{aligned}
\tag{7.57}
$$

Since the two sets $[\lambda_1, \lambda_2, \cdots, \lambda_n]$ and $[\lambda_1^r, \lambda_2^r, \cdots, \lambda_n^r]$ are the same. So, from Equations (7.56) and (7.57), it follows that $|\xi|$ is $\lambda_k > 0 \quad (1 \le k \le n)$ or zero. So, the theorem is drawn.

7.2.4. *Simulation*

In order to evaluate RNN (7.21), a numerical simulation is provided, and Matlab is used to generate the simulation.

Example: For Equation (7.24), A is randomly generated as

$$
A = \begin{pmatrix}
0 & -0.0511 & 0.2244 & -0.0537 & 0.0888 & -0.1191 & 0.1815 \\
0.0511 & 0 & 0.1064 & 0.2901 & -0.0073 & 0.0263 & 0.2322 \\
-0.2244 & -0.1064 & 0 & 0.1406 & -0.0206 & 0.1402 & -0.0910 \\
0.0537 & -0.2901 & -0.1406 & 0 & -0.2708 & -0.0640 & -0.2373 \\
-0.0888 & 0.0073 & 0.0206 & 0.2708 & 0 & 0.1271 & 0.1094 \\
0.1191 & -0.0263 & -0.1402 & 0.0640 & -0.1271 & 0 & -0.1200 \\
-0.1815 & -0.2322 & 0.0910 & 0.2373 & -0.1094 & 0.1200 & 0
\end{pmatrix},
$$

and the initial value is

$$
x(0) = \begin{pmatrix}
0.0511-0.2244i \\
-0.1064i \\
0.1064 \\
0.2901+0.1406i \\
-0.0073-0.0206i \\
0.0263+0.1402i \\
0.2322-0.0910i
\end{pmatrix}.
$$

Through simulation, the generated complex equilibrium vector is

$$\xi = \begin{pmatrix} \text{-0.1355-0.1563i} \\ \text{0.0716-0.2914i} \\ \text{0.2410-0.0716i} \\ \text{0.2840+0.3073i} \\ \text{0.1556-0.2338i} \\ \text{0.1076+0.1511i} \\ \text{0.3334-0.1507i} \end{pmatrix},$$

and the eigenvalue is

$$\begin{aligned} \lambda_1^s \mathrm{i} &= \xi^T \bar{\xi}\, \mathrm{i} \\ &= 0.6182\ \mathrm{i} \end{aligned}$$

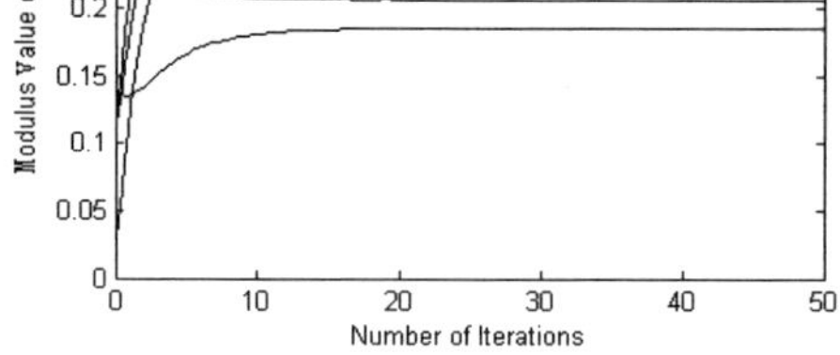

Fig. 7.11. The trajectories of modulus of components of x when A is replaced with B.

The trajectories of the modulus values of the components of $x(t)$ and $x^T(t)\,\bar{x}(t)$ approaching λ_1 are shown in Figs 7.11 and 7.12. Use Matlab to directly compute the eigenvalues and eigenvectors, the ground truth values are follows:

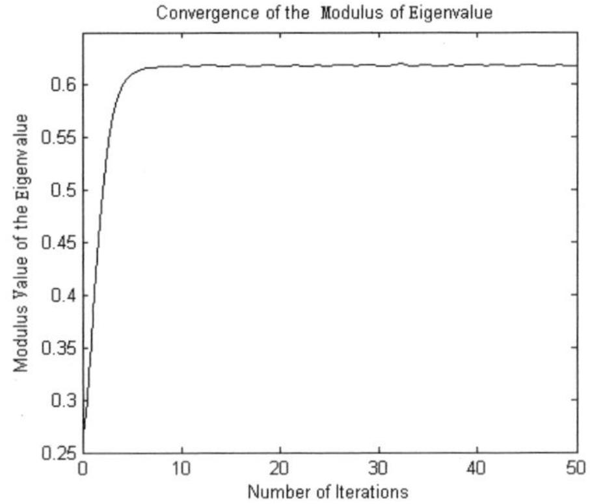

Fig. 7.12. The trajectory of $x^T(t)x(t)$ when A is replaced with B.

$$\mu_1 = \begin{pmatrix} -0.2630 - 0.0084i \\ -0.2105 - 0.3184i \\ 0.1411 - 0.2869i \\ 0.5322 \\ -0.0841 - 0.3471i \\ 0.2340 + 0.0299i \\ 0.1470 - 0.4415i \end{pmatrix}, \quad \mu_3 = \begin{pmatrix} 0.5318 \\ 0.0207 - 0.4494i \\ -0.0997 + 0.3784i \\ 0.2835 - 0.1898i \\ -0.2272 - 0.0857i \\ -0.1797 - 0.3099i \\ 0.2063 + 0.1246i \end{pmatrix},$$

$$\mu_5 = \begin{pmatrix} 0.1852 + 0.2252i \\ 0.0424 + 0.0809i \\ 0.2436 + 0.3907i \\ -0.2443 + 0.1977i \\ -0.2995 + 0.1881i \\ 0.4992 \\ 0.0769 - 0.4644i \end{pmatrix}, \quad \mu_7 = \begin{pmatrix} 0.3549 \\ -0.5360 \\ -0.2557 \\ -0.0568 \\ 0.6138 \\ 0.3656 \\ 0.0880 \end{pmatrix}.$$

$\mu_2 = \bar{\mu}_1$, $\mu_4 = \bar{\mu}_3$, $\mu_6 = \bar{\mu}_5$, $\lambda_1 i = 0.6184i$, $\lambda_2 i = -0.6184i$, $\lambda_3 i = 0.3196i$, $\lambda_4 i = -0.3196i$, $\lambda_5 i = 0.0288i$, $\lambda_6 i = -0.0288i$ and $\lambda_7 i = 0$.

When $\lambda_1^s i$ is compared with $\lambda_1 i$, the difference is

$$\begin{aligned} \Delta\lambda_1 &= \lambda_1^s i - \lambda_1 i \\ &= 0.6182i - 0.6184i. \\ &= -0.0002i \end{aligned}$$

The modulus value of $\Delta\lambda_1$ is very small, which means that the eigenvalue computed by RNN (7.21) is very close to the true value. This verifies the validity of RNN (7.21) for computing eigenvalues. On the other side, it may be noticed that the eigenvector ξ computed by RNN (7.21) is different from μ_k $1 \leq k \leq n$. Compute the inner product between ξ and μ_k, we get: $U_1 = \langle \xi, \mu_1 \rangle = 0.5336$ -0.5775i, $U_2 = \langle \xi, \mu_2 \rangle = 2.7411 \times 10^{-6}$-$1.1816 \times 10^{-6}$i, $U_3 = \langle \xi, \mu_3 \rangle = 6.8277 \times 10^{-8} + 7.7934 \times 10^{-8}$i, $U_4 = \langle \xi, \mu_4 \rangle = 1.9873 \times 10^{-13} + 1.2935 \times 10^{-13}$i, $U_5 = \langle \xi, \mu_5 \rangle = 3.4937 \times 10^{-15} + 9.1108 \times 10^{-15}$i, $U_6 = \langle \xi, \mu_6 \rangle = -9.7491 \times 10^{-16} + 1.1172 \times 10^{-15}$i, $U_7 = \langle \xi, \mu_7 \rangle = -5.5511 \times 10^{-17} + 5.0307 \times 10^{-17}$i. Obviously, U_k $(2 \leq k \leq n)$ is nearly close zero, and U_1 is not zero. Hence, ξ belongs to the subspace corresponding to λ_1, i.e.

$$\xi \in V_1.$$

Thus the eigenvector ξ computed by RNN (7.21) is equivalent to μ_1, both of which belong to the same subspace V_1.

When $x(0)$ is changed into other wholly generated values, the trajectories of modulus values of components of $x(t)$ vary. The values of ξ vary too, but ξ still belongs to V_1, and $\xi^T \bar{\xi}\,\mathrm{i}$ is still very close to $\lambda_1 \mathrm{i} = 0.6184\mathrm{i}$.

Clearly $\overline{\lambda_1^s \mathrm{i}}$ is very close to λ_2i, and $\bar{\xi}$ is the corresponding eigenvector.

This example verifies that it is effective to use RNN (7.21) to compute the eigenvalues and eigenvectors of real anti-symmetric matrices.

7.2.5. *Section summary*

Many researches have been focused on using a neural network to compute eigenvalues and eigenvectors of real symmetric matrices. In this section, a new neural network modal was presented so that eigenvalues and eigenvectors of a real anti-symmetric matrix can be computed. The network was transformed into a differential equation, and the complex analytic solution of the equation was derived. Based on the solution, the convergence behavior of the neural network was analyzed. In order to examine the proposed neural network, a 7×7 real anti-symmetric matrix was randomly generated and used. The eigenvalue computed by the network was very close to the ground true values, which were computed using Matlab functions directly. Although the eigenvector was different from the corresponding eigenvector of the ground truth eigenvalue, they both belong to the same subspace and were equivalent. Therefore, the network is effective to compute eigenvalues and eigenvectors of real anti-symmetric matrices.

It remains a problem on using this neural network to compute all eigenvalues of real anti-symmetric matrices. And it is also unsolved on using neural networks to compute eigenvalues of non-symmetric and non-anti-symmetric matrices. These problems inspire further research interests and in Section 7.4 we will introduce some of our efforts on computing eigenvalues and eigenvectors of real and *general* matrices using neural networks.

7.3. A Concise Recurrent Neural Network Computing the Largest Modulus Eigenvalues and Their Corresponding Eigenvectors of a Real Skew Matrix

As extraction of eigenstructure has many applications such as the fast retrieval of structural patterns [15], hand-written digits recognition [16] etc., many techniques have been proposed to accelerate the computation speed [4, 17]. There are also many works on applying artificial neural networks (ANNs) to calculate eigenpairs for the concurrent and asynchronous running manner of ANNs [1, 2, 4–9, 11, 13, 14, 17–24].

Generally, the techniques can be categorized into three types. Firstly, an energy function is constructed from the relations between eigenpairs and the matrix, and a differential system which can be implemented by ANNs is formed. At the equilibrium state of the system, one or more eigenpairs is computed [19, 20]. Secondly, a special neural network is constructed, originating from Oja's algorithms to extract some eigenstructure. Most of these kinds of methods [1, 2, 4–6, 8, 9, 13, 14, 18, 24] need the input matrix to be symmetric, such as the autocorrelation matrix. Finally, a differential system implemented by artificial recurrent neural networks is formulated purely for calculating eigenstructure of a special matrix [21–23]. Ordinarily, the computation burden of the first two types is heavy and the realization circuit is complex. In the framework of the last type of technique, the neural network can be flexibly designed. The concise expression of the differential system is a significant factor affecting the neural network's implementation in hardware. In Section 7.2 we have introduced a recurrent neural network adaptive to real anti-symmetric matrices. In this section, we will propose an even more concise recurrent neural network (RNN) to complete the calculation,

$$\frac{dv(t)}{dt} = [A' - B(t)] \ v(t) \tag{7.58}$$

where $t \geq 0$, $v(t) \in R^{2n}$, $A' = \begin{pmatrix} I_0 & A \\ -A & I_0 \end{pmatrix}$, $B(t) = \begin{pmatrix} IU^n v(t) & -IU_n v(t) \\ IU_n v(t) & IU^n v(t) \end{pmatrix}$.

I is a $n \times n$ unit matrix. I_0 is a $n \times n$ zero matrix. $U^n = (\underbrace{1, \cdots, 1}_{n}, \underbrace{0, \cdots, 0}_{n})$, $U_n = (\underbrace{0, \cdots, 0}_{n}, \underbrace{1, \cdots, 1}_{n})$. A is the real skew matrix. When $v(t)$ is assumed as the states of neurons, $[A' - B(t)]$ being taken as synaptic connection weights, and the activation functions are supposed as pure linear functions, Equation (7.58) describes a continuous time recurrent neural network.

Let $v(t) = \left(x^T(t)\, y^T(t)\right)^T$, $x(t) = (x_1(t), x_2(t), \cdots, x_n(t))^T \in R^n$ and $y(t) = (y_1(t), y_2(t), \cdots, y_n(t))^T \in R^n$. Rewrite Equation (7.58) as

$$\begin{cases} \frac{dx(t)}{dt} = Ay(t) - \sum_{j=1}^{n} x_j(t)x(t) + \sum_{j=1}^{n} y_j(t)y(t) \\ \frac{dy(t)}{dt} = -Ax(t) - \sum_{j=1}^{n} y_j(t)x(t) - \sum_{j=1}^{n} x_j(t)y(t) \end{cases}. \tag{7.59}$$

Let

$$z(t) = x(t) + \mathrm{i}y(t), \tag{7.60}$$

where i denotes imaginary unit. Equation (7.59) can be transformed into

$$\frac{dx(t)}{dt} + \mathrm{i}\frac{dy(t)}{dt} = -A\mathrm{i}\left[x(t) + \mathrm{i}y(t)\right] - \sum_{j=1}^{n}\left[x_j(t) + y_j(t)\mathrm{i}\right]\left[x(t) + \mathrm{i}y(t)\right],$$

that is,

$$\frac{dz(t)}{dt} = -Az(t)\,\mathrm{i} - \sum_{j=1}^{n} z_j(t)z(t). \tag{7.61}$$

From Equations (7.58), (7.59) and (7.61), we know that analyzing the convergence properties of Equation (7.61) is equal to analyzing those of RNN (7.58).

Actually, RNN (7.58) could easily transform to another neural network, with only matrix B changed to $B(t) = \begin{pmatrix} -IU^n v(t) & IU_n v(t) \\ -IU_n v(t) & -IU^n v(t) \end{pmatrix}$ while all the other components remain the same with RNN (7.58). Similar to what will be discussed in this section, the theoretical analysis and numerical valuation of this new form of neural network can be found in [25] in detail.

7.3.1. *Preliminaries*

We will use some similar preliminaries here as in Section 7.2. Thus we only give these Lemmas and please refer back to Lemmas 7.2, 7.3 and 7.4 for proof of these Lemmas.

Lemma 7.5. *The eigenvalues of A are pure imaginary numbers or zero.*

Lemma 7.6. *If eigenvalue $\eta\,i$ and μ construct an eigenpair of A, then $-\eta\,i$ and $\bar{\mu}$ also constitute an eigenpair of A.*

Lemma 7.7. *If $\lambda_k\,i \neq \lambda_m\,i$, then $\mu_k \perp \mu_m$, i.e. $\langle \mu_k, \mu_m \rangle = 0$, $k, m \in [1, n]$.*

Using Lemma 7.7 gives that if $\lambda_k\,\mathrm{i} \neq \lambda_m\,\mathrm{i}$, then $V_k \perp V_m$. When $\lambda_k\,\mathrm{i} = \lambda_m\,\mathrm{i}$, i.e. the algebraic multiplicity of $\lambda_k\,\mathrm{i}$ is more than one, two subspaces orthogonal to each other can be specially determined. Thus

$$V_1 \perp, \cdots, \perp V_n. \tag{7.62}$$

Let $\xi \in C^n$ denote the equilibrium vector, when ξ exists, there exists

$$\xi = \lim_{t \to \infty} z(t). \tag{7.63}$$

From (7.61), it follows that

$$-A\xi\,\mathrm{i} = \sum_{j=1}^{n} \xi_j \xi, \tag{7.64}$$

When ξ is an eigenvector of A, $\lambda\,\mathrm{i}\,(\lambda \in R)$ denote the associate eigenvalue, we have

$$A\xi = \lambda\,\mathrm{i}\xi. \tag{7.65}$$

From (7.64) and (7.65), it follows that

$$\lambda = \sum_{j=1}^{n} \xi_j. \tag{7.66}$$

7.3.2. *Analytic solution*

Theorem 7.13. *Let $S_k = \mu_k / |\mu_k|$, $z_k(t)$ denotes the projection value of $z(t)$ onto S_k, then*

$$z_k(t) = \frac{z_k(0)\exp(\lambda_k t)}{1 + \sum\limits_{l=1}^{n} z_l(0) \int_0^t \exp(\lambda_l \tau)\, d\tau} \tag{7.67}$$

for $t \geq 0$.

Proof: By using the ideas in proving Theorem 7.9, this theorem can be proved.

7.3.3. Convergence analysis of RNN

Theorem 7.14. *If $x_l(0) < 0$ and $y_l(0) = 0$ for $l = 1, 2, \cdots n$, there must exist overflow.*

Proof: When $y_l(0) = 0$ for $l = 1, 2, \cdots n$, from Theorem 7.1, it follows that

$$\begin{aligned}\sum_{k}^{n} z_k(t) &= \sum_{k=1}^{n} \frac{z_k(0)\exp(\lambda_k t)}{1+\sum_{l=1}^{n} z_l(0)\int_0^t \exp(\lambda_l \tau)d\tau} \\ &= \sum_{k=1}^{n} x_k(0)\exp(\lambda_k t)\frac{1}{1+\sum_{l=1}^{n} x_l(0)\int_0^t \exp(\lambda_l \tau)d\tau}\end{aligned} \tag{7.68}$$

When $x_l(0) < 0$, whether $\lambda_l = 0$ or $\lambda_l > 0$, it follows that

$$\sum_{l=1}^{n} x_l(0)\int_0^t \exp(\lambda_l \tau)\, d\tau < 0,$$

Let $F(t) = 1 + \sum_{l=1}^{n} x_l(0)\int_0^t \exp(\lambda_l \tau)\, d\tau$. Evidently $F(t) < 1$ and $\dot{F}(t) = \sum_{l=1}^{n} x_l(0)\exp(\lambda_l t) < 0$, that is, there must exist a time t_g which leads to

$$1 + \sum_{l=1}^{n} x_l(0)\int_0^{t_g} \exp(\lambda_l \tau)\, d\tau = 0,$$

i.e. at time t_g RNN (7.58) enters into overflow state. This theorem is proved.

Theorem 7.15. *If $z(0) \in V_m$ and $x(0) > 0$, when $\xi \neq 0$, then $i\sum_{k=1}^{n}\xi_k = \lambda_m i$.*

Proof: Using Lemma 7.3, it gives that $V_m \bot V_k$ $(1 \le k \le n, k \neq m)$, so $z_k(0) = 0$, $(1 \le k \le n, k \neq m)$. Using Theorems 7.1 and 7.8 gives that

$$\begin{aligned}\sum_{k=1}^{n} \xi_k &= \lim_{t\to\infty} \sum_{k=1}^{n} \frac{z_k(0)\exp(\lambda_k t)}{1+\sum_{l=1}^{n} z_l(0)\int_0^t \exp(\lambda_l \tau)d\tau} \\ &= \lim_{t\to\infty} \frac{z_m(0)\exp(\lambda_m t)}{1+z_m(0)\int_0^t \exp(\lambda_m \tau)d\tau}\end{aligned}. \tag{7.69}$$

When $\lambda_m \le 0$, it easily follows that $\sum_{k=1}^{n} \xi_k = 0$, i.e. $\xi = 0$, which contradicts $\xi \neq 0$. So $\lambda_m > 0$. In this instance, using Equation (7.69), it gives that

$$\sum_{k=1}^{n} \xi_k = \lim_{t\to\infty} \frac{z_m(0)}{\exp(-\lambda_m t)+\frac{1}{\lambda_m} z_m(0)[1-\exp(-\lambda_m t)]}, \\ = \lambda_m$$

i.e. $\mathrm{i}\sum_{\mathrm{k}=1}^{n} \xi_k = \lambda_m \mathrm{i}$. This theorem is proved.

Theorem 7.16. *If* $z(0) \notin V_m \quad (m = 1, \cdots, n)$ *and* $x_l(0) \geq 0$ *(*$l = 1, 2, \cdots n$*), then* $\xi \in V_1$*, and* $\sum\limits_{k=1}^{n} \xi_k\, i = \lambda_1 i$*.*

Proof: Since $z(0) \notin V_m$ and Equation (7.62), so $z_l(0) \neq 0$. By the result of $x_l(0) \geq 0$ and Theorem 7.2, it can be concluded that there does not exist overflow. Using Theorems 7.1 and 7.8 gives that

$$\xi = \lim_{t\to\infty} \frac{z_1(0)\exp(\lambda_1 t)S_1 + z_2(0)\exp(\lambda_2 t)S_2 + \cdots + z_n(0)\exp(\lambda_n t)S_n}{1 + \sum\limits_{l=1}^{n} z_l(0)\int_0^t \exp(\lambda_l \tau)d\tau} \\ = \lim_{t\to\infty} \frac{z_1(0)S_1 + z_2(0)\exp[(\lambda_2-\lambda_1)t]S_2 + \cdots + z_n(0)\exp[(\lambda_n-\lambda_1)t]S_n}{\exp(-\lambda_1 t) + \frac{1}{\lambda_1} z_l(0)[1-\exp(-\lambda_1 t)] + \sum\limits_{l=2}^{n} z_l(0)\int_0^t \exp(\lambda_l \tau)d\tau}, \\ = \lambda_1 S_1 \in V_1$$

obviously $\sum\limits_{k=1}^{n} \xi_k \mathrm{i} = \lambda_1 \mathrm{i}$.

Corollary 7.1. $\bar{\xi}$ *is an eigenvector corresponding to* $\lambda_2 i$*.*

Proof: Using Equation (7.64), it gives that

$$A\bar{\xi}\mathrm{i} = \sum_{j=1}^{n} \bar{\xi}_j \bar{\xi}. \tag{7.70}$$

Since $\sum\limits_{j=1}^{n} \bar{\xi}_j = \overline{\sum\limits_{j=1}^{n} \xi_j} = \overline{\lambda_1} = \lambda_1$, $\lambda_2 = -\lambda_1$ and Equation (7.70),

$$A\bar{\xi}\mathrm{i} = -\lambda_2 \bar{\xi},$$

i.e.

$$A\bar{\xi} = \lambda_2 \mathrm{i}\, \bar{\xi}.$$

So, this corollary can be drawn.

Theorem 7.17. *If* $\lambda_{l1} = \lambda_{l2} = \cdots = \lambda_{lp} \geq 0$*, nonzero* $z(0) \in V_{l1} \oplus V_{l2} \oplus \cdots \oplus V_{lp}$ *and* $x_{lk}(0) \geq 0$ *(*$k = 1, 2, \cdots p$*), then* $\xi \in V_{l1} \oplus V_{l2} \oplus \cdots \oplus V_{lp}$*, and* $\sum\limits_{k=1}^{n} \xi_k\, i = \lambda_{l1}\, i = \lambda_{l2}\, i = \cdots = \lambda_{lp}\, i$ *(*$l1, l2, \cdots, lp \in [1, n]$*).*

Proof: Since $z(0) \in V_{l1} \oplus V_{l2} \oplus \cdots \oplus V_{lp}$, so at least there exists one component $z_k \neq 0$ for $k \in (l_1, l_2, \cdots, l_p)$ and $z_{k'} = 0 \quad k' \notin (l_1, l_2, \cdots, l_p)$. Let λ_l denote $\lambda_{l1} = \lambda_{l2} = \cdots = \lambda_{lp}$. Using Theorem 7.1 and Equation (7.63), it gives that

$$\begin{aligned}
\sum_{k=1}^{n} \xi_k &= \lim_{t\to\infty} \sum_{k=1}^{n} \frac{z_k(0)\exp(\lambda_k t)}{1+\sum\limits_{l=1}^{n} z_l(0)\int_0^t \exp(\lambda_l \tau)d\tau} \\
&= \lim_{t\to\infty} \frac{\sum\limits_{k\in(l1,l2,\cdots,lp)}^{n} z_k(0)\exp(\lambda_k t) + \sum\limits_{k\notin(l1,l2,\cdots,lp)}^{n} z_k(0)\exp(\lambda_k t)}{1+\sum\limits_{k\in(l1,l2,\cdots,lp)}^{n} z_k(0)\int_0^t \exp(\lambda_k\tau)d\tau + \sum\limits_{k\notin(l1,l2,\cdots,lp)}^{n} z_k(0)\int_0^t \exp(\lambda_k\tau)d\tau}, \\
&= \lim_{t\to\infty} \frac{\sum\limits_{k\in(l1,l2,\cdots,lp)}^{n} z_k(0)\exp(\lambda_k t)}{1+\sum\limits_{k\in(l1,l2,\cdots,lp)}^{n} z_k(0)\int_0^t \exp(\lambda_k\tau)d\tau}
\end{aligned} \tag{7.71}$$

if $\lambda_l = 0$, using Equation (7.71), it gives that

$$\sum_{k=1}^{n} \xi_k = \lim_{t\to\infty} \frac{\sum\limits_{k\in(l1,l2,\cdots,lp)}^{n} z_k(0)}{1+\sum\limits_{k\in(l1,l2,\cdots,lp)}^{n} z_k(0)\,t} = 0 = \lambda_l,$$

and if $\lambda_l > 0$, Equation (7.71) gives that

$$\begin{aligned}
\sum_{k=1}^{n} \xi_k &= \lim_{t\to\infty} \frac{\sum_{k\in(l1,l2,\cdots,lp)}^{n} z_k(0)\exp(\lambda_l t)}{1+\sum\limits_{k\in(l1,l2,\cdots,lp)}^{n} z_k(0)\int_0^t \exp(\lambda_k\tau)d\tau} \\
&= \lim_{t\to\infty} \frac{\sum_{k\in(l1,l2,\cdots,lp)}^{n} z_k(0)}{\exp(-\lambda_l t)+\frac{1}{\lambda_l}\sum\limits_{k\in(l1,l2,\cdots,lp)}^{n} z_k(0)[1-\exp(-\lambda_l t)]}. \\
&= \lambda_l
\end{aligned} \tag{7.72}$$

From Equations (7.71) and (7.72), this theorem is proved.

7.3.4. *Simulation*

In order to evaluate RNN (7.58), we provide two examples here. One will demonstrate the effectiveness of RNN (7.58), and the other will illustrate that the convergence behavior remains good for large dimension matrices.

Example 1: let

$$A = \begin{pmatrix} 0 \text{ -0.2564 } 0.2862 \text{ -0.0288 } 0.4294 \\ 0.2564 \text{ 0 -0.1263 -0.1469 -0.1567} \\ \text{-0.2862 } 0.1263 \text{ 0 -0.2563 -0.1372} \\ 0.0288 \text{ } 0.1469 \text{ } 0.2563 \text{ 0 -0.0657} \\ \text{-0.4294 } 0.1567 \text{ } 0.1372 \text{ } 0.0657 \text{ 0} \end{pmatrix}.$$

The equilibrium vector is

$\xi = (0.1587\text{-}0.5258\text{i-}0.3023+0.1154\text{i } 0.2279+0.2702\text{i } 0.0998+0.0171\text{i } 0.4470+0.1231\text{i})^T$

and

$$\lambda_1 \mathrm{i} = \mathrm{i}\sum_{k=1}^{5} \xi_k = 0.6311\,\mathrm{i}.$$

The trajectories of the real parts of the components of $z(t)$ are illustrated in Fig. 7.13 and the trajectory of $\sum_{k=1}^{n} z_k(t)$ is shown in Fig. 7.14.

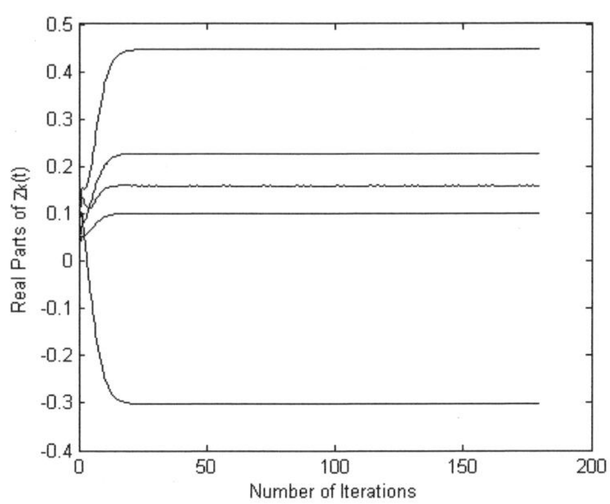

Fig. 7.13. The trajectories of real part of $Z_k(t)$.

The largest modulus true eigenvalues directly computed by Matlab as the ground truth are $\lambda_1 \mathrm{i} = 0.6310\,\mathrm{i}$, $\lambda_2 \mathrm{i} = -0.6310\,\mathrm{i}$. The corresponding eigenvectors are

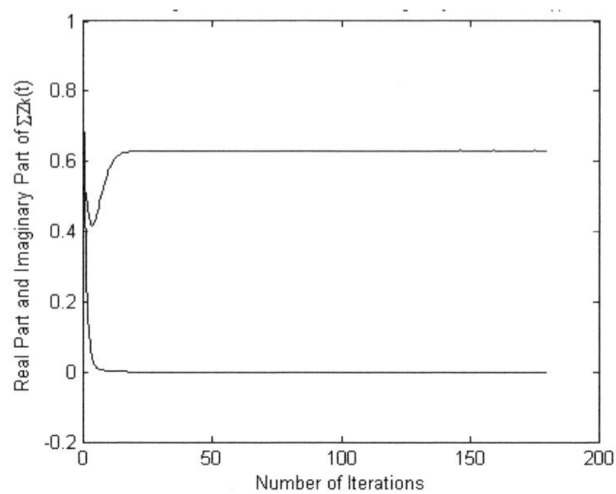

Fig. 7.14. The trajectories of real part and imaginary part of $\sum_{i=1}^{5} z_i(t)$.

$$S_1 = \begin{pmatrix} 0.6315 \\ \text{-0.2274-0.2944i} \\ \text{-0.2217+0.3406i} \\ \text{0.0143+0.1155i} \\ \text{0.0130+0.5329i} \end{pmatrix}, \quad S_2 = S_1,$$

$$S_3 = \begin{pmatrix} 0.0024 + 0.2991\text{i} \\ 0.1267 + 0.2947\text{i} \\ -0.0802 + 0.5391\text{i} \\ 0.6904 \\ \text{-0.0284-0.1817i} \end{pmatrix}, \quad S_4 = S_3 \quad \text{and } S_5 = \begin{pmatrix} 0.1533 \\ 0.7193 \\ -0.2749 \\ -0.1397 \\ 0.6033 \end{pmatrix}.$$

When λ_1i is compared with $\tilde{\lambda}_1$i, it can be seen that their difference is trivial. Therefore, RNN (7.58) is effective to compute the largest modulus eigenvalues $\tilde{\lambda}_1$i and $\tilde{\lambda}_2$i. Since $\xi^T \bar{S}_2 = \xi^T \bar{S}_3 = \xi^T \bar{S}_4 = \xi^T \bar{S}_5 = 0$ and $\xi^T \bar{S}_1 = 0.2513 + 0.8327\,\text{i}$, ξ is equivalent to S_1. As $\bar{\xi}^T \bar{S}_1 = \bar{\xi}^T \bar{S}_3 = \bar{\xi}^T \bar{S}_4 = \bar{\xi}^T \bar{S}_5 = 0$ and $\bar{\xi}^T \bar{S}_2 = 0.2513 - 0.8327\,\text{i}$, so $\bar{\xi}$ is equivalent to S_2. Therefore the largest modulus eigenvalues ($\tilde{\lambda}_1$i, $\tilde{\lambda}_2$i) and their corresponding eigenvectors are computed.

The above results are obtained when the initial vector is $z(0) = (0.1520\text{i}\ 0.2652\text{i}\ 0.1847\text{i}\ 0.0139\text{i}\ 0.2856\text{i})^T$. When the initial vector is replaced with other random values, the results have trvial changes and keep being very close to the corresponding ground truth values.

Example 2: Let $A \in R^{85\times 85}$, $A(j,i) = -A(i,j) = -(\sin(i) + \sin(j))/2$ and $z(0) = (\sin(1)\,\text{i}\ \sin(2)\,\text{i} \cdots \sin(85)\,\text{i})^T$. The calculated largest modulus eigenvalue is 19.6672i which is very close to the corresponding

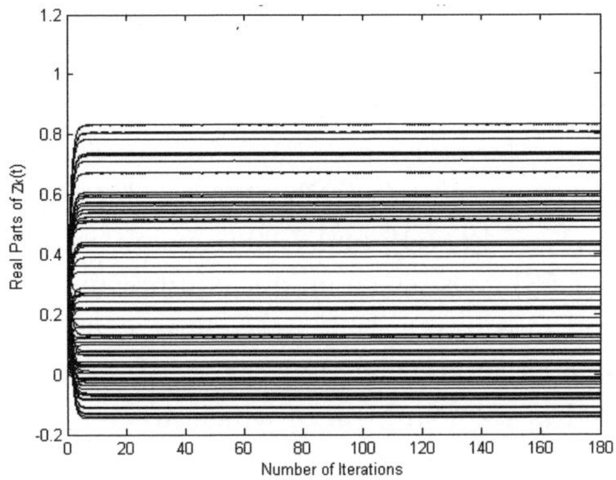

Fig. 7.15. The trajectories of real part of $z_k(t)$.

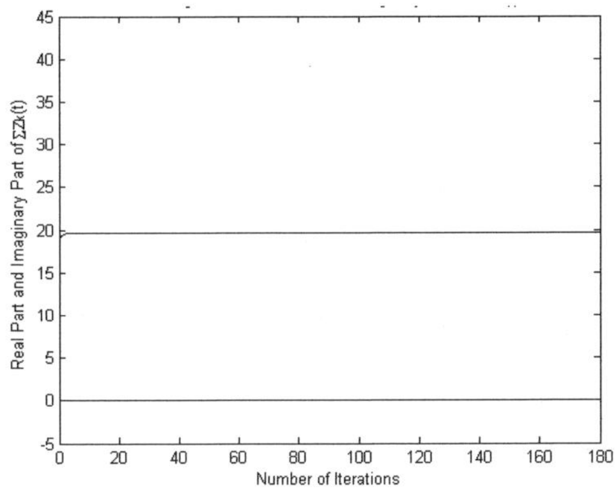

Fig. 7.16. The trajectories of real and imaginary parts of $\sum_{i=1}^{85} z_i(t)$.

ground truth value 19.6634i. Convergence behaviors are shown in Figs 7.15 and 7.16. From these figures, we can see that the iteration numbers do not increase with the dimension, and that this method is still effective even when the dimension number is very large.

7.3.5. *Comparison with other methods and discussions*

When RNN (7.58) is to be implemented by hardwares, some techniques about discretization must be considered [26]. In the Matlab environment, operating on a single central processing unit, the feature of parallel running of ANN does not exhibit as the nodes of the network cannot run synchronously. But for the stand power method [10, 17], as it serially runs in nature, it can achieve high performance in a serial running platform. To compare RNN (7.58) with the stand power method, let $A \in R^{15\times 15}$, $A(j,i) = -A(i,j) = -(\cos(i) + \sin(j))/2$ for $i \neq j$ and $A(i,i) = 0$. The simulated results corresponding to RNN (7.58) and the stand power method are shown in Figs 7.17, 7.18, 7.19 and 7.20 respectively. From Fig. 7.17, we can see that RNN (7.58) goes into a unique equilibrium state fast, while the stand power method falls into a cycle procedure, which can be seen in Fig. 7.19. The eigenvalue calculated by RNN (7.58) is 4.0695i, and that by the stand power method is 4.0693i, both of which are very close to the ground truth value 4.0693i. The convergence behaviors of these two methods are shown in Figs 7.18 and 7.20, respectively. Also from Figs 7.18 and 7.20, we can see that the convergence rates of the two methods are similar. After around five iterations, the calculated values approach to the ground truth eigenvalue.

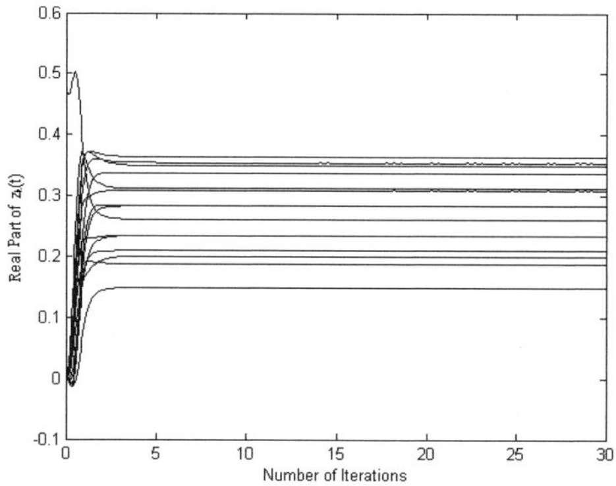

Fig. 7.17. The trajectories of the real parts of $z_i(t)$ for $1 \leq i \leq 15$ by RNN (7.58).

With an autocorrelation matrix, Fa-Long Luo introduced two algorithms: with one calculating the principal eigenvectors [4], and the other extracting the eigenvectors corresponding to the smallest eigenvalues [2]. He also proposed a real-time neural computation approach to extract the largest eigenvalue of a positive matrix [9]. Compared with these references, the electronic circuits of RNN (7.58) may be more complex because it considers the question in complex space, but is more suitable for a real skew matrix. As for reference [9], if the eigenvalue was a complex number, the computation model would fail. The approach proposed by

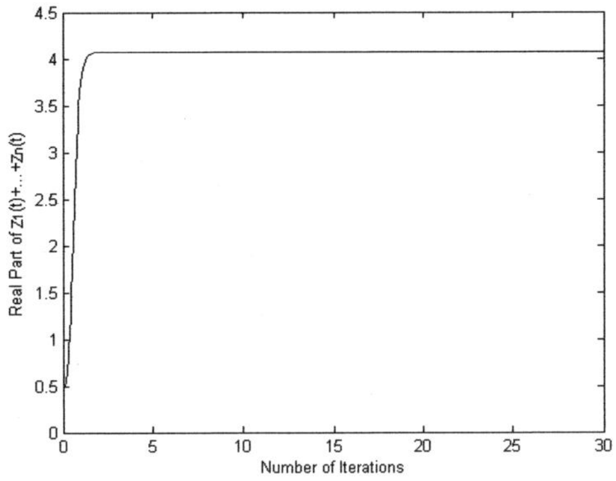

Fig. 7.18. The trajectory of $\sum_{i=1}^{15} z_i(t)$ by RNN (7.58).

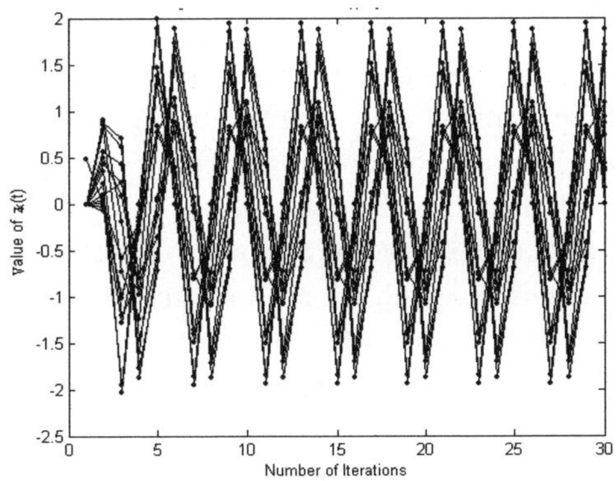

Fig. 7.19. The trajectories of the components of $z(t)$ by the standard power method.

reference [13, 14] involves a neural network model which is different from RNN (7.58), and the scheme extracting eigen-parameters in these two references would fail when the matrix had repeated eigenvalues and the initial state was not specially restricted. References [8, 21, 22] are only suitable for a real symmetric matrix. RNN (7.58) is more concise than the model in reference [23] since RNN (7.58) does not include the computation of $|z(t)|^2$. Briefly speaking, compared with the published methods, our one has some novelties in different aspects.

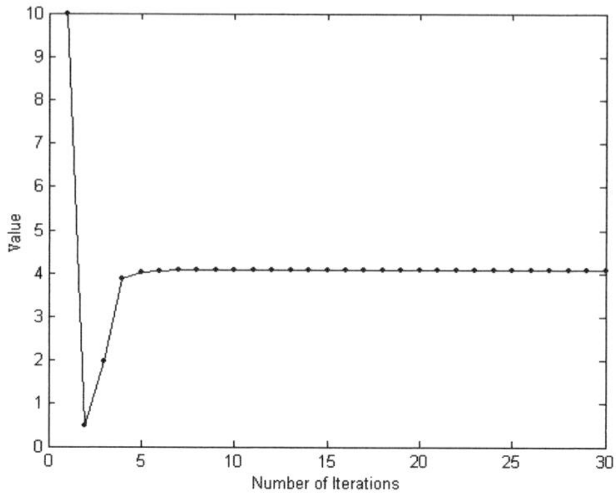

Fig. 7.20. The trajectory of the variable which converges to the largest modulus eigenvalue by the standard power method.

7.3.6. *Section summary*

A new concise recurrent neural network model adaptive to compute largest modulus eigenvalues and corresponding eigenvectors of a real anti-symmetric matrix was proposed in this section. When the model was given, it was equivalently transformed into a complex dynamical system depicted by a complex differential equation. With the analytic solution of the equation, the convergence behaviors were analyzed in detail. Simulation results verified the effectiveness of the method to calculate the eigenvalues and corresponding eigenvectors. The obtained eigenvectors were proved equivalent to the corresponding ground truth. Compared with other neural networks used in the same field, the proposed model is concise and adaptive to real anti-symmetric matrices, with good convergence property.

7.4. A Recurrent Neural Network Computing the Largest Imaginary or Real Part of Eigenvalues of a General Real Matrix

In the first three sections of this chapter, we have introduced how to use neural networks to solve the problems of computing the eigenpairs of real symmetric or anti-symmetric matrices, which have been popular research topics in the past few years. Reference [27] generalized the well-known Oja network to compute non-symmetrical matrices. Liu *et al.* [21] meliorated the model in [8] and introduced a simpler model to accomplish analogous calculations. Reference [23] introduced an RNN model to compute the largest modulus eigenvalues and their corresponding eigenvectors of an anti-symmetric matrix. It is found that most of the recent efforts have mainly been focused on solving eigenpairs of real symmetric, or anti-symmetric, matrices. Although [27] involved non-symmetric matrices, its section "The nonlinear homogeneous case" has the assumption of $\alpha(w) \in R$, which requires the matrix occupy real eigenvalues. Following a search of the relevant literature, we were unable to locate a neural network-based method to calculate eigenvalues of a general real matrix, whether the eigenvalue is a real or general complex number. Thus, in this section, a recurrent neural network-based approach will be proposed (Equation (7.73)) to estimate the largest modulus of eigenvalues of a *general real matrix.*

$$\frac{dv(t)}{dt} = A' v(t) - |v(t)|^2 \, v(t), \tag{7.73}$$

where $t \geq 0$, $v(t) \in R^{2n}$, $A' = \begin{pmatrix} 0 & A \\ -A & 0 \end{pmatrix}$, A is the general real matrix requiring calculation. $|v(t)|$ denotes the modulus of $v(t)$. When $v(t)$ is seen as the states of neurons, with $\left[A' - |v(t)|^2 U\right]$ (U denotes a suitable dimensional identity matrix) being regarded as synaptic connection weights and the activation functions being assumed to be pure linear functions, Equation (7.73) describes a continuous time recurrent neural network.

Let $v(t) = \left(x^T(t)\, y^T(t)\right)^T$, $x(t) = (x_1(t), x_2(t), \cdots, x_n(t))^T \in R^n$ and $y(t) = (y_1(t), y_2(t), \cdots, y_n(t))^T \in R^n$. From Equation (7.73), it follows that

$$\begin{cases} \frac{dx(t)}{dt} = Ay(t) - \sum\limits_{j=1}^{n} \left[x_j^2(t) + y_j^2(t)\right] x(t) \\ \frac{dy(t)}{dt} = -Ax(t) - \sum\limits_{j=1}^{n} \left[x_j^2(t) + y_j^2(t)\right] y(t) \end{cases}. \tag{7.74}$$

Let

$$z(t) = x(t) + \mathrm{i}y(t), \tag{7.75}$$

with i denoting the imaginary unit, it can be easily followed from Equation (7.74) that

$$\frac{dx(t)}{dt} + \mathrm{i}\frac{dy(t)}{dt} = -A\mathrm{i}\left[x(t) + \mathrm{i}y(t)\right] - \sum_{j=1}^{n} \left[x_j^2(t) + y_j^2(t)\right] \left[x(t) + \mathrm{i}y(t)\right],$$

i.e.

$$\frac{dz(t)}{dt} = -Az(t)\,\mathrm{i} - z^T(t)\,\bar{z}(t)\,z(t), \tag{7.76}$$

where $\bar{z}(t)$ denotes the complex conjugate vector of $z(t)$. Obviously, Equation (7.76) is a complex differential system. A set of ordinary differential equations is just a model which may approximate the real behavior of some neural networks, although there are differences between them. In the following subsections, we will discuss the convergence properties of Equation (7.76) instead of RNN (7.73).

7.4.1. *Analytic expression of* $|z(t)|^2$

All eigenvalues of A are denoted as $\lambda_1^R + \lambda_1^I\mathrm{i}, \lambda_2^R + \lambda_2^I\mathrm{i}, \cdots, \lambda_n^R + \lambda_n^I\mathrm{i}$ ($\lambda_k^R, \lambda_k^I \in R$, $k = 1, 2, \cdots, n$), and the corresponding complex eigenvectors are denoted as $\mu_1, \cdots, \mu_n$.

With any general real matrix A, there are two cases for $\mu_1, \cdots, \mu_n$:

1) when the rank of A is deficient, some of $\lambda_1^R+\lambda_1^I\mathrm{i}, \lambda_2^R+\lambda_2^I\mathrm{i}, \cdots, \lambda_n^R+\lambda_n^I\mathrm{i}$ may be zeros. When $\lambda_j^R + \lambda_j^I\mathrm{i} = 0$, u_j can be randomly chosen ensuring $\mu_1, \cdots, \mu_n$ construct a basis in $C^{n\times n}$;

2) When A is full rank, $\mu_1, \cdots, \mu_n$ are decided by A. Although they may not be orthogonal to each other, they can still construct a basis in $C^{n\times n}$.

Let $S_k = \mu_k/|\mu_k|$, obviously $S_1, \cdots, S_n$ construct a normalized basis in $C^{n\times n}$.

Theorem 7.18. *Let $z_k(t) = x_k(t) + i\,y_k(t)$ denote the projection value of $z(t)$ onto S_k. The analytic expression of $|z(t)|^2$ is*

$$|z(t)|^2 = \frac{\sum\limits_{k=1}^{n} \exp\left(2\lambda_k^I t\right)\left[x_k^2(0) + y_k^2(0)\right]}{1 + 2\sum\limits_{j=1}^{n}\left[x_j^2(0) + y_j^2(0)\right]\int_0^t \exp\left(2\lambda_j^I \tau\right)d\tau} \tag{7.77}$$

for $t \geq 0$.

Proof: the proof of this theorem is similar to that of Theorem 7.7.9 and omitted here.

7.4.2. *Convergence analysis*

If an equilibrium vector of RNN (7.73) exists, let ξ denote it, and there exists

$$\xi = \lim_{t\to\infty} z(t)\,. \tag{7.78}$$

Theorem 7.19. *If each eigenvalue is a real number, then* $|\xi| = 0$.

Proof: From Theorem 7.1, we know

$$|z| = \sqrt{\frac{\sum\limits_{k=1}^{n} \exp\left(2\lambda_k^I t\right)\left[x_k^2(0) + y_k^2(0)\right]}{1 + 2\sum\limits_{j=1}^{n}\left[x_j^2(0) + y_j^2(0)\right]\int_0^t \exp\left(2\lambda_j^I \tau\right) d\tau}}\,. \tag{7.79}$$

Thus,

$$|\xi| = \lim_{t\to\infty} |z(t)| = \lim_{t\to\infty} \sqrt{\frac{\sum\limits_{k=1}^{n} \exp\left(2\lambda_k^I t\right)\left[x_k^2(0) + y_k^2(0)\right]}{1 + 2\sum\limits_{j=1}^{n}\left[x_j^2(0) + y_j^2(0)\right]\int_0^t \exp\left(2\lambda_j^I \tau\right) d\tau}}\,. \tag{7.80}$$

Since each eigenvalue is real, so

$$\lambda_1^I = \lambda_2^I = \cdots = \lambda_n^I = 0. \tag{7.81}$$

From Equations (7.80) and (7.81), it follows that

$$|\xi| = \lim_{t\to\infty} \sqrt{\frac{\sum\limits_{k=1}^{n} \left[x_k^2(0) + y_k^2(0)\right]}{1 + 2\sum\limits_{j=1}^{n}\left[x_j^2(0) + y_j^2(0)\right]\, t}} = 0\,.$$

This theorem is proved. This theorem implies that if a matrix only has real eigenvalues, RNN (7.73) will converge to zero point, which is independent of the initial complex vector.

Theorem 7.20. *Denote* $\lambda_m^I = \max\limits_{1\le k\le n} \lambda_k^I$*. If* $\lambda_m^I > 0$*, then* $\xi^T\bar{\xi} = \lambda_m^I$.

Proof: Using Equation (7.78) and Theorem 7.1 gives that

$$\xi^T\bar{\xi} = \lim_{t\to\infty} |z(t)|^2 = \lim_{t\to\infty} \frac{\sum\limits_{k=1}^{n} \exp\left(2\lambda_k^I t\right)\left[x_k^2(0) + y_k^2(0)\right]}{1 + 2\sum\limits_{j=1}^{n}\left[x_j^2(0) + y_j^2(0)\right]\int_0^t \exp\left(2\lambda_j^I \tau\right) d\tau}\,,$$

i.e.

$$\xi^T\bar{\xi} = \lim_{t\to\infty} \frac{\exp\left(2\lambda_m^I t\right)\left[x_m^2(0)+y_m^2(0)\right] + \sum\limits_{k=1,k\neq m}^{n} \exp\left(2\lambda_k^I t\right)\left[x_k^2(0)+y_k^2(0)\right]}{1+2[x_m^2(0)+y_m^2(0)]\int_0^t \exp(2\lambda_m^I\tau)d\tau + 2\sum\limits_{j=1,j\neq m}^{n}\left[x_j^2(0)+y_j^2(0)\right]\int_0^t\exp\left(2\lambda_j^I\tau\right)d\tau}$$

$$= \lim_{t\to\infty} \frac{\left[x_m^2(0)+y_m^2(0)\right] + \sum\limits_{k=1,k\neq m}^{n} \exp\left[2\left(\lambda_k^I-\lambda_m^I\right)\, t\right]\,\left[x_k^2(0)+y_k^2(0)\right]}{\exp(-2\lambda_m^I t)+\frac{1}{\lambda_m^I}[x_m^2(0)+y_m^2(0)][1-\exp(-2\lambda_m^I t)]+2\sum\limits_{j=1,j\neq m}^{n}\left[x_j^2(0)+y_j^2(0)\right]\int_0^t\exp\left(2\lambda_j^I\tau-\right.}$$

$$= \lambda_m^I.$$

This theorem is proved. From this theorem, we know that when the maximal imaginary part of eigenvalues is positive, RNN (7.73) will converge to a nonzero equilibrium vector. In addition, the square modulus of the vector is equal to the largest imaginary part.

Theorem 7.21. *If A' is replaced by $\begin{pmatrix} A & 0 \\ 0 & A \end{pmatrix}$, then*

$$|z(t)|^2 = \frac{\sum\limits_{k=1}^{n} \exp\left(2\lambda_k^R t\right)\left[x_k^2(0)+y_k^2(0)\right]}{1+2\sum\limits_{j=1}^{n}\left[x_j^2(0)+y_j^2(0)\right]\int_0^t\exp\left(2\lambda_j^R\tau\right)\,d\tau}.$$

Proof: When $A' = \begin{pmatrix} A & 0 \\ 0 & A \end{pmatrix}$, by a similar way of obtaining Equation (7.76), RNN (7.73) is transformed into

$$\frac{dz(t)}{dt} = Az(t) - z^T(t)\,\bar{z}(t)\,z(t)\,. \tag{7.82}$$

Using the denotations of $x_k(t)$ and $y_k(t)$, we have

$$\frac{d}{dt}x_k(t) = \lambda_k^R x_k(t) - \lambda_k^I y_k(t) - \sum_{j=1}^{n}\left[x_j^2(t)+y_j^2(t)\right]x_k(t)\,, \tag{7.83}$$

$$\frac{d}{dt}y_k(t) = \lambda_k^I x_k(t) + \lambda_k^R y_k(t) - \sum_{j=1}^{n}\left[x_j^2(t)+y_j^2(t)\right]y_k(t)\,. \tag{7.84}$$

From Equations (7.83) and (7.84), it follows that

$$\frac{d}{dt}\left[x_k^2(t)+y_k^2(t)\right]=2\lambda_k^R\left[x_k^2(t)+y_k^2(t)\right]-2\sum_{j=1}^{n}\left[x_j^2(t)+y_j^2(t)\right]\left[x_k^2(t)+y_k^2(t)\right]. \tag{7.85}$$

The remaining procedures can refer to the proof of Theorem 7.9.

This theorem provides a way to extract the maximal real part of all eigenvalues through rearranging the connection weights.

Theorem 7.22. *Let* $\lambda_m^R=\max\limits_{1\le k\le n}\lambda_k^R$. *When* A' *is replaced by* $\begin{pmatrix} A & 0\\ 0 & A\end{pmatrix}$, *if* $\lambda_m^R\le 0$, *then* $\xi^T\bar{\xi}=0$. *If* $\lambda_m^R>0$, *then* $\xi^T\bar{\xi}=\lambda_m^R$.

Proof: Using Equation (7.78) and Theorem 7.21 gives that

$$\xi^T\bar{\xi}=\lim_{t\to\infty}|z(t)|^2=\lim_{t\to\infty}\frac{\sum\limits_{k=1}^{n}\exp\left(2\lambda_k^Rt\right)\left[x_k^2(0)+y_k^2(0)\right]}{1+2\sum\limits_{j=1}^{n}\left[x_j^2(0)+y_j^2(0)\right]\int_0^t\exp\left(2\lambda_j^R\tau\right)d\tau}. \tag{7.86}$$

From Equation (7.86), if $\lambda_m^R<0$, it easily follows that

$$\xi^T\bar{\xi}=0, \tag{7.87}$$

if $\lambda_m^R=0$, it follows that

$$\begin{aligned}\xi^T\bar{\xi}&=\lim_{t\to\infty}\frac{\exp\left(2\lambda_m^Rt\right)\left[x_k^2(0)+y_k^2(0)\right]+\sum\limits_{k=1,k\ne m}^{n}\exp\left(2\lambda_k^Rt\right)\left[x_k^2(0)+y_k^2(0)\right]}{1+2\left[x_j^2(0)+y_j^2(0)\right]\int_0^t\exp(2\lambda_m^R\tau)d\tau+2\sum\limits_{j=1,j\ne m}^{n}\left[x_j^2(0)+y_j^2(0)\right]\int_0^t\exp\left(2\lambda_j^R\tau\right)d\tau}\\&=\lim_{t\to\infty}\frac{\left[x_k^2(0)+y_k^2(0)\right]+\sum\limits_{k=1,k\ne m}^{n}\exp\left(2\lambda_k^Rt\right)\left[x_k^2(0)+y_k^2(0)\right]}{1+2\left[x_j^2(0)+y_j^2(0)\right]t+2\sum\limits_{j=1,j\ne m}^{n}\left[x_j^2(0)+y_j^2(0)\right]\int_0^t\exp\left(2\lambda_j^R\tau\right)d\tau}\\&=0,\end{aligned} \tag{7.88}$$

and if $\lambda_m^R>0$, like the deductive procedures of Theorem 7.3, it follows that

$$\xi^T\bar{\xi}=\lambda_m^R. \tag{7.89}$$

From Equations (7.87), (7.88) and (7.89), we know the theorem is proved. This theorem indicates that when the largest real part of all eigenvalues is positive, the slightly changed RNN (7.73) converges to a nonzero equilibrium vector, the square modulus of which is equal to the maximal real part.

7.4.3. *Simulations and discussions*

To evaluate the method, two examples are given. Example 1 uses a 7×7 matrix to show the effectiveness. A 50×50, and a 100×100, matrices are exploited to test the method when the dimensionality is very large in Example 2. The simulation platform is Matlab.

Example 1: A is randomly generated like

$$A = \begin{bmatrix} 0.1347 & 0.0324 & 0.8660 & 0.8636 & 0.6390 & 0.1760 & 0.4075 \\ 0.0225 & 0.7339 & 0.2542 & 0.5676 & 0.6690 & 0.0020 & 0.4078 \\ 0.2622 & 0.5365 & 0.5695 & 0.9805 & 0.7721 & 0.7902 & 0.0527 \\ 0.1165 & 0.2760 & 0.1593 & 0.7918 & 0.3798 & 0.5136 & 0.9418 \\ 0.0693 & 0.3685 & 0.5944 & 0.1526 & 0.4416 & 0.2132 & 0.1500 \\ 0.8529 & 0.0129 & 0.3311 & 0.8330 & 0.4831 & 0.1034 & 0.3844 \\ 0.1803 & 0.8892 & 0.6586 & 0.1919 & 0.6081 & 0.1573 & 0.3111 \end{bmatrix}.$$

The eigenvalues directly computed by Matlab functions are $\lambda_1 = 2.9506$, $\lambda_2 = 0.7105$, $\lambda_3 = -0.3799 + 0.4808i$, $\lambda_4 = \bar{\lambda}_3$, $\lambda_5 = 0.0286 + 0.5397i$, $\lambda_6 = \bar{\lambda}_5$ and $\lambda_7 = 0.1274$. so $\lambda_m^I = 0.5397$ and $\lambda_m^R = 2.9506$.

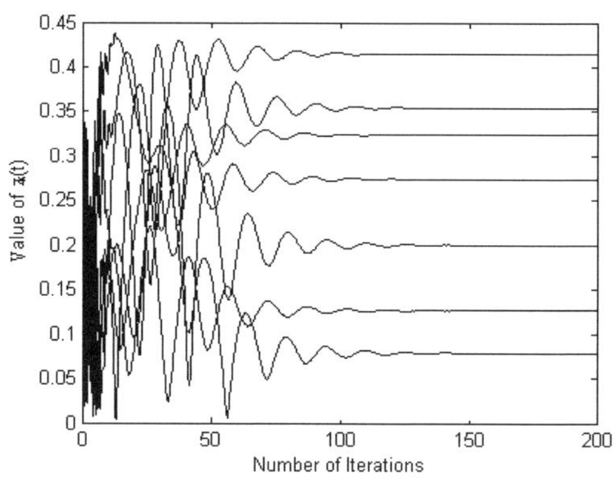

Fig. 7.21. The trajectories of $|z_k(t)|$ in searching λ_m^I when $n = 7$.

When the initial vector is

$$z(0) = [0.0506 + 0.0508i\ 0.2690 + 0.1574i\ 0.0968 + 0.1924i\ 0.2202 + 0.0049i\ 0.1233 + 0.2511i\ 0.1199 + 0.2410i\ 0.1517 + 0.2093i]^T,$$

we get the equilibrium vector

$$\xi = [0.1335 - 0.1489i\ 0.0204 + 0.1250i\ 0.3471 + 0.0709i\ -0.1727 + 0.3771i\ -0.0531 - 0.2687i\ - 0.0719 - 0.0317i\ - 0.0970 - 0.3091i]^T.$$

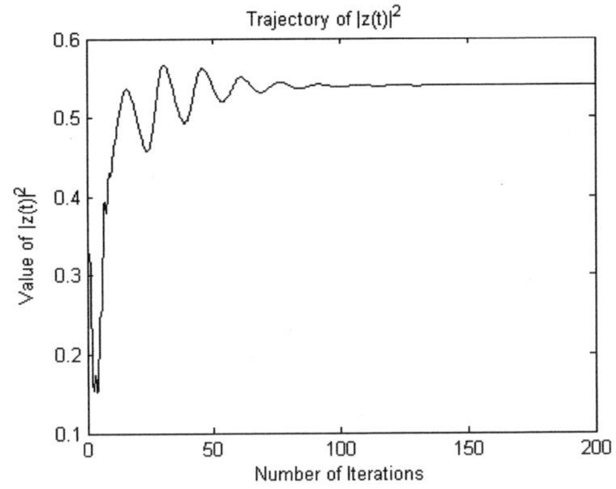

Fig. 7.22. The trajectory of $|z(t)|^2$ in searching λ_m^I when $n = 7$.

Hence the computed maximum imaginary part is

$$\lambda_m^I = \xi^T \bar{\xi} = 0.5397.$$

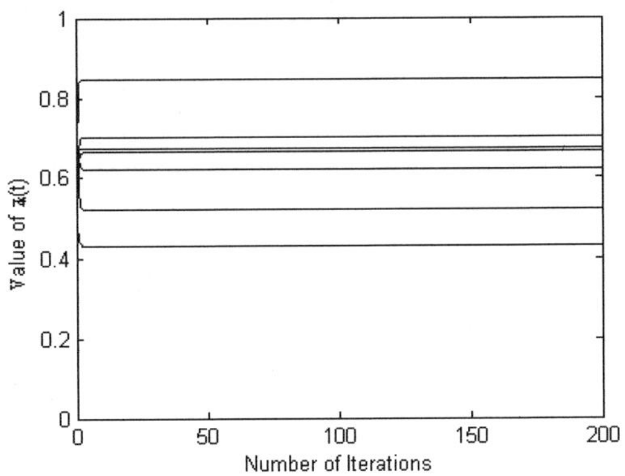

Fig. 7.23. The trajectories of $|z_k(t)|$ in searching λ_m^R when $n = 7$.

When λ_m^I is compared with λ_m^I, it can be easily seen that they are very close. The trajectories of $|z_k(t)|$ $(k = 1, 2, \cdots, 7)$ and $z^T(t)\,\bar{z}(t)$ which will approach λ_m^I are shown in Figs 7.21 and 7.22.

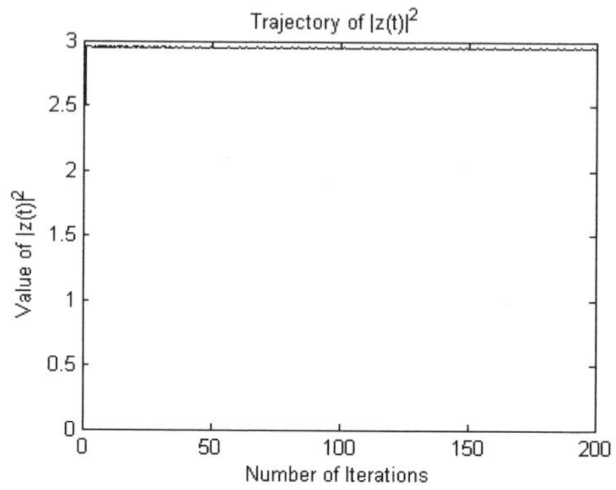

Fig. 7.24. The trajectory of $|z(t)|^2$ in searching λ_m^R when $n = 7$.

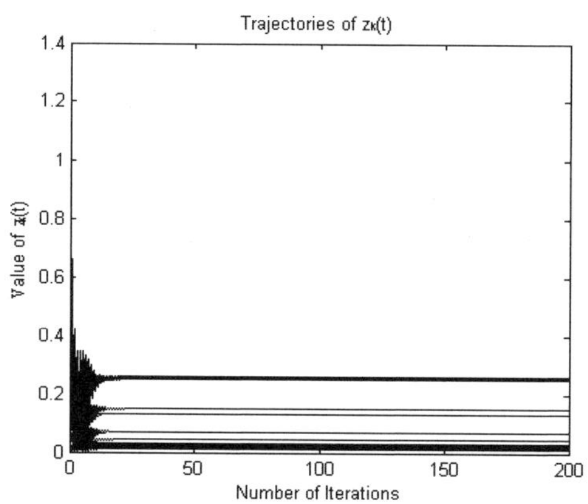

Fig. 7.25. The trajectories of $|z_k(t)|$ in searching λ_m^I when $n = 50$.

When $A' = \begin{pmatrix} A & 0 \\ 0 & A \end{pmatrix}$, the computed maximum real part is

$$\begin{aligned}\lambda_m^R &= |(0.4981 + 0.4949\text{i}\ 0.3701 + 0.3678\text{i}\ 0.6003 + 0.5965\text{i} \\ &\quad 0.4773 + 0.4742\text{i}\ 0.3059 + 0.3039\text{i}\ 0.4719 + 0.4689\text{i}\ 0.4418 + 0.4390\text{i})^T|^2 \\ &= 2.9504.\end{aligned}$$

When λ_m^R is compared with λ_m^R, the absolute difference value is

$$\Delta\lambda_m^R = \left|\lambda_m^R - \lambda_m^R\right| = |2.9506 - 2.9504| = 0.0002,$$

meaning that λ_m^R is very close to λ_m^R. The trajectories of $|z_k(t)|$ $(k = 1, 2, \cdots, 7)$ and $z^T(t)\,\bar{z}(t)$ are shown in Figs 7.23 and 7.24.

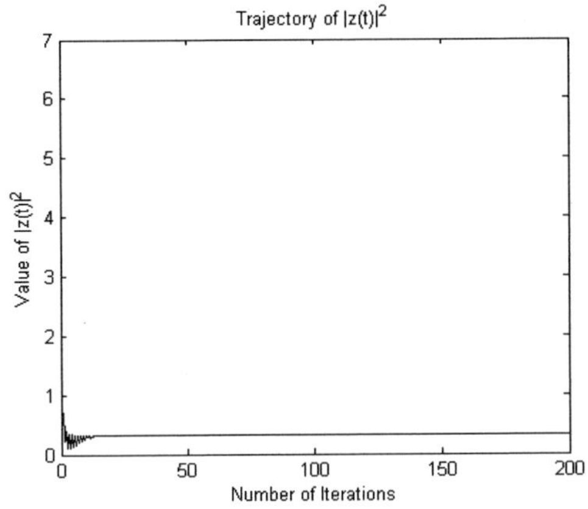

Fig. 7.26. The trajectory of $|z(t)|^2$ in searching λ_m^I when $n = 50$.

With the variation of $z(0)$, the trajectories of $|z_k(t)|$ $(k = 1, 2, \cdots, 7)$ and $z^T(t)\,\bar{z}(t)$ will vary. But λ_m^I and λ_m^R do insistently approach the corresponding ground truth values.

Example 2: How does the approach behave when the dimensionality increases? If a 50×50 matrix is randomly produced, the expression may be too long to write, thus a 50×50 matrix is specially given as

$$a_{ij} = \begin{cases} (-1)^i(50 - i)/100, & i = j \\ (1 - i/50)^i - (j/50)^j, & i \neq j \end{cases}.$$

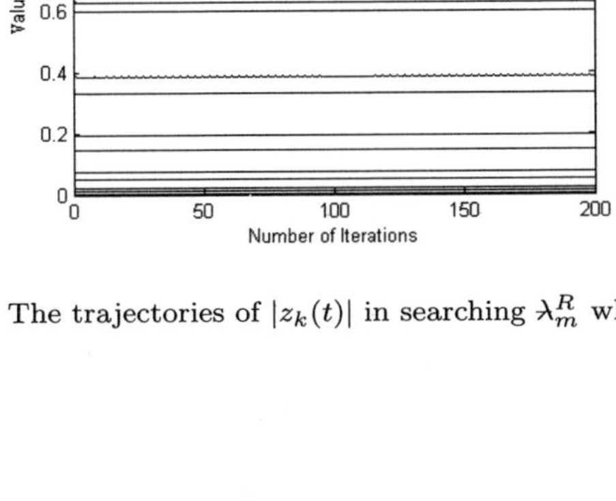

Fig. 7.27. The trajectories of $|z_k(t)|$ in searching λ_m^R when $n = 50$.

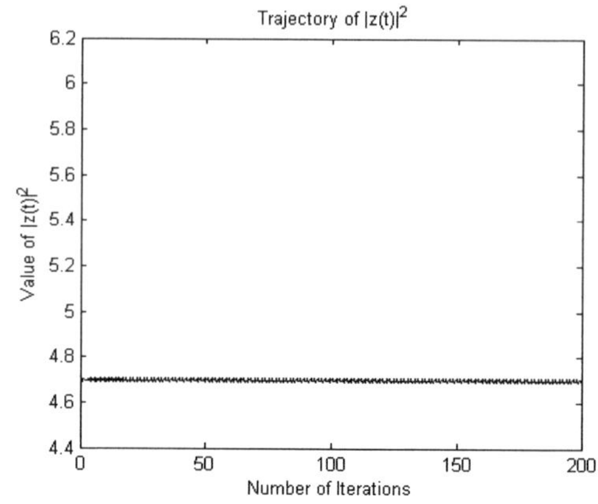

Fig. 7.28. The trajectory of $|z(t)|^2$ in searching λ_m^R when $n = 50$.

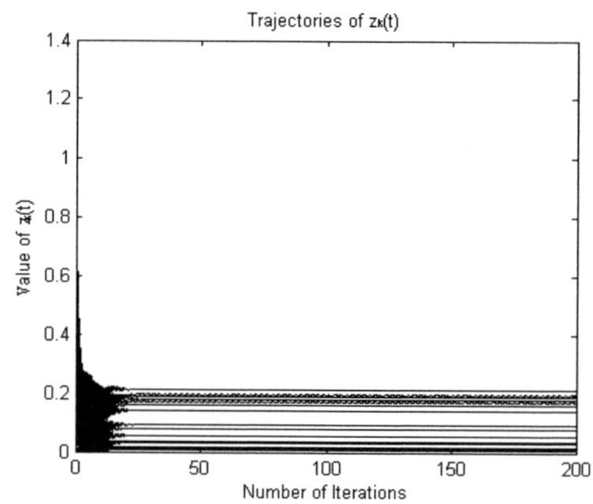

Fig. 7.29. The trajectories of $|z_k(t)|$ in searching λ_m^I when $n = 100$.

The calculated results are $\lambda_m^I = 0.3244$ and $\lambda_m^R = 4.6944$. Convergence behaviors of $|z_k(t)|$ and $z^T(t)\,\bar{z}(t)$ in searching λ_m^I and λ_m^R are shown in Figs 7.25 to 7.28. Comparing λ_m^I and λ_m^R with corresponding true ones $\lambda_m^I = 0.3246$ and $\lambda_m^R = 4.7000$, we find each pair in comparison is very

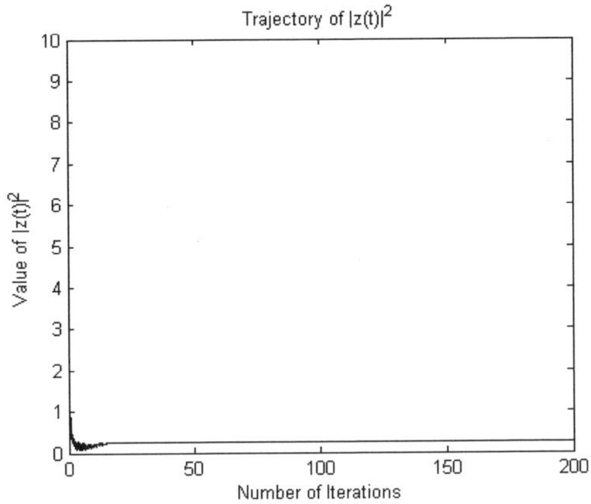

Fig. 7.30. The trajectory of $|z(t)|^2$ in searching λ_m^I when $n = 100$.

close. From Figs 7.25 to 7.28, we can also see the system gets to equilibrium state fast though the dimensionality has reached 50.

In order to ulteriorly show the effectiveness of this approach when dimensionality becomes large, let $n = 100$. The corresponding convergence behaviors are shown in Figs 7.29 to 7.32. $\lambda_m^R = 7.3220$ keeps very close to $\lambda_m^R = 7.3224$, and $\lambda_m^I = 0.2541$ is very close to $\lambda_m^I = 0.2540$. From Figs 7.25 to 7.32, we can see that the iteration number at which the system enters into equilibrium state is not sensitive to dimensionality.

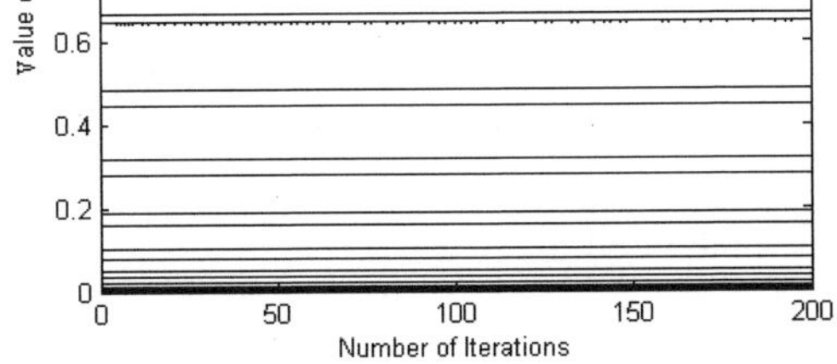

Fig. 7.31. The trajectories of $|z_k(t)|$ in searching λ_m^R when $n = 100$.

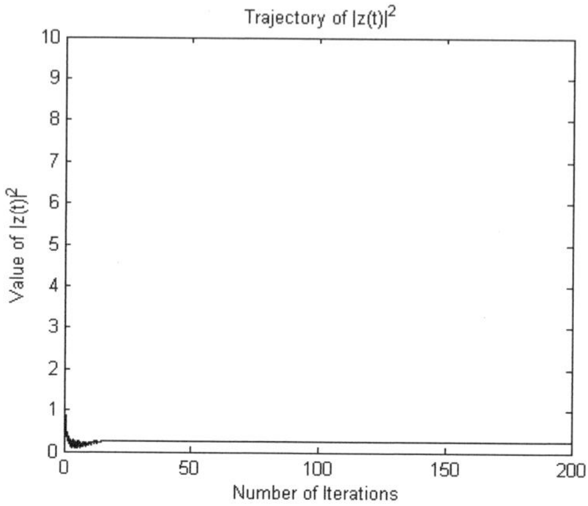

Fig. 7.32. The trajectory of $|z(t)|^2$ in searching λ_m^R when $n = 100$.

7.4.4. *Section summary*

Although many research works have been focused on using neural networks to compute eigenpairs of a real symmetric, or anti-symmetric matrix, similar efforts toward computation of a general real matrix are seldom found in relevant literatures. Therefore, in this section a recurrent neural network model was proposed to calculate the largest imaginary, or real part, of a general real matrix's eigenvalues. The network was described by a set of differential equations, which was transformed into a complex differential system. After obtaining the squared module of the system variable, the convergence behavior of the network was discussed in detail. Using a 7×7 general real matrix for numerical testing, the results indicated that the computed values were very close to the corresponding ground truth ones. In order to show the approach's performance when the dimensionality is large, a 50×50 and a 100×100 matrices were used for testing respectively. The calculated results were quite close to the ground truth values as well. It was also seen from the results that the iteration number at which the network enters into equilibrium state is not sensitive to the dimension number. This approach can thus be of potential use to estimate the largest modulus of a general real matrix's eigenvalues.

7.5. Conclusions

Using neural networks to compute eigenpairs has advantages such as being able to run in parallel and fast. Quick extraction of eigenpairs from matrices has many significant applications such as principal component analysis (PCA), real-time image compression and adaptive signal processing etc. In this chapter, we have presented a few RNNs for computation of eigenvalues and eigenvectors of different kinds of matrices. These matrices, in terms of level of processing difficulty, are classified into three types, i.e. symmetric matrices, anti-symmetric matrices and general real matrices. The procedures of how we use different RNNs to handle each type of matrices have been presented carefully in one or two sections respectively. Generally speaking, we have formulated each RNN as an individual differential equation. Subsequently, each analytic solution to the individual differential equation has been derived. Next, the convergence properties of the neural network models have been fully discussed based on these solutions. Finally, in order to evaluate the performance of each model, numerical simulations have been provided. The computational results from these models have been compared with those computed directly from Matlab functions, which are used as ground truth values. Comparison has revealed that the results from the proposed models are highly close to the ground truth values. In some sections, very large dimensional matrices have been used for rigorous testing and the results still approach the ground truth values closely. Thus, the conclusion can be made that with the use of specially designed neural networks, the computation of eigenpairs of symmetric, anti-symmetric and general real matrices is really possible.

References

[1] N. Li, A matrix inverse eigenvalue problem and its application, *Linear Algebra And Its Applications.* **266**(15), 143–152, (1997).

[2] F.-L. Luo, R. Unbehauen, and A. Cichocki, A minor component analysis algorithm, *Neural Networks.* **10**(2), 291–297, (1997).

[3] C. Ziegaus and E. Lang, A neural implementation of the jade algorithm (njade) using higher-order neurons, *Neurocomputing.* **56**, 79–100, (2004).

[4] F.-L. Luo, R. Unbehauen, and Y.-D. Li, A principal component analysis algorithm with invariant norm, *Neurocomputing.* **8**(2), 213–221, (1995).

[5] J. Song and Y. Yam, Complex recurrent neural network for computing the inverse and pseudo-inverse of the complex matrix, *Applied Mathematics and Computing.* **93**(2–3), 195–205, (1998).

[6] H. Kakeya and T. Kindo, Eigenspace separation of autocorrelation memory matrices for capacity expansion, *Neural Networks.* **10**(5), 833–843, (1997).

[7] M. Kobayashi, G. Dupret, O. King, and H. Samukawa, Estimation of singular values of very large matrices using random sampling, *Computers And Mathematics With Applications.* **42**(10–11), 1331–1352, (2001).

[8] Y. Zhang, F. Nan, and J. Hua, A neural networks based approach computing eigenvectors and eigenvalues of symmetric matrix, *Computers And Mathematics With Applications.* **47**(8–9), 1155–1164, (2004).

[9] F.-L. Luo and Y.-D. Li, Real-time neural computation of the eigenvector corresponding to the largest eigenvalue of positive matrix, *Neurocomputing.* **7**(2), 145–157, (1995).

[10] V. U. Reddy, G. Mathew, and A. Paulraj, Some algorithms for eigensubspace estimation, *Digital Signal Processing.* **5**(2), 97–115, (1995).

[11] R. Perfetti and E. Massarelli, Training spatially homogeneous fully recurrent neural networks in eigenvalue space, *Neural Networks.* **10**(1), 125–137, (1997).

[12] Y. Liu and Z. You, A concise functional neural network for computing the extremum eigenpairs of real symmetric matrices, *Lecture Notes in Computer Science.* (3971), 405–413, (2006).

[13] Y. Tan and Z. Liu, On matrix eigendecomposition by neural networks, *Neural Networks World.* **8**(3), 337–352, (1998).

[14] Y. Tan and Z. He, Neural network approaches for the extraction of the eigenstructure, *Neural Networks for Signal Processing VI–Proceedings of the 1996 IEEE Workshop, Kyoto, Japan.* 23–32, (1996).

[15] L. Xu and I. King, A PCA approach for fast retrieval of structural patterns in attributed graphs, *IEEE Transactions on Systems, Man, and Cybernetics–Part B: Cybernetics.* **31**, 812–817, (2001).

[16] B. Zhang, M. Fu, and H. Yan, A nonlinear neural network model of mixture of local principal component analysis: application to handwritten digits recognition, *Pattern Recognition.* **34**, 203–214, (2001).

[17] U. Helmke and J. B. Moore, *Optimization and dynamical systems.* (Springer–Verlag:, London, 1994).

[18] T. Chen, Modified oja's algorithms for principal subspace and minor subspace extraction, *Neural Processing Letters.* **5**, 105–110, (1997).

[19] A. Cichocki and R. Unbehauen, Neural networks for computing eigenvalues and eigenvectors, *Biological Cybernetics.* **68**, 155–164, (1992).

[20] A. Cichocki, Neural network for singular value decomposition, *Electronics Letters.* **28**(8), 784–786, (1992).

[21] Y. Liu, Z. You, and L. Cao, A simple functional neural network for computing the largest and smallest eigenvalues and corresponding eigenvectors of a real symmetric matrix, *Neurocomputing.* **67**, 369–383, (2005).

[22] Y. Liu, Z. You, L. Cao, and X. Jiang, A neural network algorithm for computing matrix eigenvalues and eigenvectors, *Journal of Software* [in Chinese]. **16**(6), 1064–1072, (2005).

[23] Y. Liu, Z. You, and L. Cao, A functional neural network for computing the largest modulus eigenvalues and their corresponding eigenvectors of an anti-symmetric matrix, *Neurocomputing.* **67**, 384–397, (2005).

[24] A neural network for computing eigenvectors and eigenvalues, *Biological Cybernetics.* **65**, 211–214, (1991).

[25] Y. Liu, Z. You, and L. Cao, A functional neural network computing some eigenvalues and eigenvectors of a special real matrix, *Neural Networks.* (18), 1293–1300, (2005).

[26] Y. Nakamura, K. Kajiwara, and H. Shiotani, On an integrable discretization of rayleigh quotient gradient system and the power method with a shift, *Journal of Computational and Applied Mathematics.* **96**, 77–90, (1998).

[27] J. M. Vegas and P. J. Zufiria, Generalized neural networks for spectral analysis: dynamics and liapunov functions, *Neural Networks.* **17**, 233–245, (2004).

Chapter 8

Automated Screw Insertion Monitoring Using Neural Networks: A Computational Intelligence Approach to Assembly in Manufacturing

Bruno Lara, Lakmal D. Seneviratne and Kaspar Althoefer

King's College London, Department of Informatics,
Strand, London WC2R 2LS, UK
k.althoefer@kcl.ac.uk

Threaded fastenings are a widely used industrial method to clamp components together. The method is successfully employed in many industries including car manufacturing, toy manufacturing and electronic component assembly - the method is popular because it is a low-cost assembly process and permits easy disassembly for maintenance, repair, relocation and recycling. Particularly, the usage of self-tapping screws has gained wide-spread recognition, because of the cost savings that can be achieved when preparing for the fastening process - the components to be clamped together need to be only equipped with holes and as such the more complicated and costly placing of threaded holes as is required for non-self-tapping bolts can be avoided. However, the process of inserting self-tapping screws is more complicated and typically carried out manually. This chapter discusses the study of methods of automation for the insertion of self-tapping screws.

Contents

8.1. Introduction

Automation of the assembly process is an important research topic in many manufacturing sectors, including the automotive industry, toy manufacturers and household appliance producing industries. With the current trend moving from fixed mass manufacturing toward flexible manufacturing methods, ones that can adapt to changes in the production lines and can cope more easily with a greater variation in the product palette and approaches that employ adaptive models and learning paradigms become more and more attractive for the manufacturing industries.

Considering that in quite a number of manufacturing industries around 25% of all assembly processes involve some kind of a threaded fastening approach, it is of great importance to research this particular assembling method in detail. Advances in the understanding of screw insertion, screw advancing and screw tightening will undoubtedly have the potential to advance the relevant manufacturing sectors. Enhanced monitoring capabilities based on comprehensive knowledge of an assembly process, such as screw fastening, will enable direct improvements in quality assurance even in the face of product variation and uncertainty. With the current interest in model predictive control, modeling the assembly process of screw fastening will certainly impact positively on modern, model-based control architectures for manufacturing allowing greater flexibility.

Screw fastenings or, more generally, threaded fastenings have proved to be a popular assembly method. The integrity of the achieved joint is defined by a number of factors including the tightening torque, the travel of the screw, the strength and quality of the fasteners and the prepared holes [1]. Compared to gluing, welding and other joining techniques, threaded fastenings have the great advantage of allowing the assembled components to be disassembled again relatively easily for the purpose of repair, maintenance, relocation or recycling. Another advantage is that the forces between joined components can be controlled to a very high degree of accuracy, if required for specific applications such as shear pins on a rocket body. A number of manufacturing industries, such as Desoutters [2], have shown a keen interest in intelligent systems for automated screw fastening, as the factory floor implementation of such systems will improve a number of aspects of this assembly process including the insertion quality, the completion of successful insertions and the working conditions of human operators. A number of research studies have drawn attention to the advantages and financial benefits of advanced insertion systems in a manufacturing environment [3–5].

With the view set on minimizing assembly costs, a particularly economical form of threaded fastenings has established itself in a number of manufacturing processes: self-tapping screws [6]. A self-tapping screw cuts a thread in the part to be fastened, avoiding the need to create pre-tapped holes prior to the screw insertion process and thus simplifying and shortening the overall assembly task. However, self-tapping insertions are more difficult to control and have an increased risk of failure, since a thread has to be formed whilst the screw is advanced into one of the joint components.

However, in many cases the fastening process based on self-tapping screws is made more difficult by the fact that handheld power tools or numerically controlled column power screwdrivers are used. A human operator has good control of the insertion process when using a simple non-motorized screwdriver; however, when employing a powered screwdriver, the control is limited, mainly owing to the high speed of the tool and reduced force feedback from the interaction between screw and surrounding material. In such a situation, the operator is usually not capable of assessing the insertion process and the overall quality of the created screw coupling.

A number of research studies have provided insight into the mechanisms that define the processes of thread cutting, advance and tightening for self-tapping screws [7–9]. Still, most of today's power screwdrivers employ basic maximum-torque mechanisms to stop the insertion process, once the desired tightening torque has been reached. Such simple methods do not lend themselves to appropriately monitoring the insertion process and fail to determine issues such as cross-threading, loose screws and other insertion failures.

The automation of the screw insertion monitoring process is of great interest for many sectors of the manufacturing industry. However, the methods being used for the accomplishment and monitoring of screw insertions or bolt tightenings are still fairly simple. These methods, such as the so-called "Teach Method", are suitable for large batch operations that do not require any changes of the assembly process, e.g. the production of high-volume products as needed for the automotive industry. The teach method is based on the assumption that a specific screw insertion process will have a unique signature based on the measured "Torque-Insertion Depth" curve. Comparing signals that are acquired on-line during the screw insertion process to signals that were recorded during a controlled insertion phase (teaching phase) differences can be easily flagged and a match between on-line signals and signals from the teaching phase indicates a correct insertion. Such methods have usually no adaptive or learning capabilities and require a labor-intensive set-up before production can commence. Improvements to the standard teach method were proposed and implemented, e.g. the "Torque-Rate" approach [10]. For this approach, the measured insertion signals need to fall within a-priori-defined torque rate levels and has shown to be capable of coping with a number of often-occurring faults such as stripped threads, excessive yielding of bolts, crossed threads, presence of foreign materials in the thread, insufficient thread cut and burrs. Despite the improvements this approach has no generalization capabilities and thus cannot cope with unknown, new cases that have not been part of the original training set. In a number of cases, the required tools such as screwdrivers can be specifically set-up to carry out the required fastening process to join components by means of screws or bolts and are economical if the components and the screw fastening requirements do not change. However, for small-batch production this approach is prohibitive because a "re-teaching" is required every time the components or fastening requirements change. Where smaller production runs are the norm, e.g. for wind turbine manufacturing, the industry is still relying on human operators to a great extent. These operators insert and fasten screws and bolts manually or by means of handheld power tools. With a view to create flexible manufacturing approaches, this book chapter discusses novel, intelligent monitoring methods for screw insertion and bolt tightening capable of adapting to uncertainty and changes in the involved components.

This book chapter investigates novel neural-network-based systems for the monitoring of the insertion of self-tapping screws. Section 8.2 provides an overview of the screw insertion process. Section 8.3 describes the methodology behind the process. Section 8.4 discusses the results from simulations. Section 8.5 presents an in-depth experimental study and discusses the results obtained. Conclusions are drawn in Section 8.6.

8.2. Background

8.2.1. *The screw insertion process: modelling and monitoring*

Screw insertion can be divided into two categories: the first describes the insertion of self-tapping screws into holes that have not been threaded; the second deals with the insertion of screws or bolts into pre-threaded holes or fixed nuts. The advantage of the first approach lies in its simplicity when preparing the components for joining – a hole in each of the components is the only requirement. The latter approach needs to undergo a more complex preparatory step, in addition to drilling holes threads have to be cut or nuts to be attached. Industry is progressively employing more of the former as it is more cost-effective, more generally applicable and allows for more rapid insertion of screws as possible with the other approach. However, the downside is that the approach based on self-tapping screws is in need of a more advanced control policy to ensure that the screw thread cuts an appropriate groove through at least one of the components during the insertion process. Owing to its complexity, the process of inserting self-tapping screws is usually carried out by human operators who can ensure that an appropriate and precise screw advancement is guaranteed, making good use of the multitude of tactile and force sensors as well as feedback control loops they have available.

In order to develop an advanced monitoring strategy for the insertion of self-tapping screws, a proper theoretical understanding of the underlying behavior of the insertion process is needed [11]. At King's College London, mathematical models, based on an equilibrium analysis of forces and describing the insertion of self-tapping screws into metal and plastic components, have been created to identify the importance of the torque-vs.-insertion-depth profile as a good representation for the five distinct stages of the insertion process, Fig. 8.2 [12]. Existing knowledge on screw advance and screw tightening of screws in pre-tapped holes is included in the proposed model for the relevant stages of the overall process [9, 10, 13–15]. The key points of this profile – representative for the five main stages occurring during the insertion – are defined as shown below.

(1) *Screw engagement* represents the stage of the insertion process lasting from the moment where the tip of the screw touches the tap plate (on the top component) until the moment when the cutting portion of the conical screw taper has been completely inserted into the hole,

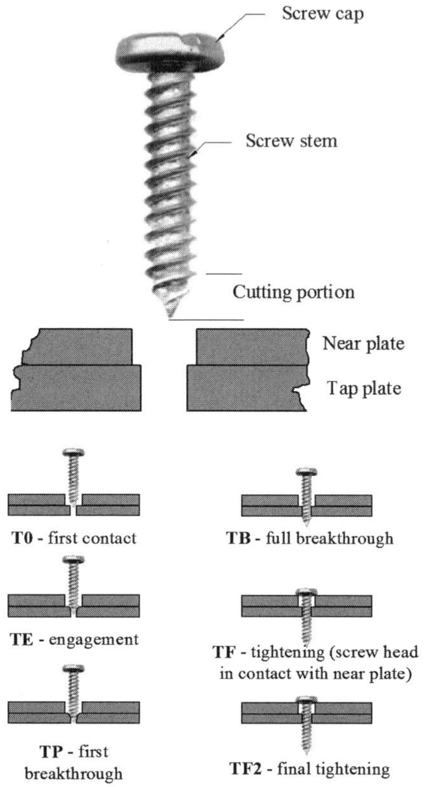

Fig. 8.1. (left) Notation for self-tapping screw insertions; (right) Key stages of the screw insertion in a two-plate joint [1].

effectively resulting in an entire turn of the screw taper penetrating through the tap plate. The screw is said to be engaged at this point, denoted TE, Figs 8.1 and 8.2. Mainly shear forces are experienced during this stage, due to the cutting of a helical groove in the hole wall.

(2) *Cutting* describes the subsequent interval from completion of screw engagement (TE) until the completion of a cut of a groove into the wall by the screw thread (TP). The main forces are due to friction and cutting. From this stage onwards (i.e. the cutting portion of the screw has completely passed through the hole in the tap plate (screw breakthrough)), cutting or shear forces have an insignificant impact on the screw advancement.

(3) *Transition from cutting to screw advance* is an intermediate stage continuing from TP to TB in the mathematical insertion model (Figs 8.1 and 8.2); a mixture of cutting and friction forces can be observed.

(4) *Screw advance or rundown* is the fourth stage where the screw moves forward in the previously-cut groove. Screw advance continues until the lower side of the screw cap touches the near plate (TF). Here, the main forces observable are friction forces owing to the movement of the screw's thread along the surface of the groove of the hole. The forces of this stage are known to be constant (see constant torque between TB and TF in Fig. 8.2 [11]).

(5) *Screw tightening* is the fifth and final stage, commencing the moment that the screw cap gets into contact with the near plate (TF) and completing when a predetermined clamping force is achieved (TF2). The main forces concerned are tightening forces, made up entirely from friction components that can be divided in two categories, firstly, forces between screw thread and hole groove, and secondly, forces occurring between screw cap and near plate.

When comparing the processes of inserting screws into pre-tapped holes, on the one hand, and inserting self-tapping screws, on the other, one recognises a clear similarity between the two processes over a range of stages. Compared to self-tapping screws, pre-tapped insertions lack the two stages from TE to TB, because cutting is not required. For screws inserted into pre-tapped holes, a short engagement stage is experienced, then transitioning rapidly to the advance or rundown stage [9, 10, 13–16]. After this, the two mathematical screw insertion models are indistinguishable.

The forces acting on the screw during the different stages are examined using fundamental stress analysis concepts [17, 18]. Each stage of the insertion process can be represented by an appropriate equation describing the relationship between screw advancement (insertion depth) and resultant torque values. It has been shown that those stages can be modeled as simple straight-line segments shown in Fig. 8.2 [11]. All other parameters depend on screw and hole geometry, material properties and friction. The overall set of equations (submodels) describing the five stages of the process of inserting self-tapping screws is as follows [11]:

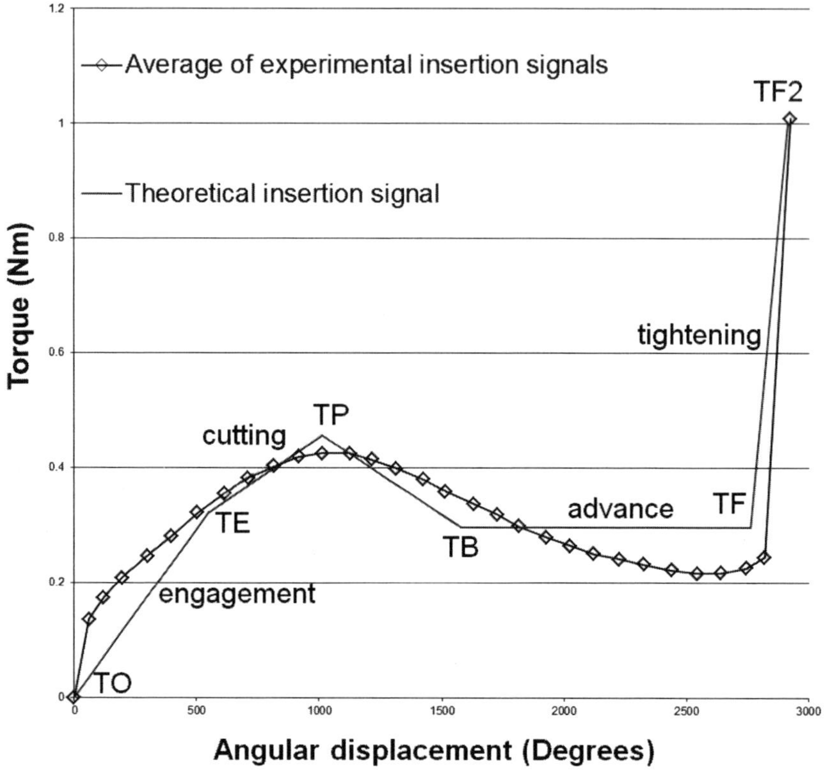

Fig. 8.2. Average experimental torque profile of an insertion on two-joint plate and the corresponding theoretical prediction [1].

$$T_1 = (\frac{\cos\beta}{64\pi L_t\sqrt{3}})(D_s^2 - D_h^2)\sigma_{uts}(D_f D_s P + \pi\mu L_t(D_s + D_h))\{\theta + \frac{4\pi L_t h}{PD_s}\} \tag{8.1}$$

$$T_2 = (\frac{\cos\beta}{16\sqrt{3}})(D_s^2 - D_h^2)\sigma_{uts}(D_f(D_s - D_h) + \frac{\mu\pi L_t(D_s^2 - D_h^2)}{2D_s P} + \mu R_f\theta) \tag{8.2}$$

$$\begin{aligned} T_3 = (\frac{\cos\beta}{32L_t\sqrt{3}})(D_s^2 - D_h^2)\sigma_{uts}\{(2R_f\mu L_t - \frac{D_f D_s P}{\pi})\theta \\ + \frac{2t}{P}(2R_f\mu\pi L_t - D_f D_s P)\} \end{aligned} \tag{8.3}$$

$$T_4 = (\frac{\cos\beta}{32P\sqrt{3}})\pi t\mu\sigma_{uts}(D_s^3 - D_s D_h^2 + D_h D_s^2 - D_h^3) \tag{8.4}$$

$$T_5 = \frac{\mu EP(D_{sh}^3 - D_s^3)(\theta - \frac{\pi}{4}(D_{sh}^2 - D_s^2))}{24l} \tag{8.5}$$

where T_1 to T_5 are the torques required for stages one to five respectively, θ is the angle of rotation of the screw, L_s is the screw length, L_t is the taper length, D_s is the major screw diameter, D_m is the minor screw diameter, D_h is the lower hole diameter, t is the lower plate thickness, l is the total plate thickness, D_{sh} is the screw head diameter, P is the pitch of the thread, β is the thread angle, μ is the friction coefficient between the screw and plate material and σ_{uts} is the ultimate tensile strength of the plate material. All the parameters are constant and depend on the screw and hole dimensions, as well as on the friction and material properties.

Realistically modeling a common manufacturing process, the process of inserting self-tapping screws can be experimentally investigated in a test environment with two plates (representing two manufacturing components) to be united [11]. As part of the experimental study, holes are drilled into the plates to be joined; the latter are then clamped together such that the hole centers of the top plate (also called near plate) are in line with the centers of the holes of the second plate (also called tap plate), Fig. 8.1. A self-tapping screw is then inserted into a hole during an experiment and screwed in, applying appropriate axial force and torque values. Ngemoh showed that the axial insertion force does not influence the advancement of the screw very much, even if it varies over quite a wide range as long as it does not go beyond a maximum value whereby the threads of the screw and/or the hole are in danger of being destroyed [11]. During this insertion process a helical groove is cut into the far plate's hole and forces as described above are experienced across the five main stages of the insertion process until the screw head is finally tightened against the near plate [11].

Based on the modeling and practical knowledge of the screw insertion and fastening process monitoring strategies can be created [12, 19]. The signature that is obtained when recording the torque-vs.-insertion-depth throughout the insertion process provides important clues on the final outcome of the overall process and its likelihood of success. The resultant torques can be best estimated if the signature is closest to its ideal one. This book chapter presents monitoring methods that are capable of predicting to what extend a pre-set final clamping torque is achieved by employing artificial intelligence in the form of an artificial neural network that uses online torque-vs.-indentation-depth insertion profiles as input. In contrast to monitoring approaches that measure the final clamping torque only, the proposed method has another advantage, faults can be detected early on and a screw insertion process can be interrupted in order to initiate remedial actions.

8.2.2. *Screw insertion process: monitoring*

A number of screw insertion monitoring techniques have established themselves in the manufacturing industry. One of the commonly employed methods is the "teach method" [10]. This method is active during the insertion of a screw, monitoring online the profile of the occurring forces during the insertion process. The teach method presumes a particular screw insertion operation to follow a unique "torque-insertion depth" signature signal that was taught before the actual assembly process commenced. Following this approach involves long set-up times, involving teaching the torque/depth profile for each insertion when the production run changes. The teach method is mainly limited by its inflexibility and the lack of generalization ability. To combat this, Smith *et al.* proposed various enhancements to the standard teach method, including the "torque-rate" approach [10]. His approach requires the correct fastening signatures to fall within pre-defined torque rate windows. This approach can deal with a range of common faults including stripped threads, excessive yielding of bolts, crossed threads, presence of foreign materials in the threads, insufficient thread cuts and burrs. However, Smith's approaches lack the flexibility to generalize when insertion cases differ from those used to define the windows.

Other efforts have focused on developing online torque estimation strategies correlating the electrical screwdriver's current to the torque at the tip of the screwdriver [8, 15, 20], and increasing the reliability during the tightening of the screw insertion process [8, 9]. However, it is noted that the start of the insertion process, in particular when using self-tapping screws, is a research area not investigated in detail. Other, more advanced techniques, such as the one presented by Dhayagude *et al.* [21] employs fuzzy logic providing a robust tool for monitoring the screw insertion process, even in the presence of noisy signals or screw alignment inaccuracies with the capability for early detection of insertion faults. However, the proposed computer simulation model used for testing ignores a variety of factors that define the torque requirements of a screw insertion.

8.3. Methodology

8.3.1. *Screw insertion signature classification: successful insertion and type of failure*

Since the process of inserting a self-tapping screw and the subsequent fastening can be modeled by a torque-insertion depth signature signal [11], intelligent model-inspired monitoring strategies can be created that are capable of separating successful from failed insertions. With the profile of the insertion signature depending mainly on the geometrical and mechanical properties of the involved components (screw and parts to be joined), commonly-occurring property variations invariably lead to deviations from the ideal torque signature profile. Theoretically and under the assumption that any given insertion case will produce a unique torque-insertion depth signature, any such deviations from the ideal signature can be employed to predict failure and type of failure. However, in practice, even the signature of a successful insertion may diverge by a small amount from the ideal signature, owing to signal parameter variations. Hence, any intelligent monitoring approach needs be capable of recognizing an insertion signature as successful even if diverging from the ideal one within some boundaries. Intelligent methods such as artificial neural networks have generalization capabilities and are thus suitable to cope with this type of uncertainty. Neural networks have also been proved to be good classifiers and thus can be used to develop the failure type. The proposed monitoring strategy is particularly beneficial for insertion processes as it can predict a failure before the completion of the insertion and can be used to invoke the appropriate, failure type dependent corrective action, when available.

In this study artificial neural networks (ANNs) based on the principle of radial basis functions (RBFs) are used [22, 23]. The following classification tasks are performed to validate the monitoring concept:

(a) *Single insertion case*
The ANN is to differentiate between signals from successful and failed insertions. The ANN is subjected to a phase of learning (using successful and unsuccessful insertions signals either simulated or from real sensor readings), and then tested with unknown signals. These test signals can only be correctly categorized if the ANN is capable of generalizing, which is necessary to cope with the random noise, added to the outputs from the mathematical model and the one inherent to real sensor data.

(b) *Multiple insertion cases*
The ability of the network to handle multiple insertion cases and to cope with cases not seen during training is investigated. Four insertion cases, corresponding to four different hole diameters, 3.7 mm, 3.8 mm, 3.9 mm and 4.0 mm, are examined, Column 2 of Table 8.1. The ANN is trained on insertion signals from the smallest hole (six signals) and the widest hole (six signals), as indicated by asterisks in Table 8.1. The ANN is also trained on eight signals representing failed insertions. However, during testing the network has, in addition, been presented with signals from insertions into the two middle-sized holes. The test set consists of 14 successful signals (2 from a 3.7 mm hole, 2 from a 4.0 mm hole, 5 from a 3.8 mm hole, and 5 from a 3.9 mm hole) and 8 unsuccessful signals. Here, the network is required to interpolate from cases learnt during training. All the signals are correctly classified after a relatively modest training period of four cycles, Fig. 8.4.

(c) *Multiple output classifications*
The aim of this classification experiment is to separate successful signals from unsuccessful signals as before and, in addition, to further classify the successful signals into different classes. Three different insertion classes are investigated in this experiment (Column 3 of Table 8.1). Here, an ANN with four nodes in the output layer is used; three to distinguish between the three different insertion classes (Classes A to C), and one to indicate unsuccessful insertions. Given an input signal, the trained network is expected to output a value close to one at a single output node, while all other output nodes should have values close to zero.

8.3.2. *Radial basis function neural network for error classification*

A radial basis function (RBF) neural network is used to classify between the different cases outlined in Section 8.3.1 [24]. After training, the network is expected to distinguish between successful insertions and failed ones, and being capable of separating successful insertions into one of the three insertion classes, Section 8.3.1 [25]. Choosing the most appropriate neural network architecture was mainly guided by the relevant literature and previous experience using neural networks for the problem of screw insertion classification.

Computer simulations based on the screw insertion model introduced in Section 8.2.1, allow the network designer to determine the most appropriate RBF network structure with respect to numbers of nodes in the input and the hidden layer by investigating a range of diverse insertion cases. As a result of a detailed computer-based investigation that aimed to optimize the network's robustness and generalization capacity as a function of the number of network nodes, an appropriate network structure was found (for more details see Section 8.3.3), Fig. 8.5. The number of nodes of the output layer is defined by the number of output categories required: one output node for (a) single insertion case and (b) multiple insertion case, and five output nodes for (c) where the network is required to distinguish between different types of successful insertions and failed insertions. Here, the neural network has a two dimensional input space that is made up of 30 discrete values of each of the two main insertion parameters, insertion depth and torque, as output by the model and acquired from sensors attached to a real screwdriver, respectively.

The function of the RBF network can be summarized as follows. After receiving input signals at the network's input nodes, the signals are weighted and passed to the network's hidden layer. Formed from Radial Basis Functions, the hidden layer nodes perform a nonlinear mapping from the input space to the output space. The results of the computations in the hidden layer nodes are weighted, added up and forwarded to the network's output layer. The task of the output layer is to categorize the signals either as successfully/unsuccessfully inserted or to distinguish between a number of different insertion types. In the output nodes, a logistic function limiting the final output of each node to a value between zero and one, denoting disagreement (zero) and agreement (one) with the specified target.

In this research, a supervised, batch mode training approach has been adopted, which has been demonstrated to be more robust and reliable than online learning [2, 26]. Here, the overall torque/insertion depth signature signal data set is divided into a training set comprising the input signals and the corresponding target outputs and a test set employed to evaluate the network's classification and generalization capabilities with regards to unknown data.

In preparation for training, the centres of the radial basis functions are initialized to values evenly collected from the set of teaching data of torque and insertion depth signals [2, 26]. The widths of the hidden layer nodes are initialized with random values between zero and one, and the weights between hidden and output nodes are also randomly initialized.

During the learning phase, training data is propagated through the ANN repeatedly; each time this happens the sum-squared error (SSE) is computed. The SSE is the difference between actual output of the network and the target output. It is then the aim of the training algorithm to modify the free parameters of the network to be updated such that the SSE is minimized [27].

After completing the learning phase, the network's performance is evaluated using data that were not seen by the network previously. It can then be seen how well the network is trained (i.e. how well it can predict the various insertion cases) and how well it is able to generalize (i.e. can cope with noisy data and variations introduced by unseen data, e.g. hole diameters that were not part of the training set).

8.3.3. *Simulations and experimental study*

Simulations were conducted to obtain the optimal ANN with regards to network learning needs, quality of screw insertion monitoring and power to generalize over the given insertion cases and possible insertion failures.

This work focuses on (a) *single insertion case*, (b) *multiple insertion cases*, and (c) *multiple output classifications*, in order to validate the proposed screw insertion monitoring method.

Based on the mathematical model (Section 8.2.1) torque-insertion-depth signals are produced for the testing and evaluation of the ANN-based monitoring strategy using a computer implementation of the developed screw insertion equations, (8.1) to (8.5) [11].

Since measurement noise is expected during the real experiments, random noise is added to the signal acquired from the mathematical model in an attempt to make the simulated study as realistic as possible and train the ANN on a set of signals as close as possible to the real data, Fig. 8.8. Noise of up to 0.2 Nm (up to 15% of the highest generated torque) was superimposed. Without impacting on generality, simulation and experimental studies were conducted without near plate.

Wide-ranging simulation sequences were conducted and revealed the most suitable architectures for the RBF ANN. In all three cases (single insertion, generalization ability, multi-case insertion), it was most suitable to equip the input layer with 60 nodes (to be fed with 30 pairs of torque/insertion-depth signals during learning and testing). With regards to the studies on the single insertion case and the network's generalization ability, it was most appropriate to employ 15 nodes in the hidden layer and 1 node in the output layer. For the multi-classification problem, a network with 20 nodes in the hidden layer and 4 nodes in the output layer proved to give the best results. The same ANN structures were employed in the experimental study where signals from the torque sensor and insertion-depth sensor attached to an electric screwdriver were used. Table 8.1 summarizes the simulation and experimental studies carried out.

While a computer-based implementation of the mathematical model (described in Section 8.3.1) was used for the simulation study, an electric screwdriver (Desoutter, Model S5) was utilized during the experimental study. Care was taken to design both studies such that they were as compatible and comparable as possible. The test rig used during this experimental study is based on the screwdriver equipped with a rotary torque sensor (maximum range: 1.9 Nm) and an optical encoder (measuring angular position in a range from 0 to 3000 degrees with a resolution of 60 degrees) attached to the screwdriver's shaft. [2] During a common screw insertion experiment, up to 50 data point pairs of torque and angular signals are recorded. The acquired angular signals are transformed into insertion-depth values exploiting knowledge of the pitch of the given screw. It was found that for ANN learning and subsequent testing reduced data sets of 30 torque/insertion-depth pairs were sufficient.

8.4. Results of Simulation Study

8.4.1. *Single insertion case*

The task of the ANN is to distinguish between successful and unsuccessful insertion signals (Column 1 of Table 8.1). During training (employing signals from ten successful insertions and eight unsuccessful insertions), the network performance in response to unseen test data is monitored. To correctly classify this set, the network requires a certain degree of generalization, since these signals would be different to those in the training set due to random noise superimposed on the theoretical curve. Figure 8.3 shows that after moderate training (three cycles), there is a clear separation between the output values of the five successful and eight unsuccessful signals in the test set, and that the ANN can efficiently distinguish between successful and unsuccessful insertion signals.

Table 8.1. Simulation and experimental study. The table shows the parameters for all screws used in this study. Results with regards to the number of successful/unsuccessful insertion signals per training/test set are shown. Generalization capabilities are investigated by training the ANN on two hole diameters (*) and testing it on intermediate hole diameters (see also Sections 8.4 and 8.5) [1].

	Simulation Study					Experimental Study				
Section	8.4.1	8.4.2	8.4.3			8.5.1	8.5.2	8.5.3		
Plate material	Polycarbonate	Polycarbonate	Aluminium	Brass	Mild Steel	Acrylic	Polycarbonate	Acrylic	Acrylic	Acrylic
Screw type	8	8	4	6	8	4	6	4	6	8
Far plate thickness (mm)	6.0	6.0	3.0	3.0	3.0	3.0	6.0	3.0	5.0	5.0
Hole diameter (mm)	3.8	3.7* 3.8 3.9 4.0	2.7	3.2	3.9	1.0	1.0* 1.5 2.0*	1.5	2.5	3.5
Training set: successful	10	12	6	6	6	6	10	5	5	5
Training set: unsuccessful	8	8		8		8	8		16	
Test set: successful	5	14	4	4	4	6	12	4	4	4
Test set: unsuccessful	8	8		8		8	8		16	
Classification	binary	binary	Four classes: A | B | C | unsuccessful			binary	binary	Four classes: A | B | C | unsuccessful		

8.4.2. *Generalization ability*

The ability of the network to handle multiple insertion cases and to cope with cases not seen during training is investigated. Four insertion cases, corresponding to four different hole diameters, 3.7 mm, 3.8 mm, 3.9 mm and 4.0 mm, are examined (Column 2 of Table 8.1). The network is only trained on insertion signals from the smallest (3.7 mm, 6 signals) and the widest hole (4.0 mm, 6 signals) as well as 8 signals representing unsuccessful insertions. However, during testing the network has, in addition, been presented with signals from insertions into the 2 middle-sized holes (3.8 and 3.9 mm). The test set consists of 22 signals including 14 successful signals (2 from a 3.7 mm hole, 2 from a 4.0 mm hole, 5 from a 3.8 mm hole and 5 from a 3.9 mm hole) and 8 unsuccessful signals. Hence, the network is required to interpolate from cases learnt during training. All the signals are correctly classified after a relatively modest training period of four cycles (including initialization), Fig. 8.4.

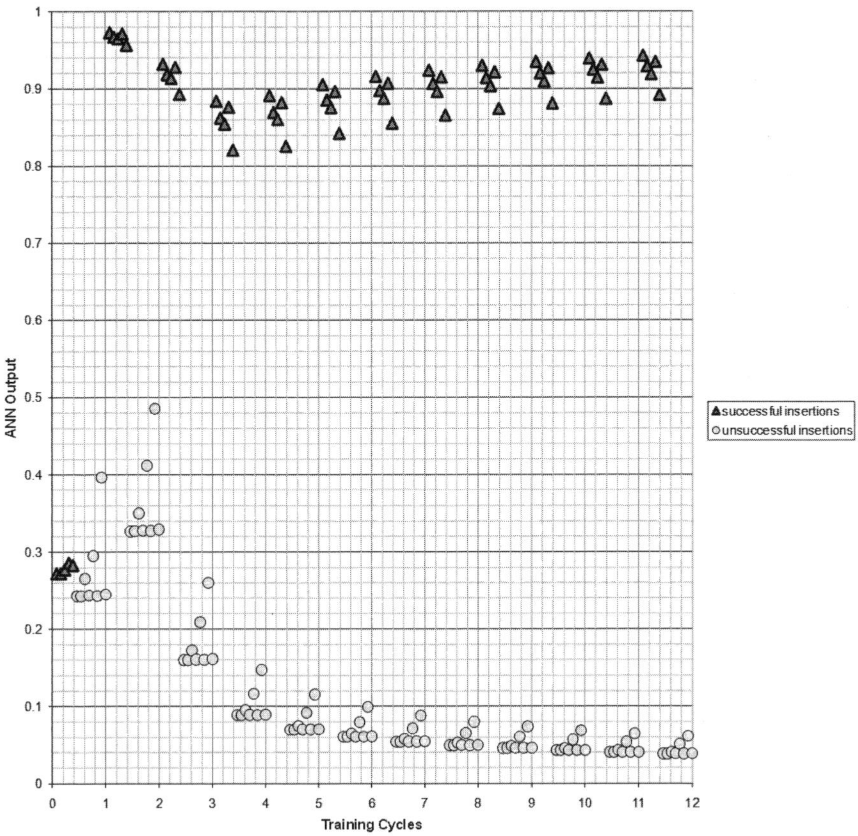

Fig. 8.3. Output values as training evolves (Simulated insertion signals). Single case experiment [1].

8.4.3. *Multi-case classification*

The aim of this classification experiment is to separate successful signals from unsuccessful signals as before and, in addition, to further classify the successful signals into different classes. Three different insertion classes are investigated in this experiment, Column 3 of Table 8.1. Here, an ANN with four nodes in the output layer is used; three to distinguish between the three different insertion classes (Classes A to C), and one to indicate unsuccessful insertions. Given an input signal, the trained network is expected to output a value close to one at a single output node, while all other output nodes should have values close to zero. During training, it was observed that the

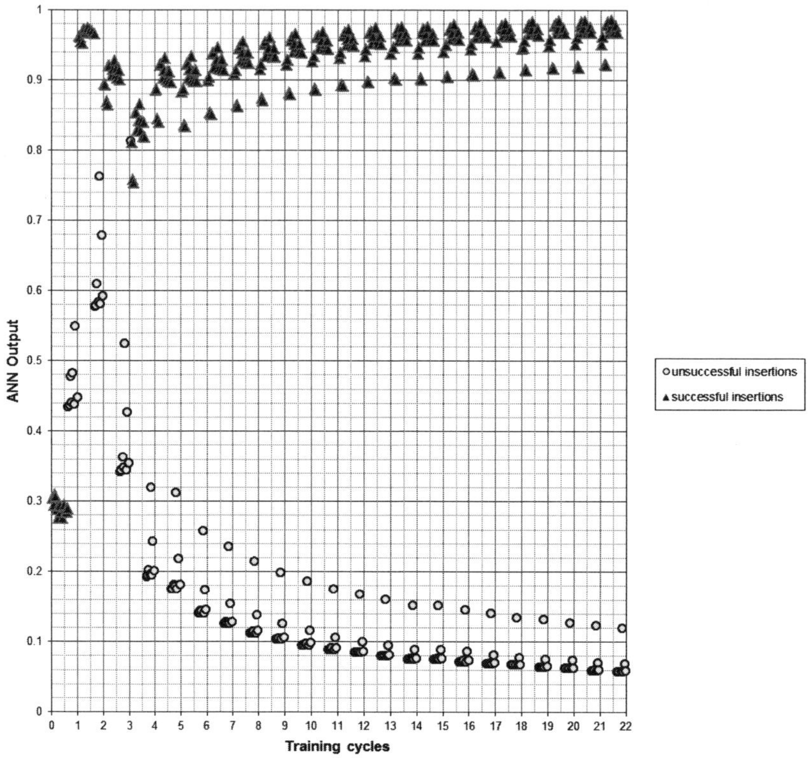

Fig. 8.4. Output values as training evolves (Simulated insertion signals). Variation of hole diameter experiment [1].

sum squared error (SSE) of the network reduces quickly to relatively low values indicating a good and steady training behavior. Figure 8.5 shows the ANN output in response to the test set after 20 training cycles. Signals 1 to 4, 5 to 8 and 9 to 12 are correctly classified as the insertions of Classes A, B and C, respectively, and the remaining signals are correctly classified as unsuccessful insertions.

8.5. Results of Experimental Study

8.5.1. *Single insertion case*

As in Section 8.4.1, the task of the network is to distinguish between successful and unsuccessful insertions for a single insertion case, for the set of parameters given in column 4 of Table 8.1. Based on the results of

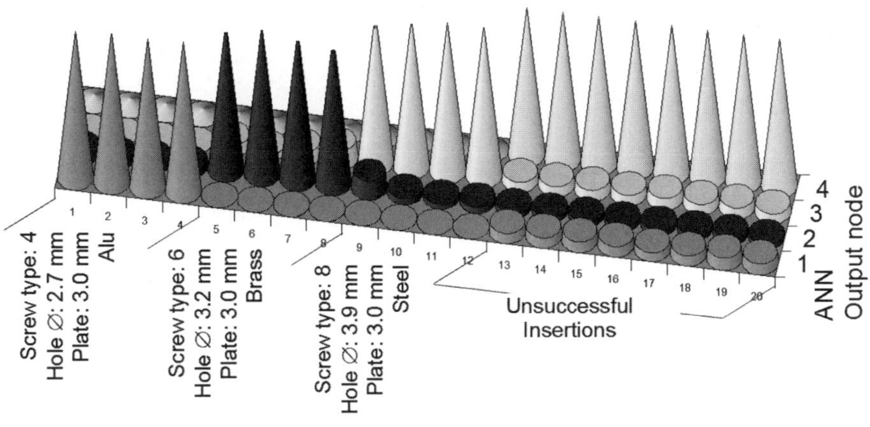

Fig. 8.5. Activation output on test set after 20 training cycles. Four-output classification experiment using simulated signals [1].

the simulation study, a network with 60 input nodes, 15 hidden layer nodes and 1 output node is used. After initialization, the network is trained over 22 cycles, Fig. 8.6. After a modest training period (eight cycles including initialization), the network output clearly differentiates between successful and unsuccessful insertions.

8.5.2. *Generalization ability*

As in Section 8.4.2, the network is trained on signals acquired during insertions of screws into the smallest (1.0 mm, 5 signals) and widest (2.0 mm, 5 signals) hole as well as on signals from eight unsuccessful insertions, Column 5 of Table 8.1. During testing (employing four successful insertion signals from each of the three holes and eight unsuccessful insertion signals), it is analyzed whether the network is capable of interpolating and correctly classifying the signals corresponding to the medium-sized hole (1.5 mm). Figure 8.7 shows the acquired insertion signals for the three different cases used in this experiment. The network is trained using 26 cycles, and the test set is presented to the network after initialization and after each training cycle, Fig. 8.8. It is seen that after a modest period of training (nine cycles), the network correctly classifies successful and unsuccessful insertions.

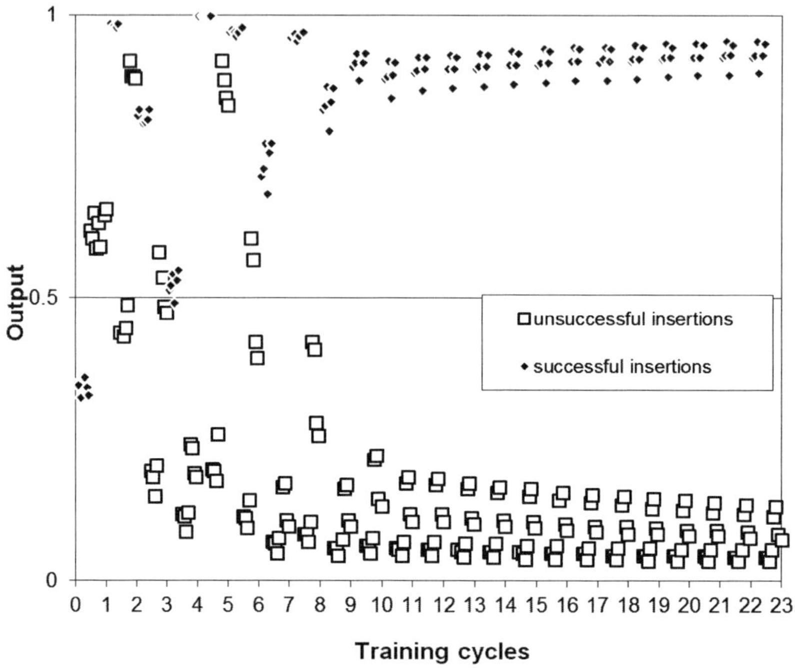

Fig. 8.6. Output values as training evolves (insertion signals recorded from electric screwdriver). Single case experiment [1].

8.5.3. *Four-output classification*

This experiment is equivalent to that performed in Section 8.4.3. The three insertion classes investigated in this experiment are shown in Column 6 of Table 8.1; the corresponding insertion signals are depicted in Fig. 8.9. The aim of the experiment is to separate successful insertions from failed insertions, and to further classify the successful signals to one of the three classes. Thus, as for the ANN in Section 8.4.3, four output nodes are used. As training evolves, output nodes one to three become more and more activated for correct signals of Classes A, B and C, respectively, while the fourth output node increases in activity for unsuccessful insertions. Tests (involving 12 signals representing successful insertions (4 for each class) and 16 signals from unsuccessful insertions) have shown that the SSE decreases relatively rapidly and smoothly to low values. At different training stages, the training and the test sets were presented to the network. When presented with the training set after 50 iterations, the network is

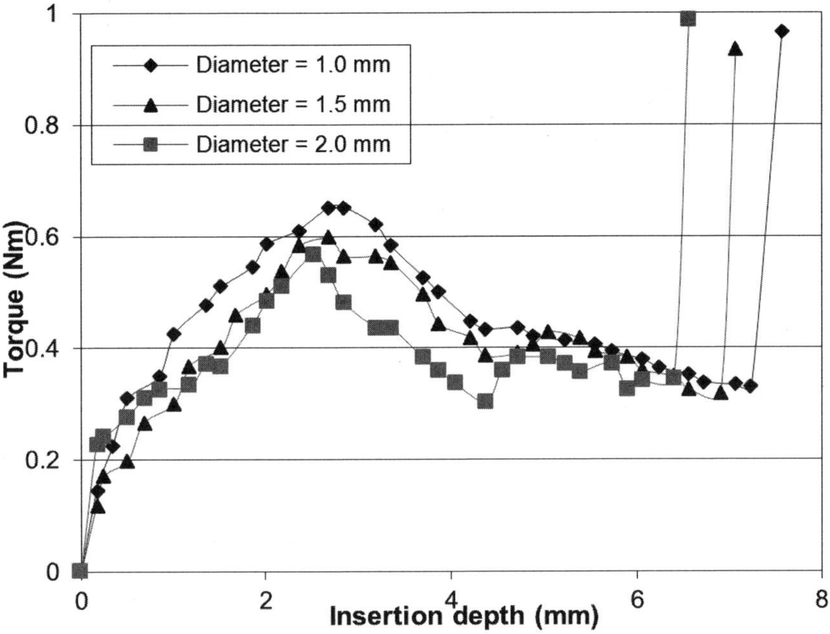

Fig. 8.7. Insertion signals from screwdriver. Variation of hole diameter [1].

able to correctly classify all 31 training signals. However, when presented with the test set, the network fails to classify one of the signals properly. However, after continued training (200 and more training cycles), the network correctly classifies all the presented signals from the test set, Fig. 8.10. Signal 8 correctly activates output node 2, but also activates output node 1; however, to a lesser extent. Also, for signals 9, 10 and 17 an increased output activity is observed. This is probably due to the proximity of the different classes. However, choosing the output node with the maximum activity will give the correct answer for all signals after 200 training cycles.

8.6. Conclusions

The main contribution of this chapter is the development of a new methodology, based on RBF ANNs, for monitoring the insertion of self-tapping screws. Its main advantage is its capability to generalize and to correctly classify unseen insertion signals. This level of classification

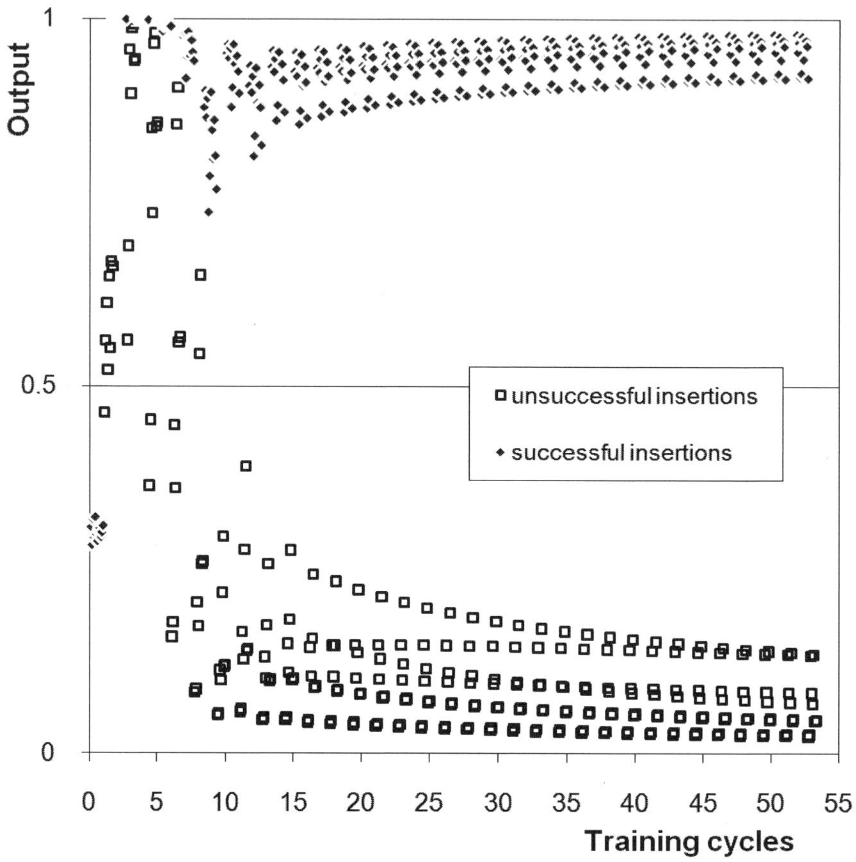

Fig. 8.8. Output values as training evolves (real insertion signals). Variation of hole diameter experiment [1].

cannot be achieved with standard methods such as the teach method and is particularly useful where insertions have to be logged as is the case where high safety standards are required.

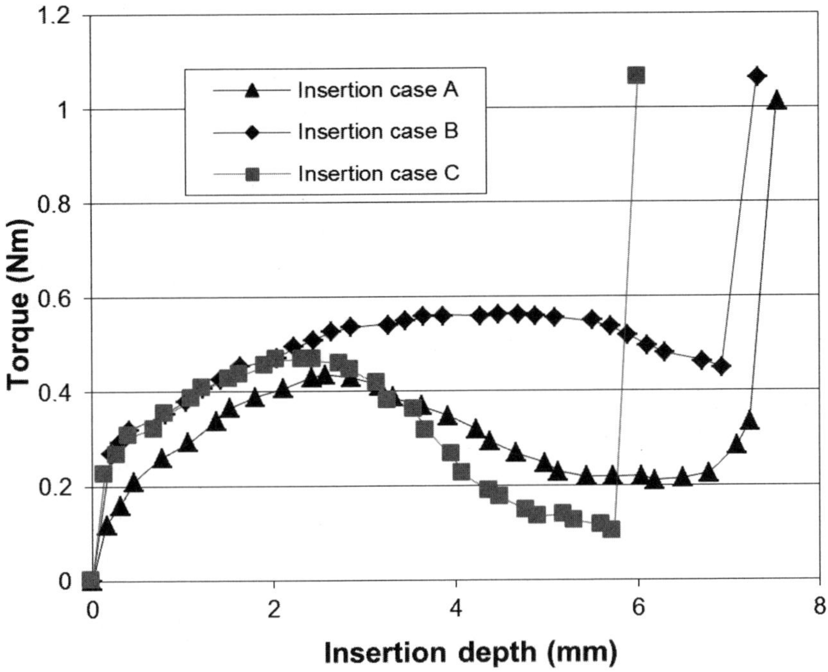

Fig. 8.9. Insertion signals from screwdriver. Four-output classification experiment [1].

This chapter investigates the ability of the ANN to classify signals belonging to a single insertion case. Both the computer simulation and experimental results show that after a modest training period (eight cycles when using real data), the network is able to correctly classify torque signature signals.

Further, the ability of the network to cope with unseen test signals is investigated, using signatures acquired from insertion into holes with different diameters. The network is trained with signals from the smallest and largest hole, and tested using signals from all insertions including those from the unseen middle-sized holes. It is shown that after a modest training period (10 cycles when using real data), the network is able to classify all test signals, including those belonging to unseen signatures. To classify signals of the unseen insertion cases, the network has to interpolate from insertion cases learnt during training, demonstrating its generalization ability.

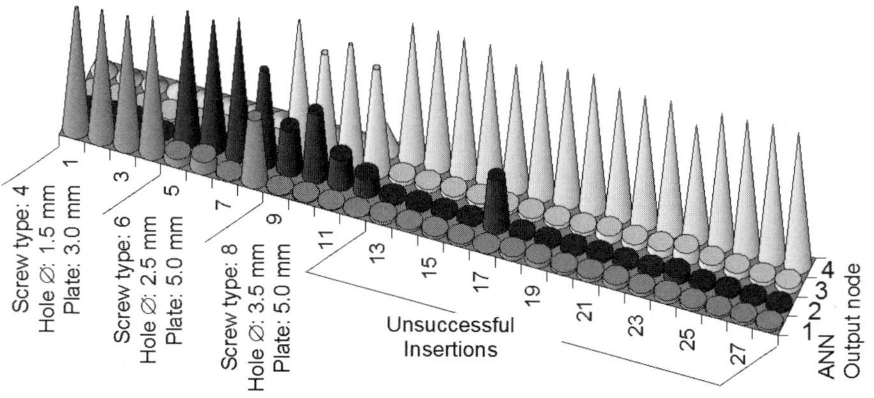

Fig. 8.10. Network activation output for the test set after 200 training cycles. Four-output classification experiment using real insertion signals. All signals are correctly attributed [1].

Finally, the ability of the network to classify into multiple categories is investigated. The classification task is to separate correct signals from faulty signals, and to further classify the correct signals into one of three classes. Although the training requirements for this case are higher than in the previous experiments (200 cycles to ensure correct classification when using real data), after training, the network is able to classify all test signals accurately. The considerably extensive training required for this experiment is due to the higher complexity of the task at hand as compared to the previous experiments.

Current research focuses on developing advanced preprocessing techniques that will provide a better separation of the essential features of the torque-insertion depth profiles into the different cases aiming to improve the multi-output classification. Work is underway on creating estimation techniques to determine the parameters of the analytical model with respect to real insertion signals [28].

Acknowledgments

The research leading to these results has been partially supported by the COSMOS project, which has received funding from the European Community's Seventh Framework Programme (FP7-NMP-2009-SMALL-3, NMP-2009-3.2-2) under grant agreement 246371-2. The work of Dr. Lara was funded by CONACYT. I also thank Allen Jiang for compositing this chapter.

References

[1] K. Althoefer, B. Lara, and L. D. Seneviratne, Monitoring of self-tapping screw fastenings using artificial neural networks, *ASME Journal of Manufacturing Science and Engineering.* **127**, 236–247, (2005).

[2] B. Lara Guzman. *Intelligent Monitoring of Screw Insertions.* PhD thesis, King's College, University of London, (2005).

[3] A. S. Kondoleon. Application of technology-economic model of assembly techniques to programmable assembly machine configuration. SM thesis. Master's thesis, Mechanical Engineering Department, Massachusetts Institute of Technology, (1976).

[4] P. M. Lynch. *Economic-Technological Modeling and Design Criteria for Automated Assembly.* PhD thesis, Mechanical Engineering Department, Massachusetts Institute of Technology, (1977).

[5] D. E. Whitney and J. L. Nevins, Computer-Controlled Assembly, *Scientific American.* **238**(2), 62–74, (1978).

[6] L. D. Seneviratne, F. A. Ngemoh, and S. W. E. Earles, An experimental investigation of torque signature signals for self-tapping screws, *Proceedings of the Institution of Mechanical Engineers, Part C: Journal of Mechanical Engineering Science.* **214**(2), 399–410, (2000).

[7] L. D. Seneviratne, P. Visuwan, and K. Althoefer. Monitoring of threaded fastenings in automated assembly using artificial neural networks. In *Intelligent assembly and disassembly: (IAD 2001): a proceedings volume from the IFAC workshop, Camela, Brazil, 5-7 November 2001*, 61–65, (2002).

[8] M. Matsumura, S. Itou, H. Hibi, and M. Hattori, Tightening torque estimation of a screw tightening robot, *Proceedings of the 1995 IEEE International Conference on Robotics and Automation.* **2**, 2108–2112, (1995).

[9] K. Ogiso and M. Watanabe, Increase of reliability in screw tightening, *Proceedings of the 4th International Conference on Assembly Automation, Tokyo, Japan.* 292–302, (1982).

[10] S. K. Smith, Use of a microprocessor in the control and monitoring of air tools while tightening threaded fasteners, *Proceedings of the Society of Manufacturing Engineers, Dearborn, Michigan.* **2**, 397–421, (1980).

[11] F. A. Ngemoh. *Modelling the Automated Screw Insertion Process.* PhD thesis, King's College, University of London, (1997).

[12] L. D. Seneviratne, F. A. Ngemoh, and S. W. E. Earles, Theoretical modelling of screw tightening operations, *Proceedings of Engineering Systems Design and Analysis, American Society of Mechanical Engineers, Istanbul, Turkey.* **47**(1), 301–310, (1992).

[13] E. J. Nicolson and R. S. Fearing, Compliant control of threaded fastener insertion, *Proceedings of the 1993 IEEE International Conference on Robotics and Automation.* 484–490, (2002).

[14] G. P. Peterson, B. D. Niznik, and L. M. Chan, Development of an automated screwdriver for use with industrial robots, *IEEE Journal of Robotics and Automation.* **4**(4), 411–414, (1988).

[15] T. Tsujimura and T. Yabuta, Adaptive force control of screwdriving with a positioning-controlled manipulator, *Robotics and Autonomous Systems.* **7** (1), 57–65, (1991).

[16] F. Mrad, Z. Gao, and N. Dhayagude, Fuzzy logic control of automated screw fastening, *Conference Record of the 1995 IEEE Industry Applications Conference, 1995. Thirtieth IAS Annual Meeting, IAS'95.* **2**, 1673–1680, (2002).

[17] A. P. Boresi, R. J. Schmidt, and O. M. Sidebottom, *Advanced Mechanics of Materials.* (John Wiley, New York, 1993).

[18] S. P. Timoshenko and J. N. Goodier, *Theory of Elasticity.* (McGraw, New York, 1970).

[19] B. Lara, K. Althoefer, and L. D. Seneviratne, Automated robot-based screw insertion system, *Proceedings of the 24th Annual Conference of the IEEE Industrial Electronics Society IECON'98.* **4**, 2440–2445, (2002).

[20] K. Althoefer, L. D. Seneviratne, and R. Shields, Mechatronic strategies for torque control of electric powered screwdrivers, *Proceedings of the Institution of Mechanical Engineers, Part C: Journal of Mechanical Engineering Science.* **214**(12), 1485–1501, (2000).

[21] N. Dhayagude, Z. Gao, and F. Mrad, Fuzzy logic control of automated screw fastening, *Robotics and Computer-Integrated Manufacturing.* **12**(3), 235–242, (1996).

[22] L. Bruzzone and D. F. Prieto, Supervised training technique for radial basis function neural networks, *Electronics Letters.* **34**(11), 1115–1116, (1998).

[23] C. M. Bishop, *Neural Networks for Pattern Recognition.* (Oxford University Press, New York, 1995).

[24] M. T. Musavi, W. Ahmed, K. H. Chan, K. B. Faris, and D. M. Hummels, On the training of radial basis function classifiers, *Neural networks.* **5**(4), 595–603, (1992).

[25] B. Lara, K. Althoefer, and L. D. Seneviratne, Artificial neural networks for screw insertions classification, *Proceedings of the IEEE International Conference on Robotics and Automation (ICRA), San Francisco, CA.* 1912–1917, (2000).

[26] B. Lara, K. Althoefer, and L. D. Seneviratne, Use of artificial neural networks for the monitoring of screw insertions, *Proceedings of the 1999 IEEE/RSJ International Conference on Intelligent Robots and Systems, 1999, IROS'99.* **1**, 579–584, (2002).

[27] A. Zell, G. Mamier, and *et al.*, SNNS: Stuttgart Neural Network Simulator. User Manual, Version 4.1, *Institute for Parallel and Distributed High Performance Systems, Technical Report.* (1995).

[28] M. Klingajay, L. Seneviratne, and K. Althoefer, Identification of threaded fastening parameters using the Newton Raphson Method, *Proceedings of the 2003 IEEE/RSJ International Conference on Intelligent Robots and Systems, IROS 2003.* **2**, 2055–2060, (2003).

PART 4

Support Vector Machines and their Applications

Chapter 9

On the Applications of Heart Disease Risk Classification and Hand-written Character Recognition using Support Vector Machines

S.R. Alty, H.K. Lam and J. Prada

Department of Electronic Engineering, King's College London
Strand, London, WC2R 2LS, United Kingdom
steve.alty@kcl.ac.uk
hak-keung.lam@kcl.ac.uk
jpradasanchez@gmail.com

Over the past decade or so, support vector machines have established themselves as a very effective means of tackling many practical classification and regression problems. This chapter relates the theory behind both support vector classification and regression, including an example of each applied to real-world problems. Specifically, a classifier is developed which can accurately estimate the risk of developing heart disease simply from the signal derived from a finger-based pulse oximeter. The regression example shows how SVMs can be used to rapidly and effectively recognize hand-written characters particularly designed for the so-called graffiti character set.

Contents

9.1. Introduction

This chapter relates the rise in interest, largely over the past decade, of supervised learning machines that employ a hypothesis space of linear discriminant functions in a higher dimensional feature space, trained and optimized from theory based on *statistical learning theory*. Vladimir Vapnik is largely credited with introducing this learning methodology that since its inception has outperformed many other systems in a broad selection of applications. We refer, of course, to support vector machines.

9.1.1. *Introduction to support vector machines*

Support vector machines (SVMs) [1–4] have attracted a significant amount of attention in the field of machine learning over the past decade by proving themselves to be very effective in a variety of real-world pattern classification and regression tasks. In the literature, they have been successfully applied to many problems ranging from face recognition, to bioinformatics and hand-written character recognition (amongst many others). In this chapter we give a brief introduction to the mathematical basis of SVMs for both classification and regression problems and give an example application for each. For a complete treatment of the background theory please see [4].

9.1.2. *The maximum-margin classifier*

Although the theory can be extended to accommodate multiple classes, without loss of generality let us first consider a binary classification task assuming we have linearly separable set of data samples

$$S = \{ (\mathbf{x}_1, y_1) \cdots (\mathbf{x}_m, y_m) \}, \tag{9.1}$$

where $\mathbf{x} \in \mathbb{R}^d$, i.e. $\mathbf{x}$ lies in a d-dimensional input space, and y_i is the class label such that $y_i \in \{-1, 1\}$. Since SVMs are principally based on linear discriminant functions, a suitable classifier could then be defined as:

$$f(\mathbf{x}) = sgn(\langle \mathbf{w}, \mathbf{x} \rangle + b) \ . \tag{9.2}$$

Where vector $\mathbf{w}$ determines the orientation of a discriminant plane (or hyperplane), $\langle \mathbf{w}, \mathbf{x} \rangle$ is the inner product of the vectors, $\mathbf{w}$ and $\mathbf{x}$ and b is the *bias* or offset from the origin. It is clear that there exists an infinite number of possible planes that could correctly dichotomize the training data. Simple intuition would lead one to expect the choice of a line drawn through the "middle", between the two classes, to be a suitable choice. As this would imply small disturbances of each data point would likely not affect the resulting classification significantly. This concept then suggests

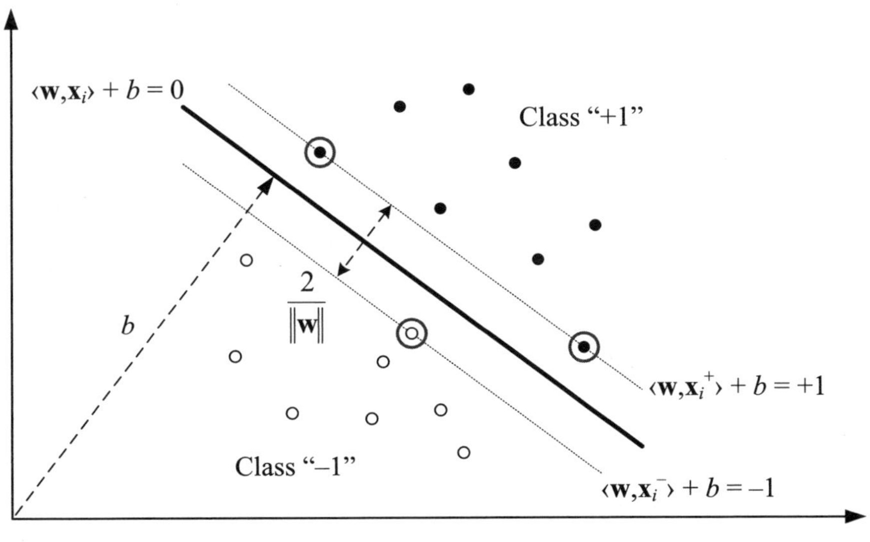

Fig. 9.1. Maximum-margin classifier with no errors showing *optimal separating hyperplane* (solid line) with canonical hyperplanes on either side (dotted lines). It can be shown that the margin is equal to $2/||\mathbf{w}||$. The support vectors are encircled.

that a good separating plane is one that works well at *generalizing*, this implies a plane which has a higher probability of correctly classifying new, unseen, data. Hence, an optimal classifier is one which finds the best generalizing hyperplane that maximizes the margin between each class of data points. This paradigm results in the selection of a single hyperplane dependent solely on the "support vectors" (these are the data points that *support* the so-called canonical hyperplanes) by maximizing the size of the margin. It is this characteristic that forms the key to the robustness of SVMs, as they rely solely on this sparse data set, and will not be affected by perturbations in any of the remainder of the test data. In this manner, SVMs are based on so-called Structural Risk Minimisation (SRM) [1] and not Empirical Risk Minimisation (ERM) on which other traditional classification techniques such as Neural Networks rely.

9.1.3. *The soft-margin classifier*

More often than not, however, real-world data sets are typically not linearly separable in input space, meaning that the maximum margin classifier model is no longer valid and a new approach must be introduced. This is achieved by relaxing the constraints a little to tolerate a small amount of misclassification. Points that subsequently fall on the wrong side of the margin, therefore, are treated as errors. The error vectors are assigned a

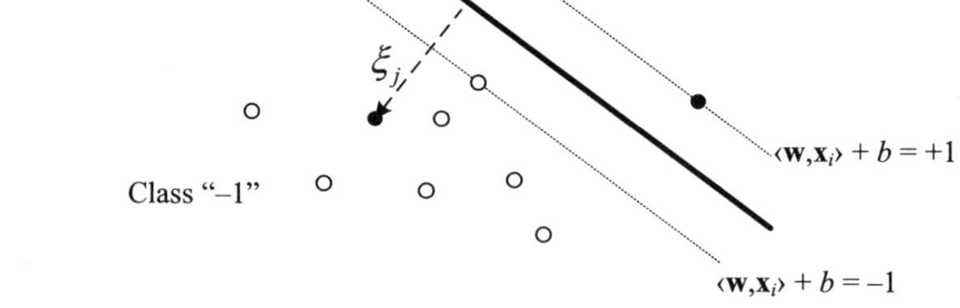

Fig. 9.2. Soft-margin classifier with some errors denoted by the slack variables ξ which represent the errors.

lower influence (determined by a preset *slack variable*) on the position of the hyperplane. Optimization of the soft-margin classifier is now achieved by maximizing the margin whilst at the same time allowing the margin constraints to be violated according to the preset slack variables ξ_i. Leading to the minimization of: $\frac{1}{2}\|\mathbf{w}\|^2+C\sum_{i=1}^{m}\xi_i$ subject to $y_i(\langle\mathbf{w},\mathbf{x}_i\rangle+b)\geq 1-\xi_i$ and $\xi_i \geq 0$ for $i = 1,\ldots,m$. Lagrangian duality theory [4] is typically applied to solve the minimization problems presented by linear inequalities. Thus, one can form the primal Lagrangian, $L(\mathbf{w},b,\boldsymbol{\xi},\boldsymbol{\alpha},\boldsymbol{\beta})$

$$= \frac{1}{2}\|\mathbf{w}\|^2 + C\sum_{i=1}^{m}\xi_i - \sum_{i=1}^{m}\beta_i\xi_i - \sum_{i=1}^{m}\alpha_i\left[y_i(\langle\mathbf{w},\mathbf{x}_i\rangle + b) - 1 + \xi_i\right], \quad (9.3)$$

where α_i and β_i are independent undetermined *Lagrangian multipliers.* The *dual-form* Lagrangian can be found by calculating each of the partial derivatives of the primal and equating to zero in turn thus,

$$\mathbf{w} = \sum_{i=1}^{m} y_i\alpha_i\mathbf{x}_i \quad (9.4)$$

and

$$0 = \sum_{i=1}^{m} y_i\alpha_i\ , \quad (9.5)$$

these are then re-substituted into the primal, which then yields,

$$L(\mathbf{w},b,\boldsymbol{\xi},\boldsymbol{\alpha},\boldsymbol{\beta}) = \sum_{i=1}^{m}\alpha_i - \frac{1}{2}\sum_{i,j=1}^{m} y_iy_j\alpha_i\alpha_j\langle\mathbf{x}_i,\mathbf{x}_j\rangle\ . \quad (9.6)$$

We note that this result is the same as for the maximum-margin classifier. The only difference is the constraint $\boldsymbol{\alpha}+\boldsymbol{\beta}=C$, where both $\boldsymbol{\alpha}$ and $\boldsymbol{\beta}\geq 0$, hence $0\leq\boldsymbol{\alpha},\boldsymbol{\beta}\leq C$. Thus, the value C sets an upper limit on the size of the Lagrangian optimization variables α_i and β_i, this limit is sometimes referred to as the *box constraint.* The selection of the value of C results in a trade-off between accuracy of data fit and regularization. The optimum choice of C will depend on the underlying data and nature of the problem and is usually found by experimental *cross-validation* (whereby the data is divided into a training set and testing or hold-out set and the classifier is tested on the hold-out set alone). This is best performed on a number of different sets (sometimes referred to as *folds*) of unseen data, leading to so-called "multi-folded cross-validation". Quadratic Programming (QP) algorithms are typically employed to solve these equations and calculate the Lagrangian multipliers. There are many online resources of such algorithms available for download, see website referred to in the excellent book by Cristianini and Shawe-Taylor [4] for an up to date listing.

9.1.4. *Support vector regression*

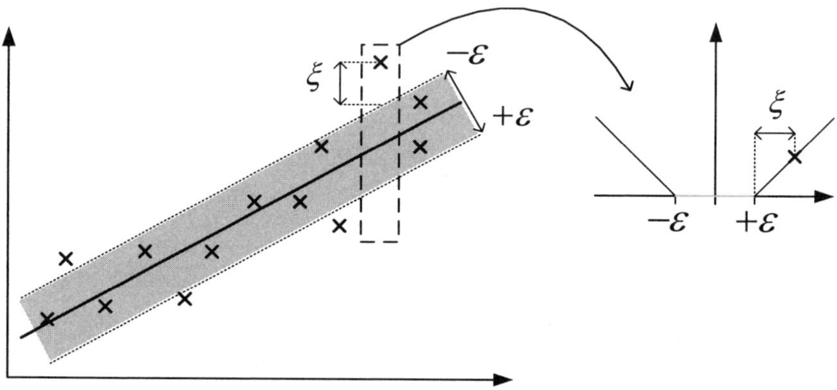

Fig. 9.3. Support vector regression showing the linear ε-insensitive loss function "tube" with width 2ε. Only those points lying outside the tube are considered support vectors.

SVMs can also lend themselves easily to the task of regression with only a simple extension to the theory. In so doing, they allow for real-valued targets to be estimated by modeling a linear function (see Fig. 9.3) in *feature space* (see Section 9.1.5). The same concept of maximizing the margin is retained but it is extended by a so-called *loss function*; which can take on different forms. The loss functions can be linear or quadratic or more usefully allow for an insensitive region whereby training data points that lie within this insensitive range then no error is deemed to have occurred. In a manner similar to the soft-margin classifier, errors are accounted for by the inclusion of slack variables that tolerate data points that violate this constraint to a limited extent. This then leads to a modified set of constraints requiring the minimization of: $\frac{1}{2}\|\mathbf{w}\|^2 + C\sum_{i=1}^{m}(\xi_i + \xi_i^*)$ subject to $y_i - \langle \mathbf{w}, \mathbf{x}_i \rangle - b \leq \varepsilon + \xi_i$ and $\langle \mathbf{w}, \mathbf{x}_i \rangle + b - y_i \leq \varepsilon + \xi_i^*$ with $\xi_i, \xi_i^* \geq 0$ for $i = 1, \ldots, m$. The solution for the above QP problem is provided once again by the use of Lagrangian duality theory, however, we have omitted a full derivation for the sake of brevity (please see the tutorial by Smola and Schölkopf [5] and the references therein). The above Fig. 9.3 shows only the linear loss function whereby the points that are further than $|\varepsilon|$ from the optimal line are apportioned weight in a linearly increasing fashion. There are, however, numerous different types of loss functions in the literature, including the quadratic and Huber's loss function among others which is in fact a hybrid or piecewise combination of quadratic and linear functions. Whilst most of them include an insensitive region to facilitate sparseness of solution this is not always the case. Figure 9.4 shows the quadratic and

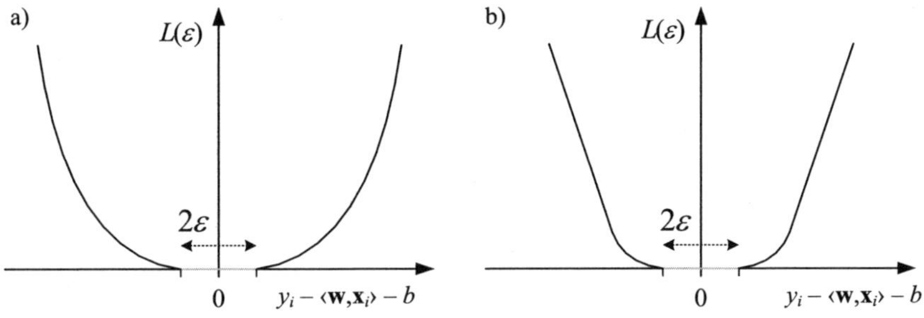

Fig. 9.4. Quadratic (a) and Huber (b) type loss functions with ε-insensitive regions.

Huber's loss function. Hence, when training an SV-based regressor one must optimize for both the box constraint, C, the parameters of the Kernel function used and ε. Typically, this is achieved by performing a grid search for all hyper-parameters during cross-validation.

9.1.5. *Kernel functions*

Often, real-world data is not readily separable using a linear hyperplane but it may exhibit a natural underlying nonlinear characteristic. Kernel mappings offer an efficient method of projecting input data into a higher dimensional *feature space* where a linear hyperplane can successfully separate classes. Kernel functions must obey Mercer's Theorem, and as such they offer an implicit mapping into feature space. This means that the explicit mapping need not be computed, rather the calculation of a simple inner-product is sufficient to facilitate the mapping. This reduces the burden of computation significantly and in combination with SVM's inherent generality, greatly mitigates the so-called "*curse of dimensionality*". Furthermore, the input feature inner-product from (9.6) can simply be substituted with the appropriate Kernel function to obtain the mapping whilst having no effect on the Lagrangian optimization theory. Hence, the relevant classifier function then becomes:

$$f(\mathbf{x}_j) = sgn\left[\sum_{i=1}^{nSVs} y_i \alpha_i K(\mathbf{x}_i, \mathbf{x}_j) + b\right] \tag{9.7}$$

and for regression

$$f(\mathbf{x}_j) = \sum_{i=1}^{nSVs} (\alpha_i - \alpha_i^*) K(\mathbf{x}_i, \mathbf{x}_j) + b \ , \tag{9.8}$$

where $nSVs$ denotes the number of support vectors, y_i are the labels, α_i and α_i^* are the Lagrangian multipliers, b the bias, $\mathbf{x}_i$ the *Support Vectors* previously identified through the training process and $\mathbf{x}_j$ the test data vector. The use of Kernel functions transforms a simple linear classifier into a powerful and general nonlinear classifier (or regressor). There are a number of different Kernel functions available, here are few popular types [4]:

$$\textit{Linear function: } K(\mathbf{x}_i, \mathbf{x}_j) = \langle \mathbf{x}_i, \mathbf{x}_j \rangle + c \tag{9.9}$$

$$\textit{Polynomial function: } K(\mathbf{x}_i, \mathbf{x}_j) = (\langle \mathbf{x}_i, \mathbf{x}_j \rangle + c)^d \tag{9.10}$$

$$\textit{Gaussian radial basis function: } K(\mathbf{x}_i, \mathbf{x}_j) = exp\left[\frac{-\|\mathbf{x}_i - \mathbf{x}_j\|^2}{2\sigma^2}\right] \tag{9.11}$$

$$\begin{aligned}\textit{Spline function: } K(\mathbf{x}_i, \mathbf{x}_j) = \prod_{k=1}^{10} \Big(1 + x_{ik} \cdot x_{jk} + \frac{1}{2} x_{ik} \cdot x_{jk} \min(x_{ik}, x_{jk}) \\ - \frac{1}{6} \min(x_{ik}, x_{jk})^3\Big)\end{aligned} \tag{9.12}$$

where c is an arbitrary constant parameter (often c is simply set to zero or unity), d is the degree of the polynomial Kernel and σ controls the width of the Gaussian radial basis function. When experimenting with training and cross-validation it is common practice to perform a *grid search* over these Kernel parameters along with the box constraint, C, for the lowest classification error within a given training set.

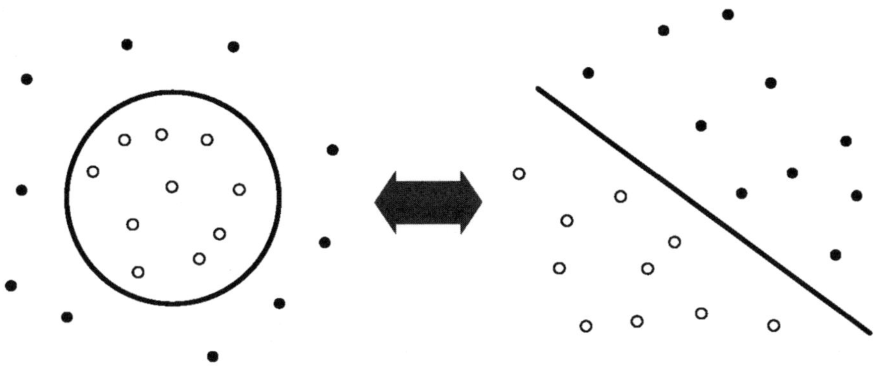

Fig. 9.5. Kernel functions generate implicit nonlinear mappings, enabling SVMs to operate on a linear separating hyperplane in higher dimensional feature space.

9.2. Application: Biomedical Pattern Classification

Cardiovascular disease (CVD) is the leading cause of mortality in the developed world [6]. In 2004 alone approximately 17 million people died from some form of CVD (largely from stroke and myocardial infarction). The World Health Organisation (WHO), suggests that this figure is expected to exceed 23 million by the year 2030. There are a number of established risk factors for CVD such as sex, age, tobacco smoking, high blood pressure, blood serum cholesterol and the presence of diabetes mellitus. Current methods for estimating the risk of a CVD event (such as a myocardial infarction or a stroke) within an individual, rely on the use of these factors in a so-called "risk calculator". This calculator is based on regression equations relating levels of individual risk factors to CVD events in various prospective follow-up studies such as the Framingham Heart study [7] or the Cox model study [8]. Such risk calculators, however, fail to identify a significant minority of subjects who subsequently go on to develop some form of CVD. Events typically occur as a result of arteriosclerosis and/or atherosclerosis, inflammatory and degenerative conditions of the arterial wall. Early on, changes occur at the cellular level but this leads to changes in the mechanical properties of the arterial wall. Hence, the possibility that biophysical measures of the mechanical properties of the arterial wall may provide a measure of CVD risk has received a great deal of attention. Currently, one of the most promising measurements is *arterial stiffness.* Arteries naturally tend to stiffen with age and premature stiffening may result from a combination of arteriosclerosis and atherosclerosis. Additionally, arterial stiffening leads to systolic hypertension and increased loading on the heart. Simple measurement of Brachial (upper arm) blood pressure may not, however, reveal this condition as central blood pressure can differ markedly from that measured in the periphery. A number of studies [9, 10] indicate that large artery stiffness, as measured by pulse wave velocity (see below) has proved to be a powerful and independent predictor of CVD events, more closely related to CVD risk than the traditional risk factors.

9.2.1. *Pulse wave velocity*

Determining arterial stiffness directly by simultaneous measurement of the change in arterial diameter with pressure is technically challenging and the most practical technique employed to measure stiffness is the estimation of arterial *Pulse Wave Velocity* (PWV). PWV is the speed at which the pressure pulse propagates through the arterial tree and is directly related to arterial stiffness. Measuring PWV from the Carotid artery (in the neck) to the Femoral artery (in the thigh) is the measurement that has been used in most outcome studies to date. It includes the Aorta and large elastic arteries that are most susceptible to age-related stiffening. Carotid-femoral PWV is often determined by placement of a tonometer (a non-invasive pressure sensor) over the Carotid and Femoral arteries. The time delay between the pressure pulse arriving at the Carotid and Femoral arteries is measured and then divided by the path length which is estimated from distance between the two sites of application of the sensors. Hence, Pulse Wave Velocity is determined in ms^{-1}.

9.2.2. *Digital volume pulse analysis*

Determination of PWV as described above, whilst non-invasive, involves the subject undressing to allow access to the Femoral artery and requires specialized equipment and a skilled technician. An alternative, simpler and quicker technique would be of great advantage in screening for CVD. We have previously proposed that the shape of the digital volume pulse (DVP) may be used to estimate arterial stiffness [11–14]. The DVP can be easily and rapidly acquired (without the need for a skilled technician) by measuring absorption of infra-red light across the finger pulp (which is technically termed *photoplethysmography*). This varies with red blood

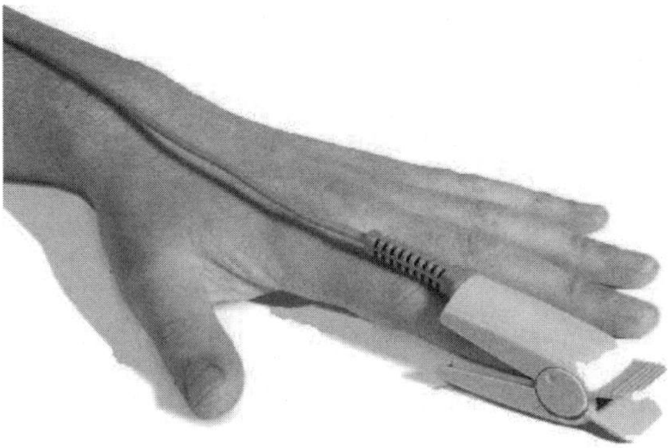

Fig. 9.6. The Photoplethysmograph device used to acquire the DVP waveform attached to the index finger.

density and hence with blood vessel diameter during the cardiac cycle. Typically the DVP waveform (see Fig. 9.7) exhibits an initial systolic peak followed by a diastolic peak. The time between these two peaks, called the *peak-to-peak time* (PPT), is related to the time taken for the pressure wave to propagate from the heart to the peripheral blood vessels and back again. Thus PPT is related to PWV in the large arteries. This has led to the development of the so-called *stiffness index* (SI), which is simply the ratio of PPT divided by the subject height and can be used as a crude estimate of PWV. Older subjects, however, and in subjects with premature arterial stiffening, the systolic and diastolic peaks in the DVP become difficult to distinguish and SI cannot be used to estimate arterial stiffness.

9.2.3. *Study population and feature extraction*

A group of 461 subjects were recruited from the local area of South East London. None of the subjects had a previous history of cardiovascular disease or were receiving heart medication. The subjects ranged from 16 to 81 years of age, with an average age of 50 and standard deviation of 13.6 years. The DVP waveform was measured for each of the subjects along with their PWV and a number of other basic physiological measures such as systolic and diastolic blood pressure, their height and weight. There are various ways in which features can be derived from the DVP waveform. Previous work in this field [13] has led to the selection of what we have come to term *Physiological Features* [15]. Essentially, these are parameters associated with the physiological properties of the aorta and arterial characteristics in general. More recently, we have focused our attention on exploiting features that do not assume an underlying physiological basis but instead are selected by applying information theoretic approaches to the DVP waveform and we refer to these as *Signal-Based Features.*

9.2.3.1. *Physiological features*

After a great deal of experimentation comparing the significance of many of the physiological features, it was found that, in fact, a specific set of four of these features gave the best classification of high or low PWV. Interestingly, two of these features have been independently cited in the literature [11, 13, 16] as having a bearing on cardiovascular pathology. Dillon and Hertzman are credited [16] with first measuring the DVP in 1941,

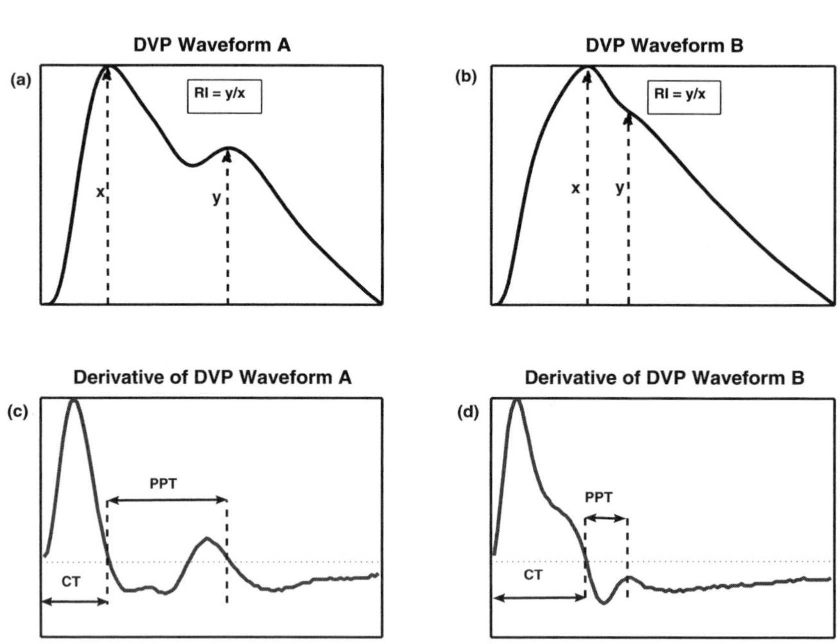

Fig. 9.7. Digital Volume Pulse waveforms as extracted from the Photoplethysmograph device and their derivatives. Labeled to show various features, e.g. PPT, RI and CT.

and they observed that subjects with hypertension or arterial heart disease exhibited an "increase in the crest time" compared to healthy subjects. The *Crest Time* (CT), is the time from the foot of the DVP waveform to its peak (as shown in Figs 9.7c and d) and it has proved to be a useful feature for the classifier. Also *Peak-to-Peak Time* (PPT), defined as the time between the first peak and the second peak or inflection point of the DVP waveform (see Figs 9.7c and d). As mentioned previously in the introduction, the second peak/inflection point on the DVP is generally accepted to be due to reflected waves. So its timing would be related to arterial stiffness and PWV. The definition of PPT depends on the DVP waveform as its contour varies with subjects. When there is a second peak as is the case with "Waveform A" in Fig. 9.7a, PPT is defined as time between the two maxima. Hence, the time between the two positive to negative zero-crossings of the derivative can be considered to be the PPT. In some DVP waveforms, however, the second peak is not distinct as in "Waveform B" in Fig. 9.7b. When this occurs, the time between the peak of the waveform and the inflection point on the downward going slope of the waveform (which is a local maximum of the first derivative, as shown in Fig. 9.7d) is defined as the PPT. Another measurement extracted from the DVP used in the classifier, is the so-called *Reflection Index* (RI), which is the ratio of relative amplitudes of the first and second peaks (see Figs 9.7a and b). These four features then: PPT, CT, RI and SI were empirically found [14] to be amongst the best physiologically motivated features for successful classification of PWV.

9.2.3.2. *Signal-based features*

These features were extracted by applying established signal processing techniques to reduce the dimensionality of the waveform to a standardized set of features without making any assumptions about the physical generation of the waveform. After much experimentation it was found that a certain range of the eigenvalues of the covariance matrix (formed 0by the autocorrelation of the DVP waveform with its mean removed) outperformed all the other features and methods by some margin. Essentially, the covariance matrix, **A**, formed from the DVP waveform (one per subject) is decomposed using Eigenvalue Decomposition such that

$$\mathbf{A} = \mathbf{V}\boldsymbol{\Sigma}\mathbf{V}^{-1}. \tag{9.13}$$

Here $\mathbf{V}$ is the matrix of orthonormal *eigenvectors* of $\mathbf{A}$ and $\mathbf{\Sigma}$ its *eigenvalues*, where $\mathbf{\Sigma} = diag\{\sigma_1, \sigma_2, \ldots, \sigma_n\}$. Specifically, the range of eigenvalues $\hat{\mathbf{\Sigma}} = \{\sigma_3, \ldots, \sigma_9\}$ inclusive were found, during experimentation, to give the best results. It is thought that the first two eigenvalues, σ_1 and σ_2, primarily represent the signal subspace data, which is essentially common to all of the waveforms in the database, and hence discarding these features enhanced the separability of the data and its subsequent classification.

9.2.4. *Results*

This section contains the best results obtained after thorough experimentation of the Support Vector classifier. Results are presented in percentages with overall (or "total" rate) then the *sensitivity* or "true positive" rate followed by the *specificity* or "true negative" rate. In actual fact, a wide range of possible feature sets and combinations exist that performed the required tasks satisfactorily, however, for ease of readability and conciseness we have selected those which we found to perform the best overall. The results presented here are based on the best two sets of each of the physiologically motivated features, two sets of signal subspace-based features and finally the two best combinations of the each type of feature set. During experimentation, the two sets of physiologically-based features that performed the best were found to be: P1 = {CT, PPT} and P2 = {CT, PPT, SI}. The two sets of signal subspace-based features that performed the best were also found accordingly, $\Sigma 1 = \{\sigma_3, \ldots, \sigma_9\}$ and $\Sigma 2 = \{\sigma_2, \ldots, \sigma_9\}$. The original cohort contained 461 subjects, both their complete DVP waveform data and PWV measurements were available to this study. The mean PWV value of our cohort was found to be around 10 ms^{-1}, hence, a binary target label was determined according to this threshold. The cohort was gapped to remove those subjects with PWV of between 9 and 11 ms^{-1} to avoid ambiguity of the target classes. The remaining 315 records were used to train and test the classifier using a three fold cross-validation regimen, where 90% of the data were used for training and 10% for testing in any given fold. A binary classifier was developed using the Ohio State University SVM toolbox for Matlab [17], the classifier was trained and tested using a number of different kernel functions. The so-called "ν-SVM" type of classifier was employed and differs from conventional C-SVM only in the way the box constraint is implemented. Instead of having an infinite range like that of the value of C, ν varies

Table 9.1. SVM classification rates % and (SD) for various data sets using GRBF kernel.

	Data sets					
	Physiological		**Eigenvalues**		**Combinations**	
	P1	**P2**	**Σ1**	**Σ2**	**Σ1+P1**	**Σ1+P2**
Total	84.0 (0.5)	84.0 (0.5)	85.1 (1.4)	85.3 (1.6)	86.1 (0.9)	**87.5** (0.0)
Sens	**90.3** (2.0)	88.2 (2.1)	**90.3** (3.3)	**90.3** (4.0)	86.7 (1.4)	87.5 (0.0)
Spec	77.4 (0.5)	79.9 (1.0)	80.2 (2.8)	80.5 (3.4)	85.3 (2.5)	**87.5** (0.0)

between the limits zero and one, thus simplifying the grid search somewhat. Experimentation revealed that the Gaussian RBF kernel performed as well or better than the others and hence the results in Table 9.1 are based on this kernel (the performance of the other kernels is compared below in Table 9.2). After performing thorough model hyper-parameter grid searches (see Fig. A.1 in Appendix A), results were averaged from a "block" of nine individual results obtained from a range of both constraint factor, ν, and GRBF width, γ. This technique was applied to all the results to mitigate against over-training of the model parameters, ensuring a more general classifier and more realistic results. As shown in Table 9.1, the SVM method using the *physiological* feature set P1 alone, gives a fairly high degree of classification accuracy, with a significantly high sensitivity of 90.3% achieved. There was a slightly lower result of only 77.4% specificity. Hence, the overall average successful classification rate becomes 84.0%. The results for the *signal subspace-based features*, are better still, showing a distinct improvement in the specificity when compared with those of the physiologically motivated features. It is readily possible to achieve sensitivities in the region of 90%, with specificities of over 80%, bringing overall classification to 85.3%. Finally, combinations of both feature sets were tested and it was found that two pairs gave good results whilst the other two combinations were less effective. In fact, the combinations of Σ1+P1 and Σ1+P2 gave the best results overall. The latter set giving an overall classification rate of 87.5%, with an equal rate for both sensitivity and specificity. This is definitely the best classification rate achieved in this study so far and is a very high classification rate for PWV based solely on features extracted from the DVP waveform. Further tests were performed with different kernel functions to compare with those of the GRBF kernel; linear and second and third order polynomial kernels were tested but the GRBF kernel consistently outperformed them for all of the data sets (see Table 9.2). For a complete treatment of this work please see Alty et al [6].

Table 9.2. Overall SVM classification rates % and (SD) for various Kernel functions for each data set.

	Data sets					
	Physiological		Eigenvalues		Combinations	
Kernel	**P1**	**P2**	**Σ1**	**Σ2**	**Σ1+P1**	**Σ1+P2**
Linear	84.0 (0.5)	83.3 (0.0)	82.3 (0.9)	80.9 (0.5)	84.4 (0.0)	85.8 (0.5)
Poly2	83.9 (0.8)	84.0 (0.5)	83.9 (1.4)	84.5 (1.1)	86.0 (1.2)	86.8 (0.5)
Poly3	83.7 (0.9)	83.9 (1.1)	85.0 (0.9)	84.6 (1.4)	86.1 (0.9)	86.5 (0.0)
GRBF	84.0 (0.5)	84.0 (0.5)	85.1 (1.4)	85.3 (1.6)	86.1 (0.9)	**87.5** (0.0)

9.3. Application: Hand-written Graffiti Recognition

In this section, the problem of recognizing one-stroke hand-written graffiti [18–20] is handled by the SVRs [1, 2]. The hand-written graffiti include digits zero to nine and three commands, i.e. backspace, carriage return and space, which are shown in Fig. 9.3. Some feature points are extracted from each graffiti for the training of the SVRs. With the feature points as the input, an SVR-based recognizer is proposed to recognize the hand-written graffiti. The recognition performance of the proposed SVR-based graffiti recognizer, with various kernels (linear function, spline function, radial basis function and polynomial function) and parameters, is investigated.

Table 9.3. Hand-written one-stroke digits and commands. The dot denotes the starting point of the character.

Class No.	Class Name	Strokes	Class No.	Class Name	Strokes
1	0(a)	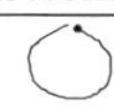	9	6	
2	0(b)		10	7	
3	1		11	8(a)	
4	2		12	8(b)	
5	3		13	9	
6	4		14	Backspace	
7	5(a)		15	Carriage Return	
8	5(b)		16	Space	

9.3.1. *Data acquisition and feature extraction*

The features of the hand-written graffiti play an important role in the recognition process. By employing meaningful features which represent the characteristic of the hand-written graffiti, it is possible to achieve a high recognition rate even using a simple structure of recognizer. In this application, 10 sample points of a hand-written graffiti will be obtained as the feature vector, which will serve as the input of the SVR-based graffiti recognizer for the training and recognition processes.

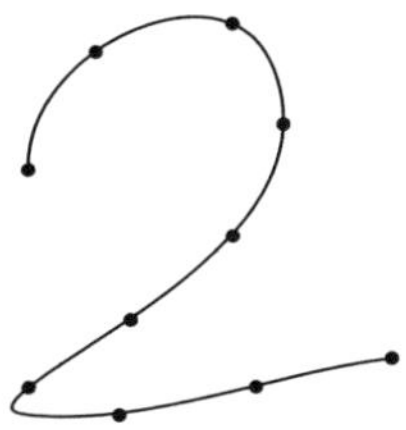

Fig. 9.8. Written trace of digit "2" (solid line) and 10 feature points characterized by coordinate (ϕ_k, β_k) (indicated by dots).

The following approach [18–20] is employed to obtain the feature vector of a graffiti. It is assumed that a graffiti is drawn in a square drawing area with dimension of $\phi_{max} \times \beta_{max}$ (in pixels). Each point in the square drawing area is characterized by a coordinate (ϕ, β) where $0 \leq \phi \leq \phi_{max}$ and $0 \leq \beta \leq \beta_{max}$. The bottom left corner is considered as the origin denoted by the coordinate (0, 0).

Figure 9.8 illustrates a hand-written digit "2" with trace in solid line and 10 sampled points (denoted by dots) taken in uniform distance characterized by coordinates (ϕ_k, β_k), $k = 1, 2, \cdots, 10$. By using the coordinate of the points to form the feature vector, we have 20 numerical values as the input for the SVR-based graffiti recognizer. Theoretically, it is feasible and the training of the SVRs will be done in the same way. However, the complexity of the SVR can be reduced if a smaller number of feature points is employed and thus it is possible to reduce the implementation complexity and cost of the hand-written graffiti recognizer.

In order to take more information about the graffiti and reduce the number of feature points, the following algorithm is proposed. Denote the feature vector as $\rho = [\rho_1 \quad \rho_2 \quad \cdots \quad \rho_{10}]$. The first five points, i.e. (ϕ_k, β_k), $k = 1, 3, 5, 7$ and 9, taken alternatively are converted to five numerical values, respectively, using the formula $\rho_k = \phi_k\phi_{max} + \beta_k$. The other five points, (ϕ_k, β_k), $k = 2, 4, 6, 8$ and 10, are converted to another five numerical values, respectively, using the formula $\rho_k = \beta_k\beta_{max} + \phi_k$. The second formula is a kind of transformation to obtain the feature points simply by rotating the square writing area by 90 degrees. The main reason for transforming the feature points is to enlarge the difference between each graffiti, particularly for those graffiti resembling each others, to improve the recognition performance. It can be imagined that the first formula look at the graffiti from the x-axis direction while the second one from the y-axis direction. Consequently, as some graffiti look like others in the x-axis but may not look like others in y-axis, the feature vectors for different graffiti will be situated far apart from each other in the feature space and benefit the recognition process. Different transformation techniques may lead to different recognition results. In the following, as more than one feature vector will be used, an index i is introduced to denote the feature vector number. Hence, we have the feature vector in the form of $\rho_i = [\rho_{i1} \quad \rho_{i2} \quad \cdots \quad \rho_{i10}]$.

It should be noted that the feature vector ρ_i provides the coordinate information of the graffiti, it is thus very sensitive to the position and size of the graffiti appearing in the square writing area. For example, the feature vector of a small size of digit "2" in the top right corner of the square writing area will be very different from a large size of digit "2" right in the middle. In order to reduce the effect of the position and size information of the graffiti to the recognition performance, a normalization process is proposed and defined as follows:

$$\mathbf{x}_i = \frac{\rho_i}{\parallel \rho_i \parallel} \tag{9.14}$$

where $\parallel \cdot \parallel$ denotes the l_2 norm. The feature vector $\mathbf{x}_i$ is taken as the input for the SVR-based graffiti recognizer.

9.3.2. *SVR-based recognizer*

An SVR-based graffiti recognizer with the block diagram shown in Fig. 9.9 is proposed for recognition of hand-written graffiti. Referring to Fig. 9.9, it consists of M SVR-based sub-recognizers. In this example, 16 graffiti as shown in Table 9.3 are to be recognized, hence, we have $M = 16$. The SVR-based graffiti recognizer takes the feature vector $\mathbf{x}_i$ as an input and then distributes it to all sub-recognizers for further processing. Corresponding to the sub-recognizer j ($j = 1, 2, \cdots, 16$), an output vector

$\mathbf{y}_{ij} \in \Re^{10}$ will be produced. All output vectors $\mathbf{y}_{ij}$ are fed to the class determiner simultaneously for determination of the most likely input graffiti indicated by an integer in the output. The integer from the output of the class determiner is in range of 1 and 16 indicating the class label of the possible input graffiti as shown in Table 9.3.

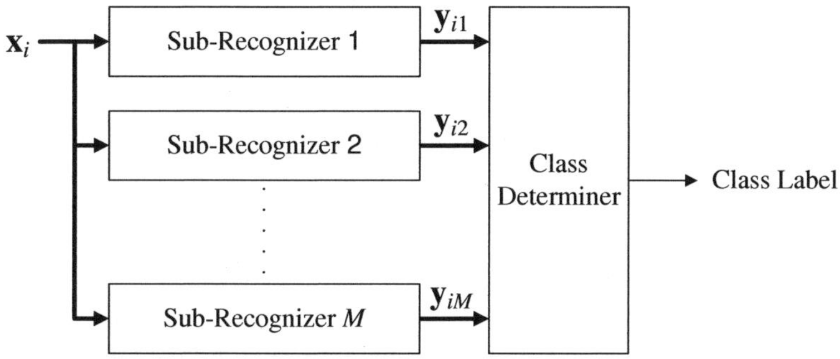

Fig. 9.9. An SVR-based recognizer for hand-written graffiti.

The SVR-based graffiti recognizer shown in Fig. 9.9 consists of 16 SVR-based sub-recognizers. Each SVR-based sub-recognizer is constructed by 10 SVRs (due to 10 feature points are taken as input) as shown in Fig. 9.10. Denote the 10 SVRs as SVR k, the normalized feature vector $\mathbf{x}_i = [x_{i1} \quad x_{i2} \quad \cdots \quad x_{i10}]$ and the output vector $\mathbf{y}_{ij} = [y_{ij1} \quad y_{ij2} \quad \cdots \quad y_{ij10}]$. As it can be seen from Fig. 9.10, the SVR k takes x_{ik} as an input and produces y_{ijk} as an output. Defining the target output of the SVR k as its input, i.e. x_{ik}, the SVR k is trained to minimize the difference between actual and target outputs according to the chosen loss function. In other words, the SVR k is trained to reproduce its input.

The sub-recognizer j, ($j = 1, 2, \cdots, 16$), will be trained using the normalized feature vector $\mathbf{x}_i$ corresponding to the j-th graffiti. For example, the sub-recognizer 1 is trained using the feature vectors corresponding to the 0(a) (graffiti "0" drawn from left to right as shown in Table 9.3). According to the training data and the training objective, the input-output difference of the SVR k will be smaller when the input x_{ik} is corresponding to the graffiti k compared to other graffiti. This characteristic of the trained SVR k offers a nice property to make the graffiti recognition possible by the class determiner in the subsequent stage.

The class determiner takes all $\mathbf{y}_{ij}$ as input. To determine the possible input graffiti, the class determiner computes a scalar similarity value s_{ij}

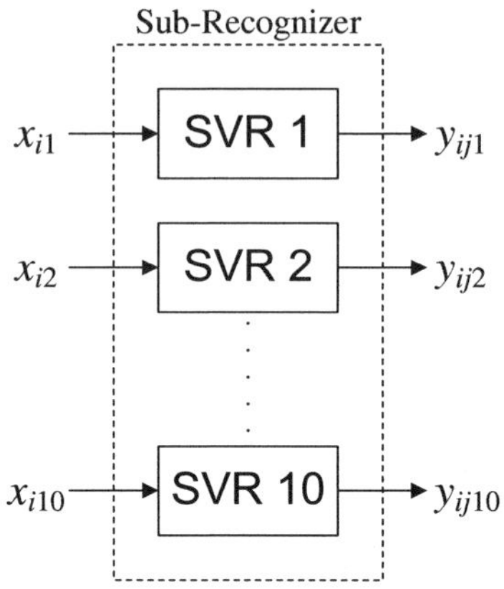

Fig. 9.10. Structure of SVR-based sub-recognizer.

for each SVR-based sub-recognizer according to the following formula.

$$s_{ij} = \left\| \mathbf{x}_i - \frac{\mathbf{y}_{ij}}{\| \mathbf{y}_{ij} \|} \right\| \in [0, 1] \tag{9.15}$$

The similarity value s_{ij} indicates the level of the input and output that the SVR-based sub-recognizer resemble each other. The higher level of similarity is indicated by a similarity value of $s_j(t)$ closer to zero, otherwise, one. The class determiner is based on the similarity values making the recognition decision by picking the SVR sub-recognizer which produces the smallest value of s_{ij} and produces the value of index j as the output. The index j showing in the output indicates that the graffiti j is the possible input graffiti.

9.3.3. *Simulation results*

The proposed SVR-based recognizer under different settings will be trained and tested in this section and the recognition performance in terms of recognition rate will be investigated. The training and testing data sets for each graffiti consist of 100 and 50 patterns, respectively. For the purposes of training, we consider four kernel functions, namely, linear, spline, polynomial and radial basis functions, for the SVRs (see (9.9), (9.10), (9.11) and (9.12) in section 9.1.5).

To perform the training, we consider the SVRs with different kernel functions, c, σ, loss functions, ε and C as shown in Table 9.4. The recognition performances of the SVR-based graffiti recognizers under different settings are shown in the tables in the appendices at the end of this chapter. The value of ε is chosen to be zero for quadratic loss function. It is found experimentally that the recognition performance of the SVR-based graffiti recognizers with ε-insensitive loss function subject to $\varepsilon = 0.01$ or $\varepsilon = 0.1$ is not comparable to $\varepsilon = 0.05$. Thus, the tables (in the appendices) showing the recognition rate for $\varepsilon = 0.01$ and $\varepsilon = 0.1$ are omitted. Referring to the tables, the training and testing recognition rates for each sub-recognizer j, $j = 1, 2, \cdots, 16$, and the average training and testing recognition rates of the SVR-based recognizer are illustrated. The worst recognition rates given by the sub-recognizers and the best average recognition rate are highlighted in bold under different settings and parameters.

Table 9.4. Settings and parameters of SVRs.

Kernel functions	Linear ($c = 0$), spline, polynomial, radial basis kernel functions
c, *sigma*	1, 2, 5, 10
Loss functions	Quadratic ($\varepsilon = 0$), ε-insensitive loss functions
ε	0.01, 0.05, 0.1 (for ε-insensitive loss functions)
C	0.01, 0.1, 1, 10, 100, ∞

To summarize the results, the SVR-based graffiti recognizers with both average training and testing recognition rates over 99% under different settings and parameters are tabulated in Table 9.5. In total, we have 23 cases satisfying the criterion. Comparing the cases among the kernel functions without parameter c or σ, namely, linear and spline kernel functions, the SVR-based graffiti recognizer with spline kernel function performs better in general in the sense of higher average recognition rate. Comparing the cases among the kernel functions with parameter c or σ, namely, polynomial and radial basis functions, the radial basis function demonstrates a better potential to produce acceptable recognition performance. Referring to Table 9.5, the radial basis function offers 13 cases with average recognition rate over 99% while only 5 cases for the polynomial function. It can be seen from the table that the recognition performance offered by the radial basis function is less sensitive to the parameters c, σ and C.

In general, the kernel functions with extra parameter c or σ are able to offer a better recognition performance due to the extra parameter giving one more degree of freedom for transformation of the feature space. It is noted that the average training recognition rate is always higher than the average

Table 9.5. Recognition performance of SVR-based graffiti recognizers with the average recognition rate over 99% for both training and testing data.

Case	Kernel[♭]	Loss Function[♯]	c, σ	C	Average (%)[†]	Worst (%)[*]
1	Linear	Quadratic	0	0.1	99.2500/99.0000	93(5)/96(1,11,12)
2	Linear	ϵ-insensitive	0	0.01	99.0000/99.0000	**92**(5)/96(1,11)
3	Spline	Quadratic	–	0.1	99.2500/99.0000	93(5)/96(1,11,12)
4	Spline	ϵ-insensitive	–	0.1	99.5625/99.1250	95(5)/**94**(1)
5	Poly	Quadratic	1	0.1	99.2500/99.0000	93(5)/96(1,11,12)
6	Poly	Quadratic	2	0.1	99.3750/99.0000	94(5)/**94**(12)
7	Poly	ϵ-insensitive	1	0.1	99.6250/99.0000	96(5)/**94**(1)
8	Poly	ϵ-insensitive	2	0.01	99.3750/**99.2500**	94(5)/96(1,11)
9	Poly	ϵ-insensitive	2	0.1	**99.8125**/99.0000	98(5)/**94**(8)
10	RB	Quadratic	2	1	99.3125/99.0000	93(5)/96(1,11,12)
11	RB	Quadratic	5	10	99.3750/99.0000	94(5)/**94**(1)
12	RB	Quadratic	10	10	99.2500/99.0000	93(5)/96(1,11,12)
13	RB	ϵ-insensitive	1	0.01	99.1875/99.0000	93(5)/96(1,11)
14	RB	ϵ-insensitive	1	0.1	99.5625/99.1250	96(5)/96(1,11)
15	RB	ϵ-insensitive	2	0.01	99.1250/99.0000	**92**(5)/96(1,11)
16	RB	ϵ-insensitive	2	0.1	99.1875/99.0000	93(5)/96(1,11)
17	RB	ϵ-insensitive	5	0.01	99.1250/99.0000	**92**(5)/96(1,11)
18	RB	ϵ-insensitive	5	0.1	99.0625/99.0000	**92**(5)/96(1,11)
19	RB	ϵ-insensitive	5	1	99.2500/99.1250	93(5)/96(1,11)
20	RB	ϵ-insensitive	10	0.01	99.1250/99.0000	**92**(5)/96(1,11)
21	RB	ϵ-insensitive	10	0.1	99.0625/99.0000	**92**(5)/96(1,11)
22	RB	ϵ-insensitive	10	1	99.0625/99.0000	**92**(5)/96(1,11)
23	RB	ϵ-insensitive	10	10	99.5000/99.0000	95(5)/**94**(1)

[♭] Poly and RB stand for polynomial and radial basis functions, respectively.
[♯] When ϵ-insensitive loss function is employed, $\varepsilon = 0.05$ is used.
[†] Average recognition rate in the format of A/B. A is for the training data and B is for the testing data.
[*] The worst recognition rate in the format of $A(a)/B(b)$. A is for the training data and B is for the testing data. a and b denote the class labels of the graffiti.

testing recognition rate. The highest average training recognition rate is 99.8125% (case 9) while the highest testing recognition rate is 99.2500% (case 8). It is interestingly found that both cases are for the SVR-based graffiti recognizer with polynomial function. It is noted that the worst training recognition rate is 92% for the graffiti with the class label 5 while the worst testing recognition rate is 94% for the graffiti with the class labels 1, 11 and 12. The graffiti labels 1, 5, 11 and 12 are corresponding to the digits 0, 3, 8 (written in both left and right directions). They have a similar characteristic in the shapes leading to the feature vectors looking like each other. Thus, it makes the recognition process more difficult and degrades the recognition performance. The result gives a clue to improve the recognition performance by employing a better transformation to obtain the feature vectors such that they are far apart from each other in the feature space.

Among the 23 cases, we are going to to come up with one which offers the best recognition performance. We define the overall recognition rate as the average of the average training and testing recognition rates. Considering the cases where the overall recognition rate is over 99.3000% or the average testing recognition rate is equal to or greater than 99.1250%, we come up with 6 cases, i.e. cases 4, 7, 8, 9 14 and 19. By considering the worst training and testing recognition rates, the SVR-based graffiti recognizer of case 14 offers the best performance. The worst training and testing recognition rates are both 96% which is the highest compared to other chosen cases.

The number of support vectors corresponding to cases 4, 7, 8, 9, 14 and 19 is tabulated in Table 9.6. The number of support vectors for each sub-recognizer j, $j = 1, 2, \cdots, 16$, is the sum of the support vectors of the 10 SVRs shown in Fig. 9.10. It can be seen that the sub-recognizer 5 corresponding to digit "3" produces the largest number of support vectors while the sub-recognizer 14 corresponding to the command "backspace" produces the smallest number for all cases. Of the cases 4, 7, 8, 9, 14 and 19, case 8 produces the highest average number of support vectors, i.e. 251.9375 while case 9 produces the smallest average number of support vectors, i.e. 143.000. From the point of view of the recognizer complexity, the SVR-based graffiti recognizer for case 9 with the smallest average number of support vectors is recommended.

9.4. Conclusion

This chapter has given a basic introduction to SVMs. Some properties and theories have been presented to support the design of SVMs dealing with some practical problems. Two applications have been considered in this chapter, namely, classification of heart disease risk and recognition of hand-written characters. On the application of the classification of heart disease, a classifier has been developed using the support vector classifiers to accurately estimate the risk of developing heart disease by using the signal derived from a finger-based pulse oximeter. On the application of recognition of hand-written characters, a recognizer has been developed using the support vector regressors. Simulation results have been shown to illustrate the effectiveness of the proposed approaches.

Table 9.6. Number of support vectors for cases 4, 7, 8, 9 14 and 19.

Sub-Recognizer	Case 4	Case 7	Case 8	Case 9	Case 14	Case 19
1	145	160	282	93	184	228
2	340	356	295	286	375	420
3	87	89	164	67	99	94
4	336	344	374	285	372	409
5	**342**	**358**	**406**	**292**	**387**	**442**
6	95	103	216	58	113	116
7	306	325	351	261	345	389
8	158	162	187	146	172	172
9	112	116	214	80	133	157
10	133	152	246	89	173	225
11	201	211	230	168	231	256
12	216	229	282	178	251	281
13	218	232	358	176	262	301
14	**17**	**17**	**120**	**13**	**22**	**6**
15	80	80	130	71	89	76
16	34	41	176	25	62	74
Average	176.2500	185.9375	251.9375	**143.0000**	204.3750	227.8750

Acknowledgements

The work described in this paper was supported by the Division of Engineering, King's College London. The authors would like to thank the patients of St. Thomas' Hospital who were involved in this study for allowing their data to be collected and analyzed.

References

[1] V. N. Vapnik, *The Nature of Statistical Learning Theory.* (Springer–Verlag, Berlin, 2000).

[2] C. J. C. Burges, A tutorial on support vector machines for pattern recognition, *Data Mining and Knowledge Discovery.* **2**(2), 121–167, (1998).

[3] S. R. Gunn, Support vector machines for classification and regression, *ISIS Technical Report.* **14**, (1998).

[4] N. Cristianini and J. Shawe-Taylor, *An Introduction to Support Vector Machines.* (Cambridge University Press, Cambridge, 2000).

[5] A. J. Smola and B. Schölkopf, A tutorial on support vector regression, *Statistics and Computing.* **14**(3), 199–222, (2004).

[6] S. R. Alty, N. Angarita-Jaimes, S. C. Millasseau, and P. J. Chowienczyk, Predicting arterial stiffness from the digital volume pulse waveform, *IEEE Transactions on Biomedical Engineering.* **54**(12), 2268–2275, (2007).

[7] K. M. Anderson, P. M. Odell, P. W. F. Wilson, and W. B. Kannel, Cardiovascular disease risk profiles, *American Heart Journal.* **121**(1), 293–298, (1991).
[8] S. M. Grundy, R. Pasternak, P. Greenland, S. Smith Jr, and V. Fuster, AHA/ACC scientific statement: Assessment of cardiovascular risk by use of multiple-risk-factor assessment equations: a statement for healthcare professionals from the American Heart Association and the American College of Cardiology, *Journal of the American College of Cardiology.* **34** (4), 1348–1359, (1999).
[9] J. Blacher, R. Asmar, S. Djane, G. M. London, and M. E. Safar, Aortic pulse wave velocity as a marker of cardiovascular risk in hypertensive patients, *Hypertension.* **33**(5), 1111–1117, (1999).
[10] P. Boutouyrie, A. I. Tropeano, R. Asmar, I. Gautier, A. Benetos, P. Lacolley, and S. Laurent, Aortic stiffness is an independent predictor of primary coronary events in hypertensive patients: a longitudinal study, *Hypertension.* **39**(1), 10–15, (2002).
[11] P. J. Chowienczyk, R. P. Kelly, H. MacCallum, S. C. Millasseau, T. L. G. Andersson, R. G. Gosling, J. Ritter, and E. Anggard, Photoplethysmographic assessment of pulse wave reflection: blunted response to endothelium-dependent beta2-adrenergic vasodilation in type II diabetes mellitus, *Journal of the American College of Cardiology.* **34**(7), 2007–2014, (1999).
[12] S. C. Millasseau, F. G. Guigui, R. P. Kelly, K. Prasad, J. R. Cockcroft, J. M. Ritter, and P. J. Chowienczyk, Noninvasive assessment of the digital volume pulse: comparison with the peripheral pressure pulse, *Hypertension.* **36**(6), 952–956, (2000).
[13] S. C. Millasseau, R. P. Kelly, J. M. Ritter, and P. J. Chowienczyk, Determination of age-related increases in large artery stiffness by digital pulse contour analysis, *Clinical Science.* **103**(4), 371–378, (2002).
[14] N. Angarita-Jaimes. Support Vector Machines for Improved Cardiovascular Disease Risk Prediction. Master's thesis, Department of Electronic Engineering, Kings College London, (2005).
[15] N. Angarita-Jaimes, S. R. Alty, S. C. Millasseau, and P. J. Chowienczyk, Classification of aortic stiffness from eigendecomposition of the digital volume pulse waveform. **2**, 2416–2419, (2006).
[16] J. B. Dillon and A. B. Hertzman, The form of the volume pulse in the finger pad in health, arteriosclerosis and hypertension, *American Heart Journal.* **21**, 172–190, (1941).
[17] J. Ma, Y. Zhao, and S. Ahalt, *OSU SVM Classifier Matlab Toolbox (version 3.00).* (Ohio State University, Columbus, USA, 2002).
[18] H. K. Lam and F. H. F. Leung, Digit and command interpretation for electronic book using neural network and genetic algorithm, *IEEE Transactions on Systems, Man, and Cybernetics, Part B: Cybernetics.* **34** (6), 2273–2283, (2004).
[19] K. F. Leung, F. H. F. Leung, H. K. Lam, and S. H. Ling, On interpretation of graffiti digits and characters for eBooks: Neural-fuzzy network and genetic

algorithm approach, *IEEE Transactions on Industrial Electronics.* **51**(2), 464–471, (2004).

[20] H. K. Lam and J. Prada, Interpretation of handwritten single-stroke graffiti using support vector machines, *International Journal of Computational Intelligence and Applications.* **8**(4), 369–393, (2009).

Appendix A. Grid search shown in three dimensions for SVM-based DVP classifier with Gaussian Radial Basis function kernel

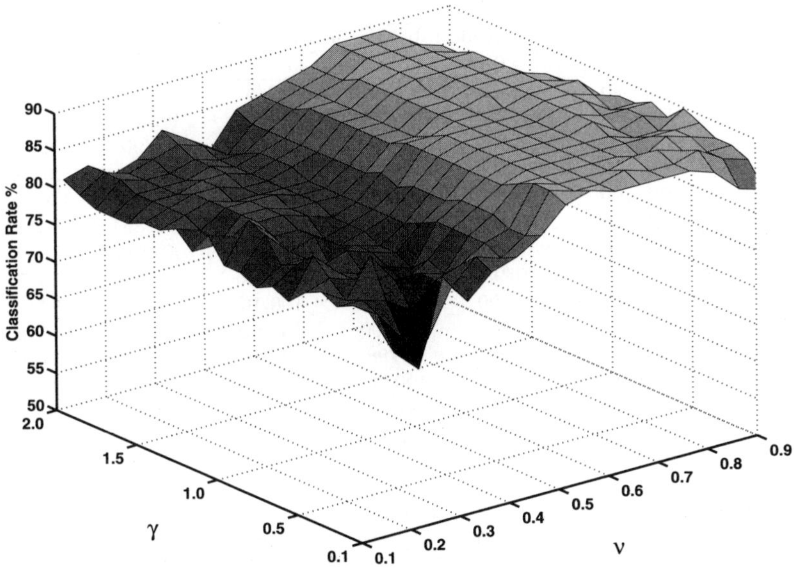

Fig. A.1. Grid search for optimal hyperparameters during training, showing values of γ and ν versus overall classification rate.

Appendix B. Tables of recognition rate for SVR-based graffiti recognizer with linear kernel function

Table B.1. Training and testing results with *linear* kernel function, *quadratic* loss function and various values of C.

Class No.	Recognition rate (%) (Training/Testing phase)					
	$C = 0.01$	$C = 0.1$	$C = 1$	$C = 10$	$C = 100$	$C = \text{Inf}$
1	100/**96**	100/**96**	100/96	100/88	98/78	98/76
2	100/100	100/100	100/100	99/94	98/70	98/64
3	100/100	100/100	100/100	98/96	93/90	92/88
4	97/100	99/100	99/100	99/100	96/100	96/100
5	**93**/100	**93**/100	**95**/100	98/100	100/100	100/100
6	100/98	100/98	100/98	98/94	94/86	93/84
7	98/100	98/100	100/100	98/100	90/100	86/96
8	100/98	100/98	100/**94**	100/86	99/76	99/76
9	100/100	100/100	100/100	100/92	94/86	94/82
10	99/100	99/100	99/100	**97/80**	**75/36**	**55/34**
11	99/**96**	99/**96**	99/98	99/100	97/98	97/98
12	100/**96**	100/**96**	100/96	100/96	100/96	100/96
13	100/98	100/100	100/100	100/100	100/100	100/100
14	100/100	100/100	100/100	100/100	97/66	82/40
15	100/100	100/100	100/100	100/100	99/96	96/96
16	100/100	100/100	100/100	100/92	100/78	100/76
Average	99.1250/ 98.8750	99.2500/ **99.0000**	**99.5000**/ 98.8750	99.1250/ 94.8750	95.6250/ 84.7500	92.8750/ 81.6250

Table B.2. Training and testing results with *linear* kernel function, ϵ-*insensitive* loss function ($\epsilon = 0.05$) and various values of C.

	Recognition rate (%) (Training/Testing phase)					
Class No.	$C = 0.01$	$C = 0.1$	$C = 1$	$C = 10$	$C = 100$	$C = \text{Inf}$
1	100/**96**	100/90	97/70	100/98	100/98	100/98
2	100/100	100/100	100/100	100/100	100/100	100/100
3	100/100	100/100	**31/22**	100/100	100/100	100/100
4	97/100	99/100	97/100	100/100	100/100	100/100
5	**92**/100	96/100	97/98	98/100	98/100	98/100
6	99/98	**86**/96	100/98	100/98	100/98	100/98
7	98/100	99/100	69/98	**91**/94	**91**/94	**91**/94
8	100/98	100/98	98/70	99/**74**	99/**74**	99/**74**
9	100/100	100/100	97/100	100/98	100/98	100/98
10	99/100	99/100	98/96	100/100	100/100	100/100
11	99/**96**	99/98	91/80	99/98	99/98	99/98
12	100/98	99/**84**	100/96	100/96	100/96	100/96
13	100/98	100/100	99/88	100/100	100/100	100/100
14	100/100	100/100	100/100	100/100	100/100	100/100
15	100/100	100/100	100/100	100/100	100/100	100/100
16	100/100	100/100	100/98	100/94	100/94	100/94
Average	99.0000/ **99.0000**	98.5625/ 97.8750	92.1250/ 88.3750	**99.1875**/ 96.8750	99.1875/ 96.8750	99.1875/ 96.8750

Appendix C. Tables of recognition rate for SVR-based graffiti recognizer with spline kernel function

Table C.1. Training and testing results with *spline* kernel function, *quadratic* loss function and various values of C.

	Recognition rate (%) (Training/Testing phase)					
Class No.	$C = 0.01$	$C = 0.1$	$C = 1$	$C = 10$	$C = 100$	$C = \text{Inf}$
1	100/**96**	100/**96**	100/96	100/94	100/92	96/96
2	100/100	100/100	100/100	**98**/96	100/100	100/100
3	100/100	100/100	100/100	99/98	100/100	100/100
4	98/100	99/100	99/100	99/100	100/100	100/90
5	**93**/100	**93**/100	**96**/100	98/100	97/100	66/46
6	100/98	100/98	100/98	100/94	97/94	**4/20**
7	98/100	98/100	99/100	99/100	99/98	67/98
8	100/98	100/98	100/**94**	100/86	99/74	100/74
9	100/100	100/100	100/100	100/96	97/92	100/84
10	98/100	99/100	99/100	98/**84**	**95/68**	99/98
11	99/**96**	99/**96**	99/98	99/100	99/98	100/96
12	100/**96**	100/**96**	100/94	100/96	100/96	99/94
13	100/98	100/100	100/100	100/100	100/100	100/100
14	100/100	100/100	100/100	100/100	100/100	100/100
15	100/100	100/100	100/100	100/100	100/100	100/100
16	100/100	100/100	100/100	100/94	100/98	100/78
Average	99.1250/ 98.8750	99.2500/ **99.0000**	**99.5000**/ 98.7500	99.3750/ 96.1250	98.9375/ 94.3750	89.4375/ 85.8750

Table C.2. Training and testing results with *spline* kernel function, ϵ-*insensitive* loss function ($\epsilon = 0.05$) and various values of C.

Class No.	Recognition rate (%) (Training/Testing phase)					
	$C = 0.01$	$C = 0.1$	$C = 1$	$C = 10$	$C = 100$	$C = \text{Inf}$
1	100/**96**	100/**94**	100/100	100/100	100/100	100/100
2	100/100	100/100	100/100	100/100	100/100	100/100
3	100/100	100/100	100/100	100/100	100/100	100/100
4	98/100	99/100	100/100	100/100	100/100	100/100
5	**93**/100	**95**/100	**97**/100	97/100	97/100	97/100
6	100/98	100/100	100/98	100/98	100/98	100/98
7	98/100	100/100	100/100	**96**/98	**96**/98	**96**/98
8	100/98	100/98	100/**88**	100/**80**	100/**80**	100/**80**
9	100/100	100/100	100/98	100/96	100/96	100/96
10	99/100	100/100	100/100	100/100	100/100	100/100
11	99/**96**	99/98	99/100	99/100	99/100	99/100
12	100/**96**	100/96	100/96	100/96	100/96	100/96
13	100/98	100/100	100/100	100/100	100/100	100/100
14	100/100	100/100	100/100	100/100	100/100	100/100
15	100/100	100/100	100/100	100/100	100/100	100/100
16	100/100	100/100	100/98	100/94	100/94	100/94
Average	99.1875/ 98.8750	99.5625/ **99.1250**	**99.7500**/ 98.6250	99.5000/ 97.6250	99.5000/ 97.6250	99.5000/ 97.6250

Appendix D. Tables of recognition rate for SVR-based graffiti recognizer with polynomial kernel function

Table D.1. Training and testing results with *polynomial* function ($c = 1$), *quadratic* loss function and various values of C.

Class No.	Recognition rate (%) (Training/Testing phase)					
	$C = 0.01$	$C = 0.1$	$C = 1$	$C = 10$	$C = 100$	$C = \text{Inf}$
1	100/**96**	100/**96**	100/96	100/90	98/78	98/76
2	100/100	100/100	100/100	98/90	98/70	98/64
3	100/100	100/100	100/100	98/96	93/90	92/88
4	98/100	99/100	99/100	99/100	96/100	96/100
5	**93**/100	**93**/100	**95**/100	98/100	100/100	100/100
6	100/98	100/98	100/98	99/94	94/86	93/84
7	98/100	98/100	99/100	98/100	90/100	86/96
8	100/98	100/98	100/**94**	100/86	99/76	99/76
9	100/100	100/100	100/100	100/94	94/86	94/82
10	98/100	99/100	99/100	**97/80**	**75/36**	**55/34**
11	99/**96**	99/**96**	99/98	99/100	97/98	97/98
12	100/**96**	100/**96**	100/**94**	100/96	100/96	100/96
13	100/98	100/100	100/100	100/100	100/100	100/100
14	100/100	100/100	100/100	100/100	97/66	82/40
15	100/100	100/100	100/100	100/100	99/96	96/96
16	100/100	100/100	100/100	100/92	100/78	100/76
Average	99.1250/ 98.8750	99.2500/ **99.0000**	**99.4375**/ 98.7500	99.1250/ 94.8750	95.6250/ 84.7500	92.8750/ 81.6250

Table D.2. Training and testing results with *polynomial* function ($c = 2$), *quadratic* loss function and various values of C.

Class No.	Recognition rate (%) (Training/Testing phase)					
	$C = 0.01$	$C = 0.1$	$C = 1$	$C = 10$	$C = 100$	$C = \text{Inf}$
1	100/98	100/96	100/96	100/94	100/86	99/68
2	100/100	100/100	99/96	98/96	100/100	100/96
3	99/100	100/100	100/100	98/96	100/100	100/100
4	98/100	99/100	100/100	99/100	99/100	99/100
5	**94**/100	**94**/100	**96**/100	100/100	98/100	92/96
6	100/98	100/100	100/98	97/94	97/92	94/90
7	99/100	99/100	99/100	98/100	98/96	97/96
8	100/98	100/98	100/94	100/86	99/76	**76/20**
9	100/100	100/100	100/100	99/94	97/92	95/86
10	98/100	99/100	98/100	**96/72**	**96/72**	93/64
11	99/96	99/96	99/98	99/100	99/98	98/96
12	100/**94**	100/**94**	100/**92**	100/96	100/96	100/96
13	100/98	100/100	100/100	100/100	100/100	100/96
14	100/100	100/100	100/100	100/100	100/100	100/88
15	100/100	100/100	100/100	100/100	100/100	100/100
16	100/100	100/100	100/100	100/92	100/98	100/84
Average	99.1875/ 98.8750	99.3750/ **99.0000**	**99.4375**/ 98.3750	99.0000/ 95.0000	98.9375/ 94.1250	96.4375/ 86.0000

Table D.3. Training and testing results with *polynomial* function ($c = 5$), *quadratic* loss function and various values of C.

Class No.	Recognition rate (%) (Training/Testing phase)					
	$C = 0.01$	$C = 0.1$	$C = 1$	$C = 10$	$C = 100$	$C = \text{Inf}$
1	100/92	100/92	100/98	100/92	100/94	100/68
2	97/98	98/**86**	98/88	99/100	100/100	100/100
3	96/100	99/100	99/100	100/100	100/100	100/100
4	98/100	99/100	**97**/100	100/100	100/100	99/80
5	**91**/100	**96**/100	97/100	99/100	99/100	73/68
6	100/100	100/100	100/96	100/94	96/94	97/92
7	96/**88**	98/92	98/98	**98**/96	99/98	90/72
8	100/98	100/96	100/90	100/82	**94/60**	**15/8**
9	100/100	100/100	99/98	98/94	97/90	93/92
10	98/98	98/100	98/90	98/**76**	99/78	86/86
11	99/90	99/90	98/94	99/100	99/98	100/94
12	99/90	99/90	100/**82**	100/94	100/96	100/96
13	100/98	100/98	100/100	100/100	100/100	100/98
14	100/100	100/100	100/100	100/100	100/100	100/100
15	99/100	99/100	99/100	100/100	100/100	100/100
16	100/100	100/100	100/94	100/98	100/96	100/84
Average	98.3125/ **97.0000**	99.0625/ 96.5000	98.9375/ 95.5000	**99.4375**/ 95.3750	98.9375/ 94.0000	90.8125/ 83.6250

Table D.4. Training and testing results with *polynomial* function ($c = 10$), *quadratic* loss function and various values of C.

Class No.	Recognition rate (%) (Training/Testing phase)					
	$C = 0.01$	$C = 0.1$	$C = 1$	$C = 10$	$C = 100$	$C = \text{Inf}$
1	99/**78**	99/**68**	100/**76**	100/96	100/96	100/80
2	98/82	98/70	98/78	100/94	100/100	100/100
3	**92**/98	98/100	100/100	100/100	100/100	100/100
4	96/100	98/100	100/100	100/100	100/100	100/88
5	94/100	97/100	**92**/96	98/100	**96**/100	98/84
6	100/98	100/96	100/96	100/94	**96**/92	98/94
7	99/96	96/84	98/96	100/98	98/98	**76**/64
8	100/98	100/92	100/90	98/**52**	98/**78**	**76/50**
9	100/98	99/98	100/98	**96**/84	99/96	94/96
10	98/98	98/100	98/86	**96**/80	100/88	84/84
11	99/98	99/98	99/98	97/88	98/98	100/94
12	100/100	98/82	100/**76**	100/94	100/94	100/96
13	100/98	**95**/96	100/100	100/100	99/100	100/100
14	100/100	100/100	100/100	100/100	100/100	100/100
15	99/100	99/100	99/100	100/100	100/100	100/100
16	100/82	100/96	100/100	100/96	100/98	100/80
Average	98.3750/ 95.2500	98.3750/ 92.5000	99.0000/ 93.1250	**99.0625**/ 92.2500	99.0000/ **96.1250**	95.3750/ 88.1250

Table D.5. Training and testing results with *polynomial* function ($c = 1$), *ϵ-insensitive* loss function ($\epsilon = 0.05$) and various values of C.

Class No.	Recognition rate (%) (Training/Testing phase)					
	$C = 0.01$	$C = 0.1$	$C = 1$	$C = 10$	$C = 100$	$C = \text{Inf}$
1	100/**96**	100/**94**	100/96	100/98	100/98	100/98
2	100/100	100/100	100/100	100/100	100/100	100/100
3	100/100	100/100	100/100	100/100	100/100	100/100
4	98/100	99/100	100/100	100/100	100/100	100/100
5	**93**/100	**96**/100	**98**/100	97/100	97/100	97/100
6	100/98	100/100	100/98	100/98	100/98	100/98
7	98/100	100/100	100/100	**94**/98	**94**/98	**94**/98
8	100/98	100/98	100/**88**	99/**80**	99/**80**	99/**80**
9	100/100	100/100	100/98	100/96	100/96	100/96
10	99/100	100/100	100/100	100/100	100/100	100/100
11	99/**96**	99/96	99/98	99/100	99/100	99/100
12	100/**96**	100/96	100/96	100/96	100/96	100/96
13	100/98	100/100	100/100	100/100	100/100	100/100
14	100/100	100/100	100/100	100/100	100/100	100/100
15	100/100	100/100	100/100	100/100	100/100	100/100
16	100/100	100/100	100/98	100/94	100/94	100/94
Average	99.1875/ 98.8750	99.6250/ **99.0000**	**99.8125**/ 98.2500	99.3125/ 97.5000	99.3125/ 97.5000	99.3125/ 97.5000

Table D.6. Training and testing results with *polynomial* function ($c = 2$), ϵ-*insensitive* loss function ($\epsilon = 0.05$) and various values of C.

Class No.	Recognition rate (%) (Training/Testing phase)					
	$C = 0.01$	$C = 0.1$	$C = 1$	$C = 10$	$C = 100$	$C = \text{Inf}$
1	100/**96**	100/96	100/100	100/100	100/100	100/100
2	100/100	100/100	100/100	100/100	100/100	100/100
3	100/100	100/100	100/100	100/100	100/100	100/100
4	99/100	100/100	100/100	100/100	100/100	100/100
5	**94**/100	**98**/100	98/100	97/100	97/100	97/100
6	100/100	100/100	100/98	100/98	100/98	100/98
7	99/100	100/100	**96**/100	**93**/98	**93**/98	**93**/98
8	100/98	100/**94**	100/**82**	99/**74**	99/**74**	99/**74**
9	100/100	100/100	100/94	100/94	100/94	100/94
10	99/100	100/100	100/100	100/100	100/100	100/100
11	99/**96**	99/98	99/100	99/100	99/100	99/100
12	100/98	100/96	100/98	100/98	100/98	100/98
13	100/100	100/100	100/100	100/100	100/100	100/100
14	100/100	100/100	100/100	100/100	100/100	100/100
15	100/100	100/100	100/100	100/100	100/100	100/100
16	100/100	100/100	100/98	100/98	100/98	100/98
Average	99.3750/ **99.2500**	**99.8125**/ 99.0000	99.5625/ 98.1250	99.2500/ 97.5000	99.2500/ 97.5000	99.2500/ 97.5000

Table D.7. Training and testing results with *polynomial* function ($c = 5$), ϵ-*insensitive* loss function ($\epsilon = 0.05$) and various values of C.

Class No.	Recognition rate (%) (Training/Testing phase)					
	$C = 0.01$	$C = 0.1$	$C = 1$	$C = 10$	$C = 100$	$C = \text{Inf}$
1	100/92	100/96	100/96	100/96	100/96	100/96
2	98/**88**	100/90	100/88	100/88	100/88	100/88
3	99/100	100/100	100/100	100/100	100/100	100/100
4	98/100	100/100	100/100	100/100	100/100	100/100
5	**96**/100	97/100	99/100	99/100	99/100	99/100
6	100/100	100/98	100/98	100/98	100/98	100/98
7	98/92	98/94	98/98	98/98	98/98	98/98
8	100/96	100/90	100/**76**	100/**76**	100/**76**	100/**76**
9	100/100	100/96	98/88	98/88	98/88	98/88
10	98/100	100/98	100/94	100/94	100/94	100/94
11	99/90	**96/78**	**97**/90	**97**/90	**97**/90	**97**/90
12	99/90	100/90	100/96	100/96	100/96	100/96
13	100/98	100/100	100/100	100/100	100/100	100/100
14	100/100	100/100	100/100	100/100	100/100	100/100
15	99/100	99/100	100/100	100/100	100/100	100/100
16	100/100	100/96	100/98	100/98	100/98	100/98
Average	99.0000/ **96.6250**	99.3750/ 95.3750	**99.5000**/ 95.1250	99.5000/ 95.1250	99.5000/ 95.1250	99.5000/ 95.1250

Table D.8. Training and testing results with *polynomial* function ($c = 10$), ϵ-*insensitive* loss function ($\epsilon = 0.05$) and various values of C.

Class No.	Recognition rate (%) (Training/Testing phase)					
	$C = 0.01$	$C = 0.1$	$C = 1$	$C = 10$	$C = 100$	$C = \text{Inf}$
1	100/74	97/**66**	98/76	98/76	98/76	98/76
2	99/**66**	99/72	94/**60**	93/**60**	94/**60**	93/**60**
3	95/98	98/98	98/98	98/98	98/98	98/98
4	98/100	98/100	99/100	99/100	99/100	99/100
5	98/100	100/100	99/98	99/98	99/98	99/98
6	100/96	100/96	100/96	100/96	100/96	100/96
7	97/90	97/96	97/98	97/98	97/98	97/98
8	94/94	100/90	100/82	100/82	100/82	100/82
9	99/96	**96**/88	**92**/80	**92**/80	**92**/80	**92**/80
10	98/98	99/84	99/84	99/84	99/84	99/84
11	99/98	99/100	99/100	99/100	99/100	99/100
12	99/90	100/98	100/100	100/100	100/100	100/100
13	**93**/90	**96**/98	96/96	96/96	96/96	96/96
14	99/86	100/94	100/96	100/96	100/96	100/96
15	99/100	100/100	100/98	100/98	100/98	100/98
16	98/72	100/92	99/86	99/86	99/86	99/86
Average	97.8125/ 90.5000	**98.6875**/ **92.0000**	98.1250/ 90.5000	98.0625/ 90.5000	98.1250/ 90.5000	98.0625/ 90.5000

Appendix E. Tables of recognition rate for SVR-based graffiti recognizer with radial basis kernel function

Table E.1. Training and testing results with *radial basis* kernel function ($\sigma = 1$), *quadratic* loss function and various values of C.

	Recognition rate (%) (Training/Testing phase)					
Class No.	$C = 0.01$	$C = 0.1$	$C = 1$	$C = 10$	$C = 100$	$C = \text{Inf}$
1	100/**96**	100/**96**	100/96	100/90	99/78	100/90
2	100/100	100/100	100/100	98/90	98/68	100/100
3	100/100	100/100	100/100	98/96	95/90	100/100
4	97/100	99/100	99/100	99/100	100/100	100/100
5	**93**/100	**93**/100	**95**/100	99/100	100/100	**99**/100
6	100/98	100/98	100/98	99/94	96/96	100/98
7	98/100	98/100	99/100	98/100	90/90	100/98
8	100/98	100/98	100/**94**	100/86	99/76	100/**80**
9	100/100	100/100	100/100	100/92	95/90	100/96
10	99/100	99/100	99/100	**97/78**	**82/60**	100/88
11	99/**96**	99/**96**	99/98	99/100	97/92	100/100
12	100/**96**	100/**96**	100/96	100/96	100/92	100/92
13	100/98	100/98	100/100	100/100	100/98	100/100
14	100/100	100/100	100/100	100/100	100/100	100/100
15	100/100	100/100	100/100	100/100	99/100	100/100
16	100/100	100/100	100/100	100/94	100/96	100/100
Average	99.1250/ **98.8750**	99.2500/ 98.8750	99.4375/ 98.8750	99.1875/ 94.7500	96.8750/ 89.1250	**99.9375**/ 96.3750

Table E.2. Training and testing results with *radial basis* kernel function ($\sigma = 2$), *quadratic* loss function and various values of C.

Class No.	Recognition rate (%) (Training/Testing phase)					
	$C = 0.01$	$C = 0.1$	$C = 1$	$C = 10$	$C = 100$	$C = \text{Inf}$
1	100/**96**	100/**96**	100/**96**	100/92	100/84	100/100
2	100/100	100/100	100/100	100/100	98/80	100/94
3	100/100	100/100	100/100	100/100	95/94	97/92
4	97/100	98/100	99/100	100/100	98/100	100/100
5	**93**/100	**93**/100	**93**/100	**97**/100	100/100	97/100
6	100/98	100/98	100/98	100/98	97/92	99/96
7	98/100	98/100	99/100	100/100	95/100	81/**72**
8	100/98	100/98	100/98	100/**90**	99/76	98/72
9	100/100	100/100	100/100	100/100	98/88	99/88
10	99/100	99/100	99/100	99/100	**92/64**	**79**/82
11	99/**96**	99/**96**	99/**96**	99/98	99/100	100/98
12	100/**96**	100/**96**	100/**96**	100/96	100/96	100/98
13	100/98	100/98	100/100	100/100	100/100	99/100
14	100/100	100/100	100/100	100/100	100/96	100/98
15	100/100	100/100	100/100	100/100	99/100	100/100
16	100/100	100/100	100/100	100/98	100/88	100/88
Average	99.1250/ 98.8750	99.1875/ 98.8750	99.3125/ **99.0000**	**99.6875**/ 98.2500	98.1250/ 91.1250	96.8125/ 92.3750

Table E.3. Training and testing results with *radial basis* kernel function ($\sigma = 5$), *quadratic* loss function and various values of C.

Class No.	Recognition rate (%) (Training/Testing phase)					
	$C = 0.01$	$C = 0.1$	$C = 1$	$C = 10$	$C = 100$	$C = \text{Inf}$
1	100/**96**	100/**96**	100/**96**	100/**94**	100/92	100/90
2	100/100	100/100	100/100	100/100	100/98	100/100
3	100/100	100/100	100/100	100/100	100/100	100/100
4	97/100	97/100	98/100	99/100	99/100	100/100
5	**93**/100	**93**/100	**93**/100	**94**/100	**98**/100	**98**/100
6	100/98	100/98	100/98	100/98	100/94	100/96
7	98/100	98/100	98/100	99/100	100/100	99/94
8	100/98	100/98	100/98	100/98	100/**90**	100/**74**
9	100/100	100/100	100/100	100/100	100/96	100/96
10	99/100	99/100	99/100	99/100	**98**/100	99/98
11	99/**96**	99/**96**	99/**96**	99/96	99/98	99/96
12	100/**96**	100/**96**	100/**96**	100/98	100/96	100/98
13	100/98	100/98	100/98	100/100	100/100	100/100
14	100/100	100/100	100/100	100/100	100/100	100/100
15	100/100	100/100	100/100	100/100	100/100	100/100
16	100/100	100/100	100/100	100/100	100/94	100/100
Average	99.1250/ 98.8750	99.1250/ 98.8750	99.1875/ 98.8750	99.3750/ **99.0000**	99.6250/ 97.3750	**99.6875**/ 96.3750

Table E.4. Training and testing results with *radial basis* kernel function ($\sigma = 10$), *quadratic* loss function and various values of C.

Class No.	Recognition rate (%) (Training/Testing phase)					
	$C = 0.01$	$C = 0.1$	$C = 1$	$C = 10$	$C = 100$	$C = \text{Inf}$
1	100/**96**	100/**96**	100/**96**	100/**96**	100/96	100/96
2	100/100	100/100	100/100	100/100	100/100	100/100
3	100/100	100/100	100/100	100/100	100/100	100/100
4	97/100	97/100	97/100	99/100	99/100	99/100
5	**93**/100	**93**/100	**93**/100	**93**/100	**95**/100	**97**/100
6	100/98	100/98	100/98	100/98	100/98	100/96
7	98/100	98/100	98/100	98/100	100/100	98/98
8	100/98	100/98	100/98	100/98	100/**94**	100/**90**
9	100/100	100/100	100/100	100/100	100/100	100/100
10	99/100	99/100	99/100	99/100	99/100	98/98
11	99/**96**	99/**96**	99/**96**	99/**96**	99/98	99/98
12	100/**96**	100/**96**	100/**96**	100/**96**	100/96	100/94
13	100/98	100/98	100/98	100/100	100/100	100/100
14	100/100	100/100	100/100	100/100	100/100	100/100
15	100/100	100/100	100/100	100/100	100/100	100/100
16	100/100	100/100	100/100	100/100	100/100	100/98
Average	99.1250/ 98.8750	99.1250/ 98.8750	99.1250/ 98.8750	99.2500/ **99.0000**	**99.5000**/ 98.8750	99.4375/ 98.0000

Table E.5. Training and testing results with *radial basis* kernel function ($\sigma = 1$), *ϵ-insensitive* loss function ($\epsilon = 0.05$) and various values of C.

Class No.	Recognition rate (%) (Training/Testing phase)					
	$C = 0.01$	$C = 0.1$	$C = 1$	$C = 10$	$C = 100$	$C = \text{Inf}$
1	100/**96**	100/**96**	100/94	100/98	100/98	100/98
2	100/100	100/100	100/100	100/100	100/100	100/100
3	100/100	99/100	100/100	100/100	100/100	100/100
4	98/100	99/100	100/100	100/100	100/100	100/100
5	**93**/100	**96**/100	**98**/100	97/100	97/100	97/100
6	100/98	100/98	100/98	100/98	100/98	100/98
7	98/100	100/100	100/100	**94**/98	**94**/98	**94**/98
8	100/98	100/98	100/**86**	99/**74**	99/**74**	99/**74**
9	100/100	100/100	100/98	100/96	100/96	100/96
10	99/100	100/100	100/100	100/100	100/100	100/100
11	99/**96**	99/**96**	99/98	99/100	99/100	99/100
12	100/98	100/98	100/98	100/96	100/96	100/96
13	100/98	100/100	100/100	100/100	100/100	100/100
14	100/100	100/100	100/100	100/100	100/100	100/100
15	100/100	100/100	100/100	100/100	100/100	100/100
16	100/100	100/100	100/98	100/94	100/94	100/94
Average	99.1875/ 99.0000	99.5625/ **99.1250**	**99.8125**/ 98.1250	99.3125/ 97.1250	99.3125/ 97.1250	99.3125/ 97.1250

Table E.6. Training and testing results with *radial basis* kernel function ($\sigma = 2$), *ϵ-insensitive* loss function ($\epsilon = 0.05$) and various values of C.

	Recognition rate (%) (Training/Testing phase)					
Class No.	$C = 0.01$	$C = 0.1$	$C = 1$	$C = 10$	$C = 100$	$C = \text{Inf}$
1	100/**96**	100/**96**	100/96	100/98	100/98	100/98
2	100/100	100/100	100/100	100/100	100/100	100/100
3	100/100	100/100	99/100	100/100	100/100	100/100
4	98/100	98/100	100/100	100/100	100/100	100/100
5	**92**/100	**93**/100	**98**/100	97/100	97/100	97/100
6	100/98	100/98	100/98	100/98	100/98	100/98
7	98/100	98/100	100/100	**94**/98	**94**/98	**94**/98
8	100/98	100/98	100/**94**	99/**74**	99/**74**	99/**74**
9	100/100	100/100	100/100	100/96	100/96	100/96
10	99/100	99/100	100/100	100/100	100/100	100/100
11	99/**96**	99/**96**	99/98	99/100	99/100	99/100
12	100/98	100/98	100/96	100/96	100/96	100/96
13	100/98	100/98	100/100	100/100	100/100	100/100
14	100/100	100/100	100/100	100/100	100/100	100/100
15	100/100	100/100	100/100	100/100	100/100	100/100
16	100/100	100/100	100/98	100/94	100/94	100/94
Average	99.1250/ **99.0000**	99.1875/ 99.0000	**99.7500**/ 98.7500	99.3125/ 97.1250	99.3125/ 97.1250	99.3125/ 97.1250

Table E.7. Training and testing results with *radial basis* kernel function ($\sigma = 5$), *ϵ-insensitive* loss function ($\epsilon = 0.05$) and various values of C.

	Recognition rate (%) (Training/Testing phase)					
Class No.	$C = 0.01$	$C = 0.1$	$C = 1$	$C = 10$	$C = 100$	$C = \text{Inf}$
1	100/**96**	100/**96**	100/**96**	100/96	100/98	100/98
2	100/100	100/100	100/100	100/100	100/100	100/100
3	100/100	100/100	100/100	100/100	100/100	100/100
4	98/100	98/100	99/100	100/100	100/100	100/100
5	**92**/100	**92**/100	**93**/100	**98**/100	97/100	97/100
6	100/98	99/98	100/98	100/98	100/98	100/98
7	98/100	98/100	98/100	100/100	**94**/98	**94**/98
8	100/98	100/98	100/98	100/**92**	99/**74**	99/**74**
9	100/100	100/100	100/100	100/100	100/96	100/96
10	99/100	99/100	99/100	100/100	100/100	100/100
11	99/**96**	99/**96**	99/**96**	99/98	99/100	99/100
12	100/98	100/98	100/98	100/96	100/96	100/96
13	100/98	100/98	100/100	100/100	100/100	100/100
14	100/100	100/100	100/100	100/100	100/100	100/100
15	100/100	100/100	100/100	100/100	100/100	100/100
16	100/100	100/100	100/100	100/98	100/94	100/94
Average	99.1250/ 99.0000	99.0625/ 99.0000	99.2500/ **99.1250**	**99.8125**/ 98.6250	99.3125/ 97.1250	99.3125/ 97.1250

Table E.8. Training and testing results with *radial basis* kernel function ($\sigma = 10$), ϵ-*insensitive* loss function ($\epsilon = 0.05$) and various values of C.

	Recognition rate (%) (Training/Testing phase)					
Class No.	$C = 0.01$	$C = 0.1$	$C = 1$	$C = 10$	$C = 100$	$C =$ Inf
1	100/**96**	100/**96**	100/**96**	100/**94**	100/94	100/98
2	100/100	100/100	100/100	100/100	100/100	100/100
3	100/100	100/100	100/100	99/100	100/100	100/100
4	98/100	98/100	98/100	99/100	100/100	100/100
5	**92**/100	**92**/100	**92**/100	**95**/100	**98**/100	97/100
6	100/98	99/98	99/98	100/98	100/98	100/98
7	98/100	98/100	98/100	100/100	99/100	**94**/98
8	100/98	100/98	100/98	100/98	100/**86**	99/**74**
9	100/100	100/100	100/100	100/100	100/98	100/96
10	99/100	99/100	99/100	100/100	100/100	100/100
11	99/**96**	99/**96**	99/**96**	99/96	99/98	99/100
12	100/98	100/98	100/98	100/98	100/96	100/96
13	100/98	100/98	100/98	100/100	100/100	100/100
14	100/100	100/100	100/100	100/100	100/100	100/100
15	100/100	100/100	100/100	100/100	100/100	100/100
16	100/100	100/100	100/100	100/100	100/98	100/94
Average	99.1250/ **99.0000**	99.0625/ 99.0000	99.0625/ 99.0000	99.5000/ 99.0000	**99.7500**/ 98.0000	99.3125/ 97.1250

Chapter 10

Nonlinear Modeling Using Support Vector Machine for Heart Rate Response to Exercise

[*]Weidong Chen, [†‡]Steven W. Su, [†]Yi Zhang, [§]Ying Guo, [†]Nghir Nguyen, [#‡]Branko G. Celler and [†]Hung T. Nguyen

Faculty of Engineering and Information Technology,
University of Technology,
Sydney, Australia
Steven.Su@uts.edu.au

In order to accurately regulate cardiovascular response to exercise for an individual exerciser, this study proposed a control oriented modeling approach to depict nonlinear behavior of heart rate response at both the onset and offset of treadmill exercise. With the aim of capturing nonlinear dynamic behaviors, a well designed exercise protocol has been applied for a healthy male subject. Non-invasively measured variables, such as ECG,, body movements and oxygen saturation (S_pO_2), have been reliably monitored and recorded. Based on several sets of experimental data, both steady state gain and time constant of heart rate response are identified. The nonlinear models relating to steady state gain and time constant (vs. walking speed) were built up based on support vector machine regression (SVR). The nonlinear behaviors at both onset and offset of exercise have been well described by using the established SVR models. The model provides the fundamentals for the optimization of exercise efforts by using model-based optimal control approaches, which is the following step of this study.

[*]Department of Automation, Shanghai Jiao Tong University, Shanghai, China.
[†]Centre for Health Technologies, Faculty of Engineering and Information Technology, University of Technology, Sydney, Australia.
[‡]Human Performance Group, Biomedical Systems Lab, School of Electrical Engineering and Telecommunications, University of New South Wales, UNSW Sydney N.S.W. 2052 Australia.
[#]College of Health and Science, University of Western Sydney, UWS Penrith NSW 2751 Australia.
[§]Autonomous Systems Lab, CSIRO ICT Center, Sydney, Australia.

Contents

10.1. Introduction

Heart rate, as we know, has been extensively applied to evaluate cardio-respiratory response [1–5] to exercise as it can be easily measured by cheap wireless portable non-invasive sensors. In this sense, therefore, developing nonlinear models with respect to the analysis of dynamic characteristics of heart rate response is the starting point of this project. Based on the model, a nonlinear switching model predictive control approach will be developed to optimize exercise effects while keeping the level of exercise intensity within the safe range [6].

There are plenty of papers [7, 8] about the analysis of steady state characteristics of heart rate response. Nonlinear behavior has been detected and nonlinear models have been established for response analysis when response entering steady state. During medical diagnosis and analysis of cardio-respiratory kinetics, however, transient response of heart rate is more valuable as it contains indicators of current disease or warnings about impending cardiac diseases [9]. Although both linear and nonlinear modeling approaches [10, 11] have been applied to explore dynamic characteristics of heart response to exercise, few papers focus on the variation of dynamic characteristics under different exercise intensities for both onset and offset of exercise. For moderate exercise, literatures often assume heart rate dynamics can be described by linear time invariant models. In this study, it was observed that the time constant of heart response to exercise not only depends on exercise intensity but also varies at the onset and offset of exercise. Papers [12–14] prove that exercise effects can be optimized by regulating heart rate following a pre-defined exercise protocol. It is well known that higher control performance can be obtained if the model contains less uncertainty. Therefore, it is worthwhile to establish a more accurate dynamical model to enhance the controller design of heart rate regulation. In this study, we designed a treadmill walking exercise protocol to analyze step response of heart rate. During experiments, ECG, body movement and oxygen saturation were recorded by using portable non-invasive sensors: Alive ECG monitor, Micro Inertial Measurement Unit (IMU) and Alive Pulse Oximeter. It was confirmed that time constants are not invariant especially when walking speed is faster than three miles/hour. Time constants for offset of exercises are normally bigger than those of onset of exercises. Steady state gain variation under different exercise intensity has also been visibly observed. Furthermore, the experiment results indicate that it is difficult to describe the variation of the transient parameters (such as time constant) by using a simple linear model. We applied the novel machine learning method, support vector machine (SVM) ,to depict the nonlinear relationship.

Support vector machine-based regression [15] (Support Vector Regression (SVR)) has been successfully applied to nonlinear function estimation. Vapnik *et al.* [2, 16, 17] established the foundation of SVM. The formulation of SVM [18, 19] embodies the structure of the risk minimization principle, which has been shown to be superior to other traditional empirical risk minimization principles [20]. Support vector machine-based regression applies the kernel methods implicitly to transform data into a feature space (this is known as a kernel trick [21]), and uses linear regression to get a nonlinear function approximation in the feature space. By using RBF kernel , this study efficiently established the nonlinear relationship between time constant and exercise intensity for both onset and offset of exercises.

This chapter is organized as follows. Section 10.2 provides preliminary knowledge of SVM-based regression. Section 10.3 describes the experimental equipments and exercise protocol. Data analysis and modeling results are given in Section 10.4. Lastly, Section 10.5 gives conclusions.

10.2. SVM Regression

Let $\{u_i, y_i\}_{i=1}^{N}$ be a set of inputs and outputs data points ($u_i \in U \subseteq R^d, y_i \in Y \subseteq R$, N is the number of points). The goal of the support vector regression is to find a function $f(u)$ which has the following form

$$f(u) = w \cdot \phi(u) + b, \tag{10.1}$$

where $\phi(u)$ is the high-dimensional feature spaces which are nonlinearly transformed from u. The weight vector w and bias b are defined as the hyperplane by the equation $\langle w \cdot \phi(u) \rangle + b = 0$. The hyperplane is estimated

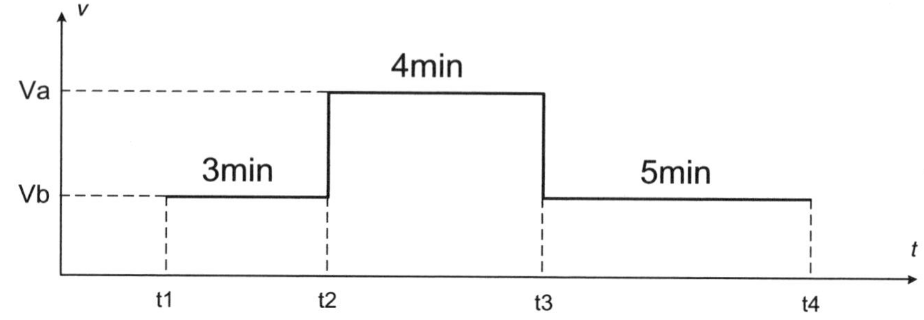

Fig. 10.1. Experiment protocol.

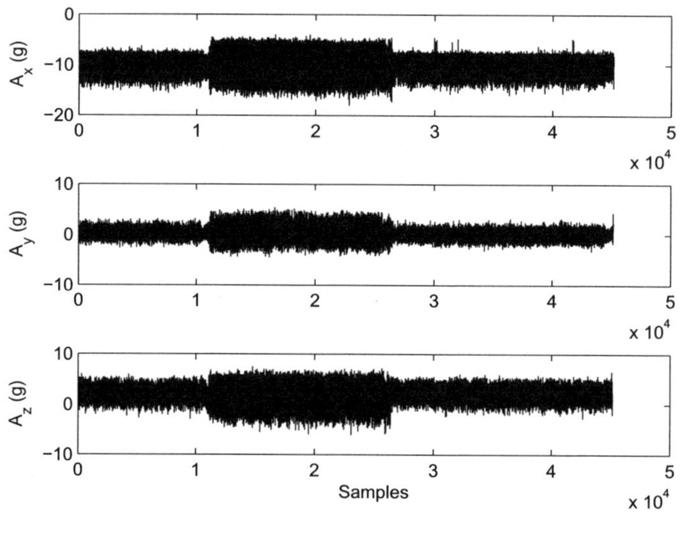

Fig. 10.2. Accelerations of three axes provided by the Micro IMU.

by minimizing the regularized risk function:

$$\frac{1}{2}\|w\|^2 + C\frac{1}{N}\sum_{i=1}^{N} L_\varepsilon(y_i, f(u_i)). \tag{10.2}$$

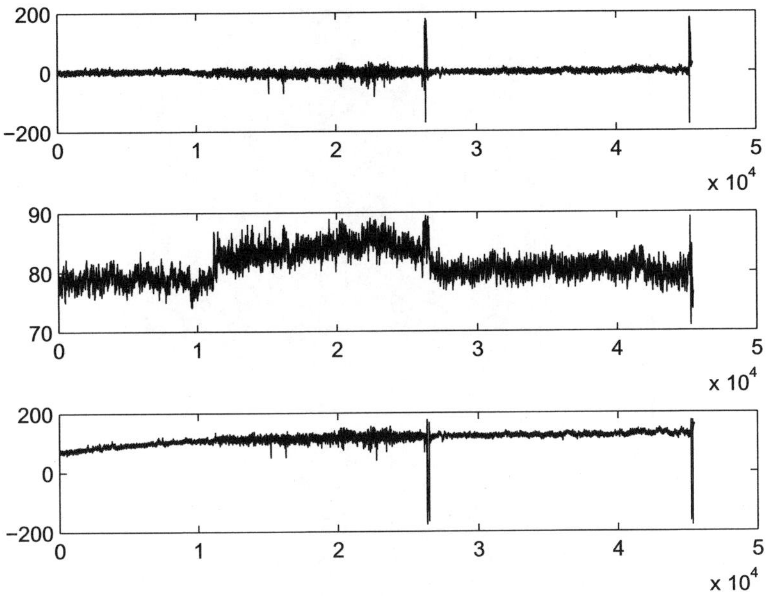

Fig. 10.3. Roll, pitch and yaw angles provided by the Micro IMU.

The first term is called the regularized term. The second term is the empirical error measured by ε-insensitivity loss function which is defined as:

$$L_\varepsilon(y_i, f(u_i)) = \begin{cases} \mid y_i - f(u_i) \mid -\varepsilon, \mid y_i - f(u_i) \mid > \varepsilon \\ 0, \qquad\qquad \mid y_i - f(u_i) \mid \leq \varepsilon. \end{cases} \tag{10.3}$$

This defines an ε tube. The radius ε of the tube and the regularization constant C are both determined by user.

The selection of parameter C depends on application knowledge of the domain. Theoretically, a small value of C will under-fit the training data because the weight placed on the training data is too small, thus resulting in large values of MSE (mean square error) on the test sets. However, when C is too large, SVR will over-fit the training set so that $\frac{1}{2}\|w\|^2$ will lose its meaning and the objective goes back to minimize the empirical risk only. Parameter ε controls the width of the ε-insensitive zone. Generally, the larger the ε the fewer number of support vectors and thus the sparser the representation of the solution. However, if the ε is too large, it can deteriorate the accuracy on the training data.

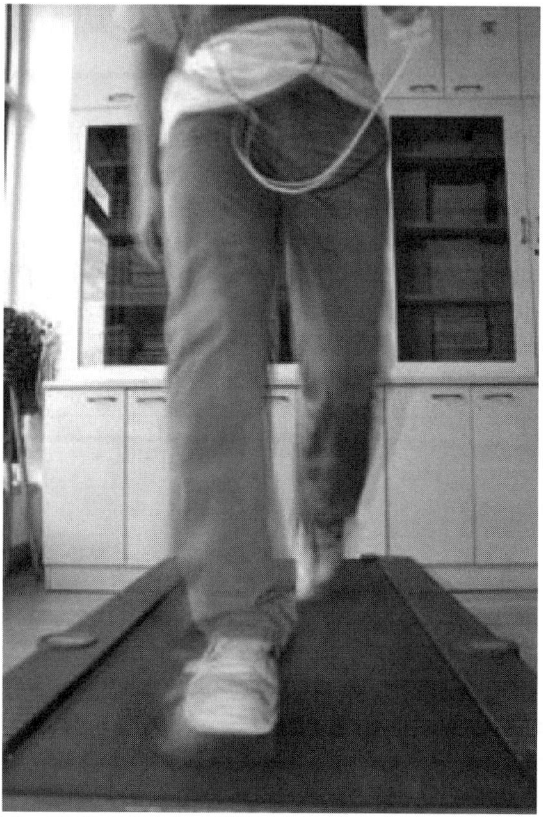

Fig. 10.4. Experimental scenario.

By solving the above constrained optimization problem, we have

$$f(u) = \sum_{i=1}^{N} \beta_i \phi(u_i) \cdot \phi(u_i) + b. \tag{10.4}$$

As mentioned above, by the use of kernels, all necessary computations can be performed directly in the input space, without having to compute the map $\phi(u)$ explicitly. After introducing kernel function $k(u_i, u_j)$, the above equation can be rewritten as follows:

$$f(u) = \sum_{i=1}^{N} \beta_i k(u_i, u) + b, \tag{10.5}$$

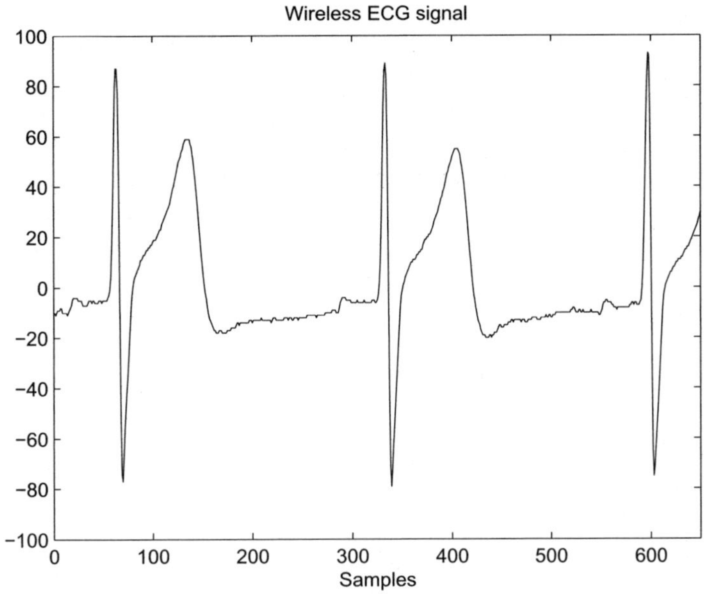

Fig. 10.5. Original ECG signal.

where the coefficients β_i correspond to each (u_i, y_i). The support vectors are the input vectors u_j whose corresponding coefficients $\beta_j \neq 0$. For linear support regression, the kernel function is thus the inner product in the input space:

$$f(u) = \sum_{i=1}^{N} \beta_i \langle u_i, u \rangle + b. \tag{10.6}$$

For nonlinear SVR, there are a number of kernel functions which have been found to provide good generalization capabilities, such as polynomials, radial basis function (RBF), sigmod. Here we present the polynomials and RBF kernel functions as follows:

Polynomial kernel: $k(u, u') = ((u \cdot u') + h)^p$.

RBF Kernel: $k(u, u') = exp(-\frac{\|u - u'\|^2}{2\sigma^2})$.

Details about SVR, such as the selection of radius ε of the tube, kernel function and the regularization constant C, can be found in [18] [21].

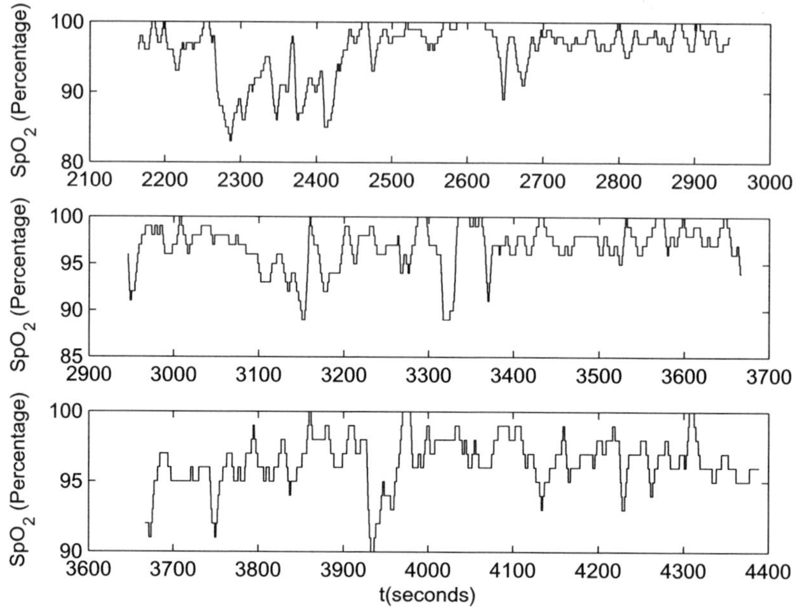

Fig. 10.6. The recording of SpO_2.

Table 10.1. The values of walking speed V_a and V_b.

	Set 1	Set 2	Set 3	Set 4	Set 5	Set 6
V_b (m/h)	0.5	1.5	2	2.5	3	3.5
V_a (m/h)	1.5	2.5	3	3.5	4	4.5

10.3. Experiment

A 41-year-old healthy male joined the study. He was 178 cm tall and 79 kg heavy. Experiments were performed in the afternoon, and the subject was allowed to have a light meal one hour before the measurements. After walking for about 10 minutes on the treadmill to get acquainted with this kind of exercise, the subject walked at six sets of exercise protocol (see Fig. 10.1) to test step response. The values of walking speed V_a and V_b were designed to vary exercise intensity and are listed in Table 10.1. To properly identify time constants for onset and offset of exercise, the recorded data should be precisely synchronized. Therefore, time instants t_1, t_2, t_3, and t_4 should be identified and marked accurately. In this study,

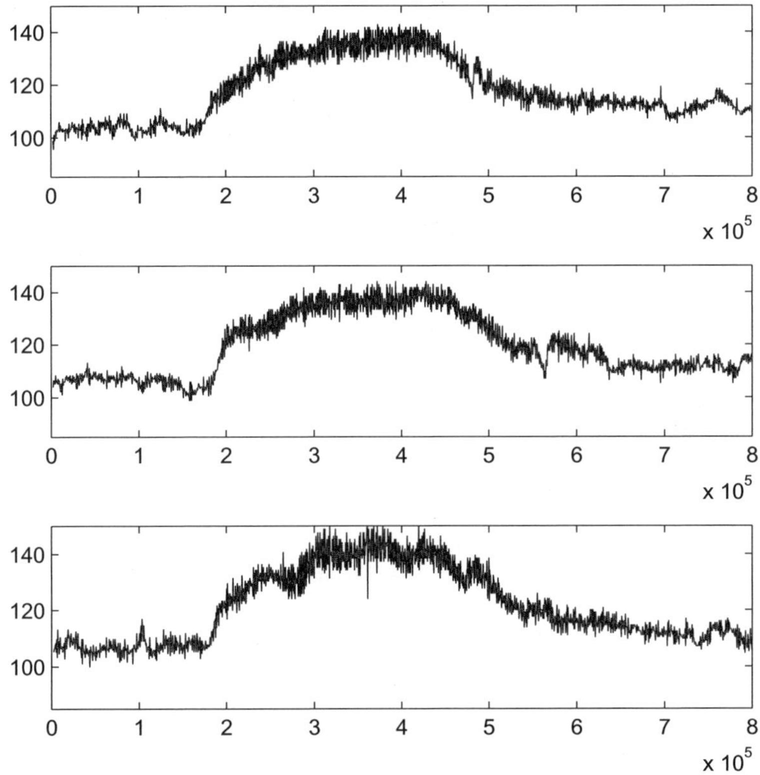

Fig. 10.7. A measured heart rate step response signal.

we applied a Micro Inertial Measurement Unit (Xsens MTi-G IMU) to fulfil this requirement. We compared both attitude information (roll, pitch and yaw angles) and acceleration information provided by the Micro IMU. It was observed that acceleration information alone is sufficient to identify these time instants (see Fig. 10.2 and Fig. 10.3).

During experiments, continuous measurements of ECG, body movement and S_pO_2 (oxygen saturation) were made by using portable non-invasive sensors. Specifically, ECG was recorded by using Alive ECG Monitor. Body movement was measured by using the Xsens MTi-G IMU. S_pO_2 was monitored by using Alive Pulse Oximeter to guarantee the safety of the subject. The experimental scenario is shown in Fig. 10.4.

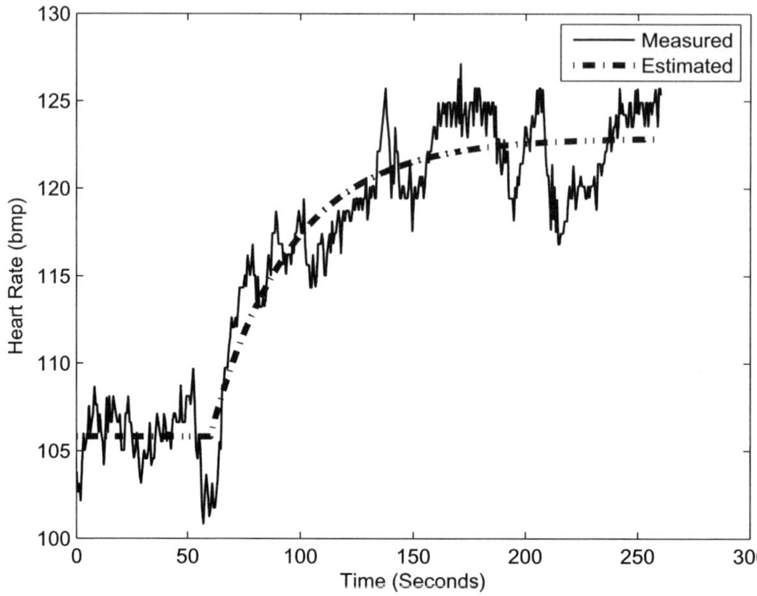

Fig. 10.8. A typical curve fitting result.

10.4. Data Analysis and Discussions

Original signals of IMU, ECG and S_pO_2 are shown in Figs 10.3, 10.5 and 10.6 respectively. It is well known that even in the absence of external interference the heart rate can vary substantially over time under the influence of various internal or external factors. [12] As mentioned before, in order to reduce the variance, designed experimental protocol has been repeated three times. Experimental data of these repeated experiments has been synchronized and averaged.

A typical measured heart rate response is shown in Fig. 10.7. Paper [12] found that heart rate response to exercise can be approximated as first order process from a control application point of view. Therefore we established first order model for six averaged step response data by using Matlab System Identification Toolbox [22].

Table 10.2 shows the identified steady state gain (K) and time constant (T) by using averaged data of three sets of experimental data. A typical curve fitting result is shown in Fig. 10.8. From Table 10.2, we can clearly

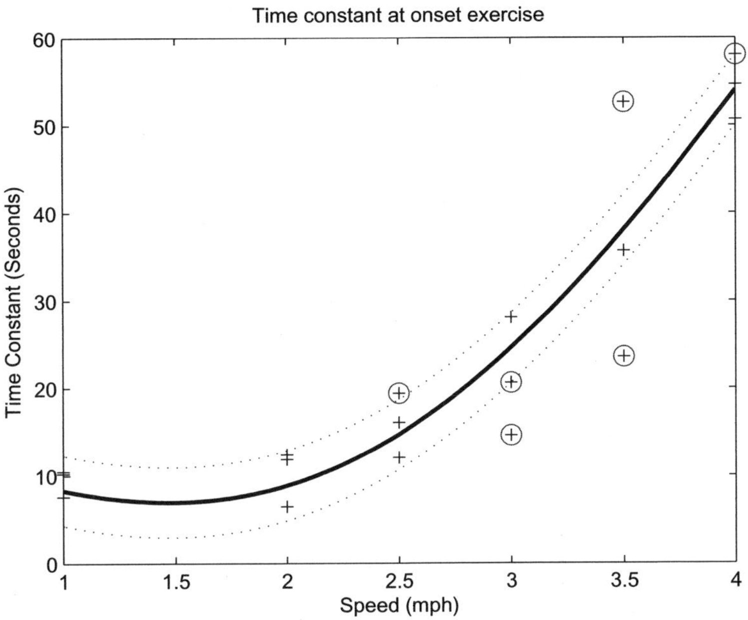

Fig. 10.9. SVM regression results for time constant at onset of exercise.

see that both steady state gain and time constant vary when walking speed V_a and V_b change. Furthermore, time constants of the offset of exercise are noticeably bigger than those of the onset of exercise. However, it should be pointed out that the variants of time constants are not distinctly dependent on walking speed when walking speed is less than three miles/hour. Overall, experimental results indicate that heart rate dynamics at the onset and offset of exercise exhibit high nonlinearity when walking speed is higher than three miles/hour.

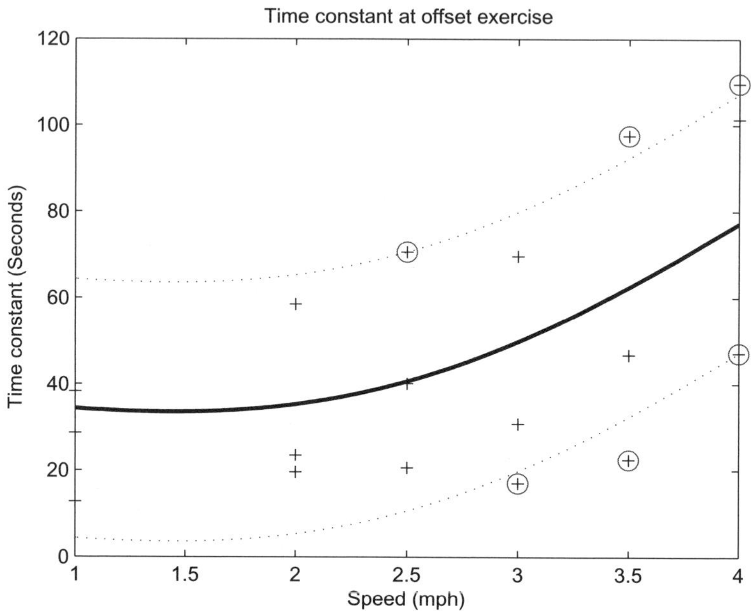

Fig. 10.10. SVM regression results for time constant at offset of exercise.

Table 10.2. The identified time constants and steady state gains by using averaged data.

Sets	Onset		Offset	
	DC gain	Time constant	DC gain	Time constant
1	9.2583	9.4818	7.9297	27.358
2	11.264	10.193	9.8561	27.365
3	10.006	13.659	8.9772	26.741
4	12.807	18.618	12.087	30.865
5	17.753	38.192	17.953	48.114
6	32.911	55.974	25.733	81.693

In order to quantitatively describe the detected nonlinear behaviour, we employed the novel machine learning modeling method, SVR, to model time constant and DC gain of heart rate dynamics.

The time constant regression results at onset and offset of exercise are shown in Figs 10.9 and 10.10 respectively. In these figures, the continuous curve stands for the estimated input-output steady state relationship. The dotted lines indicate the ε-insensitivity tube. The plus markers are the

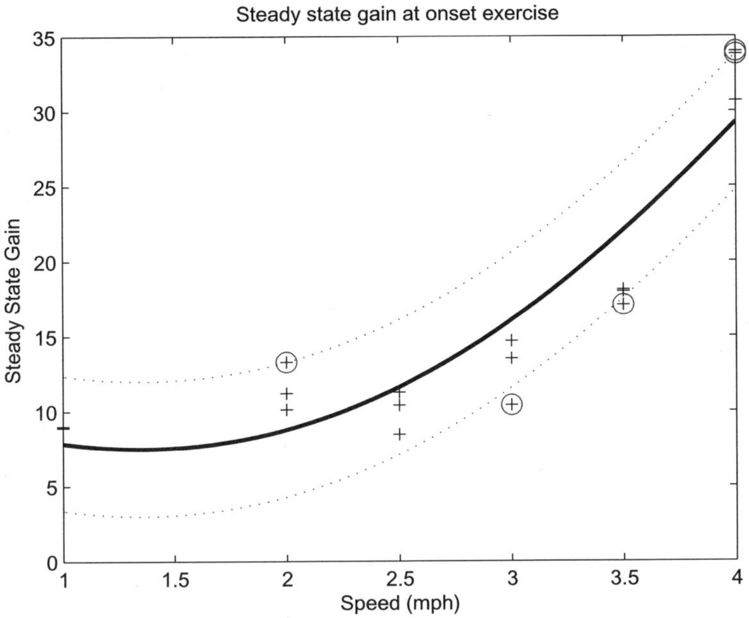

Fig. 10.11. SVM regression results for DC gain at onset of exercise.

points of input–output data. The circled plus markers are the support points. It should be emphasized that ε-insensitive SVR uses just less than 30% of total points to sparsely describe the nonlinear relationship efficiently.

It can be seen that the time constant at the offset of exercise is bigger than that at the onset of exercise. It can also be observed that the time constant at the onset of exercise is more accurately identified than that at the offset of exercise. This is indicated by the ε tube (or the width of the ε-nsensitive zone). It is probable that the recovery stage can be influenced by other exercise-unrelated factors than those at the onset of exercise.

The SVM regression results for DC gain at the onset and offset of exercise are shown in Figs 10.11 and 10.12. It can be observed that the DC gain for recovery stage is less than that at the onset of exercise, especially when walking speed is greater than three miles/hour.

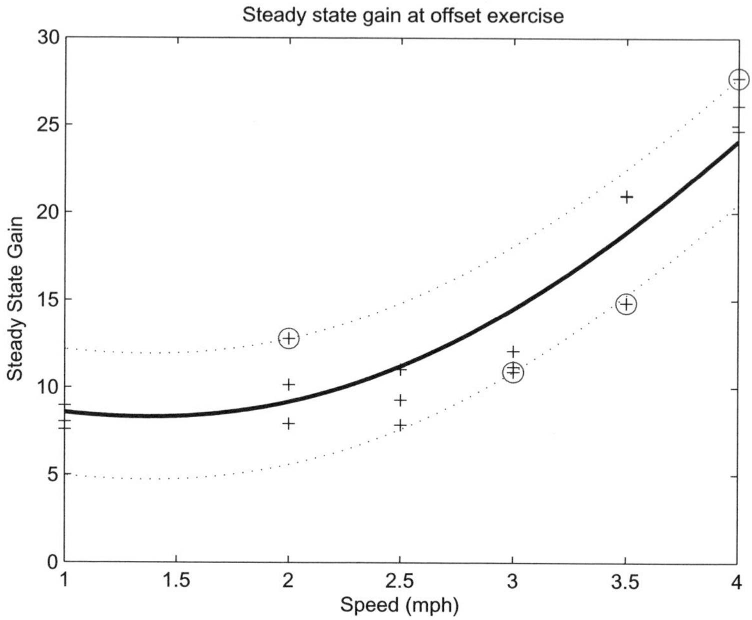

Fig. 10.12. SVM regression results for DC gain at offet of exercise.

10.5. Conclusion

This study aims to capture the nonlinear behavior of heart rate response to treadmill walking exercises by using support vector machine-based analysis. We identified both steady state gain and the time constant under different walking speeds by using the data from a healthy middle-aged male subject. Both steady state gain and the time constant are variant under different walking speeds. The time constant for the recovery stage is longer than that at the onset of exercise as predicted. In this study, these nonlinear behaviors have been quantitatively described by using an effective machine learning-based approach, named SVM regression. Based on the established model, we have already developed a new switching control approach which will be reported somewhere else. We believe this integrated modeling and control approach can be utilized to a broad range of process control. [6] In the next step of this study, we are planning to recruit more subjects to test the established nonlinear modeling and control approach further.

References

[1] S. W. Su, B. G. Celler, A. Savkin, H. T. Nguyen, T. M. Cheng, Y. Guo, and L. Wang, Transient and steady state estimation of human oxygen uptake based on noninvasive portable sensor measurements, *Medical & Biological Engineering & Computing.* **47**(10), 1111–1117, (2009).

[2] S. W. Su, L. Wang, B. Celler, E. Ambikairajah, and A. Savkin, Estimation of walking energy expenditure by using Support Vector Regression, *Proceedings of the 27th Annual International Conference of the IEEE Engineering in Medicine and Biology Society (EMBS).* pp. 3526–3529, (2005).

[3] M. S. Fairbarn, S. P. Blackie, N. G. McElvaney, B. R. Wiggs, P. D. Pare, and R. L. Pardy, Prediction of heart rate and oxygen uptake during incremental and maximal exercise in healthy adults, *Chest.* **105**, 1365–1369, (1994).

[4] P. O. Astrand, T. E. Cuddy, B. Saltin, and J. Stenberg, Cardiac output during submaximal and maximal work, *Journal of Applied Physiology.* **9**, 268–274, (1964).

[5] M. E. Freedman, G. L. Snider, P. Brostoff, S. Kimelblot, and L. N. Katz, Effects of training on response of cardiac output to muscular exercise in athletes, *Journal of Applied Physiology.* **8**, 37–47, (1955).

[6] Y. Zhang, S. W. Su, H. T. Nguyen, and B. G. Celler, Machine learning based nonlinear model predictive control for heart rate response to exercise, in H. K. Lam and S. H. Ling and H. T. Nguyen (Eds), *Computational Intelligence and its Applications: Evolutionary Computation, Fuzzy Logic, Neural Network and Support Vector Machine Techniques.* pp. 271–285, (World Scientific, Singapore, 2011).

[7] V. Seliger and J. Wagner, Evaluation of heart rate during exercise on a bicycle ergometer, *Physiology Boheraoslov.* **18**, 41, (1969).

[8] Y. Chen and Y. Lee, Effect of combined dynamic and static workload on heart rate recovery cost, *Ergonomics.* **41**(1), 29–38, (1998).

[9] R. Acharya, A. Kumar, I. P. Bhat, L. Choo, S. Iyengar, K. Natarajan, and S. Krishnan, Classification of cardiac abnormalities using heart rate signals, *Medical & Biological Engineering & Computing.* **42**(3), 288–293, (2004).

[10] M. Hajek, J. Potucek, and V. Brodan, Mathematical model of heart rate regulation during exercise, *Automatica.* **16**, 191–195, (1980).

[11] T. M. Cheng, A. V. Savkin, B. G. Celler, S. W. Su, and L. Wang, Nonlinear modelling and control of human heart rate response during exercise with various work load intensities, *IEEE Transactions on Biomedical Engineering.* **55**(11), 2499–2508, (2008).

[12] S. Su, L. Wang, B. Celler, A. Savkin, and Y. Guo, Identification and control for heart rate regulation during treadmill exercise, *IEEE Transactions on Biomedical Engineering.* **54**(7), 1238–1246, (2007).

[13] R. A. Cooper, T. L. Fletcher-Shaw, and R. N. Robertson, Model reference adaptive control of heart rate during wheelchair ergometry, *IEEE Transactions on Control Systems Technology.* **6**(4), 507–514, (1998).

[14] R. Eston, A. Rowlands, and D. Ingledew, Validity of heart rate, pedometry, accelerometry for predicting the energy cost of children's activities, *Journal of Applied Physiology.* **84**, 362–371, (1998).

[15] H. Drucker, C. Burges, L. Kaufman, A. Smola, and V. Vapnik, *Support vector regression machines*, in M. Mozer, M. Jordan, and T. Petsche (Eds), *Advances in Neural Information Procession Systems*, pp. 57–86 (Elsevier, Cambridge, MA, 1997).

[16] I. Goethals, K. Pelckmans, J. Suykens, and B. D. Moor, Identification of MIMO Hammerstein models using least squares support vector machines, *Automatica.* **41**, 1263–1272, (2005).

[17] J. Suykens, V. Gestel, J. D. Brabanter, B. D. Moor, and J. Vandewalle, *Least squares support vector machines.* (World Scientific, Singapore, 2002).

[18] V. Vapnik, *The Nature of Statistical Learning Theory.* (Springer, New York, 1995).

[19] V. Vapnik and A. Lerner, Pattern recognition using generalized portrait method, *Automation and Remote Control.* **24**, 774–780, (1963).

[20] S. Gunn, M. Brown, and K. Bossley, Network performance assessment for neuro-fuzzy data modelling, *Intelligent Data Analysis.* **1280**, 313–323, (1997).

[21] B. Schlkopf and A. Smola, *Learning with kernels.* (MIT Press, Cambridge, MA, 2002).

[22] L. Ljung, *System Identication Toolbox V4.0 for Matlab.* (The MathWorks, Inc, Natick, MA, 1995).

Chapter 11

Machine Learning-based Nonlinear Model Predictive Control for Heart Rate Response to Exercise

[†]Yi Zhang, [†‡]Steven W. Su, [#‡]Branko G. Celler and [†]Hung T. Nguyen

Steven.Su@eng.uts.edu.au

This study explores control methodologies to handle time variant behavior for heart rate dynamics at onset and offset of exercise. To achieve this goal, a novel switching model predictive control (MPC) algorithm is presented to optimize the exercise effects at both onset and offset of exercise. Specifically, dynamic matrix control (DMC), one of the most popular MPC control algorithms, has been employed as the essential of the optimization of process regulation while switching strategy has been adopted during the transfer between onset and offset of exercise. The parameters of the DMC/MPC controller have been well tuned based on a previously established SVM-based regression model relating to both onset and offset of treadmill walking exercises. The effectiveness of the proposed modeling and control approach has been shown from the regulation of dynamical heart rate response to exercise through simulation using Matlab.

Contents

[†]Centre for Health Technologies, Faculty of Engineering and Information Technology, University of Technology, Sydney, Australia.
[‡]Human Performance Group, Biomedical Systems Lab, School of Electrical Engineering and Telecommunications, University of New South Wales, Sydney NSW 2052 Australia.
[#]College of Health and Science, University of Western Sydney, Penrith NSW 2751 Australia.

11.1. Introduction

As heart rate was found to be a predictor of major ischemic heart disease events, cardiovascular mortality and sudden cardiac death, [1, 2] many scholars have been interested in monitoring it to evaluate the cardiovascular fitness. [3–7] Heart rate is determined by the number of heartbeats per unit of time, typically expressed as beats per minute (BPM), and can vary as the body's need for oxygen changes during exercise.

SVM regression offers a solution for nonlinear behavior description of heart rate response to moderate exercise as shown in the previous chapter [8]. This SVM-based model for heart rate estimation can be used to implicitly indicate some key cardio-respiratory responses to exercise, such as oxygen uptake as discussed in [9] and [10]. In our previous study [8], it is shown that time constants of heart rate response are variant. It is often bigger at the offset of exercise than at the onset of exercise. The captured difference leads to setting up two nonlinear models separately to present the dynamic characteristics of heart rate at the onset and offset of exercise.

One process possessing two or more quite different characteristics is quite common not only for human body responses but also for some industrial processes. For instance, the boiler is widely used in live stream sector which is a closed vessel where water or other liquid is heated. It may only take a few minutes to heat the water (or other liquid) up to 100 °C, but it may take several hours to cool down in general. Although it is evident that using different models for different stages (as shown in [8]) may provide a more precise description of the process, it requires a more advanced control strategy to handle this complicated mechanism.

MPC is a family of control algorithms that employ an explicit model to predict the future behavior of the process over a prediction horizon. The controller output is calculated by minimizing a pre-defined objective function over a control horizon. Figure 11.1 illustrates the "moving horizon" technique used in MPC. Recently, MPC has established itself in industry as an important form of advance control [11] due to its advantages over traditional controllers. [12, 13] MPC displays improved performance because the process model allows current computations to consider future dynamic events. This provides benefits when controlling processes with large dead times or non-minimum phase behavior. MPC also allows for the incorporation of hard and soft constraints directly in the objective function. In addition, the algorithm provides a convenient architecture for handling multivariable control due to the superposition of linear models within the controller.

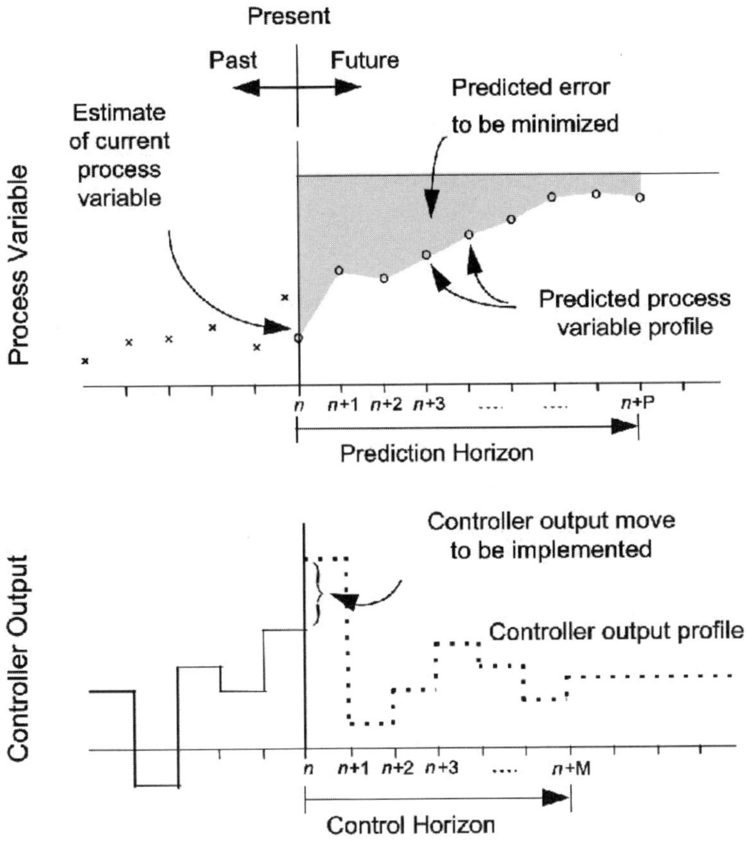

Fig. 11.1. The "moving horizon" concept of model predictive control.

In this study, one of the most popular MPC algorithms, Dynamic Matrix Control, is selected to control the heart rate responses based on previously established SVM-based nonlinear time variant model. The major benefit of using a DMC controller is its simplicity and efficiency for the computation of optimal control action, which is essentially a least-square optimization problem.

To handle different dynamic characteristics at the onset and offset of exercise, the switching control strategy has been implemented during the transmission between the onset and offset of treadmill exercises. By integrating the proposed modeling and control methods, heart rate response to exercise has been optimally regulated at both the onset and offset of exercise.

The organization of this chapter is as follows. The preliminaries of DMC/MPC are clarified in Section 11.2. The proposed switching DMC control approach is discussed in Section 11.3, which is followed by simulation results. Conclusions are given in Section 11.4.

11.2. Background

11.2.1. *Model-based predictive control (MPC)*

11.2.1.1. *MPC structure*

The basic structure of the MPC controller consists of two main elements as depicted in Fig. 11.2. The first element is the predicted model of the process to be controlled. Further, if any measurable disturbance or noise exists in the process it can be added to the model of the system for compensation. The second element is the optimizer that calculates the future control action to be executed in the next step while taking into account the cost function and constraints [14].

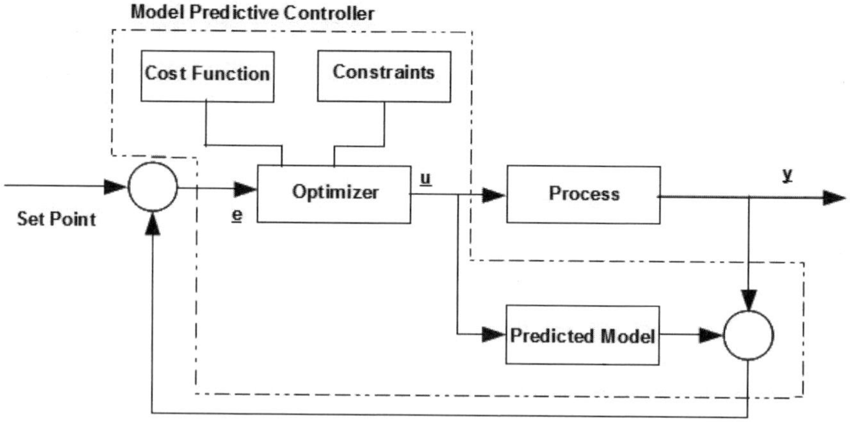

Fig. 11.2. Structure of model predictive control.

11.2.2. *Dynamic matrix control (DMC)*

DMC uses a linear finite step response model of the process to predict the process variable profile, $\hat{y}(k+j)$ over j sampling instants ahead of the current time, k:

$$\hat{y}(k+j) = y_0 + \underbrace{\sum_{i=1}^{j} A_i \triangle u(k+j-i)}_{\text{Effect of current and future moves}} + \underbrace{\sum_{i=j+1}^{N-1} P_i \triangle u(k+j-i)}_{\text{Effect of past moves}}$$
$$j = 1, 2 \cdots P \quad N: Model\ Horizon, \tag{11.1}$$

where P is the prediction horizon and represents the number of sampling intervals into the future over which DMC predicts the future process variable [15]. In (11.1), y_0 is the initial condition of the process variable, $\triangle u_i = u_i - u_{i-1}$ is the change in the controller output at the i-th sampling instant, A_i and P_i are composed by the i-th unit step response coefficient of the process, and N is the model horizon and represents the number of sampling intervals of past controller output moves used by DMC to predict the future process variable profile.

The current and future controller output moves have not been determined and cannot be used in the computation of the predicted process variable profile. Therefore, (11.1) reduces to

$$\hat{y}(k+j) = y_0 + \sum_{i=j+1}^{N-1} (P_i \triangle u(k+j-i)) + d(k+j), \tag{11.2}$$

where the term $d(k+j)$ combines the unmeasured disturbances and the inaccuracies due to plant–model mismatch. Since future values of the disturbances are not available, $d(k+j)$ over future sampling instants is assumed to be equal to the current value of the disturbance, or

$$d(k+j) = d(k) = y(k) - y_0 - \sum_{i=1}^{N-1} (H_i \triangle u(k-j)), \tag{11.3}$$

where $y(k)$ is the current process variable measurement.

The goal is to compute a series of controller output moves such that

$$R_{sp}(k+j) - \hat{y}(k+j) = 0. \tag{11.4}$$

Substituting (11.1) in (11.4) gives

$$\underbrace{R_{sp}(k+j) - y_0 - \sum_{i=j+1}^{N-1} P_i \triangle u(k+j-i) - d(k+j)}_{\text{Predicted error based on past moves, e(k+j)}} = \underbrace{\sum_{i=1}^{j} A_i \triangle u(k+j-i)}_{\text{Effect of current and future moves to be determined}} \quad . \tag{11.5}$$

Equation (11.5) is a system of linear equations that can be represented as a matrix equation of the form

$$\begin{bmatrix} e(k+1) \\ e(k+2) \\ e(k+3) \\ \vdots \\ e(k+M) \\ \vdots \\ e(k+P) \end{bmatrix}_{P\times 1} = \begin{bmatrix} a_1 & 0 & 0 & \dots & 0 \\ a_2 & a_1 & 0 & \dots & 0 \\ a_3 & a_2 & a_1 & \dots & 0 \\ \vdots & \vdots & \vdots & \ddots & \vdots \\ a_M & a_{M-1} & a_{M-2} & & a_1 \\ \vdots & \vdots & \vdots & \ddots & \vdots \\ a_P & a_{P-1} & a_{P-2} & \dots & a_{P-M+1} \end{bmatrix}_{P\times M} \times \begin{bmatrix} \triangle u(k) \\ \triangle u(k+1) \\ \triangle u(k+2) \\ \vdots \\ \triangle u(k+M-1) \end{bmatrix}_{M\times 1} \tag{11.6}$$

or in a compact matrix notation as [15]

$$\bar{e} = A \triangle \bar{u}, \tag{11.7}$$

where $\bar{e}$ is the vector of predicted errors over the next P sampling instants, A is the dynamic matrix and $\triangle\bar{u}$ is the vector of controller output moves to be determined.

An exact solution to (11.7) is not possible since the number of equations exceeds the degrees of freedom ($P > M$). Hence, the control objective is posed as a least squares optimization problem with a quadratic performance objective function of the form determined.

$$\min_{\triangle \bar{u}} J = [\bar{e} - A \triangle \bar{u}]^T [\bar{e} - A \triangle \bar{u}]. \tag{11.8}$$

The DMC control law of this minimization problem is

$$\triangle\bar{u} = (A^T A)^{-1} A^T \bar{e}. \tag{11.9}$$

Implementation of DMC with the control law in (11.9) results in excessive control action, especially when the control horizon is greater than one. Therefore, a quadratic penalty on the size of controller output moves is introduced into the DMC performance objective function. The modified objective function has the form

$$\min_{\triangle\bar{u}} J = [\bar{e} - A \triangle \bar{u}]^T [\bar{e} - A \triangle \bar{u}] + [\triangle\bar{u}]^T \lambda [\triangle\bar{u}], \tag{11.10}$$

where λ is the move suppression coefficient (controller output weight). This weighting factor plays a crucial role on the optimizer of DMC. If the value of λ is large enough, the optimizer attaches more importance to the effects of $\triangle u$, so that the robustness of output moves of the process is straightly improved, but the accuracy of output moves along with reference profile might be sacrificed. In the same way to reduce the value of λ, to optimize the effect of $\bar{e}$ has higher priority than that of $\triangle u$. Accuracy of system becomes more significant than robustness.

In the unconstrained case, the modified objective function has a closed form solution of [16, 17]

$$\triangle\bar{u} = (A^T A + \lambda I)^{-1} A^T \bar{e}. \tag{11.11}$$

Adding constraints to the classical formulation given in (11.10) produces the quadratic dynamic matrix control (QDMC) [18, 19] algorithm. The constraints considered in this work include:

$$\hat{y}_{min} \le \hat{y} \le \hat{y}_{max}; \tag{11.12a}$$

$$\triangle\bar{u}_{min} \le \triangle\bar{u} \le \triangle\bar{u}_{max}; \tag{11.12b}$$

$$\bar{u}_{min} \le \bar{u} \le \bar{u}_{max}. \tag{11.12c}$$

11.3. Control Methodologies Design

11.3.1. *Discrete time model*

From the previous studies, [8] heart rate response to exercise can be approximated as a first order process, which is expressed in S-domain as (11.13)

$$H(s) = \frac{Y(s)}{U(s)} = \frac{K}{Ts+1}. \tag{11.13}$$

For obtaining the discrete time model, (11.13) has to be transformed to z-domain by

$$s = \frac{1 - z^{-1}}{T_s}, \tag{11.14}$$

T_s is the sample time.

To bring (11.14) to (11.13), this model in z-domain will be followed as (11.15)

$$(\frac{T}{T_s} + 1)y = \frac{T}{T_s}yz^{-1} + Ku. \tag{11.15}$$

According to $y(k)z^{-1} = y(k-1)$ (k: the kth sample time), (11.15) is transformed to the discrete time form

$$y(k) = \frac{T}{T + T_s}y(k-1) + \frac{T_s K}{T + T_s}u(k). \tag{11.16}$$

In (11.16), T and K are the only parameters to be defined for describing the first order model. It can be regarded as a nonlinear model when the set of parameters K and T varies as $u(k)$ does change. This is exactly what the mathematic model of the dynamic characteristics of cardio-respiratory response to exercise is. The relationships between the transient parameters (K and T) and $u(k)$ relating to SVR results can be found in [8].

11.3.2. *Switching control method*

If a control system has two or more than two processes, switching control would be one of the approaches commonly used in the multiply model control field. The switching control for discrete time models increases the control accuracy, lowers the system consumption and raises the efficiency of control processing. Nevertheless, it also issues the risk on system robustness, because of the existing gap between models.

By the analysis of the previous experiment results in [8], it can be seen there are two time variant models being introduced for dynamic characteristics of heart rate response at the onset and offset of exercise. Certainly, two unique DMC controllers are also established, each computing their own control actions. Although two models plus two controllers are employed in this work, the approach can easily be extended to include as many local models and controllers as the practitioner would like (see Fig. 11.3).

If $\triangle R(k) = R(k) - R(k-1)$ is the set point change, $\triangle u(k) = u(k) - u(k-1)$ is the input change of designed controller at kth sample time, u_{onset}

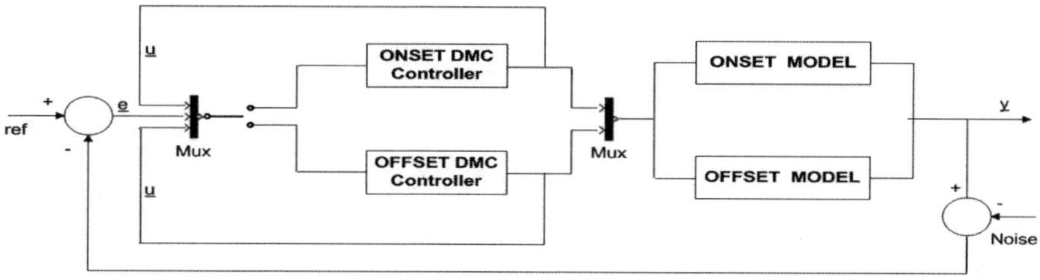

Fig. 11.3. Block diagram for double model predictive switching control system.

is the controller output for onset of exercise, u_{offset} is the controller output for offset of exercise, y_{onset} is the measured output of the process for onset of exercise and y_{offset} is the measured output of the process for offset of exercise, then

If $\triangle R(k) > 0$ then

$$u_{\text{meas}} = u_{\text{onset}}. \tag{11.17}$$

And if $\triangle u(k) > 0$

$$y_{\text{meas}} = y_{\text{onset}}. \tag{11.18}$$

Otherwise

$$y_{\text{meas}} = y_{\text{offset}}. \tag{11.19}$$

If $\triangle R(k) = 0$
And if $\triangle u(k) > 0$

$$u_{\text{meas}} = u_{\text{onset}}. \tag{11.20}$$

$$y_{\text{meas}} = y_{\text{onset}}. \tag{11.21}$$

Otherwise

$$u_{\text{meas}} = u_{\text{offset}}. \tag{11.22}$$

$$y_{\text{meas}} = y_{\text{offset}}. \tag{11.23}$$

If $\triangle R(k) < 0$ then

$$u_{\text{meas}} = u_{\text{offset}}. \tag{11.24}$$

And if $\triangle u(k) > 0$

$$y_{\text{meas}} = y_{\text{onset}}. \tag{11.25}$$

Otherwise

$$y_{\text{meas}} = y_{\text{offset}}. \tag{11.26}$$

From this point of view, y_{meas} is the actual measured output of the control system and u_{meas} is the actual controller output after which the controller is selected by the above conditions.

11.3.3. *Demonstration of tuned DMC parameters for control system of cardio-respiratory response to exercise*

The parameters to be tuned relating to this project include the sample time (T_s), prediction horizon (P), moving horizon (M), model horizon (N), move suppression coefficient (λ), peak value of the reference profile (R_p) and number of samples (S) (see Table 11.1).

Table 11.1. Tuning parameters for DMC control system of cardio-respiratory response to exercise.

	controller for onset stage	controller for offset stage
P	30	30
M	10	10
N	180	250
λ	300	3000
S	900	
R_p	30	
T_s	2	

According to previous studies [8], the range of a normal measured heart rate step response signal during the target's workout stage to treadmill exercises with the pace rate of around 3.5 m/hour is approximately from 100 *bpm* to 140 *bpm*. Therefore, the target's variant heart rate (R_p) is 30 as the simulation reference scale.

Due to the nonlinearity of this study, the DMC parameters are usually set by a combination of practical training and theoretical philosophies. [8] For example, in order to find a best value for the move suppression coefficient (λ), a test is carried out that employs 21 sets of steady state gain (K) and time constant (T) in terms of the SVR simulation results in [8]. These 21 different experiment data can be simply treated as 21 linear models. The method of practical training tends to tailor these linear models with a possible best value and evaluate them to find the final λ for nonlinear DMC controllers. The tuned values for DMC onset and offset controllers through 21 sets of test data analysis respectively amount to 300 and 3,000.

The sample time (T_s) is set as two seconds based on the general heartbeat rate of human beings. The experiment period is about 30 minutes except 10 minutes for warm-up at the beginning of exercise. Hence, the number of samples (S) is 900. Considering the larger T_s and S, prediction horizon (P) and moving horizon (M) are modulated to 30 and 10 severally. In addition, the tuned parameters T_s and N improve the system response time so the control effect can match with the sample time moves.

Model horizon (N) also needs to be tuned in order to reduce the system's computational time and enhance the efficiency of the DMC controller. In particular, N is defined as a dynamic array to keep storing and shifting the values of steady state responses of the process until it stays level. If the length of N is too long, it would be redundant. Based on experimental data analysis, the value of N at DMC onset controller would be 180, while 250 is estimated at DMC offset controller for a safe range.

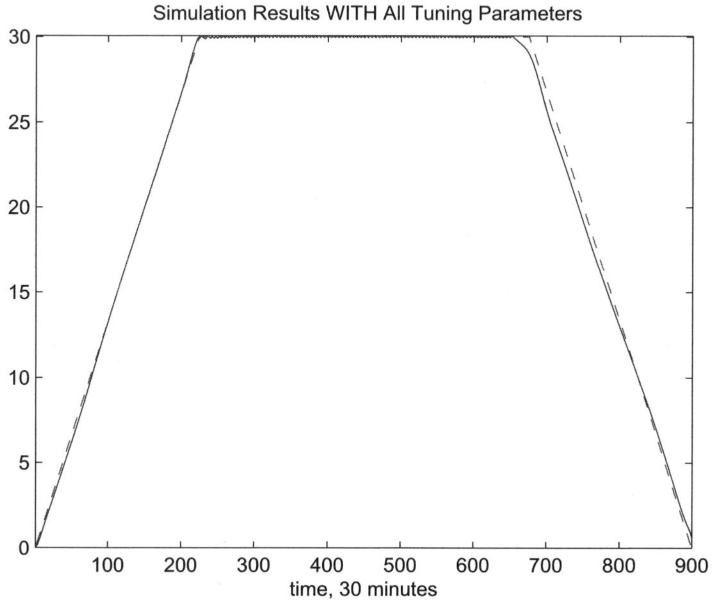

Fig. 11.4. Simulation results for machine learning-based double nonlinear model predictive switching control for cardio-respiratory response to exercise with all tuning parameters (I).

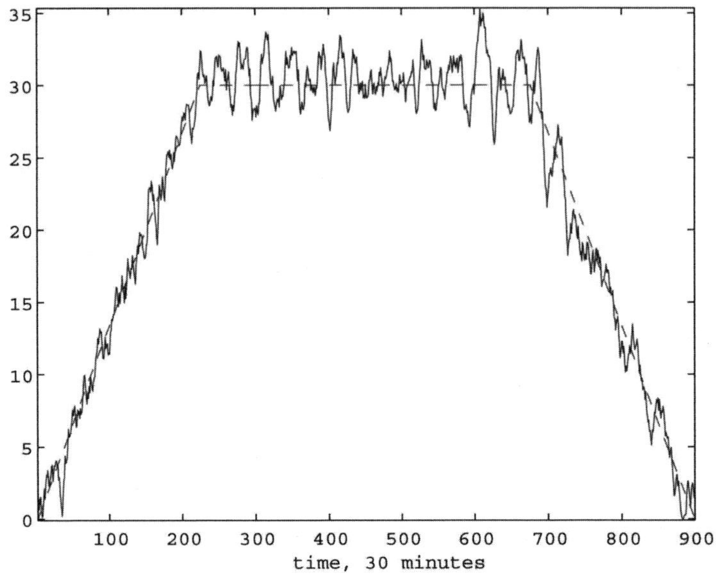

Fig. 11.5. Simulation results added noise for machine learning-based double nonlinear model predictive switching control for cardio-respiratory response to exercise with all tuning parameters.

11.3.4. *Simulation*

The simulation results for machine learning-based double nonlinear model predictive switching control for cardio-respiratory response to exercise is demonstrated in Figs 11.4 and 11.5. Based on these figures, the results are sound, even if a random disturbance is added into DMC controllers (see Fig. 11.5), which also can efficiently avoid the distortion. In the experiment results, these complex nonlinear behaviors have been qualitatively optimized with high accuracy by using the double model predictive switching control approach.

On the other hand, switching control brings slight oscillations at middle stage (see Fig. 11.6). As the amplitudes of these oscillations do not exceed the theoretical error range ($\sigma \leq 5\%$), it is acceptable to bear it in mind at the simulation stage.

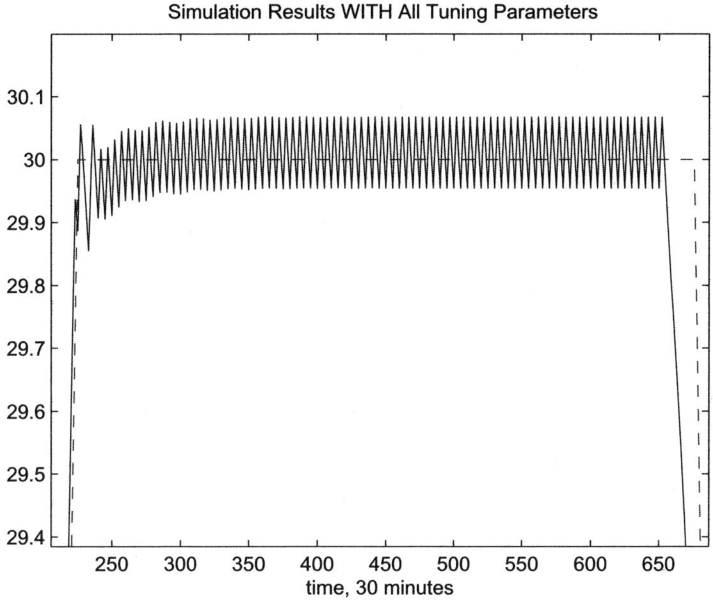

Fig. 11.6. Simulation results for machine learning-based double nonlinear model predictive switching control for cardio-respiratory response to exercise with all tuning parameters (II).

11.4. Conclusions and Outlook

In this study, a machine learning-based nonlinear model predictive control for heart rate response to exercise is introduced.

As discussed in [8], this nonlinear behavior of heart rate response to treadmill walking exercise can be effectively captured by using SVM regression. We investigated both steady state gain and the time constant under different walking speeds by using the data from an individual healthy middle-aged male subject. The experiment results demonstrate that the time constant for recovery stage is longer than that at onset of exercise, which provides the essential idea to form double models method to describe the corresponding onset or offset of exercise.

Based on the established model, a novel switching model predictive control algorithm has been developed, which applies DMC algorithm to optimize the regulation of heart rate responses at both the onset and offset of exercise.

Simulation results indicate switching DMC controller can efficiently handle the different dynamic characteristics at onset and offset of exercise. However, it should be pointed out that the proposed approach, as most switching control strategies, also suffers from transient behavior during controller switching. For example, the simulation results in transition stage ($\triangle R = 0$, Fig. 11.6; Equations (11.20), (11.21), (11.22) and (11.23)) have slight oscillation due to the quick switching between two controllers. In the next step of this study, we will develop a bump-less transfer controller to minimize the transient behavior and implement those methodologies in the real-time control of heart rate response during treadmill exercises.

References

[1] A. G. Shaper, G. Wannamethee, P. W. Macfarlane, and M. Walker, Heart rate ischaemic heart disease: sudden cardiac death in middle-aged British men, *British Heart Journal.* **70**, 49–55, (1993).

[2] R. Acharya, A. Kumar, I. P. S. Bhat, L. Choo, S. S. Iyengar, K. Natarajan, and S. M. Krishnan, Classification of cardiac abnormalities using heart rate signals, *Medical & Biological Engineering & Computing.* **42**(3), 288–293, (2004).

[3] S. W. Su, B. G. Celler, A. Savkin, H. T. Nguyen, T. M. Cheng, Y. Guo, and L. Wang, Transient and steady state estimation of human oxygen uptake based on noninvasive portable sensor measurements, *Medical & Biological Engineering & Computing.* **47**(10), 1111–1117, (2009).

[4] S. W. Su, L. Wang, B. Celler, E. Ambikairajah, and A. Savkin, Estimation of walking energy expenditure by using Support Vector Regression, *Proceedings of the 27th Annual International Conference of the IEEE Engineering in Medicine and Biology Society (EMBS).* pp. 3526–3529, (2005).

[5] M. S. Fairbarn, S. P. Blackie, N. G. McElvaney, B. R. Wiggs, P. D. Pare, and R. L. Pardy, Prediction of heart rate and oxygen uptake during incremental and maximal exercise in healthy adults, *Chest.* **105**, 1365–1369, (1994).

[6] P. O. Astrand, T. E. Cuddy, B. Saltin, and J. Stenberg, Cardiac output during submaximal and maximal work, *Journal of Applied Physiology.* **9**, 268–274, (1964).

[7] M. E. Freedman, G. L. Snider, P. Brostoff, S. Kimelblot, and L. N. Katz, Effects of training on response of cardiac output to muscular exercise in athletes, *Journal of Applied Physiology.* **8**, 37–47, (1955).

[8] W. Chen, S. W. Su, Y. Zhang, Y. Guo, N. Nguyen, B. G. Celler, and H. T. Nguyen, Nonlinear modeling using support vector machine for heart rate response to exercise, in H. K. Lam, S. H. Ling and H. T. Nguyen (Eds), *Computational Intelligence and its Applications: Evolutionary Computation, Fuzzy Logic, Neural Network and Support Vector Machine Techniques.* pp. 255–270, (Imperial College Press, London, 2012).

[9] S. W. Su, B. G. Celler, A. Savkin, H. T. Nguyen, T. M. Cheng, Y. Guo, and L. Wang, Transient and steady state estimation of human oxygen uptake based on noninvasive portable sensor measurements, *Medical & Biological Engineering & Computing.* **47**(10), 1111–1117, (2009).

[10] L. Wang, S. Su, B. Celler, G. Chan, T. Cheng, and A. Savkin, Assessing the human cardiovascular response to moderate exercise, *Physiological Measurement.* **30**, 227–244, (2009).

[11] J. Richalet, Industrial applications of model based predictive control, *Automatica.* **29**(5), 1251–1274, (1993).

[12] C. E. Garcia, D. M. Prett, and M. Morari, Model predictive control: theory and practice–a survey, *Automatica.* **25**(3), 335–348, (1989).

[13] K. R. Muske and J. L. Rawlings, Model predictive control with linear models, *AICHE Journal.* **39**, 262–287, (1993).

[14] C. Bordons and E. F. Camacho, *Model predictive control, 2nd edition.* (Springer-Verlag, London, 2004).

[15] D. Dougherty and D. Cooper, A practical multiple model adaptive strategy for single-loop MPC, *Control Engineering Practice.* **11**, 141–159, (2003).

[16] J. L. Marchetti, D. A. Mellichamp, and D. E. Seborg, Predictive control based on discrete convolution models, *Industrial & Engineering Chemistry, Processing Design and Development.* **22**, 488–495, (1983).

[17] B. A. Qgunnaike, Dynamic matrix control: A nonstochastic, industrial process control technique with parallels in applied statistics, *Industrial & Engineering Chemical Fundamentals.* **25**, 712–718, (1986).

[18] A. M. Morshedi, C. R. Cutler, and T. A. Skrovanek, Optimal solution of dynamic matrix control with linear programming techniques (LDMC), *Proceedings of the American Control Conference, New Jersey: IEEE Publications.* pp. 199–208, (1985).

[19] C. E. Garcia and A. M. Morshedi, Quadratic programming solution of dynamic matrix control (QDMC), *Chemical Engineering Communications.* **46**, 73–87, (1986).

Chapter 12

Intelligent Fault Detection and Isolation of HVAC System Based on Online Support Vector Machine

*Davood Dehestani, †Ying Guo, *Sai Ho Ling, *Steven W. Su and *Hung T. Nguyen

Faculty of Engineering and Information Technology,
University of Technology,
Sydney, Australia
Davood.Dehestani@student.uts.edu.au

Heating, Ventilation and Air Conditioning (HVAC) systems are often one of the largest energy consuming parts in modern buildings. Two focused issues of HVAC systems are energy saving and its safety. Regular checking and maintenance are usually the keys to tackle these problems. Due to the high cost of maintenance, preventive maintenance plays an important role. One cost-effective strategy is the development of analytic fault detection and isolation (FDI) modules by online monitoring of the key variables of HVAC systems. This chapter investigates real-time FDI for HVAC systems by using online support vector machine (SVM), by which we are able to train an FDI system with manageable complexity under real-time working conditions. It also proposes a new approach which allows us to detect unknown faults and update the classifier by using these previously unknown faults. Based on the proposed approach, a semi-unsupervised fault detection methodology has been developed for HVAC systems. This chapter also identifies the variables which are the indications of the particular faults we are interested in. Simulation studies are given to show the effectiveness of the proposed online FDI approach.

Contents

*Faculty of Engineering and Information Technology, University of Technology, Sydney, Australia
†Autonomous System Lab, CSIRO ICT Center, Australia

12.1. Introduction

There are not many energy systems so commonly used in both industry and domestic as HVAC systems. Moreover, HVAC systems usually consume the largest portion of energy in a building both in industry and domestically. It is reported in [1] that the air-conditioning of buildings accounts for 28% of the total energy end use of commercial sectors. From 15% to 30% of the energy waste in commercial buildings is due to the performance degradation, improper control strategy and malfunctions of HVAC systems. Regular checks and maintenance are usually the keys to reaching these goals. However, due to the high cost of maintenance, preventive maintenance plays an important role. A cost-effective strategy is the development of fault detection and isolation (FDI).

Several strategies have been employed as an FDI modular in an HVAC system. These strategies can be mainly classified in two categories: model-based strategy and signal processing-based strategy [2–4]. Model-based techniques either use a mathematical model or a knowledge model to detect and isolate the faulty modes. These techniques include but are not limited to observer-based approach [5], parity-space approach [6], and parameter identification-based methods [7]. Henao [8] reviewed fault detection based on signal processing. This procedure involves mathematical or statistical operations which are directly performed on the measurements to extract the features of faults.

Intelligent methods such as genetic algorithm (GA), neural network (NN) and fuzzy logic had been applied during the last decade for fault detection. Neural network has been used in a range of systems for fault detection even for HVAC systems [9]. Lo [10] proposed intelligent technique based on fuzzy-genetic algorithm (FGA) for automatically detecting faults on HVAC systems. However, many intelligent methods such as NN often require big data sets for training. Some of them are not fast enough to realize real-time fault detection and isolation. This chapter investigates methods with real-time operation capability and requiring less data. Support vector machine (SVM) has been extensively studied in data mining and machine learning communities for the last two decades. SVM is capable of both classification and regression. It is easy to formulate a fault detection and isolation problem as a classification problem.

SVM can be treated as a special neural network. In fact, an SVM model is equivalent to a two-layer, perceptron neural network. With using a kernel function, SVM is an alternative training method for multi-layer perceptron classifiers in which the weights of the network are identified by solving a quadratic programming problem under linear constraints, rather than by solving a non-convex unconstrained minimization problem as in standard neural network training.

Liang [2] studied FDI for HVAC systems by using standard SVM (offline). In this chapter, incremental SVM (online) has been applied. It is required to solve a quadratic programming (QP) for the training of an SVM. However, standard numerical techniques for QP are unfeasible for very large data sets which is the situation for fault detection and isolation for HVAC systems. By using online SVM, the large-scale classification problems can be implemented in real-time configuration under limited hardware and software resources. Furthermore, this chapter also provides a potential approach for the implementation of FDI under an unsupervised learning framework.

Based on the model structure given in paper [2], we constructed a HVAC model by using Matlab/Simulink and identified the variables which are more sensitive to commonly encountered HVAC faults. Finally, the effectiveness of the proposed online FDI approach has been verified and illustrated by using Simulink Simulation Platform.

12.2. General Introduction on HVAC System

In parallel to the modeling of other energy systems, HVAC modelling was developed by Arguello-Serran [11], Bourhan Tashtoush [12] and others. Gian Liang [13] developed a dynamic model of the HVAC system with single zone thermal space. A model of HVAC for thermal comfort control based on NN was also developed by Liang [13]. Based on this research [13], Liang developed a new model for fault detection and diagnosis [2].

Specifically, a few changes in control signal and model parameters have been made in order to well match real applications. Figure 12.1 shows a simple schematic of a HVAC system. It consists of three main parts: air handling unit (AHU), the chiller and the control system. When the HVAC system starts to work, fresh air passes from a heat exchanger cooling coil section to change heat between fresh air and cooling water. Cooled fresh air is forced by a supply fan to the room.

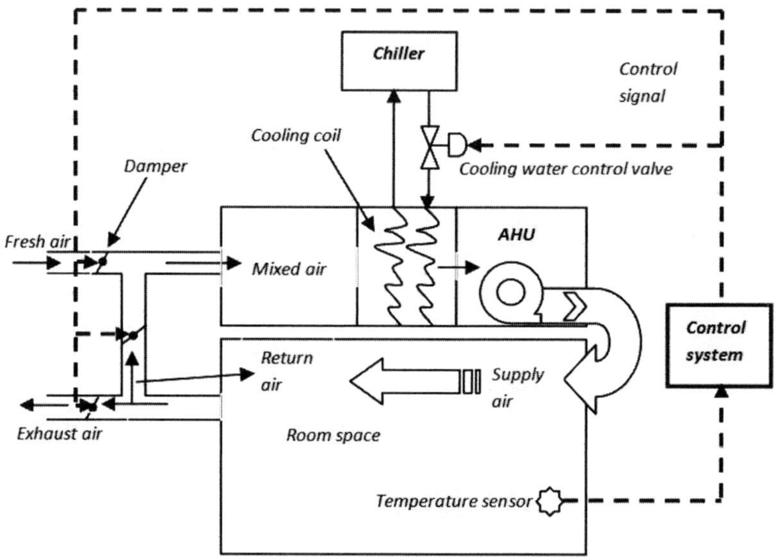

Fig. 12.1. General schematic of HVAC system.

After just a few minutes, the return damper opens to allow room air to come back to AHU. Then the mixing air passes from the cooling coil section to decrease its temperature and humidity. A trade off among exhaust, fresh and return air is decided by the control unit. Also the temperature of the room is regulated by adjusting the flow rate of cooling water by a certain control valve. Figure 12.2 shows the block diagram of the HVAC system with a simple PI controller. The model consists of eight variables in which six variables define as state variables.

Two pressures (air supply pressure P_s and room air pressure P_a) and four temperatures (wall temperature T_w, cooling coil temperature T_{cc}, air supply temperature T_s and room air temperature T_a) are considered as six states. Cooling water flow rate f_{cc} is considered as control signal. Also all six mentioned state variables with cooling water outlet temperature $T_{waterout}$ are considered as system outputs. But just one of them (room temperature T_a) acts as feedback signa. It should be noted that outlet water temperature is not used as a state variable in this modeling and it is just used as an auxiliary parameter for finding faults. The states, control input and controlled output are listed as follows:

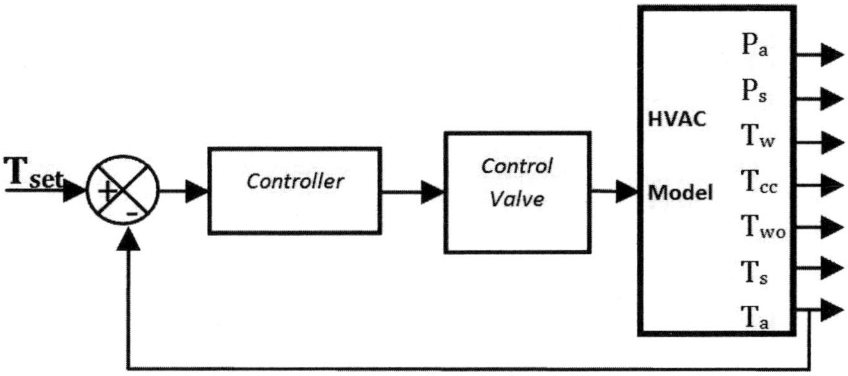

Fig. 12.2. Block diagram of HVAC model with PI controller.

$$X = [P_a; P_s; T_w; T_{cc}; T_s; T_a]$$
$$U = [f_{cc}]$$
$$Y = [P_a; P_s; T_w; T_{cc}; T_s; T_a]$$

For the control of HVAC systems, the most popular method is Proportion-Integration (PI) control with the flow rate f_cc served as the control input. In this study, we therefore select a PI controller, and tune the controller by using the Ziegler–Nichols method (Reaction Curve Method). In order to simulate the environmental disturbance in real application, two disturbances are considered in the model: outdoor temperature and outdoor heating (or cooling) load. Outdoor heat/cool loading will disturb the system but it cannot be measured directly. Though it can be estimated based on the supply/return air temperature/humidity via a load observer [11], but for convenience, it is assumed that the two disturbances are sinusoidal functions.

12.3. HVAC Parameter Setting

Table 12.1 shows some major parameters used in this simulation. Without loss of generality, the simulation runs in cooling mode. It is easy to consider heating mode just by changing some parameters in Table 12.1. Range of disturbances are 24 to 30 °C and 0.8-1 kW for outside temperature and heat loading respectively. Mixed air ratio for this model is a constant value when the system is working in steady state mode. The inlet water temperature is set as $T_{water-in} = 7$ °C whilst the outlet water temperature is set as $T_{water-out} = 9$ °C which may be disturbed by the cooling load.

Table 12.1. Main parameters of HVAC system.

Parameter definition	Setting value
Temperature set point	27.5 °C
Room space dimension	$5m \times 5m \times 3m$
Indoor cooling load range	0.8-1 kW
Outdoor temperature range	24-30 °C
Outdoor humidity	$55 - 75\%$
Max chilled water flow rate	0.5 kg/s
Air flow rate	980 m3/h
Mixed air ratio	4
Noise of temperature	5% mean value
Air handling unit volume	$2m \times 1m \times 1m$
Outside pressure	1 atm.
Inlet water temperature	7 °C

As with other intelligent systems, the parameters of an online SVM classifier should be determined at first. First parameter is maximum penalty. By defining the maximum penalty of 10 we could achieve the best margin for SVM. Based on the testing of different kernel functions, Gaussian function is chosen as the best kernel function with regard to its perfect response to the HVAC problem.

12.4. HVAC Model Simulation

All initial values of temperature are set at the morning time. Mathematical model simulated for 12 hours (from 8 am to 8 pm). The output temperature for normal condition (without fault) is shown in Fig. 12.3. The first half hour of simulation is the transient mode of the system. We can see room temperature could stay in the desired value (set point) but other temperatures change with noise profile due to their effort for adjusting the room temperature with the set point. It is clear that wall temperature is a function of outside temperature as it follows outdoor temperature profile. But other internal temperatures follow an inverse profile of outdoor temperature.

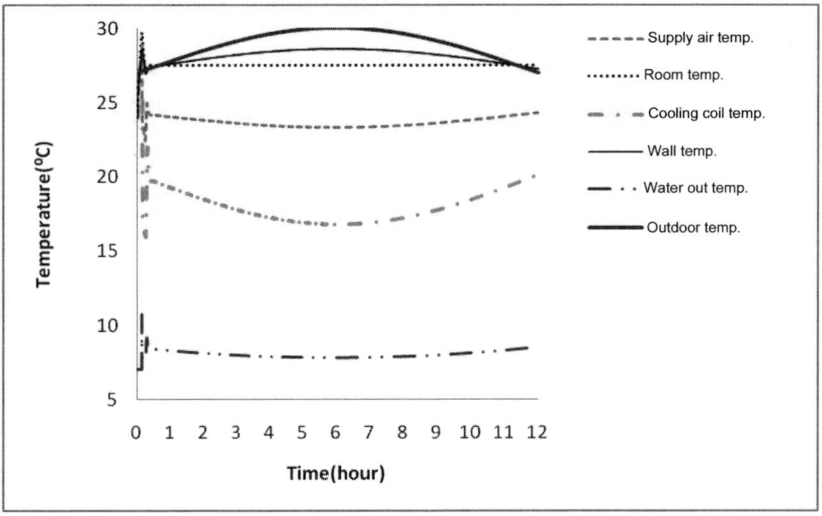

Fig. 12.3. Temperatures in normal condition of HVAC.

Figure 12.4 shows the control signal during simulation time. This flow rate is controlled by a control valve in which the control valve signal generated from the PI controller. Cooling water flow rate reaches its maximum value at noon due to highest value of outlet heat and temperature at this time. Some fluctuation in control signal and other variables at the beginning time of the simulation is related to transient behaviors of the system.

12.5. Fault Introduction

HVAC systems may suffer from many faults or malfunctions during operation. Three commonly encountered faults are defined in this simulation:

- Supply fan fault
- Return damper fault
- Cooling coil pipes fouling

Usage of these faults is just to test the performance of the proposed fault detector system. Incipient faults are applied to test the proposed fault detector due to its difficulty of detection. Four different models consisting of one healthy model and three faulty models are generated. Figure 12.5

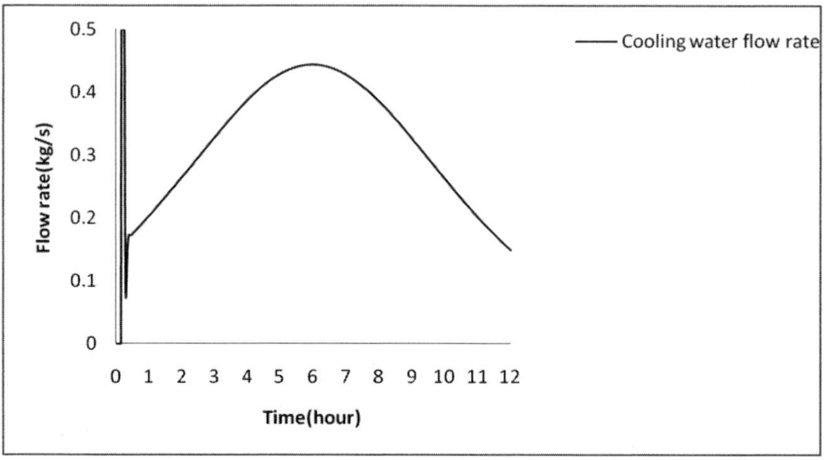

Fig. 12.4. Water flow rate as the function of control signal.

shows the general profile of the fault during one day. The amplitude of the faults gradually increases for six hours to reach their maximum values then they stay in this state for four hours and finally return gradually to normal condition during the last six hours.

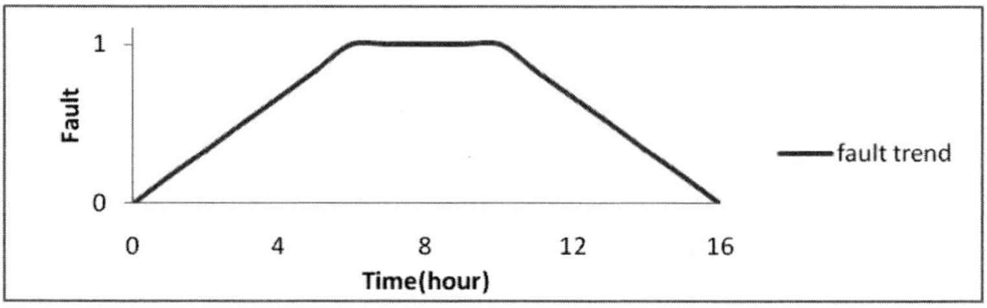

Fig. 12.5. Fault trend during one day.

This fault profile has been applied for each fault with some minor changes. In the air supply fan fault this profile is used with gain of 10. In damper fault it is used with gain of -2 and shift point of $+4$. For the pipe fault it is used with gain -0.3 and shift point of $+1$. The most sensitive parameters have been identified for each fault. For the air supply fan fault the most sensitive parameter is the air supply pressure that changes between 0 to 10 Pascal during fault period. The mixed air ratio is selected as the indicator of the damper fault that decreases from four to two. Cooling water flow rate decreases from f_{cc} to $0.7f_{cc}$ in the cooling coil tube fault.

12.6. Parameter Sensitivity

The sensitivity of variables in respect of each fault is analyzed in this subsection. Figure 12.6 shows sensitivity of cooling water flow rate with respect to different faulty modes. It is sensitive to all three faults (damper fault, supply fan fault and cooling water tube fault) with sensitivity of 0.03 kg/s, 0.07 kg/s and 0.08 kg/s.

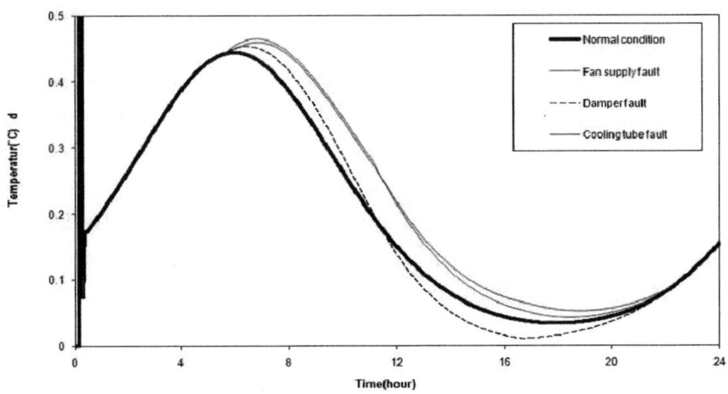

Fig. 12.6. Cooling water flow rate changes.

Other analysis shows cooling coil temperature and outlet water temperature are sensitive to both supply fan fault and return damper fault. Based on this sensitivity analysis, six parameters consisting of air supply, room pressure, air supply temperature, cooling coil temperature, outlet water temperature and water flow rate are used for training of supply fan fault. Also three parameters consisting of cooling coil temperature, outlet water temperature and water flow rate are applied for training of return damper fault but only water flow rate is used for training of the third fault (cooling coil pipes fouling).

12.7. Incremental–Decremental Algorithm of SVM

The main advantages of SVM include the usage of kernel trick (no need to know the nonlinear mapping function), the global optimal solution (quadratic problem) and the generalization capability obtained by optimizing the margin [14]. However, for very large data sets, standard numeric techniques for QP become unfeasible. An online alternative, that formulates the (exact) solution for ℓ+1 training data in terms of that for ℓ data and one new data point, is presented in online incremental method. Training an SVM incrementally on new data by discarding all previous data except their support vectors, gives only approximate results [15]. Cauwenberghs [16] consider incremental learning as an exact online method to construct the solution recursively, one point at a time. The key is to retain the Kuhn–Tucker (KT) conditions on all previous data, while adiabatically adding a new data point to the solution. Leave-one-out is a standard procedure in predicting the generalization power of a trained classifier, both from a theoretical and empirical perspective [17].

Giving n data, $S = \{x_i, y_i\}$ and $y_i \in \{+1, -1\}$ where x_i represents the condition attributes, y_i is the class label (correct label is +1 and faulty label is -1) and i is the number of data for training. The decision hyperplane of SVM can be defined as (w,b), where w is a weight vector and b a bias. Let w_0 and b_0 denote the optimal values of the weight vector and bias. Correspondingly, the optimal hyperplane can be written as:

$$w_0{}^T + b_0 = 0. \tag{12.1}$$

To find the optimum values of w and b, it is necessary to solve the following optimization problem:

$$min_{w,b,\xi}, \quad 1/2w^T w + C\sum_i \xi_i, \tag{12.2}$$

subject to

$$y_i(w^T \varphi(x_i) + b) \geq \ 1 - \xi_i, \tag{12.3}$$

where ξ is the slack variable, C is the user-specified penalty parameter of the error term ($C > 0$) and φ is the kernel function. SVM can change the original nonlinear separation problem into a linear separation case by mapping input vector on to a higher feature space. On the feature space, the two-class separation problem is reduced to find the optimal hyperplane that linearly separates the two classes transformed into a quadratic optimization problem. Depending on problem type, several kernel functions are used. Two best kernel functions for classification problems are Radial Basis Function (RBF) and Gaussian function regard to nonlinearity consideration. Equation (12.4) shows RBF as the important function for nonlinear classification.

$$K(x_i, x_j) = exp\{-\gamma\|x_i - x_j\|^2\}, \qquad \gamma > 0. \tag{12.4}$$

In SVM classification, the optimal separating function reduces to a linear combination of kernels on the training data, $f(x) = \sum_j \alpha_j y_j k(x_j, x) + b$, with training vectors x_i and corresponding labels y_i in the dual formulation of the training problem, the coefficients α_i are obtained by minimizing a convex quadratic objective function under constraints in Equation 5.1.

$$min_{0<\alpha_i<C}, \quad w = 1/2\sum_{ij}\alpha_i Q_{ij}\alpha_j - \sum_i \alpha_i + b\sum_i y_i\alpha_i, \tag{12.5}$$

With Lagrange multiplier (and offset) b, and the symmetric positive definite kernel matrix $Q_{ij} = y_i y_j K(x_i, x_j)$ the first-order conditions on w reduce to the Kuhn–Tucker (KT) condition as described in Equations (12.6) and (12.7):

$$\frac{\partial w}{\partial \alpha_i}\begin{cases} > 0; & \alpha_i = 0 \\ = 0; & 0 < \alpha_i < C \\ < 0; & \alpha_i = C \end{cases}, \tag{12.6}$$

and

$$\frac{\partial w}{\partial b} = 0. \tag{12.7}$$

The margin vector coefficients change value during each incremental step to keep all elements in equilibrium, i.e. keep their KT conditions satisfied. It is naturally implemented by decremental unlearning, adiabatic reversal of incremental learning, on each of the training data from the full trained solution. Incremental learning and, in particular, decremental unlearning offer a simple and computationally efficient scheme for online SVM training. It has also exact leave-one-out evaluation of the generalization performance on the training data.

12.8. Algorithm of FDI by Online SVM

There are huge amounts of data generated before a fault happens as most HVAC systems are rather reliable. For large data sets, standard SVM

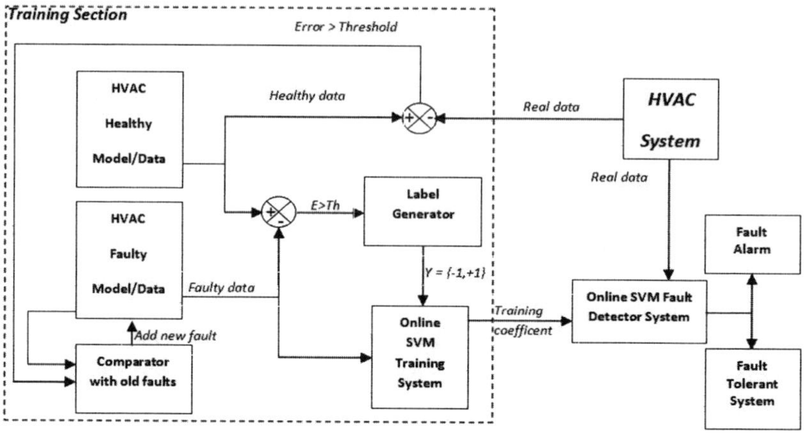

Fig. 12.7. Schematic of semi-unsupervised fault detection with online SVM.

techniques (offline SVM) become unfeasible. This motivates the usage of incremental–decremental SVM indexSVM (online SVM). Figure 12.7 shows the proposed fault detection scheme by using incremental-decremental support vector machine classification. The main purpose of the system is to detect un-known faults by monitoring key HVAC variables as discussed in previous sections during system operation. In this algorithm new faults can be detected (as unknown new faults) by comparing with the outputs of the healthy model and the real system. If the detected fault is similar to the old fault, it will be categorized by the algorithm as an existing fault. Otherwise, this data is sent to the online SVM trainer for training for the new fault. Finally the new fault will be isolated by this online SVM as a known fault. The incremental procedure is reversible and decremental unlearning of each training sample produces an exact leave-one-out estimate of faults with using all HVAC data during its operation.

The main advantage of this algorithm is usage of only a range of useful data (including healthy data, old faults and new faults) instead of whole data sets. Based on this online training procedure, a semi-unsupervised fault detection can be implemented.

Figure 12.8 shows the structure of the label generation algorithm. Here, label of y is set as $+1$ (non-faulty) when the error is smaller than a given threshold and it is set as -1 (faulty) when the error is bigger than that threshold. Labels including $y_{p1}, \cdots, y_{pn}$ are generated with n variables

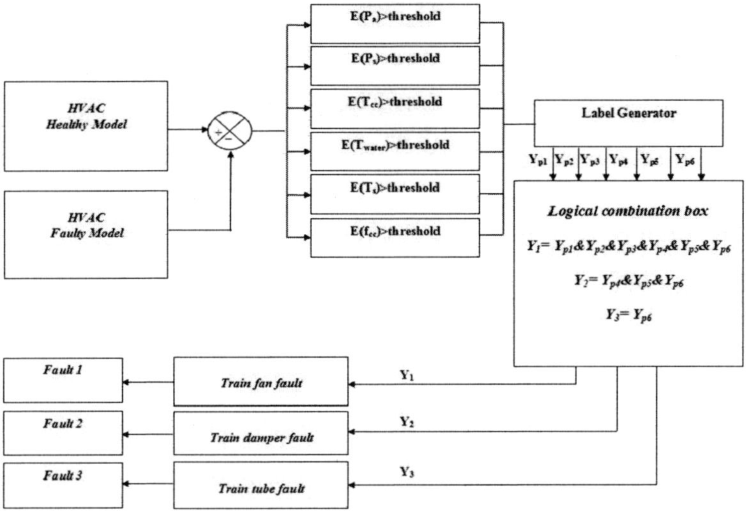

Fig. 12.8. Schematic of label generation algorithm for training system of each fault.

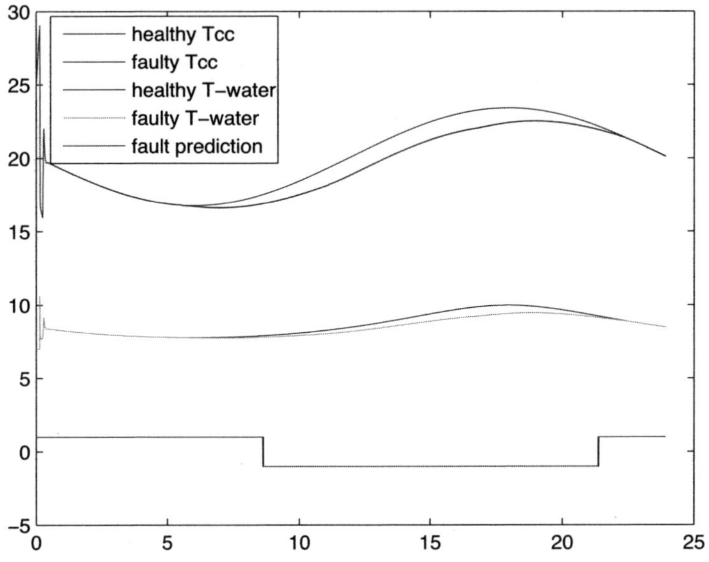

Fig. 12.9. Graduate known fault detection.

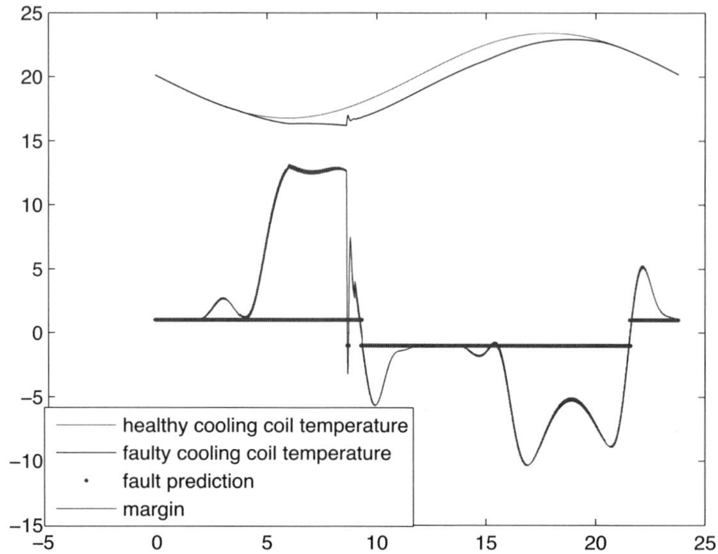

Fig. 12.10. Sudden unknown fault detection.

for each fault. For each fault all labels should be combined together in a proper logic to generate one label as one fault needs just one label for training. A combination of labels can be used to generate the final label. But for really complex HVAC systems, we recommend using a fuzzy logic membership function and some rules to the generated final label. In this chapter, a specific fault can happen if all errors of sensitive parameters can be passed from their thresholds.

12.9. FDI Simulation

Since the SVM classifier presented in the last section can only be used to deal with two-class cases, a multi-layer SVM framework has to be designed for the FDI problem with various faulty conditions. In order to use online SVM classification methods to achieve a better isolation performance, three faulty models are used in the isolation section. A four-layer SVM classifier is designed, in which the normal and three different HVAC fault conditions are all taken into consideration. Furthermore, it should be pointed out that

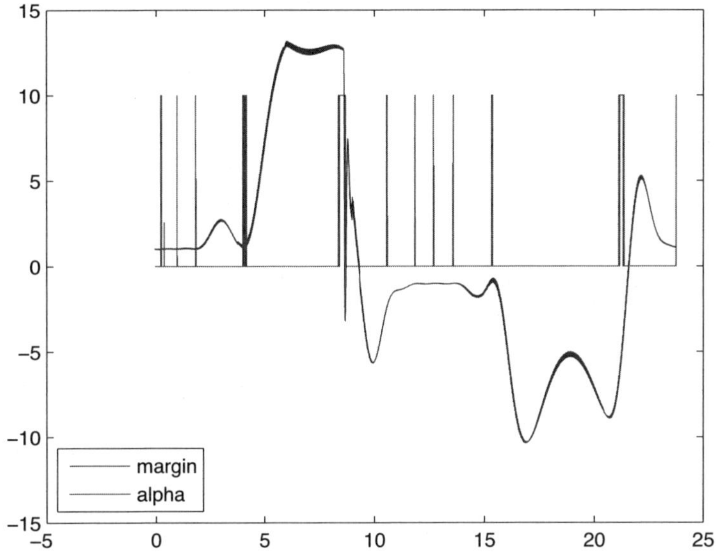

Fig. 12.11. Training coefficient via margin change.

other unknown faulty conditions can be placed in the upper layer of the FDI system. The kernel function must be properly selected for SVM classifier in order to achieve high classification accuracy. In general, linear function, polynomial function, radial basis function (RBF), sigmoid function and Gaussian function can be adopted as the kernel function. In this chapter, Gaussian function is used as it has excellent performance in the simulation.

In this research, two tests are conducted systematically. The diagnosis results and corresponding characteristics of the SVM classifiers are shown in Figs 12.9, 12.10, 12.11. Test 1 is designed to investigate the SVM classifier performance on known incipient faults. The steady-state data is used to build the four-layer SVM classifier: as mentioned in previous sections, the data within the threshold under the normal condition indicate fault free, and the data beyond the threshold indicate faults one to three. For each normal/faulty condition, two days data (20 hours data per day between 2 am and 10 pm) are used. Therefore, a total of 4 times 40 hour samples are collected. Half of the data for each condition are used as the training data, whilst the rest are used as the testing data for fault diagnosis. In

Fig. 12.9, the label changes from +1 (non-faulty situation) to -1 (faulty situation) when the fault is detected. For simplicity Fig. 12.9 only shows 2 variables when there is fault 1 in the data: the cooling coil temperature and the water outlet temperature. It is clear that the HVAC faults can be diagnosed 100% by using the SVM classifier for the testing data.

As mentioned earlier, our proposed algorithm is able to detect unknown faults in the sense of semi-unsupervised manner. To testing semi-unsupervised performances, an unknown sudden fault (at time of 9 hours) combined with previously introduced incipient faults are imposed on the system at the second test. The detection results are shown in Fig. 12.10.

It is clearly indicated that the margin changes from high level to low level when detecting incipient faults. For unknown faults this change is dramatic as unknown faults are abrupt types. To efficiently optimize the training process, samples in each normal/faulty condition should be applied. A group containing the maximum of faulty training samples is selected, and applied for training. From Fig. 12.10, it is found that the designed SVM classifier can identify the HVAC unknown fault accurately. Based on the simulation result, it is found that by using the proposed approach, the unknown faults of HVAC system can also be detected efficiently.

We can see α coefficient change with respect to margin change in Fig. 12.11. As mentioned in the previous section, this coefficient should be confined between zero and maximum penalty as shown in this figure.

12.10. Conclusion

This chapter focuses on the fault detection and isolation of HVAC systems under real-time working conditions. An online SVM FDI classifier has been developed which can be trained during the operating of the HVAC system. Different to the offline method, the proposed approach can even detect new unknown faults for the training of the classifier in real-time. Furthermore, this online approach can more efficiently train the FDI modular by throwing out unnecessary data (leave out vectors) and just using a series of data with high priority regarding classification. Due to these properties, the proposed algorithm can be implemented in a semi-unsupervised learning framework. Simulation study indicates that the proposed approach can efficiently detect and isolate typical HVAC faults. In the next step, we will validate the proposed approach by using real experimental data.

References

[1] S. W. Wang, Q. Zhou, and F. Xiao, A system-level fault detection and diagnosis strategy for HVAC systems involving sensor faults, *Energy and Buildings.* **42**(4), 447–490, (2010).

[2] J. Liang and R. Du, Model-based fault detection and diagnosis of HVAC systems using support vector machine method, *International Journal of Refrigeration.* **30**(6), 1104–1114, (2007).

[3] T. I. Salsbury and R. C. Diamond, Fault detection in HVAC systems using model-based feedforward control, *Energy and Buildings.* **33**(4), 403–415, (2001).

[4] Q. Zhou, S. W. Wang, and Z. J. Ma, A model-based fault detection and diagnosis strategy for HVAC systems, *International Journal of Energy Research.* **33**(10), 903–918, (2009).

[5] K. Zhang, B. Jiang, and P. Shi, A new approach to observer-based fault-tolerant controller design for Takagi–Sugeno fuzzy systems with state delay, *Circuits Systems and Signal Processing.* **28**(5), 679–697, (2009).

[6] P. S. Kim and E. H. Lee, A new parity space approach to fault detection for general systems, *High Performance Computing and Communications, Proceedings.* **37**(26), 535–540, (2007).

[7] Y. Dote, S. J. Ovaska, and X. Z. Gao, Fault detection using RBFN- and AR-based general parameter methods, *Proceeding of the 2001 IEEE International Conference on Systems, Man, and Cybernetics.* **1**(5), 77–80, (2002).

[8] H. Henao and G. A. Capolino, An improved signal processing-based fault detection technique for induction machine drives, *Proceeding of the 29th Annual Conference of the IEEE Industrial Electronics Society (IECON'03).* **1**(3), 1386–1389, (2003).

[9] Z. M. Du, X. Q. Jin, and B. Fan, Fault diagnosis for sensors in HVAC systems using wavelet neural network, *Proceedings of the 4th Asian Conference on Refrigeration and Air-Conditioning (ACRA 2009).* **86**(9), 409–415, (2010).

[10] C. H. Lo, Y. K. Wong, A. B. Rad, and K. L. Cheung, Fuzzy-genetic algorithm for automatic fault detection in HVAC systems, *Applied Soft Computing.* **7** (1), 554–560, (2002).

[11] B. Arguello-Serrano and M. Velez-Reyes, Nonlinear control of a heating, ventilating, and air conditioning system with thermal load estimation., *IEEE Transactions on Control Systems Technology.* **7**(1), 56–63, (1999).

[12] B. Tashtoush, M. Molhim, and M. Al-Rousan, Dynamic model of an HVAC system for control analysis, *Energy.* **30**(10), 1729–1745, (2005).

[13] L. Jian and D. Ruxu, Thermal comfort control based on neural network for HVAC application, *Proceedings of the IEEE Conference on Control Applications.* **11**(9), 819–824, (2005).

[14] A. S. Cerqueira, D. D. Ferreiraa, M. V. Ribeiroa, and C. A. Duque, Power quality events recognition using a SVM-based method, *Electric Power Systems Research.* **78**(9), 1546–1552, (2008).

[15] N. A. Syed, H. Liu, and K. K. Sung, Incremental learning with support vector machines, *Proceeding of the International Joint Conference on Artificial Intelligence (IJCAI-99).* **11**(7), 143–148, (1999).

[16] G. Cauwenberghs and T. Poggio, Incremental and decremental support vector machine learning, *Advances in Neural Information Processing Systems.* **13**(13), 409–415, (2001).

[17] V. Vapnik, *The Nature of Statistical Learning Theory.* (Springer–Verlag, New York, 1995).

Index